PHILOSOPHICAL WRITINGS OF PEIRCE

Selected and Edited
With an Introduction by
JUSTUS BUCHLER

DOVER PUBLICATIONS, INC., NEW YORK

This new Dover edition,
first published in 1955, is an unabridged
and unaltered republication of the book
first published in 1940 under the title
"The Philosophy of Peirce: Selected Writings."
It is published through special arrangement with
Routledge and Kegan Paul Ltd.

International Standard Book Number: 0-486-20217-8

Library of Congress Catalog Card Number: 56-13549

This edition is manufactured in the
United States of America and is for sale only in the
United States of America.

Dover Publications, Inc.
180 Varick Street
New York, N. Y. 10014

CONTENTS

PREFACE

I HOPE that in accordance with its purpose this volume contains Peirce's best work and is at the same time thoroughly representative of his philosophy as a whole. Intended both for new readers and those already acquainted with Peirce, it will perhaps, besides reaching many to whom his work has been inaccessible practically speaking, make possible a perspective of that work which might not otherwise have been attained. Unlike most important thinkers, Peirce profits from selection. His philosophic writings consist entirely of essays and manuscripts, many of the latter fragmentary, so that the process of selecting is no less one of organizing. There is here naturally a minimum of duplication, and of the digression which sometimes makes a paper of his so difficult to follow. It is, however, neither possible nor desirable wholly to avoid repetition of theme: his thinking is often so compressed that recurrence of an idea in more than one context is necessary if we are to grasp its full significance. Similarly, an innocuous specimen or two of his digressive habits is necessary in conformity with the purpose of this edition to represent his idiosyncrasies as well as his opinions. Omissions, where made, are such as avoid text-chopping.

With the exception of Chapter 21 and a short piece in Chapter 20 (reprinted for the first time from periodicals), the material has been selected from *Collected Papers of Charles Sanders Peirce* (six volumes, edited by Charles Hartshorne and Paul Weiss, Harvard University Press, 1931-35). All of Peirce's footnotes have been omitted in the present volume excepting a few deemed important, and these are indicated in the text by daggers. Editor's footnotes, bracketed and indicated by asterisks, give information concerning original source, date, and location in *Collected Papers* of the material constituting each chapter. (*Collected Papers* is abbreviated *CP*, "*CP* 6.522-8," for example, denoting Volume 6, paragraphs 522 to 528.) Numbers occurring in the text refer to notes in the rear, necessarily few and for the most part of a factual character. Chapter titles and sub-headings are the editor's if not otherwise specified. Peirce's capitalization and punctuation have been left intact, and his spelling, though not changed, has been made uniform. Brief minor omissions, indicated in the usual manner by successive periods, are in some cases those of *Collected Papers*. Of bracketed words in the text, added for the purpose of filling lacunae or providing synonyms, a majority already occur in *Collected Papers*.

The reader is urged to keep an eye on the dates of the various selections, in order to more readily understand changes in point of view. One or two cases, where manuscripts of different dates were printed as one piece in *Collected Papers* and are similarly printed here, call for a word. On p. 105 a distinction between *icon* and *hypoicon* in the first two paragraphs disappears in succeeding paragraphs, because the latter are of an earlier date; and on p. 108 a distinction between *index* and *subindex* likewise disappears, for the same reason. The matter is not important, but is less perplexing to the reader who recalls the explanation.

The order of the chapters has been determined partly by Peirce's classification of the sciences, but more largely by appropriateness in the unfolding of his views (or in baldly subjective terms, by my own sense of consecutiveness). The reader may wish to skip around, and needless to say no great harm will result; but he should bear in mind that later chapters as a rule assume more than earlier ones. It has been unavoidable that some terms should appear prior to the places in which they are formally introduced. If a note in the rear does not help, a glance at index or table of contents will.

I wish to thank the Harvard University Department of Philosophy, and the Harvard University Press, for permission to reprint from *Collected Papers* material previously unpublished. Such permission of course imposes no responsibility on these bodies for the character of the present edition.

This being the second Peirce book published by the International Library within the last two years, the reader interested in a critical discussion may be referred to the other, *Charles Peirce's Empiricism* by the present writer.

J. B.

INTRODUCTION

ONLY recently have we begun to explore the philosophy of Charles Sanders Peirce, a vast and fecund wealth of ideas. Peirce was both natural scientist and close student of the history of philosophy—a rare combination. But the significance of this is dwarfed by the further fact that he could critically utilize his historical study toward the achievement of imaginative depth, and his experimental science toward the development of a powerful logic. The striking originality of his thought thus grows from a broad and solid foundation, and it is the product not only of his native intellectual genius but of his moral conviction that philosophy must build as well as repair.

Peirce's literary activity began in 1867 and continued almost unceasingly until a few years before his death in 1914. From the very beginning his approach was revolutionary and constructive. He could accept none of the current intellectual influences; the sensationalism of the followers of Mill; the Scottish philosophy, inheriting in another guise the Cartesian philosophy of intuition; the swelling tide of neo-Hegelianism; Spencerian evolutionism and its concomitant dogmatic mechanism. But he could find value in all of these. Upon a synthesis of whatever healthful strains he detected in sensationalism with the older British tradition, Kantism, and the logic of science, he constructed his own empiricism, in which fallibilism replaces scepticism and pragmatism replaces positivism. Scottish common-sensism he transformed into critical common-sensism. In Hegel he discerned the germ of his principle of continuity or synechism. And he accepted evolution, not the regnant interpretation but one in which the concepts of chance and habit play a major rôle.

Among thinkers of the first rank, few have in their lifetime addressed so small a public as Peirce. His inability to secure a regular teaching position (no bright page in American academic history) and to have his work published in book form partly account for this fact, and so does his unwillingness to "water down" ideas for whatever audiences he reached. But his effect on other thinkers has been great: the philosophies of Royce, James, and Dewey would lack some of their most distinctive emphases if his influence were subtracted, and men like Schroeder and Russell learned from his contribution to logic. If American philosophy began to come of age with Peirce's friend and immediate predecessor Chauncey Wright, it had not yet freed itself from discipleship to worn traditions. In Peirce's first publications it flames into startlingly sudden distinction, propelled by a force whose full influence has been curiously suspended until the present.

The pages of Peirce vibrate with the effort to place philosophy on a scientific basis. The phrase "scientific philosophy" has acquired a hollow ring in our time. On the one hand, the claim to have achieved it is notorious among the most widely differing classical philosophers, and on the other, too many contemporary craftsmen have made philosophy scientific by simply dispensing with most of it. To Peirce the phrase has a perfectly literal implication, at once faithful to the method of science and the scope of philosophic tradition, namely, that the broadest speculative theories should be experimentally verifiable. This attitude rests on the conviction that philosophy is a branch of progressive inquiry rather than a species of art, and that the scientific method alone makes progressive inquiry possible. To Peirce the scientific method represents the antithesis of individualism. What distinguishes it from all other methods of inquiry is its coöperative or public character. It conceives of evidence as an objective factor inviting universal examination and compelling ultimate unanimity; it conceives of its results as essentially provisional or corrigible; and for these reasons it ensures measurable progress.

This attitude is inimical to philosophies in which intuitive cognition is fetish, whether in the form of self-evident *a priori* principles or in that of infallible perceptual apprehension. By the queer yet understandable twists of philosophic history such viewpoints have in their different ways purported to be scientific, apriorism confusing natural science and mathematics—in Peirce a fundamental distinction—and intuitive empiricism unduly elevating the cognitive value of sense. The result has been an abnormal veneration of science—the other extreme of the pendulum. Peirce's actual scientific experience, his comprehensive grasp of the scientific enterprise, and his analysis of induction, led him to expect no specific guarantees of unfailing correctness, no royal road, from the scientific method, but instead to understand that its power dwells in the capacity, through constant modification of its own conclusions, to approximate indefinitely to the truth. Most repugnant, perhaps, to Peirce's viewpoint is one that winks cynically at the idea of philosophic progress, abetting not a little what he has eloquently revealed to be a crime as profound as it is subtle, the obstruction of inquiry.

If philosophers have indiscriminately claimed to reflect the scientific attitude, they have in an even greater degree claimed for their opinions the sanction of common sense. In this respect too the philosophy of Peirce goes beyond verbalism. His critical theory of common sense, involving the conception of an indubitability that is relative to social and biological frameworks—for his fallibilism precludes absolute indubitability of any kind—and that must father all purposive investigation, explains how successful scientific theorizing is possible, and gives the lie to artificial scepticisms which would counsel us to doubt what we cannot help believing. At the same time, it defines the limits of common sense and is free from the naïve extremism shared by the Scottish school and various present-day common-sensists.

Peirce's theory of common sense and science receives logical expression in the most widely heralded but scarcely the best-understood of his contributions, pragmatism. In the versions of James and Schiller, a huge pragmatist offspring flourished early in this century. But the seeds of confusion and superficiality caused it to die as suddenly as it had been born. The pragmatism of Peirce, for a time obscured, has now emerged, and the differences are truly impressive. Whereas Popular pragmatism is an anti-intellectualistic revolt, an embrace of the "will to believe" pathetic in its methodological feebleness, Peircean pragmatism (pragmaticism), demonstrating the fatuity of an emphasis on mere volition or sensation, is precisely intellectualistic. Popular pragmatism is an interesting manifestation of the general empirical temper; pragmaticism is a step forward in the history of empiricism. It differs from the classical British tradition, from Kant's anti-metaphysical scepticism, and from nineteenth-century positivism, primarily in that it introduces the concept of meaning into empiricist methodology. It is the first deliberate *theory* of meaning in modern times, and it offers a *logical* technique for the clarification of ideas. It has a potential interest far greater than that of similar theories current today, for it embodies an analysis of knowledge with rich implications. Peirce maintains that in so far as thought is cognitive it must be linguistic or symbolical in character—that is, it must presuppose communication. Communication takes place by means of signs, and Peirce's theory, in its investigation of the nature and conditions of the sign-relation, endows with a new and vital significance the old truth that man is a social animal. His view differs from others in stressing that pragmatic definition cannot be in terms of individual reaction or private sensation, which are incommunicable, but of that which is public and general —a habit of action. If our language is to possess cognitive meaning, it must be defined by the ways in which it is used communicatively. In opposition to atomistic psychology Peirce demonstrates that no thought (in so far as it is a mental sign) is perfectly unitary or simple but is inseparable from interpretation by further thoughts. Thought is inferential, expectative, or predictive, and therefore always in some degree general. It is not a granular succession but a web of continuously related signs. This is really the heart of fallibilism. All science, all significant inquiry is a web with in-definite frontiers. On Peirce's view even the act of conjecture by which the hypotheses of science are born is a clearly definable species of inference. "Abduction," as he calls it, connects scientific inquiry with common thought; and to call this logical bridge the differentia of his common-sensism would not be far from correct.

A frequently repeated assertion by Peirce, that pragmaticism is not a metaphysical theory but a logical rule, directs attention to another of his path-breaking contributions, the conception of logic as the philosophy of communication, or theory of signs. Peirce's work in logic is immense in scope as well as in depth. Rare enough is the logician who has made contributions of the first importance to the two great movements in the nineteenth-century logical renaissance, the development of deductive systems and the philo-sophy of empirical science. Peirce is among the leaders in yet a third field, of even smaller company—the philosophy of logic. Seldom, in actual practice, does he separate his concern with this from his logical research proper, a policy well illustrated in his philosophy of mathematics, the principal theses of which anticipate and are interestingly germane to present-day discussion. The conception of logic as semiotic opens broad, new possibilities, toward which Peirce himself could barely do more than take the first long stride. To regard empirical science, mathematics, and the whole of human discourse as so many types of domains in which signs operate, both clarifies and fertilizes the range of logic. A consideration of the different possible classes of signs and the different possible ways in which they function, adequately com-prises the traditional problems and many more besides. In Peirce we find just recognition alike of the socio-biological and the mathematical aspects of logic. The desideratum in logical theory at present is the unification of emphases, unfortunately flourishing independently, on each of these aspects. Semiotic would appear to be the answer. It is perhaps broader and more thoroughgoing in conception than what is today called the theory of inquiry, since its analysis would penetrate not only to the standards, presuppositions, and forms of the problem-solving situation, but to those implicit in the most rudimentary types of all communication. Peirce's explorations in logical theory have a critical aspect necessarily supplementing his positive opinions. In this direction he attacked what was then (and is even at present) a widespread vogue of psychologism, substituting for subjective logical criteria his doctrine of leading principles or habits of reasoning. It is not difficult to see that the divorce of psychology from logic follows from his fundamental philosophic outlook. To found validity in reasoning on feeling or instinct is to assign individual judgment a weight which on his view it does not and cannot have.

In Peirce's labours toward a scientific philosophy, his empirical phenomenology is an essential factor. By means of this science he discriminates in all experience three basic classes—Firstness, Secondness, Thirdness. Aside from its intrinsic philosophic significance, this phenomenology is methodologically important as supplying, in the three categories, the organized matrix in terms of which the theories of metaphysics are to be tested. The special sciences, Peirce holds, appeal to special observation for the confirmation of their hypotheses, while those of metaphysics are submitted to the general observation accessible to all men but for that very reason most difficult to discern and analyze. It is a safe guess that many who are repelled by other conceptions of phenomenology will be refreshed by the clear-cut outlines of Peirce's, whatever their position with respect to his conclusions.

Peirce's vigorous opposition to the fashionable nineteenth-century tradition of mechanical determinism argues in an altogether independent manner that absolute conformity of facts to law is an assumption which actually does not rest on any empirical evidence, whereas that of chance or spontaneous departures from law does. The extent of his divergence from the orthodox metaphysics is revealed, however, hardly by this (tychism) alone but by his evolutionary idealism as a whole, which conceives laws of nature to be habits of an objective world that is essentially psychical. The existence of chance in part explains how these habits originated and develop, that is, how evolution or the progressive growth of uniformity takes place. Peirce's fundamental metaphysical hypothesis supposes a "law of mind," a tendency of all things to acquire habits. This tendency is the panpsychic counterpart of mental association, the habit-acquiring tendency of ideas or feelings: they "spread," become increasingly general, and merge in a continuum of mind. Peirce is much concerned to validate this cosmological principle as experientially verifiable. He justifies it, together with his subsidiary metaphysical hypotheses, by a principle of continuity (synechism), serving in this connection to exclude the dualism of matter and mind as creating and resting content with an inexplicability. The principle of continuity he holds to be a principle of logic, and it is, in so far, an application of pragmatism to the hypotheses of philosophy; but from another angle it is seen to function as itself a metaphysical hypothesis. Peirce caps the exposition of his cosmology by formulating its leading idea as a law of love (agapasticism), a frankly anthropomorphic representation of the evolutionary or habit-taking process. The continuity of mind, the spreading of ideas, generates a "sympathy" by means of which growth takes place. It is worth noting that Peirce introduces his agapasticism in an ethical context: the doctrine of love he regards as opposed to the ethical individualism (the "gospel of greed") springing from nineteenth-century political economy and given expression by Darwinism. But Darwinism, despite the ethical interpretation of it to which Peirce falls prey, plays a significant part in his evolutionary theory. He generalizes it and translates it metaphysically as a recognition of the chance-factor in evolution, and therefore as a constituent assumption of agapasticism.

Underlying every phase of Peirce's thought is his realism. The supposition that there are real things—the real is "that whose characters are independent of what anybody may think them to be"—he regards as the "fundamental hypothesis" of science, for it alone explains the manner in which minds are compelled to agreement. This is a realism which, by virtue of the pragmatic method, excludes the supposition of any unknowable, and is hostile to atomism, individualism, and nominalism in whatever form they may take. For Peirce the idea of the public, the general, the communal, is of primary importance in sound philosophizing. It is reflected in all of his opinions: in his opposition to methodological individualism, and his social theories of truth, reality, knowledge, and meaning; in his view of phenomenology as the analysis of common or universal experience; and in a metaphysics dominated by the ideas of continuity and generality. More specifically, it is the key to his conception of leading principles or habits in contrast to intuitive insight as the foundation of reasoning; in his conception of a scientific experiment as no isolated, self-contained process but as indissociable from a complex chain of verification; in his identification of pragmatic definition with habit rather than immediate experience; in his theory of common sense, the important word being "common"; in his theory of the generalization or habit-crystallization of feelings; in his emphasis on the reality of law. Especially prominent is the concept of habit and the forms which it assumes. In terms of it he defines cognitive meaning, leading principle, and law of nature. But to say that a philosophy is anti-individualistic does not necessarily mean that it discounts the individual element in experience, as individualistic philosophies do the general. This receives its proper attention in Peirce's category of Secondness, mirrored ontologically in specific, brute fact, psychologically in the sense of duality or reaction, and logically in the sign which he calls the "index."

Aware that recognition of his work would come late, Peirce sensed the danger that it might be unaccompanied by rigorous criticism. To be blinded by the peculiar strength of his thinking into a type of reverence that has always been common, would certainly be to violate the very spirit which animated him. First among the problems that confronts the critical reader is whether the experimentalism and the agapastic idealism of Peirce are congruous. He must separate and judge independently the arguments for the possibility of a scientific philosophy and the attempt of Peirce to achieve it. He must determine whether the anthropomorphism of Peirce is a legitimate extension of common sense or whether it borders on mythology and violates the pragmatic principle of clarity. He probably cannot avoid asking himself whether pragmaticism has been formulated too broadly or too narrowly, and whether the statement of the pragmatic criterion in terms of habit (it is not always so stated by Peirce) is a virtue or a difficulty. In the logic of science provocative questions crop up concerning the nature and interrelation of abduction, induction, and probability; for example, to what extent Peirce's claim that the success of the inductive procedure is independent of general material assumptions about the universe is justified—questions further stimulated by Peirce's ability to draw from his most technical discussions implications of broadest philosophic significance. His views on the relation between mathematics and deductive logic raise the problem not only of his justice to their respective subject-matter but of serious inconsistency in his analysis of necessary inference. In phenomenology numerous difficulties emerge, chiefly relating to the delineation of the three categories. That of Firstness suffers from considerable ambiguity, that of Thirdness from obscurity. These are a few of the general directions in which difficulties suggest themselves. Specific points that raise doubts and specific opinions that require restatement and clarification are as numerous as they must inevitably be in a creative intellect of Peirce's magnitude.

To follow Peirce's experiments in the science of philosophy is far less like strolling in green fields than like climbing a rocky slope. Those unafraid of the ascent may expect to breathe a purer atmosphere, one which discourages complacent slumber and the manufacture of neat fictions. Even to the most unsympathetic, Peirce's thought cannot fail to convey something of lasting value. It has a peculiar property, like that of the Lernæan hydra: discover a weak point, and two strong ones spring up beside it. Despite the elaborate architectonic planning of its creator, it is everywhere uncompleted, often distressingly so. There are many who have small regard for things uncompleted, and no doubt what they value is much to be valued. In his quest for magnificent array, in his design for a mighty temple that should house his ideas, Peirce failed. He succeeded only in advancing philosophy.

J. B.

I

CONCERNING THE AUTHOR *

THE reader has a right to know how the author's opinions were
formed. Not, of course, that he is expected to accept any conclusions which are not borne out by argument. But in discussions of
extreme difficulty, like these, when good judgment is a factor, and
pure ratiocination is not everything, it is prudent to take every
element into consideration. From the moment when I could think
at all, until now, about forty years, I have been diligently and incessantly occupied with the study of methods [of] inquiry, both those
which have been and are pursued and those which ought to be
pursued. For ten years before this study began, I had been in training in the chemical laboratory. I was thoroughly grounded not only
in all that was then known of physics and chemistry, but also in the
way in which those who were successfully advancing knowledge
proceeded. I have paid the most attention to the methods of the
most exact sciences, have intimately communed with some of the
greatest minds of our times in physical science, and have myself
made positive contributions—none of them of any very great importance, perhaps—in mathematics, gravitation, optics, chemistry,
astronomy, etc. I am saturated, through and through, with the
spirit of the physical sciences. I have been a great student
of logic, having read everything of any importance on the subject,
devoting a great deal of time to medieval thought, without neglecting
the works of the Greeks, the English, the Germans, the French, etc.,
and have produced systems of my own both in deductive and in
inductive logic. In metaphysics my training has been less systematic; yet I have read and deeply pondered upon all the main systems,
never being satisfied until I was able to think about them as their
own advocates thought.

The first strictly philosophical books that I read were of the
classical German schools; and I became so deeply imbued with many
of their ways of thinking that I have never been able to disabuse
myself of them. Yet my attitude was always that of a dweller in a
laboratory, eager only to learn what I did not yet know, and not that

* [Ms. c. 1897 (*CP* 1.3-14).]

of philosophers bred in theological seminaries, whose ruling impulse is to teach what they hold to be infallibly true. I devoted two hours a day to the study of Kant's *Critic of the Pure Reason* for more than three years, until I almost knew the whole book by heart, and had critically examined every section of it. For about two years, I had long and almost daily discussions with Chauncey Wright, one of the most acute of the followers of J. S. Mill.

The effect of these studies was that I came to hold the classical German philosophy to be, upon its argumentative side, of little weight; although I esteem it, perhaps am too partial to it, as a rich mine of philosophical suggestions. The English philosophy, meagre and crude, as it is, in its conceptions, proceeds by surer methods and more accurate logic. The doctrine of the association of ideas is, to my thinking, the finest piece of philosophical work of the prescientific ages. Yet I can but pronounce English sensationalism to be entirely destitute of any solid bottom. From the evolutionary philosophers, I have learned little; although I admit that, however hurriedly their theories have been knocked together, and however antiquated and ignorant Spencer's *First Principles* and general doctrines, yet they are under the guidance of a great and true idea, and are developing it by methods that are in their main features sound and scientific.

The works of Duns Scotus have strongly influenced me. If his logic and metaphysics, not slavishly worshipped, but torn away from its medievalism, be adapted to modern culture, under continual wholesome reminders of nominalistic criticisms, I am convinced that it will go far toward supplying the philosophy which is best to harmonize with physical science. But other conceptions have to be drawn from the history of science and from mathematics.

Thus, in brief, my philosophy may be described as the attempt of a physicist to make such conjecture as to the constitution of the universe as the methods of science may permit, with the aid of all that has been done by previous philosophers. I shall support my propositions by such arguments as I can. Demonstrative proof is not to be thought of. The demonstrations of the metaphysicians are all moonshine. The best that can be done is to supply a hypothesis, not devoid of all likelihood, in the general line of growth of scientific ideas, and capable of being verified or refuted by future observers.

Religious infallibilism, caught in the current of the times, shows symptoms of declaring itself to be only practically speaking infallible; and when it has thus once confessed itself subject to gradations, there will remain over no relic of the good old tenth-century infallibilism, except that of the infallible scientists, under which head I include, not merely the kind of characters that manufacture scientific catechisms and homilies, churches and creeds, and who are indeed "born missionaries," but all those respectable and cultivated persons who, having acquired their notions of science from reading, and not from research, have the idea that "science" means knowledge, while the truth is, it is a misnomer applied to the pursuit of those who are devoured by a desire to find things out. . . .

Though infallibility in scientific matters seems to me irresistibly comical, I should be in a sad way if I could not retain a high respect for those who lay claim to it, for they comprise the greater part of the people who have any conversation at all. When I say they lay claim to it, I mean they assume the functions of it quite naturally and unconsciously. The full meaning of the adage *Humanum est errare*, they have never waked up to. In those sciences of measurement which are the least subject to error—metrology, geodesy, and metrical astronomy—no man of self-respect ever now states his result, without affixing to it its *probable error*; and if this practice is not followed in other sciences it is because in those the probable errors are too vast to be estimated.

I am a man of whom critics have never found anything good to say. When they could see no opportunity to injure me, they have held their peace. The little laudation I have had has come from such sources, that the only satisfaction I have derived from it, has been from such slices of bread and butter as it might waft my way. Only once, as far as I remember, in all my lifetime have I experienced the pleasure of praise—not for what it might bring but in itself. That pleasure was beatific; and the praise that conferred it was meant for blame. It was that a critic said of me that I did not seem to be *absolutely sure of my own conclusions*. Never, if I can help it, shall that critic's eye ever rest on what I am now writing; for I owe a great pleasure to him; and, such was his evident animus, that should he find that out, I fear the fires of hell would be fed with new fuel in his breast.

My book will have no instruction to impart to anybody. Like a mathematical treatise, it will suggest certain ideas and certain reasons for holding them true; but then, if you accept them, it must be because you like my reasons, and the responsibility lies with you. Man is essentially a social animal: but to be social is one thing, to be gregarious is another: I decline to serve as bellwether. My book is meant for people who *want to find out*; and people who want philosophy ladled out to them can go elsewhere. There are philosophical soup shops at every corner, thank God!

The development of my ideas has been the industry of thirty years. I did not know as I ever should get to publish them, their ripening seemed so slow. But the harvest time has come, at last, and to me that harvest seems a wild one, but of course it is not I who have to pass judgment. It is not quite you, either, individual reader; it is experience and history.

For years in the course of this ripening process, I used for myself to collect my ideas under the designation *fallibilism*; and indeed the first step toward *finding out* is to acknowledge you do not satisfactorily know already; so that no blight can so surely arrest all intellectual growth as the blight of cocksureness; and ninety-nine out of every hundred good heads are reduced to impotence by that malady—of whose inroads they are most strangely unaware!

Indeed, out of a contrite fallibilism, combined with a high faith in the reality of knowledge, and an intense desire to find things out, all my philosophy has always seemed to me to grow. . . .

2

THE FIXATION OF BELIEF *

FEW persons care to study logic, because everybody conceives himself to be proficient enough in the art of reasoning already. But I observe that this satisfaction is limited to one's own ratiocination, and does not extend to that of other men.

We come to the full possession of our power of drawing inferences, the last of all our faculties; for it is not so much a natural gift as a long and difficult art. The history of its practice would make a grand subject for a book. The medieval schoolmen, following the Romans, made logic the earliest of a boy's studies after grammar, as being very easy. So it was as they understood it. Its fundamental principle, according to them, was, that all knowledge rests either on authority or reason; but that whatever is deduced by reason depends ultimately on a premiss derived from authority. Accordingly, as soon as a boy was perfect in the syllogistic procedure, his intellectual kit of tools was held to be complete.

To Roger Bacon, that remarkable mind who in the middle of the thirteenth century was almost a scientific man, the schoolmen's conception of reasoning appeared only an obstacle to truth. He saw that experience alone teaches anything—a proposition which to us seems easy to understand, because a distinct conception of experience has been handed down to us from former generations; which to him likewise seemed perfectly clear, because its difficulties had not yet unfolded themselves. Of all kinds of experience, the best, he thought, was interior illumination, which teaches many things about Nature which the external senses could never discover, such as the transubstantiation of bread.

Four centuries later, the more celebrated Bacon, in the first book of his *Novum Organum*, gave his clear account of experience as something which must be open to verification and reëxamination. But, superior as Lord Bacon's conception is to earlier notions, a modern reader who is not in awe of his grandiloquence is chiefly struck by the inadequacy of his view of scientific procedure.

* [This chapter, with Peirce's title, is the entire first paper of the series "Illustrations of the Logic of Science," *Popular Science Monthly* 1877. Here reprinted with the later changes (*CP* 5.358-87).]

That we have only to make some crude experiments, to draw up briefs of the results in certain blank forms, to go through these by rule, checking off everything disproved and setting down the alternatives, and that thus in a few years physical science would be finished up—what an idea! "He wrote on science like a Lord Chancellor," indeed, as Harvey, a genuine man of science said.

The early scientists, Copernicus, Tycho Brahe, Kepler, Galileo, Harvey, and Gilbert, had methods more like those of their modern brethren. Kepler undertook to draw a curve through the places of Mars, and to state the times occupied by the planet in describing the different parts of that curve; but perhaps his greatest service to science was in impressing on men's minds that this was the thing to be done if they wished to improve astronomy; that they were not to content themselves with inquiring whether one system of epicycles was better than another, but that they were to sit down to the figures and find out what the curve, in truth, was. He accomplished this by his incomparable energy and courage, blundering along in the most inconceivable way (to us), from one irrational hypothesis to another, until, after trying twenty-two of these, he fell, by the mere exhaustion of his invention, upon the orbit which a mind well furnished with the weapons of modern logic would have tried almost at the outset.†

In the same way, every work of science great enough to be well remembered for a few generations affords some exemplification of the defective state of the art of reasoning of the time when it was written; and each chief step in science has been a lesson in logic. It was so when Lavoisier and his contemporaries took up the study of Chemistry. The old chemist's maxim had been, "Lege, lege, lege, labora, ora, et relege." Lavoisier's method was not to read and pray, but to dream that some long and complicated chemical process would have a certain effect, to put it into practice with dull patience, after its inevitable failure, to dream that with some modification it would have another result, and to end by publishing the last dream as a fact: his way was to carry his mind into his laboratory, and literally to make of his alembics and cucurbits instruments of thought, giving a new conception of reasoning as something which was to be done with one's eyes open, in manipulating real things instead of words and fancies.

† I am ashamed at being obliged to confess that this volume contains a very false and foolish remark about Kepler. When I wrote it, I had never studied the original book as I have since. It is now my deliberate opinion that it is the most marvellous piece of inductive reasoning I have been able to find.—1893. [Cf. ch. 11, part II.]

The Darwinian controversy is, in large part, a question of logic. Mr. Darwin proposed to apply the statistical method to biology. The same thing has been done in a widely different branch of science, the theory of gases. Though unable to say what the movements of any particular molecule of gas would be on a certain hypothesis regarding the constitution of this class of bodies, Clausius and Maxwell were yet able, eight years before the publication of Darwin's immortal work, by the application of the doctrine of probabilities, to predict that in the long run such and such a proportion of the molecules would, under given circumstances, acquire such and such velocities; that there would take place, every second, such and such a relative number of collisions, etc.; and from these propositions were able to deduce certain properties of gases, especially in regard to their heat-relations. In like manner, Darwin, while unable to say what the operation of variation and natural selection in any individual case will be, demonstrates that in the long run they will, or would, adapt animals to their circumstances. Whether or not existing animal forms are due to such action, or what position the theory ought to take, forms the subject of a discussion in which questions of fact and questions of logic are curiously interlaced.

The object of reasoning is to find out, from the consideration of what we already know, something else which we do not know. Consequently, reasoning is good if it be such as to give a true conclusion from true premises, and not otherwise. Thus, the question of validity is purely one of fact and not of thinking. A being the facts stated in the premises and B being that concluded, the question is, whether these facts are really so related that if A were B would generally be. If so, the inference is valid; if not, not. It is not in the least the question whether, when the premises are accepted by the mind, we feel an impulse to accept the conclusion also. It is true that we do generally reason correctly by nature. But that is an accident; the true conclusion would remain true if we had no impulse to accept it; and the false one would remain false, though we could not resist the tendency to believe in it.

We are, doubtless, in the main logical animals, but we are not perfectly so. Most of us, for example, are naturally more sanguine and hopeful than logic would justify. We seem to be so constituted that in the absence of any facts to go upon we are happy and self-satisfied; so that the effect of experience is continually to contract our hopes and aspirations. Yet a lifetime of the application of this corrective does not usually eradicate our sanguine disposition. Where hope is unchecked by any experience, it is likely that our optimism is extravagant. Logicality in regard to practical matters (if this be understood, not in the old sense, but as consisting in a wise union of security with fruitfulness of reasoning) is the most useful quality an animal can possess, and might, therefore, result from the action of natural selection; but outside of these it is probably of more advantage to the animal to have his mind filled with pleasing and encouraging visions, independently of their truth; and thus, upon unpractical subjects, natural selection might occasion a fallacious tendency of thought.

That which determines us, from given premises, to draw one inference rather than another, is some habit of mind, whether it be constitutional or acquired. The habit is good or otherwise, according as it produces true conclusions from true premises or not; and an inference is regarded as valid or not, without reference to the truth or falsity of its conclusion specially, but according as the habit which determines it is such as to produce true conclusions in general or not. The particular habit of mind which governs this or that inference may be formulated in a proposition whose truth depends on the validity of the inferences which the habit determines; and such a formula is called a *guiding principle* of inference. Suppose, for example, that we observe that a rotating disk of copper quickly comes to rest when placed between the poles of a magnet, and we infer that this will happen with every disk of copper. The guiding principle is, that what is true of one piece of copper is true of another. Such a guiding principle with regard to copper would be much safer than with regard to many other substances—brass, for example.

A book might be written to signalize all the most important of these guiding principles of reasoning. It would probably be, we must confess, of no service to a person whose thought is directed wholly to practical subjects, and whose activity moves along thoroughly-beaten paths. The problems that present themselves to such a mind are matters of routine which he has learned once for all to handle in learning his business. But let a man venture into an unfamiliar field, or where his results are not continually checked by experience, and all history shows that the most masculine intellect will ofttimes lose his orientation and waste his efforts in directions which bring him no nearer to his goal, or even carry him entirely astray. He is like a ship in the open sea, with no one on board who understands the rules of navigation. And in such a case some general study of the guiding principles of reasoning would be sure to be found useful.

The subject could hardly be treated, however, without being first limited; since almost any fact may serve as a guiding principle. But it so happens that there exists a division among facts, such that in one class are all those which are absolutely essential as guiding principles, while in the others are all which have any other interest as objects of research. This division is between those which are necessarily taken for granted in asking why a certain conclusion is thought to follow from certain premises, and those which are not implied in such a question. A moment's thought will show that a variety of facts are already assumed when the logical question is first asked. It is implied, for instance, that there are such states of mind as doubt and belief—that a passage from one to the other is possible, the object of thought remaining the same, and that this transition is subject to some rules by which all minds are alike bound. As these are facts which we must already know before we can have any clear conception of reasoning at all, it cannot be supposed to be any longer of much interest to inquire into their truth or falsity. On the other hand, it is easy to believe that those rules of reasoning which are deduced from the very idea of the process are the ones which are the most essential; and, indeed, that so long as it conforms to these it will, at least, not lead to false conclusions from true premises. In point of fact, the importance of what may be deduced from the assumptions involved in the logical question turns out to be greater than might be supposed, and this for reasons which it is difficult to exhibit at the outset. The only one which I shall here mention is, that conceptions which are really products of logical reflection, without being readily seen to be so, mingle with our ordinary thoughts, and are frequently the causes of great confusion. This is the case, for example, with the conception of quality. A quality, as such, is never an object of observation. We can see that a thing is blue or green, but the quality of being blue and the quality of being green are not things which we see; they are products of logical reflections. The truth is, that common-sense, or thought as it first emerges above the level of the narrowly practical, is deeply imbued with that bad logical quality to which the epithet *metaphysical* is commonly applied; and nothing can clear it up but a severe course of logic.

We generally know when we wish to ask a question and when we wish to pronounce a judgment, for there is a dissimilarity between the sensation of doubting and that of believing.

But this is not all which distinguishes doubt from belief. There is a practical difference. Our beliefs guide our desires and shape our actions. The Assassins, or followers of the Old Man of the Mountain, used to rush into death at his least command, because they believed that obedience to him would insure everlasting felicity. Had they doubted this, they would not have acted as they did. So it is with every belief, according to its degree. The feeling of believing is a more or less sure indication of there being established in our nature some habit which will determine our actions. Doubt never has such an effect.

Nor must we overlook a third point of difference. Doubt is an uneasy and dissatisfied state from which we struggle to free ourselves and pass into the state of belief; while the latter is a calm and satisfactory state which we do not wish to avoid, or to change to a belief in anything else. On the contrary, we cling tenaciously, not merely to believing, but to believing just what we do believe.

Thus, both doubt and belief have positive effects upon us, though very different ones. Belief does not make us act at once, but puts us into such a condition that we shall behave in some certain way, when the occasion arises. Doubt has not the least such active effect, but stimulates us to inquiry until it is destroyed. This reminds us of the irritation of a nerve and the reflex action produced thereby; while for the analogue of belief, in the nervous system, we must look to what are called nervous associations—for example, to that habit of the nerves in consequence of which the smell of a peach will make the mouth water.

The irritation of doubt causes a struggle to attain a state of belief. I shall term this struggle *Inquiry*, though it must be admitted that this is sometimes not a very apt designation.

The irritation of doubt is the only immediate motive for the struggle to attain belief. It is certainly best for us that our beliefs should be such as may truly guide our actions so as to satisfy our desires; and this reflection will make us reject every belief which does not seem to have been so formed as to insure this result. But it will only do so by creating a doubt in the place of that belief. With the doubt, therefore, the struggle begins, and with the cessation of doubt it ends. Hence, the sole object of inquiry is the settlement of opinion. We may fancy that this is not enough for us, and that we seek, not merely an opinion, but a true opinion. But put this fancy to the test, and it proves groundless; for as soon as a firm belief is reached we are entirely satisfied, whether the belief be true or false. And it is clear that nothing out of the sphere of our knowledge can be our object, for nothing which does not affect the mind can be the motive for mental effort. The most that can be maintained is, that we seek for a belief that we shall *think* to be true. But we think each one of our beliefs to be true, and, indeed, it is mere tautology to say so.

That the settlement of opinion is the sole end of inquiry is a very important proposition. It sweeps away, at once, various vague and erroneous conceptions of proof. A few of these may be noticed here.

1. Some philosophers have imagined that to start an inquiry it was only necessary to utter a question whether orally or by setting it down upon paper, and have even recommended us to begin our studies with questioning everything! But the mere putting of a proposition into the interrogative form does not stimulate the mind to any struggle after belief. There must be a real and living doubt, and without this all discussion is idle.

2. It is a very common idea that a demonstration must rest on some ultimate and absolutely indubitable propositions. These, according to one school, are first principles of a general nature; according to another, are first sensations. But, in point of fact, an inquiry, to have that completely satisfactory result called demonstration, has only to start with propositions perfectly free from all actual doubt. If the premisses are not in fact doubted at all, they cannot be more satisfactory than they are.

3. Some people seem to love to argue a point after all the world is fully convinced of it. But no further advance can be made. When doubt ceases, mental action on the subject comes to an end; and, if it did go on, it would be without a purpose.

If the settlement of opinion is the sole object of inquiry, and if belief is of the nature of a habit, why should we not attain the desired end, by taking as answer to a question any we may fancy, and constantly reiterating it to ourselves, dwelling on all which may conduce to that belief, and learning to turn with contempt and hatred from anything that might disturb it? This simple and direct method is really pursued by many men. I remember once being entreated not to read a certain newspaper lest it might change my opinion upon free-trade. "Lest I might be entrapped by its fallacies and misstatements," was the form of expression. "You are not," my friend said, "a special student of political economy. You might, therefore, easily be deceived by fallacious arguments upon the subject. You might, then, if you read this paper, be led to believe in protection. But you admit that free-trade is the true doctrine; and you do not wish to believe what is not true." I have often known this system to be deliberately adopted. Still oftener, the instinctive dislike of an undecided state of mind, exaggerated into a vague dread of doubt, makes men cling spasmodically to the views they already take. The man feels that, if he only holds to his belief without wavering, it will be entirely satisfactory. Nor can it be denied that a steady and immovable faith yields great peace of mind. It may, indeed, give rise to inconveniences, as if a man should resolutely continue to believe that fire would not burn him, or that he would be eternally damned if he received his *ingesta* otherwise than through a stomach-pump. But then the man who adopts this method will not allow that its inconveniences are greater than its advantages. He will say, "I hold steadfastly to the truth, and the truth is always wholesome." And in many cases it may very well be that the pleasure he derives from his calm faith overbalances any inconveniences resulting from its deceptive character. Thus, if it be true that death is annihilation, then the man who believes that he will certainly go straight to heaven when he dies, provided he have fulfilled certain simple observances in this life, has a cheap pleasure which will not be followed by the least disappointment. A similar consideration seems to have weight with many persons in religious topics, for we frequently hear it said, "Oh, I could not believe so-and-so, because I should be wretched if I did." When an ostrich buries its head in the sand as danger approaches, it very likely takes the happiest course. It hides the danger, and then calmly says there is no danger; and, if it feels perfectly sure there is none, why should it raise its head to see? A man may go through life, systematically keeping out of view all that might cause a change in his opinions, and if he only succeeds—basing his method, as he does, on two fundamental psychological laws—I do not see what can be said against his doing so. It would be an egotistical impertinence to object that his procedure is irrational, for that only amounts to saying that his method of settling belief is not ours. He does not propose to himself to be rational, and, indeed, will often talk with scorn of man's weak and illusive reason. So let him think as he pleases.

But this method of fixing belief, which may be called the method of tenacity, will be unable to hold its ground in practice. The social impulse is against it. The man who adopts it will find that other men think differently from him, and it will be apt to occur to him, in some saner moment, that their opinions are quite as good as his own, and this will shake his confidence in his belief. This conception, that another man's thought or sentiment may be equivalent to one's own, is a distinctly new step, and a highly important one. It arises from an impulse too strong in man to be suppressed, without danger of destroying the human species. Unless we make ourselves hermits, we shall necessarily influence each other's opinions; so that the problem becomes how to fix belief, not in the individual merely, but in the community.

Let the will of the state act, then, instead of that of the individual. Let an institution be created which shall have for its object to keep correct doctrines before the attention of the people, to reiterate them perpetually, and to teach them to the young; having at the same time power to prevent contrary doctrines from being taught, advocated, or expressed. Let all possible causes of a change of mind be removed from men's apprehensions. Let them be kept ignorant, lest they should learn of some reason to think otherwise than they do. Let their passions be enlisted, so that they may regard private and unusual opinions with hatred and horror. Then, let all men who reject the established belief be terrified into silence. Let the people turn out and tar-and-feather such men, or let inquisitions be made into the manner of thinking of suspected persons, and when they are found guilty of forbidden beliefs, let them be subjected to some signal punishment. When complete agreement could not otherwise be reached, a general massacre of all who have not thought in a certain way has proved a very effective means of settling opinion in a country. If the power to do this be wanting, let a list of opinions be drawn up, to which no man of the least independence of thought can assent, and let the faithful be required to accept all these propositions, in order to segregate them as radically as possible from the influence of the rest of the world.

This method has, from the earliest times, been one of the chief means of upholding correct theological and political doctrines, and of preserving their universal or catholic character. In Rome, especially, it has been practised from the days of Numa Pompilius to those of Pius Nonus. This is the most perfect example in history; but wherever there is a priesthood—and no religion has been without one—this method has been more or less made use of. Wherever there is an aristocracy, or a guild, or any association of a class of men whose interests depend, or are supposed to depend, on certain propositions, there will be inevitably found some traces of this natural product of social feeling. Cruelties always accompany this system; and when it is consistently carried out, they become atrocities of the most horrible kind in the eyes of any rational man. Nor should this occasion surprise, for the officer of a society does not feel justified in surrendering the interests of that society for the sake of mercy, as he might his own private interests. It is natural, therefore, that sympathy and fellowship should thus produce a most ruthless power.

In judging this method of fixing belief, which may be called the method of authority, we must, in the first place, allow its immeasurable mental and moral superiority to the method of tenacity. Its success is proportionately greater; and, in fact, it has over and over again worked the most majestic results. The mere structures of stone which it has caused to be put together—in Siam, for example, in Egypt, and in Europe—have many of them a sublimity hardly more than rivalled by the greatest works of Nature. And, except the geological epochs, there are no periods of time so vast as those which are measured by some of these organized faiths. If we scrutinize the matter closely, we shall find that there has not been one of their creeds which has remained always the same; yet the change is so slow as to be imperceptible during one person's life, so that individual belief remains sensibly fixed. For the mass of mankind, then, there is perhaps no better method than this. If it is their highest impulse to be intellectual slaves, then slaves they ought to remain.

But no institution can undertake to regulate opinions upon every subject. Only the most important ones can be attended to, and on the rest men's minds must be left to the action of natural causes. This imperfection will be no source of weakness so long as men are in such a state of culture that one opinion does not influence another —that is, so long as they cannot put two and two together. But in the most priest-ridden states some individuals will be found who are raised above that condition. These men possess a wider sort of social feeling; they see that men in other countries and in other ages have held to very different doctrines from those which they themselves have been brought up to believe; and they cannot help seeing that it is the mere accident of their having been taught as they have, and of their having been surrounded with the manners and associations they have, that has caused them to believe as they do and not far differently. Nor can their candour resist the reflection that there is no reason to rate their own views at a higher value than those of other nations and other centuries; thus giving rise to doubts in their minds.

They will further perceive that such doubts as these must exist in their minds with reference to every belief which seems to be determined by the caprice either of themselves or of those who originated the popular opinions. The willful adherence to a belief, and the arbitrary forcing of it upon others, must, therefore, both be given up. A different new method of settling opinions must be adopted, that shall not only produce an impulse to believe, but shall also decide what proposition it is which is to be believed. Let the action of natural preferences be unimpeded, then, and under their influence let men, conversing together and regarding matters in different lights, gradually develop beliefs in harmony with natural causes. This method resembles that by which conceptions of art have been brought to maturity. The most perfect example of it is to be found in the history of metaphysical philosophy. Systems of this sort have not usually rested upon any observed facts, at least not in any great degree. They have been chiefly adopted because their fundamental propositions seemed "agreeable to reason." This is an apt expression; it does not mean that which agrees with experience, but that which we find ourselves inclined to believe. Plato, for example, finds it agreeable to reason that the distances of the celestial spheres from one another should be proportional to the different lengths of strings which produce harmonious chords. Many philosophers have been led to their main conclusions by considerations like this †; but this is the lowest and least developed

† Let us see in what manner a few of the greatest philosophers have undertaken to settle opinion, and what their success has been. Descartes, who would have a man begin by doubting everything, remarks that there is one thing he will find himself unable to doubt, and that is, that he does doubt ; and when he reflects that he doubts, he can no longer doubt that he exists. Then, because he is all the while doubting whether there are any such things as shape and motion, Descartes thinks he must be persuaded that shape and motion do not belong to his nature, or anything else but consciousness. This is taking it for granted that nothing in his nature lies hidden beneath the surface. Next, Descartes asks the doubter to remark that he has the idea of a Being, in the highest degree intelligent, powerful, and perfect. Now a Being would not have these qualities unless he existed necessarily and eternally. By existing necessarily he means existing by virtue of the existence of the idea. Consequently, all doubt as to the existence of this Being must cease. This plainly supposes that belief is to be fixed by what men find in their minds. He is reasoning like this : I find it written in the volume of my mind that there is something X, which is such a sort of thing that the moment it is written down it exists. Plainly, he is aiming at a kind of truth which saying so can make to be so. He gives two further proofs of God's existence. Descartes makes God easier to know than anything else ; for whatever we think He is, He is. He fails to remark that this is precisely the definition of a *figment*. In particular, God cannot be a deceiver ; whence it follows, that whatever we quite clearly and distinctly think to be true about any subject, must *be* true. Accordingly, if people will thoroughly discuss a subject, and quite clearly and distinctly make up their minds what they think about it, the desired settlement of the question will be reached. I may remark that the world has pretty thoroughly deliberated upon that theory and has quite distinctly come to the conclusion that it is utter nonsense ; whence that judgment is indisputably right.

Many critics have told me that I misrepresent the *a priori* philosophers, when I represent them as adopting whatever opinion there seems to be a form which the method takes, for it is clear that another man might find Kepler's theory, that the celestial spheres are proportional to the inscribed and circumscribed spheres of the different regular solids, more agreeable to *his* reason. But the shock of opinions will soon lead men to rest on preferences of a far more universal nature. Take, for example, the doctrine that man only acts selfishly—that is, from the consideration that acting in one way will afford him more pleasure than acting in another. This rests on no fact in the world, but it has had a wide acceptance as being the only reasonable theory.

This method is far more intellectual and respectable from the point of view of reason than either of the others which we have noticed. Indeed, as long as no better method can be applied, it ought to be followed, since it is then the expression of instinct which must be the ultimate cause of belief in all cases. But its failure has been the most manifest. It makes of inquiry something similar to

natural inclination to adopt. But nobody can say the above does not accurately define the position of Descartes, and upon what does he repose except natural ways of thinking ? Perhaps I shall be told, however, that since Kant, that vice has been cured. Kant's great boast is that he critically examines into our natural inclinations toward certain opinions. An opinion that something is *universally* true clearly goes further than experience can warrant. An opinion that something is *necessarily* true (that is, not merely is true in the existing state of things, but would be true in every state of things) equally goes further than experience will warrant. Those remarks had been made by Leibniz and admitted by Hume ; and Kant reiterates them. Though they are propositions of a nominalistic cast, they can hardly be denied. I may add that whatever is held to be precisely true goes further than experience can possibly warrant. Accepting those criteria of the origin of ideas, Kant proceeds to reason as follows : Geometrical propositions are held to be universally true. Hence, they are not given by experience. Consequently, it must be owing to an inward necessity of man's nature that he sees everything in space. Ergo, the sum of the angles of a triangle will be equal to two right angles for all the objects of our vision. Just that, and nothing more, is Kant's line of thought. But the dry-rot of reason in the seminaries has gone to the point where such stuff is held to be admirable argumentation. I might go through the *Critic of the Pure Reason*, section by section, and show that the thought throughout is precisely of this character. He everywhere shows that ordinary objects, such as trees and gold-pieces, involve elements not contained in the first presentations of sense. But we cannot persuade ourselves to give up the reality of trees and gold-pieces. There is a general inward insistence upon them, and that is the warrant for swallowing the entire bolus of general belief about them. This is merely accepting without question a belief as soon as it is shown to please a great many people very much. When he comes to the ideas of God, Freedom, and Immortality, he hesitates ; because people who think only of bread and butter, pleasure and power, are indifferent to those ideas. He subjects these ideas to a different kind of examination, and finally admits them upon grounds which appear to the seminarists more or less suspicious, but which in the eyes of laboratorists are infinitely stronger than the grounds upon which he has accepted space, time, and causality. Those last grounds amount to nothing but this, that what there is a very decided and general inclination to believe must be true. Had the development of taste; but taste, unfortunately, is always more or less a matter of fashion, and accordingly metaphysicians have never come to any fixed agreement, but the pendulum has swung backward and forward between a more material and a more spiritual philosophy, from the earliest times to the latest. And so from this, which has been called the *a priori* method, we are driven, in Lord Bacon's phrase, to a true induction. We have examined into this *a priori* method as something which promised to deliver our opinions from their accidental and capricious element. But development, while it is a process which eliminates the effect of some casual circumstances, only magnifies that of others. This method, therefore, does not differ in a very essential way from that of authority. The government may not have lifted its finger to influence my convictions; I may have been left outwardly quite free to choose, we will

Kant merely said, I shall adopt for the present the belief that the three angles of a triangle are equal to two right angles because nobody but brother Lambert and some Italian has ever called it in question, his attitude would be well enough. But on the contrary, he and those who today represent his school distinctly maintain the proposition is *proved*, and the Lambertists *refuted*, by what comes merely to general disinclination to think with them.

As for Hegel, who led Germany for a generation, he recognizes clearly what he is about. He simply launches his boat into the current of thought and allows himself to be carried wherever the current leads. He himself calls his method *dialectic*, meaning that a frank discussion of the difficulties to which any opinion spontaneously gives rise will lead to modification after modification until a tenable position is attained. This is a distinct profession of faith in the method of inclinations.

Other philosophers appeal to "the test of inconceivability of the opposite," to "presuppositions" (by which they mean *Voraussetzungen*, properly translated, *postulates*), and other devices; but all these are but so many systems of rummaging the garret of the skull to find an enduring opinion about the Universe.

When we pass from the perusal of works upholding the method of authority to those of the philosophers, we not only find ourselves in a vastly higher intellectual atmosphere, but also in a clearer, freer, brighter, and more refreshing moral atmosphere. All this, however, is beside the one significant question of whether the method succeeds in fixing men's opinions. The projects of these authors are most persuasive. One dare swear they should succeed. But in point of fact, up to date they decidedly do not; and the outlook in this direction is most discouraging. The difficulty is that the opinions which today seem most unshakable are found tomorrow to be out of fashion. They are really far more changeable than they appear to a hasty reader to be; since the phrases made to dress out defunct opinions are worn at second hand by their successors.

We still talk of "cause and effect" although, in the mechanical world, the opinion that phrase was meant to express has been shelved long ago. We now know that the acceleration of a particle at any instant depends upon its position relative to other particles at that same instant; while the old idea was that the past affects the future, while the future does not affect the past. So the "law of demand and supply" has utterly different meanings with different economists.—1893.

say, between monogamy and polygamy, and, appealing to my conscience only, I may have concluded that the latter practice is in itself licentious. But when I come to see that the chief obstacle to the spread of Christianity among a people of as high culture as the Hindoos has been a conviction of the immorality of our way of treating women, I cannot help seeing that, though governments do not interfere, sentiments in their development will be very greatly determined by accidental causes. Now, there are some people, among whom I must suppose that my reader is to be found, who, when they see that any belief of theirs is determined by any circumstance extraneous to the facts, will from that moment not merely admit in words that that belief is doubtful, but will experience a real doubt of it, so that it ceases in some degree at least to be a belief.

To satisfy our doubts, therefore, it is necessary that a method should be found by which our beliefs may be determined by nothing human, but by some external permanency—by something upon which our thinking has no effect. Some mystics imagine that they have such a method in a private inspiration from on high. But that is only a form of the method of tenacity, in which the conception of truth as something public is not yet developed. Our external permanency would not be external, in our sense, if it was restricted in its influence to one individual. It must be something which affects, or might affect, every man. And, though these affections are necessarily as various as are individual conditions, yet the method must be such that the ultimate conclusion of every man shall be the same. Such is the method of science. Its fundamental hypothesis, restated in more familiar language, is this: There are Real things, whose characters are entirely independent of our opinions about them; those Reals affect our senses according to regular laws, and, though our sensations are as different as are our relations to the objects, yet, by taking advantage of the laws of perception, we can ascertain by reasoning how things really and truly are; and any man, if he have sufficient experience and he reason enough about it, will be led to the one True conclusion. The new conception here involved is that of Reality. It may be asked how I know that there are any Reals. If this hypothesis is the sole support of my method of inquiry, my method of inquiry must not be used to support my hypothesis. The reply is this: 1. If investigation cannot be regarded as proving that there are Real things, it at least does not lead to a contrary conclusion; but the method and the conception on which it is based remain ever in harmony. No doubts of the method, therefore, necessarily arise from its practice, as is the case with all the others. 2. The feeling which gives rise to any method of fixing belief is a dissatisfaction at two repugnant propositions. But here already is a vague concession that there is some *one* thing which a proposition should represent. Nobody, therefore, can really doubt that there are Reals, for, if he did, doubt would not be a source of dissatisfaction. The hypothesis, therefore, is one which every mind admits. So that the social impulse does not cause men to doubt it. 3. Everybody uses the scientific method about a great many things, and only ceases to use it when he does not know how to apply it. 4. Experience of the method has not led us to doubt it, but, on the contrary, scientific investigation has had the most wonderful triumphs in the way of settling opinion. These afford the explanation of my not doubting the method or the hypothesis which it supposes; and not having any doubt, nor believing that anybody else whom I could influence has, it would be the merest babble for me to say more about it. If there be anybody with a living doubt upon the subject, let him consider it.

To describe the method of scientific investigation is the object of this series of papers. At present I have only room to notice some points of contrast between it and other methods of fixing belief.

This is the only one of the four methods which presents any distinction of a right and a wrong way. If I adopt the method of tenacity, and shut myself out from all influences, whatever I think necessary to doing this, is necessary according to that method. So with the method of authority: the state may try to put down heresy by means which, from a scientific point of view, seem very ill-calculated to accomplish its purposes; but the only test *on that method* is what the state thinks; so that it cannot pursue the method wrongly. So with the *a priori* method. The very essence of it is to think as one is inclined to think. All metaphysicians will be sure to do that, however they may be inclined to judge each other to be perversely wrong.· The Hegelian system recognizes every natural tendency of thought as logical, although it be certain to be abolished by counter-tendencies. Hegel thinks there is a regular system in the succession of these tendencies, in consequence of which, after drifting one way and the other for a long time, opinion will at last go right. And it is true that metaphysicians do get the right ideas at last; Hegel's system of Nature represents tolerably the science of his day; and one may be sure that whatever scientific investigation shall have put out of doubt will presently receive *a priori* demonstration on the part of the metaphysicians. But with the scientific method the case is different. I may start with known and observed facts to proceed to the unknown; and yet the rules which I follow in doing so may not be such as investigation would approve. The test of whether I am truly following the method is not an immediate appeal to my feelings and purposes, but, on the contrary, itself involves the application of the method. Hence it is that bad reasoning as well as good reasoning is possible; and this fact is the foundation of the practical side of logic.

It is not to be supposed that the first three methods of settling opinion present no advantage whatever over the scientific method. On the contrary, each has some peculiar convenience of its own. The *a priori* method is distinguished for its comfortable conclusions. It is the nature of the process to adopt whatever belief we are inclined to, and there are certain flatteries to the vanity of man which we all believe by nature, until we are awakened from our pleasing dream by rough facts. The method of authority will always govern the mass of mankind; and those who wield the various forms of organized force in the state will never be convinced that dangerous reasoning ought not to be suppressed in some way. If liberty of speech is to be untrammelled from the grosser forms of constraint, then uniformity of opinion will be secured by a moral terrorism to which the respectability of society will give its thorough approval. Following the method of authority is the path of peace. Certain non-conformities are permitted; certain others (considered unsafe) are forbidden. These are different in different countries and in different ages; but, wherever you are, let it be known that you seriously hold a tabooed belief, and you may be perfectly sure of being treated with a cruelty less brutal but more refined than hunting you like a wolf. Thus, the greatest intellectual benefactors of mankind have never dared, and dare not now, to utter the whole of their thought; and thus a shade of *prima facie* doubt is cast upon every proposition which is considered essential to the security of society. Singularly enough, the persecution does not all come from without; but a man torments himself and is oftentimes most distressed at finding himself believing propositions which he has been brought up to regard with aversion. The peaceful and sympathetic man will, therefore, find it hard to resist the temptation to submit his opinions to authority. But most of all I admire the method of tenacity for its strength, simplicity, and directness. Men who pursue it are distinguished for their decision of character, which becomes very easy with such a mental rule. They do not waste time in trying to make up their minds what they want, but, fastening like lightning upon whatever alternative comes first, they hold it to the end, whatever happens, without an instant's irresolution. This is one of the splendid qualities which generally accompany brilliant, unlasting success. It is impossible not to envy the man who can dismiss reason, although we know how it must turn out at last.

Such are the advantages which the other methods of settling opinion have over scientific investigation. A man should consider well of them; and then he should consider that, after all, he wishes his opinions to coincide with the fact, and that there is no reason why the results of those three first methods should do so. To bring about this effect is the prerogative of the method of science. Upon such considerations he has to make his choice—a choice which is far more than the adoption of any intellectual opinion, which is one of the ruling decisions of his life, to which, when once made, he is bound to adhere. The force of habit will sometimes cause a man to hold on to old beliefs, after he is in a condition to see that they have no sound basis. But reflection upon the state of the case will overcome these habits, and he ought to allow reflection its full weight. People sometimes shrink from doing this, having an idea that beliefs are wholesome which they cannot help feeling rest on nothing. But let such persons suppose an analogous though different case from their own. Let them ask themselves what they would say to a reformed Mussulman who should hesitate to give up his old notions in regard to the relations of the sexes; or to a reformed Catholic who should still shrink from reading the Bible. Would they not say that these persons ought to consider the matter fully, and clearly understand the new doctrine, and then ought to embrace it, in its entirety? But, above all, let it be considered that what is more wholesome than any particular belief is integrity of belief, and that to avoid looking into the support of any belief from a fear that it may turn out rotten is quite as immoral as it is disadvantageous. The person who confesses that there is such a thing as truth, which is distinguished from falsehood simply by this, that if acted on it should, on full consideration, carry us to the point we aim at and not astray, and then, though convinced of this, dares not know the truth and seeks to avoid it, is in a sorry state of mind indeed.

Yes, the other methods do have their merits: a clear logical conscience does cost something—just as any virtue, just as all that we cherish, costs us dear. But we should not desire it to be otherwise. The genius of a man's logical method should be loved and reverenced as his bride, whom he has chosen from all the world. He need not contemn the others; on the contrary, he may honour them deeply, and in doing so he only honours her the more. But she is the one that he has chosen, and he knows that he was right in making that choice. And having made it, he will work and fight for her, and will not complain that there are blows to take, hoping that there may be as many and as hard to give, and will strive to be the worthy knight and champion of her from the blaze of whose splendours he draws his inspiration and his courage.

3

HOW TO MAKE OUR IDEAS CLEAR *

WHOEVER has looked into a modern treatise on logic of the common sort, will doubtless remember the two distinctions between *clear* and *obscure* conceptions, and between *distinct* and *confused* conceptions. They have lain in the books now for nigh two centuries, unimproved and unmodified, and are generally reckoned by logicians as among the gems of their doctrine.

A clear idea is defined as one which is so apprehended that it will be recognized wherever it is met with, and so that no other will be mistaken for it. If it fails of this clearness, it is said to be obscure.

This is rather a neat bit of philosophical terminology; yet, since it is clearness that they were defining, I wish the logicians had made their definition a little more plain. Never to fail to recognize an idea, and under no circumstances to mistake another for it, let it come in how recondite a form it may, would indeed imply such prodigious force and clearness of intellect as is seldom met with in this world. On the other hand, merely to have such an acquaintance with the idea as to have become familiar with it, and to have lost all hesitancy in recognizing it in ordinary cases, hardly seems to deserve the name of clearness of apprehension, since after all it only amounts to a subjective feeling of mastery which may be entirely mistaken. I take it, however, that when the logicians speak of "clearness," they mean nothing more than such a familiarity with an idea, since they regard the quality as but a small merit, which needs to be supplemented by another, which they call *distinctness*.

A distinct idea is defined as one which contains nothing which is not clear. This is technical language; by the *contents* of an idea logicians understand whatever is contained in its definition. So that an idea is *distinctly* apprehended, according to them, when we can give a precise definition of it, in abstract terms. Here the professional logicians leave the subject; and I would not have troubled the reader with what they have to say, if it were not such a striking example of how they have been slumbering through ages

* [This chapter, with Peirce's title, is the entire second paper of a series (cf. ch. 2), *Popular Science Monthly* 1878. Here reprinted with the later changes (*CP* 5.388-410).]

of intellectual activity, listlessly disregarding the enginery of modern thought, and never dreaming of applying its lessons to the improvement of logic. It is easy to show that the doctrine that familiar use and abstract distinctness make the perfection of apprehension has its only true place in philosophies which have long been extinct; and it is now time to formulate the method of attaining to a more perfect clearness of thought, such as we see and admire in the thinkers of our own time.

When Descartes set about the reconstruction of philosophy, his first step was to (theoretically) permit scepticism and to discard the practice of the schoolmen of looking to authority as the ultimate source of truth. That done, he sought a more natural fountain of true principles, and thought he found it in the human mind; thus passing, in the directest way, from the method of authority to that of apriority, as described in my first paper.[1] Self-consciousness was to furnish us with our fundamental truths, and to decide what was agreeable to reason. But since, evidently, not all ideas are true, he was led to note, as the first condition of infallibility, that they must be clear. The distinction between an idea *seeming* clear and really being so, never occurred to him. Trusting to introspection, as he did, even for a knowledge of external things, why should he question its testimony in respect to the contents of our own minds? But then, I suppose, seeing men, who seemed to be quite clear and positive, holding opposite opinions upon fundamental principles, he was further led to say that clearness of ideas is not sufficient, but that they need also to be distinct, *i.e.*, to have nothing unclear about them. What he probably meant by this (for he did not explain himself with precision) was, that they must sustain the test of dialectical examination; that they must not only seem clear at the outset, but that discussion must never be able to bring to light points of obscurity connected with them.

Such was the distinction of Descartes, and one sees that it was precisely on the level of his philosophy. It was somewhat developed by Leibniz. This great and singular genius was as remarkable for what he failed to see as for what he saw. That a piece of mechanism could not do work perpetually without being fed with power in some form, was a thing perfectly apparent to him; yet he did not understand that the machinery of the mind can only transform knowledge, but never originate it, unless it be fed with facts of observation. He thus missed the most essential point of the Cartesian philosophy, which is, that to accept propositions which seem perfectly evident to us is a thing which, whether it be logical or illogical, we cannot help doing. Instead of regarding the matter in this way, he sought to reduce the first principles of science to two classes, those which cannot be denied without self-contradiction, and those which result from the principle of sufficient reason (of which more anon), and was apparently unaware of the great difference between his position and that of Descartes. So he reverted to the old trivialities of logic; and, above all, abstract definitions played a great part in his philosophy. It was quite natural, therefore, that on observing that the method of Descartes laboured under the difficulty that we may seem to ourselves to have clear apprehensions of ideas which in truth are very hazy, no better remedy occurred to him than to require an abstract definition of every important term. Accordingly, in adopting the distinction of *clear* and *distinct* notions, he described the latter quality as the clear apprehension of everything contained in the definition; and the books have ever since copied his words. There is no danger that his chimerical scheme will ever again be over-valued. Nothing new can ever be learned by analyzing definitions. Nevertheless, our existing beliefs can be set in order by this process, and order is an essential element of intellectual economy, as of every other. It may be acknowledged, therefore, that the books are right in making familiarity with a notion the first step toward clearness of apprehension, and the defining of it the second. But in omitting all mention of any higher perspicuity of thought, they simply mirror a philosophy which was exploded a hundred years ago. That much-admired "ornament of logic"—the doctrine of clearness and distinctness—may be pretty enough, but it is high time to relegate to our cabinet of curiosities the antique *bijou*, and to wear about us something better adapted to modern uses.

The very first lesson that we have a right to demand that logic shall teach us is, how to make our ideas clear; and a most important one it is, depreciated only by minds who stand in need of it. To know what we think, to be masters of our own meaning, will make a solid foundation for great and weighty thought. It is most easily learned by those whose ideas are meagre and restricted; and far happier they than such as wallow helplessly in a rich mud of conceptions. A nation, it is true, may, in the course of generations, overcome the disadvantage of an excessive wealth of language and its natural concomitant, a vast, unfathomable deep of ideas. We may see it in history, slowly perfecting its literary forms, sloughing at length its metaphysics, and, by virtue of the untirable patience which is often a compensation, attaining great excellence in every branch of mental acquirement. The page of history is not yet unrolled that is to tell us whether such a people will or will not in the long run prevail over one whose ideas (like the words of their language) are few, but which possesses a wonderful mastery over those which it has. For an individual, however, there can be no question that a few clear ideas are worth more than many confused ones. A young man would hardly be persuaded to sacrifice the greater part of his thoughts to save the rest; and the muddled head is the least apt to see the necessity of such a sacrifice. Him we can usually only commiserate, as a person with a congenital defect. Time will help him, but intellectual maturity with regard to clearness is apt to come rather late. This seems an unfortunate arrangement of Nature, inasmuch as clearness is of less use to a man settled in life, whose errors have in great measure had their effect, than it would be to one whose path lay before him. It is terrible to see how a single unclear idea, a single formula without meaning, lurking in a young man's head, will sometimes act like an obstruction of inert matter in an artery, hindering the nutrition of the brain, and condemning its victim to pine away in the fullness of his intellectual vigour and in the midst of intellectual plenty. Many a man has cherished for years as his hobby some vague shadow of an idea, too meaningless to be positively false; he has, nevertheless, passionately loved it, has made it his companion by day and by night, and has given to it his strength and his life, leaving all other occupations for its sake, and in short has lived with it and for it, until it has become, as it were, flesh of his flesh and bone of his bone; and then he has waked up some bright morning to find it gone, clean vanished away like the beautiful Melusina of the fable, and the essence of his life gone with it. I have myself known such a man; and who can tell how many histories of circle-squarers, metaphysicians, astrologers, and what not, may not be told in the old German [French!] story?

The principles set forth in the first part [1] of this essay lead, at once, to a method of reaching a clearness of thought of higher grade than the "distinctness" of the logicians. It was there noticed that the action of thought is excited by the irritation of doubt, and ceases when belief is attained; so that the production of belief is the sole function of thought. All these words, however, are too strong for my purpose. It is as if I had described the phenomena as they appear under a mental microscope. Doubt and Belief, as the words are commonly employed, relate to religious or other grave discussions. But here I use them to designate the starting of any question, no matter how small or how great, and the resolution of it. If, for instance, in a horse-car, I pull out my purse and find a five-cent nickel and five coppers, I decide, while my hand is going to the purse, in which way I will pay my fare. To call such a question Doubt, and my decision Belief, is certainly to use words very disproportionate to the occasion. To speak of such a doubt as causing an irritation which needs to be appeased, suggests a temper which is uncomfortable to the verge of insanity. Yet, looking at the matter minutely, it must be admitted that, if there is the least hesitation as to whether I shall pay the five coppers or the nickel (as there will be sure to be, unless I act from some previously contracted habit in the matter), though irritation is too strong a word, yet I am excited to such small mental activity as may be necessary to deciding how I shall act. Most frequently doubts arise from some indecision, however momentary, in our action. Sometimes it is not so. I have, for example, to wait in a railway-station, and to pass the time I read the advertisements on the walls. I compare the advantages of different trains and different routes which I never expect to take, merely fancying myself to be in a state of hesitancy, because I am bored with having nothing to trouble me. ' Feigned hesitancy, whether feigned for mere amusement or with a lofty purpose, plays a great part in the production of scientific inquiry. However the doubt may originate, it stimulates the mind to an activity which may be slight or energetic, calm or turbulent. Images pass rapidly through consciousness, one incessantly melting into another, until at last, when all is over—it may be in a fraction of a second, in an hour, or after long years—we find ourselves decided as to how we should act under such circumstances as those which occasioned our hesitation. In other words, we have attained belief.

In this process we observe two sorts of elements of consciousness, the distinction between which may best be made clear by means of an illustration. In a piece of music there are the separate notes, and there is the air. A single tone may be prolonged for an hour or a day, and it exists as perfectly in each second of that time as in the whole taken together; so that, as long as it is sounding, it might be present to a sense from which everything in the past was as completely absent as the future itself. But it is different with the air, the performance of which occupies a certain time, during the portions of which only portions of it are played. It consists in an orderliness in the succession of sounds which strike the ear at different times; and to perceive it there must be some continuity of consciousness which makes the events of a lapse of time present to us. We certainly only perceive the air by hearing the separate notes; yet we cannot be said to directly hear it, for we hear only what is present at the instant, and an orderliness of succession cannot exist in an instant. These two sorts of objects, what we are *immediately* conscious of and what we are *mediately* conscious of, are found in all consciousness. Some elements (the sensations) are completely present at every instant so long as they last, while others (like thought) are actions having beginning, middle, and end, and consist in a congruence in the succession of sensations which flow through the mind. They cannot be immediately present to us, but must cover some portion of the past or future. Thought is a thread of melody running through the succession of our sensations.

We may add that just as a piece of music may be written in parts, each part having its own air, so various systems of relationship of succession subsist together between the same sensations. These different systems are distinguished by having different motives, ideas, or functions. Thought is only one such system, for its sole motive, idea, and function is to produce belief, and whatever does not concern that purpose belongs to some other system of relations. The action of thinking may incidentally have other results; it may serve to amuse us, for example, and among *dilettanti* it is not rare to find those who have so perverted thought to the purposes of pleasure that it seems to vex them to think that the questions upon which they delight to exercise it may ever get finally settled; and a positive discovery which takes a favourite subject out of the arena of literary debate is met with ill-concealed dislike. This disposition is the very debauchery of thought. But the soul and meaning of thought, abstracted from the other elements which accompany it, though it may be voluntarily thwarted, can never be made to direct itself toward anything but the production of belief. Thought in action has for its only possible motive the attainment of thought at rest; and whatever does not refer to belief is no part of the thought itself.

And what, then, is belief? It is the demi-cadence which closes a musical phrase in the symphony of our intellectual life. We have seen that it has just three properties: First, it is something that we are aware of; second, it appeases the irritation of doubt; and, third, it involves the establishment in our nature of a rule of action, or, say for short, a *habit*. As it appeases the irritation of doubt, which is the motive for thinking, thought relaxes, and comes to rest for a moment when belief is reached. But, since belief is a rule for action, the application of which involves further doubt and further thought, at the same time that it is a stopping-place, it is also a new starting-place for thought. That is why I have permitted myself to call it thought at rest, although thought is essentially an action. The *final* upshot of thinking is the exercise of volition, and of this thought no longer forms a part; but belief is only a stadium of mental action, an effect upon our nature due to thought, which will influence future thinking.

The essence of belief is the establishment of a habit; and different beliefs are distinguished by the different modes of action to which they give rise. If beliefs do not differ in this respect, if they appease the same doubt by producing the same rule of action, then no mere differences in the manner of consciousness of them can make them different beliefs, any more than playing a tune in different keys is playing different tunes. Imaginary distinctions are often drawn between beliefs which differ only in their mode of expression;—the wrangling which ensues is real enough, however. To believe that any objects are arranged among themselves as in Fig. 1, and to believe that they are arranged [as] in Fig. 2, are one and the same belief; yet it is conceivable that a man should assert one proposition

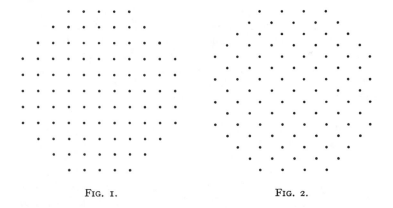

FIG. 1.   FIG. 2.

and deny the other. Such false distinctions do as much harm as the confusion of beliefs really different, and are among the pitfalls of which we ought constantly to beware, especially when we are upon metaphysical ground. One singular deception of this sort, which often occurs, is to mistake the sensation produced by our own unclearness of thought for a character of the object we are thinking. Instead of perceiving that the obscurity is purely subjective, we

fancy that we contemplate a quality of the object which is essentially mysterious; and if our conception be afterward presented to
us in a clear form we do not recognize it as the same, owing to
the absence of the feeling of unintelligibility. So long as this deception lasts, it obviously puts an impassable barrier in the way of
perspicuous thinking; so that it equally interests the opponents
of rational thought to perpetuate it, and its adherents to guard
against it.

Another such deception is to mistake a mere difference in the
grammatical construction of two words for a distinction between the
ideas they express. In this pedantic age, when the general mob of
writers attend so much more to words than to things, this error is
common enough. When I just said that thought is an *action*, and
that it consists in a *relation*, although a person performs an action
but not a relation, which can only be the result of an action, yet
there was no inconsistency in what I said, but only a grammatical
vagueness.

From all these sophisms we shall be perfectly safe so long as we
reflect that the whole function of thought is to produce habits of
action; and that whatever there is connected with a thought, but
irrelevant to its purpose, is an accretion to it, but no part of it. If
there be a unity among our sensations which has no reference to
how we shall act on a given occasion, as when we listen to a piece
of music, why we do not call that thinking. To develop its meaning,
we have, therefore, simply to determine what habits it produces, for
what a thing means is simply what habits it involves. Now, the
identity of a habit depends on how it might lead us to act, not
merely under such circumstances as are likely to arise, but under
such as might possibly occur, no matter how improbable they may
be. What the habit is depends on *when* and *how* it causes us to
act. As for the *when*, every stimulus to action is derived from
perception; as for the *how*, every purpose of action is to produce
some sensible result. Thus, we come down to what is tangible
and conceivably practical, as the root of every real distinction of
thought, no matter how subtle it may be; and there is no distinction of meaning so fine as to consist in anything but a possible
difference of practice.

To see what this principle leads to, consider in the light of it such
a doctrine as that of transubstantiation. The Protestant churches
generally hold that the elements of the sacrament are flesh and
blood only in a tropical sense; they nourish our souls as meat and
the juice of it would our bodies. But the Catholics maintain that

they are literally just meat and blood; although they possess all the sensible qualities of wafer-cakes and diluted wine. But we can have no conception of wine except what may enter into a belief, either—

1. That this, that, or the other, is wine; or,
2. That wine possesses certain properties.

Such beliefs are nothing but self-notifications that we should, upon occasion, act in regard to such things as we believe to be wine according to the qualities which we believe wine to possess. The occasion of such action would be some sensible perception, the motive of it to produce some sensible result. Thus our action has exclusive reference to what affects the senses, our habit has the same bearing as our action, our belief the same as our habit, our conception the same as our belief; and we can consequently mean nothing by wine but what has certain effects, direct or indirect, upon our senses; and to talk of something as having all the sensible characters of wine, yet being in reality blood, is senseless jargon. Now, it is not my object to pursue the theological question; and having used it as a logical example I drop it, without caring to anticipate the theologian's reply. I only desire to point out how impossible it is that we should have an idea in our minds which relates to anything but conceived sensible effects of things. Our idea of anything *is* our idea of its sensible effects; and if we fancy that we have any other we deceive ourselves, and mistake a mere sensation accompanying the thought for a part of the thought itself. It is absurd to say that thought has any meaning unrelated to its only function. It is foolish for Catholics and Protestants to fancy themselves in disagreement about the elements of the sacrament, if they agree in regard to all their sensible effects, here and hereafter.

It appears, then, that the rule for attaining the third grade of clearness of apprehension is as follows: Consider what effects, that might conceivably have practical bearings, we conceive the object of our conception to have. Then, our conception of these effects is the whole of our conception of the object.

Let us illustrate this rule by some examples; and, to begin with the simplest one possible, let us ask what we mean by calling a thing *hard*. Evidently that it will not be scratched by many other substances. The whole conception of this quality, as of every other, lies in its conceived effects. There is absolutely no difference between a hard thing and a soft thing so long as they are not brought to the test. Suppose, then, that a diamond could be crystallized in the midst of a cushion of soft cotton, and should remain there until it was finally burned up. Would it be false to say that that diamond was soft? This seems a foolish question, and would be so, in fact, except in the realm of logic. There such questions are often of the greatest utility as serving to bring logical principles into sharper relief than real discussions ever could. In studying logic we must not put them aside with hasty answers, but must consider them with attentive care, in order to make out the principles involved. We may, in the present case, modify our question, and ask what prevents us from saying that all hard bodies remain perfectly soft until they are touched, when their hardness increases with the pressure until they are scratched. Reflection will show that the reply is this: there would be no *falsity* in such modes of speech. They would involve a modification of our present usage of speech with regard to the words hard and soft, but not of their meanings. For they represent no fact to be different from what it is; only they involve arrangements of facts which would be exceedingly maladroit.[2] This leads us to remark that the question of what would occur under circumstances which do not actually arise is not a question of fact, but only of the most perspicuous arrangement of them. For example, the question of free-will and fate in its simplest form, stripped of verbiage, is something like this: I have done something of which I am ashamed; could I, by an effort of the will, have resisted the temptation, and done otherwise? The philosophical reply is, that this is not a question of fact, but only of the arrangement of facts. Arranging them so as to exhibit what is particularly pertinent to my question—namely, that I ought to blame myself for having done wrong—it is perfectly true to say that, if I had willed to do otherwise than I did, I should have done otherwise. On the other hand, arranging the facts so as to exhibit another important consideration, it is equally true that, when a temptation has once been allowed to work, it will, if it has a certain force, produce its effect, let me struggle how I may. There is no objection to a contradiction in what would result from a false supposition. The *reductio ad absurdum* consists in showing that contradictory results would follow from a hypothesis which is consequently judged to be false. Many questions are involved in the free-will discussion, and I am far from desiring to say that both sides are equally right. On the contrary, I am of opinion that one side denies important facts, and that the other does not. But what I do say is, that the above single question was the origin of the whole doubt; that, had it not been for this question, the controversy would never have arisen; and that this question is perfectly solved in the manner which I have indicated.

Let us next seek a clear idea of Weight. This is another very easy case. To say that a body is heavy means simply that, in the absence of opposing force, it will fall. This (neglecting certain specifications of how it will fall, etc., which exist in the mind of the physicist who uses the word) is evidently the whole conception of weight. It is a fair question whether some particular facts may not *account* for gravity; but what we mean by the force itself is completely involved in its effects.

This leads us to undertake an account of the idea of Force in general. This is the great conception which, developed in the early part of the seventeenth century from the rude idea of a cause, and constantly improved upon since, has shown us how to explain all the changes of motion which bodies experience, and how to think about all physical phenomena; which has given birth to modern science, and changed the face of the globe; and which, aside from its more special uses, has played a principal part in directing the course of modern thought, and in furthering modern social development. It is, therefore, worth some pains to comprehend it. According to our rule, we must begin by asking what is the immediate use of thinking about force; and the answer is, that we thus account for changes of motion. If bodies were left to themselves, without the intervention of forces, every motion would continue unchanged both in velocity and in direction. Furthermore, change of motion never takes place abruptly; if its direction is changed, it is always through a curve without angles; if its velocity alters, it is by degrees. The gradual changes which are constantly taking place are conceived by geometers to be compounded together according to the rules of the parallelogram of forces. If the reader does not already know what this is, he will find it, I hope, to his advantage to endeavour to follow the following explanation; but if mathematics are insupportable to him, pray let him skip three paragraphs rather than that we should part company here.

A *path* is a line whose beginning and end are distinguished. Two paths are considered to be equivalent, which, beginning at the same point, lead to the same point. Thus the two paths, *A B C D E* and *A F G H E* (Fig. 3), are equivalent. Paths which do *not* begin at the same point are considered to be equivalent, provided that, on moving either of them without turning it, but keeping it always parallel to its original position, when its beginning coincides with that of the other path, the ends also coincide. Paths are considered as geometrically added together, when one begins where the other ends; thus

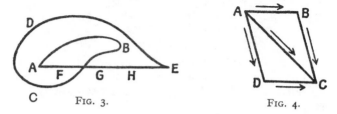

FIG. 3.   FIG. 4.

the path *A E* is conceived to be a sum of *A B*, *B C*, *C D*, and *D E*. In the parallelogram of Fig. 4 the diagonal *A C* is the sum of *A B* and *B C*; or, since *A D* is geometrically equivalent to *B C*, *A C* is the geometrical sum of *A B* and *A D*.

All this is purely conventional. It simply amounts to this: that we choose to call paths having the relations I have described equal or added. But, though it is a convention, it is a convention with a good reason. The rule for geometrical addition may be applied not only to paths, but to any other things which can be represented by paths. Now, as a path is determined by the varying direction and distance of the point which moves over it from the starting-point, it follows that anything which from its beginning to its end is determined by a varying direction and a varying magnitude is capable of being represented by a line. Accordingly, *velocities* may be represented by lines, for they have only directions and rates. The same thing is true of *accelerations*, or changes of velocities. This is evident enough in the case of velocities; and it becomes evident for accelerations if we consider that precisely what velocities are to positions—namely, states of change of them—that accelerations are to velocities.

The so-called "parallelogram of forces" is simply a rule for compounding accelerations. The rule is, to represent the accelerations by paths, and then to geometrically add the paths. The geometers, however, not only use the "parallelogram of forces" to compound different accelerations, but also to resolve one acceleration into a sum of several. Let *A B* (Fig. 5) be the path which represents a certain acceleration—say, such a change in the motion of a body that at the end of one second the body will, under the influence of that change, be in a position different from what it would have had if its motion had continued unchanged such that a path equivalent to *A B* would lead from the latter position to the former. This acceleration may be considered as the sum of the accelerations represented by *A C* and *C B*. It may also be considered as the sum of the very different accelera-tions represented by *A D* and *D B*, where *A D* is almost the opposite of *A C*. And it is clear that there is an immense variety of ways in which *A B* might be resolved into the sum of two accelerations.

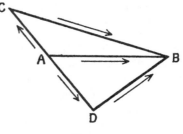

Fig. 5.

After this tedious explana-tion, which I hope, in view of the extraordinary interest of the conception of force, may not have exhausted the reader's patience, we are prepared at last to state the grand fact which this conception embodies. This fact is that if the actual changes of motion which the different par-ticles of bodies experience are each resolved in its appropriate way, each component acceleration is precisely such as is prescribed by a certain law of Nature, according to which bodies, in the relative positions which the bodies in question actually have at the moment, always receive certain accelerations, which, being compounded by geometrical addition, give the acceleration which the body actually experiences.

This is the only fact which the idea of force represents, and who-ever will take the trouble clearly to apprehend what this fact is, perfectly comprehends what force is. Whether we ought to say that a force *is* an acceleration, or that it *causes* an acceleration, is a mere question of propriety of language, which has no more to do with our real meaning than the difference between the French idiom "*Il fait froid*" and its English equivalent "*It is cold.*" Yet it is surprising to see how this simple affair has muddled men's minds. In how many profound treatises is not force spoken of as a "mysterious entity," which seems to be only a way of confessing that the author despairs of ever getting a clear notion of what the word means! In a recent admired work on *Analytic Mechanics* it is stated that we understand precisely the effect of force, but what force itself is we do not understand! This is simply a self-contradiction. The idea which the word force excites in our minds has no other function than to affect our actions, and these actions can have no reference to force otherwise than through its effects. Consequently, if we know what the effects of force are, we are acquainted with every fact which is implied in saying that a force exists, and there is nothing more to know. The truth is, there is some vague notion afloat that a question may mean something which the mind cannot conceive; and when some hair-splitting philosophers have been confronted with the absurdity of such a view, they have invented an empty distinction between positive and negative conceptions, in the attempt to give their non-idea a form not obviously nonsensical. The nullity of it is sufficiently plain from the considerations given a few pages back; and, apart from those considerations, the quibbling character of the distinction must have struck every mind accustomed to real thinking.

Let us now approach the subject of logic, and consider a conception which particularly concerns it, that of *reality*. Taking clearness in the sense of familiarity, no idea could be clearer than this. Every child uses it with perfect confidence, never dreaming that he does not understand it. As for clearness in its second grade, however, it would probably puzzle most men, even among those of a reflective turn of mind, to give an abstract definition of the real. Yet such a definition may perhaps be reached by considering the points of difference between reality and its opposite, fiction. A figment is a product of somebody's imagination; it has such characters as his thought impresses upon it. That those characters are independent of how you or I think is an external reality. There are, however, phenomena within our own minds, dependent upon our thought, which are at the same time real in the sense that we really think them. But though their characters depend on how we think, they do not depend on what we think those characters to be. Thus, a dream has a real existence as a mental phenomenon, if somebody has really dreamt it; that he dreamt so and so, does not depend on what anybody thinks was dreamt, but is completely independent of all opinion on the subject. On the other hand, considering, not the fact of dreaming, but the thing dreamt, it retains its peculiarities by virtue of no other fact than that it was dreamt to possess them. Thus we may define the real as that whose characters are independent of what anybody may think them to be.

But, however satisfactory such a definition may be found, it would be a great mistake to suppose that it makes the idea of reality perfectly clear. Here, then, let us apply our rules. According to them, reality, like every other quality, consists in the peculiar sensible effects which things partaking of it produce. The only effect which real things have is to cause belief, for all the sensations which they excite emerge into consciousness in the form of beliefs.

The question therefore is, how is true belief (or belief in the real) distinguished from false belief (or belief in fiction). Now, as we have seen in the former paper,[1] the ideas of truth and falsehood, in their full development, appertain exclusively to the experiential method of settling opinion. A person who arbitrarily chooses the propositions which he will adopt can use the word truth only to emphasize the expression of his determination to hold on to his choice. Of course, the method of tenacity never prevailed exclusively; reason is too natural to men for that. But in the literature of the dark ages we find some fine examples of it. When Scotus Erigena is commenting upon a poetical passage in which hellebore is spoken of as having caused the death of Socrates, he does not hesitate to inform the inquiring reader that Helleborus and Socrates were two eminent Greek philosophers, and that the latter, having been overcome in argument by the former, took the matter to heart and died of it! What sort of an idea of truth could a man have who could adopt and teach, without the qualification of a perhaps, an opinion taken so entirely at random? The real spirit of Socrates, who I hope would have been delighted to have been "overcome in argument," because he would have learned something by it, is in curious contrast with the naïve idea of the glossist, for whom (as for "the born missionary" of today) discussion would seem to have been simply a struggle. When philosophy began to awake from its long slumber, and before theology completely dominated it, the practice seems to have been for each professor to seize upon any philosophical position he found unoccupied and which seemed a strong one, to intrench himself in it, and to sally forth from time to time to give battle to the others. Thus, even the scanty records we possess of those disputes enable us to make out a dozen or more opinions held by different teachers at one time concerning the question of nominalism and realism. Read the opening part of the *Historia Calamitatum* of Abélard, who was certainly as philosophical as any of his contemporaries, and see the spirit of combat which it breathes. For him, the truth is simply his particular stronghold. When the method of authority prevailed, the truth meant little more than the Catholic faith. All the efforts of the scholastic doctors are directed toward harmonizing their faith in Aristotle and their faith in the Church, and one may search their ponderous folios through without finding an argument which goes any further. It is noticeable that where different faiths flourish side by side, renegades are looked upon with contempt even by the party whose belief they adopt; so completely has the idea of loyalty replaced that of truth-seeking. Since the time of Descartes, the defect in the conception of truth has been less apparent. Still, it will sometimes strike a scientific man that the philosophers have been less intent on finding out what the facts are, than on inquiring what belief is most in harmony with their system. It is hard to convince a follower of the *a priori* method by adducing facts; but show him that an opinion he is defending is inconsistent with what he has laid down elsewhere, and he will be very apt to retract it. These minds do not seem to believe that disputation is ever to cease; they seem to think that the opinion which is natural for one man is not so for another, and that belief will, consequently, never be settled. In contenting themselves with fixing their own opinions by a method which would lead another man to a different result, they betray their feeble hold of the conception of what truth is.

On the other hand, all the followers of science are animated by a cheerful hope that the processes of investigation, if only pushed far enough, will give one certain solution to each question to which they apply it. One man may investigate the velocity of light by studying the transits of Venus and the aberration of the stars; another by the oppositions of Mars and the eclipses of Jupiter's satellites; a third by the method of Fizeau; a fourth by that of Foucault; a fifth by the motions of the curves of Lissajoux; a sixth, a seventh, an eighth, and a ninth, may follow the different methods of comparing the measures of statical and dynamical electricity. They may at first obtain different results, but, as each perfects his method and his processes, the results are found to move steadily together toward a destined centre. So with all scientific research. Different minds may set out with the most antagonistic views, but the progress of investigation carries them by a force outside of themselves to one and the same conclusion. This activity of thought by which we are carried, not where we wish, but to a fore-ordained goal, is like the operation of destiny. No modification of the point of view taken, no selection of other facts for study, no natural bent of mind even, can enable a man to escape the predestinate opinion. This great hope is embodied in the conception of truth and reality. The opinion which is fated to be ultimately agreed to by all who investigate, is what we mean by the truth, and the object represented in this opinion is the real. That is the way I would explain reality.

But it may be said that this view is directly opposed to the abstract definition which we have given of reality, inasmuch as it makes the characters of the real depend on what is ultimately thought about them. But the answer to this is that, on the one hand, reality is independent, not necessarily of thought in general, but only of what you or I or any finite number of men may think about it; and that, on the other hand, though the object of the final opinion depends on what that opinion is, yet what that opinion is does not depend on what you or I or any man thinks. Our perversity and that of others may indefinitely postpone the settlement of opinion; it might even conceivably cause an arbitrary proposition to be universally accepted as long as the human race should last. Yet even that would not change the nature of the belief, which alone could be the result of investigation carried sufficiently far; and if, after the extinction of our race, another should arise with faculties and disposition for investigation, that true opinion must be the one which they would ultimately come to. "Truth crushed to earth shall rise again," and the opinion which would finally result from investigation does not depend on how anybody may actually think. But the reality of that which is real does depend on the real fact that investigation is destined to lead, at last, if continued long enough, to a belief in it.

But I may be asked what I have to say to all the minute facts of history, forgotten never to be recovered, to the lost books of the ancients, to the buried secrets.

> Full many a gem of purest ray serene
>   The dark, unfathomed caves of ocean bear;
> Full many a flower is born to blush unseen,
>   And waste its sweetness on the desert air.

Do these things not really exist because they are hopelessly beyond the reach of our knowledge? And then, after the universe is dead (according to the prediction of some scientists), and all life has ceased forever, will not the shock of atoms continue though there will be no mind to know it? To this I reply that, though in no possible state of knowledge can any number be great enough to express the relation between the amount of what rests unknown to the amount of the known, yet it is unphilosophical to suppose that, with regard to any given question (which has any clear meaning), investigation would not bring forth a solution of it, if it were carried far enough. Who would have said, a few years ago, that we could ever know of what substances stars are made whose light may have been longer in reaching us than the human race has existed? Who can be sure of what we shall not know in a few hundred years? Who can guess what would be the result of continuing the pursuit of science for ten thousand years, with the activity of the last hundred? And if it were to go on for a million, or a billion, or any number of years you please, how is it possible to say that there is any question which might not ultimately be solved?

But it may be objected, "Why make so much of these remote considerations, especially when it is your principle that only practical distinctions have a meaning?" Well, I must confess that it makes very little difference whether we say that a stone on the bottom of the ocean, in complete darkness, is brilliant or not—that is to say, that it *probably* makes no difference, remembering always that that stone *may* be fished up tomorrow. But that there are gems at the bottom of the sea, flowers in the untravelled desert, etc., are propositions which, like that about a diamond being hard when it is not pressed, concern much more the arrangement of our language than they do the meaning of our ideas.

It seems to me, however, that we have, by the application of our rule, reached so clear an apprehension of what we mean by reality, and of the fact which the idea rests on, that we should not, perhaps, be making a pretension so presumptuous as it would be singular, if we were to offer a metaphysical theory of existence for universal acceptance among those who employ the scientific method of fixing belief. However, as metaphysics is a subject much more curious than useful, the knowledge of which, like that of a sunken reef, serves chiefly to enable us to keep clear of it, I will not trouble the reader with any more Ontology at this moment. I have already been led much further into that path than I should have desired; and I have given the reader such a dose of mathematics, psychology, and all that is most abstruse, that I fear he may already have left me, and that what I am now writing is for the compositor and proofreader exclusively. I trusted to the importance of the subject. There is no royal road to logic, and really valuable ideas can only be had at the price of close attention. But I know that in the matter of ideas the public prefer the cheap and nasty; and in my next paper [3] I am going to return to the easily intelligible, and not wander from it again. The reader who has been at the pains of wading through this paper, shall be rewarded in the next one by seeing how beautifully what has been developed in this tedious way can be applied to the ascertainment of the rules of scientific reasoning.

We have, hitherto, not crossed the threshold of scientific logic. It is certainly important to know how to make our ideas clear, but they may be ever so clear without being true. How to make them so, we have next to study. How to give birth to those vital and procreative ideas which multiply into a thousand forms and diffuse themselves everywhere, advancing civilization and making the dignity of man, is an art not yet reduced to rules, but of the secret of which the history of science affords some hints.

4

THE SCIENTIFIC ATTITUDE AND FALLIBILISM *

I

IF we endeavour to form our conceptions upon history and life, we remark three classes of men. The first consists of those for whom the chief thing is the qualities of feelings. These men create art. The second consists of the practical men, who carry on the business of the world. They respect nothing but power, and respect power only so far as it [is] exercised. The third class consists of men to whom nothing seems great but reason. If force interests them, it is not in its exertion, but in that it has a reason and a law. For men of the first class, nature is a picture; for men of the second class, it is an opportunity; for men of the third class, it is a cosmos, so admirable, that to penetrate to its ways seems to them the only thing that makes life worth living. These are the men whom we see possessed by a passion to learn, just as other men have a passion to teach and to disseminate their influence. If they do not give themselves over completely to their passion to learn, it is because they exercise self-control. Those are the natural scientific men; and they are the only men that have any real success in scientific research.

If we are to define science, not in the sense of stuffing it into an artificial pigeon-hole where it may be found again by some insignificant mark, but in the sense of characterizing it as a living historic entity, we must conceive it as that about which such men as I have described busy themselves. As such, it does not consist so much in *knowing*, nor even in "organized knowledge," as it does in diligent inquiry into truth for truth's sake, without any sort of axe to grind, nor for the sake of the delight of contemplating it, but from an impulse to penetrate into the reason of things. This is the sense in which this book is entitled a History of *Science*. Science and philosophy seem to have been changed in their cradles. For it is not knowing, but the love of learning, that characterizes the scientific

* [I consists of selections from ms. of notes c. 1896 (*CP* 1.43-58, 75-6, 103-20). In II, the first selection is from ms. c. 1899, the second from ms. c. 1897 (*CP* 1.135-49).]

man; while the "philosopher" is a man with a system which he thinks embodies all that is best worth knowing. If a man burns to learn and sets himself to comparing his ideas with experimental results in order that he may correct those ideas, every scientific man will recognize him as a brother, no matter how small his knowledge may be.

But if a man occupies himself with investigating the truth of some question for some ulterior purpose, such as to make money, or to amend his life, or to benefit his fellows, he may be ever so much better than a scientific man, if you will—to discuss that would be aside from the question—but he is not a scientific man. For example, there are numbers of chemists who occupy themselves exclusively with the study of dyestuffs. They discover facts that are useful to scientific chemistry; but they do not rank as genuine scientific men. The genuine scientific chemist cares just as much to learn about erbium—the extreme rarity of which renders it commercially unimportant—as he does about iron. He is more eager to learn about erbium if the knowledge of it would do more to complete his conception of the Periodic Law, which expresses the mutual relations of the elements.

When a man desires ardently to know the truth, his first effort will be to imagine what that truth can be. He cannot prosecute his pursuit long without finding that imagination unbridled is sure to carry him off the track. Yet nevertheless, it remains true that there is, after all, nothing but imagination that can ever supply him an inkling of the truth. He can stare stupidly at phenomena; but in the absence of imagination they will not connect themselves together in any rational way. Just as for Peter Bell a cowslip was nothing but a cowslip, so for thousands of men a falling apple was nothing but a falling apple; and to compare it to the moon would by them be deemed "fanciful."

It is not too much to say that next after the passion to learn there is no quality so indispensable to the successful prosecution of science as imagination. Find me a people whose early medicine is not mixed up with magic and incantations, and I will find you a people devoid of all scientific ability. There is no magic in the medical Papyrus Ebers. The stolid Egyptian saw nothing in disease but derangement of the affected organ. There never was any true Egyptian science.

There are, no doubt, kinds of imagination of no value in science, mere artistic imagination, mere dreaming of opportunities for gain.   The scientific imagination dreams of explanations and laws.

A scientific man must be single-minded and sincere with himself. Otherwise, his love of truth will melt away, at once.   He can, therefore, hardly be otherwise than an honest, fair-minded man. True, a few naturalists have been accused of purloining specimens; and some men have been far from judicial in advocating their theories.   Both of these faults must be exceedingly deleterious to their scientific ability.   But on the whole, scientific men have been the best of men.   It is quite natural, therefore, that a young man who might develop into a scientific man should be a well-conducted person.

Yet in more ways than one an exaggerated regard for morality is unfavourable to scientific progress.   I shall present only one of those ways.   It will no doubt shock some persons that I should speak of morality as involving an element which can become bad.   To them good conduct and moral conduct are one and the same—and they will accuse me of hostility to morality.   I regard morality as highly necessary; but it is a means to good life, not necessarily coextensive with good conduct.   Morality consists in the folklore of right conduct.   A man is brought up to think he ought to behave in certain ways.   If he behaves otherwise, he is uncomfortable.   His conscience pricks him.   That system of morals is the traditional wisdom of ages of experience.   If a man cuts loose from it, he will become the victim of his passions.   It is not safe for him even to reason about it, except in a purely speculative way.   Hence, morality is essentially conservative.   Good morals and good manners are identical, except that tradition attaches less importance to the latter.   The gentleman is imbued with conservatism.   This conservatism is a habit, and it is the law of habit that it tends to spread and extend itself over more and more of the life.   In this way, conservatism about morals leads to conservatism about manners and finally conservatism about opinions of a speculative kind.   Besides, to distinguish between speculative and practical opinions is the mark of the most cultivated intellects.   Go down below this level and you come across reformers and rationalists at every turn—people who propose to remodel the ten commandments on modern science.   Hence it is that morality leads to a conservatism which any new view, or even any free inquiry, no matter how purely speculative, shocks.   The whole moral weight of such a community will be cast against science. To inquire into nature is for a Turk very unbecoming to a good

Moslem; just as the family of Tycho Brahe regarded his pursuit of astronomy as unbecoming to a nobleman. (See Thomas Nash in *Pierce Pennilesse* for the character of a Danish nobleman.)

This tendency is necessarily greatly exaggerated in a country when the "gentleman," or recognized exponent of good manners, is appointed to that place as the most learned man. For then the inquiring spirit cannot say the gentlemen are a lot of ignorant fools. To the moral weight cast against progress in science is added the weight of superior learning. Wherever there is a large class of academic professors who are provided with good incomes and looked up to as gentlemen, scientific inquiry must languish. Wherever the bureaucrats are the more learned class, the case will be still worse.

The first questions which men ask about the universe are naturally the most general and abstract ones. Nor is it true, as has so often been asserted, that these are the most difficult questions to answer. Francis Bacon is largely responsible for this error, he having represented—having nothing but his imagination and no acquaintance with actual science to draw upon—that the most general inductions must be reached by successive steps. History does not at all bear out that theory. The errors about very general questions have been due to a circumstance which I proceed to set forth.

The most abstract of all the sciences is mathematics. That this is so, has been made manifest in our day; because all mathematicians now see clearly that mathematics is only busied about *purely hypothetical questions*. As for what the truth of existence may be the mathematician does not (*qua* mathematician) care a straw. It is true that early mathematicians could not clearly see that this was so. But for all their not seeing it, it was just as true of the mathematics of early days as of our own. The early mathematician might perhaps be more inclined to assert roundly that two straight lines in a plane cut by a third so as to make the sum of the internal angles on one side less than two right angles would meet at some finite distance on that side if sufficiently produced; although, as a matter of fact, we observe no such tendency in Euclid. But however that may have been, the early mathematician had certainly no more tendency than the modern to *inquire into the truth of that postulate*; but quite the reverse. What he really did, therefore, was merely to deduce consequences of unsupported assumptions, whether he recognized that this was the nature of his business or not. Mathematics, then, really was, for him as for us, the most abstract of the sciences, cut off from all inquiry into existential truth. Consequently, the tendency to attack the most abstract problems first, not because they were *recognized* as such, but because such they *were*, led to mathematics being the earliest field of inquiry.

We find some peoples drawn more toward arithmetic; others more toward geometry. But in either case, a correct method of reasoning was sure to be reached before many centuries of real inquiry had elapsed. The reasoning would be at first awkward, and one case would be needlessly split up into several. But still all influences were pressing the reasoner to make use of a diagram, and as soon as he did that he was pursuing the correct method. For mathematical reasoning consists in constructing a diagram according to a general precept, in observing certain relations between parts of that diagram not explicitly required by the precept, showing that these relations will hold for all such diagrams, and in formulating this conclusion in general terms. All valid necessary reasoning is in fact thus diagrammatic. This, however, is far from being obviously true. There was nothing to draw the attention of the early reasoners to the need of a diagram in such reasoning. Finding that by their inward meditations they could deduce the truth concerning, for example, the height of an inaccessible pillar, they naturally concluded the same method could be applied to positive inquiries.

In this way, early success in mathematics would naturally lead to bad methods in the positive sciences, and especially in metaphysics.

We have seen how success in mathematics would necessarily create a confidence altogether unfounded in man's power of eliciting truth by inward meditation without any aid from experience. Both its confidence in what is within and the absolute certainty of its conclusions lead to the confusion of *a priori* reason with conscience. For conscience, also, refuses to submit its dicta to experiment, and makes an absolute dual distinction between right and wrong. One result of this is that men begin to rationalize about questions of purity and integrity, which in the long run, through moral decay, is unfavourable to science. But what is worse, from our point of view, they begin to look upon science as a guide to conduct, that is, no longer as pure science but as an instrument for a practical end. One result of this is that all probable reasoning is despised. If a proposition is to be applied to action, it has to be embraced, or believed without reservation. There is no room for doubt, which can only paralyze action. But the scientific spirit requires a man to be at all times ready to dump his whole cartload of beliefs, the moment experience is against them. The desire to learn forbids him to be perfectly cocksure that he knows already. Besides positive science can only rest on experience; and experience can never result in absolute certainty, exactitude, necessity, or universality. But it is precisely with the universal and necessary, that is, with Law, that [con]science concerns itself. Thus the real character of science is destroyed as soon as it is made an adjunct to conduct; and especially all progress in the inductive sciences is brought to a standstill.

The effect of mixing speculative inquiry with questions of conduct results finally in a sort of half make-believe reasoning which deceives itself in regard to its real character. Conscience really belongs to the subconscious man, to that part of the soul which is hardly distinct in different individuals, a sort of community-consciousness, or public spirit, not absolutely one and the same in different citizens, and yet not by any means independent in them. Conscience has been created by experience just as any knowledge is; but it is modified by further experience only with secular slowness.

When men begin to rationalize about their conduct, the first effect is to deliver them over to their passions and produce the most frightful demoralization, especially in sexual matters. Thus, among the Greeks, it brought about paederasty and a precedence of public women over private wives. But ultimately the subconscious part of the soul, being stronger, regains its predominance and insists on setting matters right. Men, then, continue to tell themselves they regulate their conduct by reason; but they learn to look forward and see what conclusions a given method will lead to before they give their adhesion to it. In short, it is no longer the reasoning which determines what the conclusion shall be, but it is the conclusion which determines what the reasoning shall be. This is sham reasoning. In short, as morality supposes self-control, men learn that they must not surrender themselves unreservedly to any method, without considering to what conclusions it will lead them. But this is utterly contrary to the single-mindedness that is requisite in science. In order that science may be successful, its votaries must hasten to surrender themselves at discretion to experimental inquiry, in advance of knowing what its decisions may be. There must be no reservations.

The effect of this shamming is that men come to look upon reasoning as mainly decorative, or at most, as a secondary aid in minor matters—a view not altogether unjust, if questions of conduct are alone to interest us. They, therefore, demand that it shall be plain and facile. If, in special cases, complicated reasoning is indispensable, they hire a specialist to perform it. The result of this state of things is, of course, a rapid deterioration of intellectual vigour, very perceptible from one generation to the next. This is just what is taking place among us before our eyes; and to judge from the history of Constantinople, it is likely to go on until the race comes to a despicable end.

. . . The old-fashioned political economist adored, as alone capable of redeeming the human race, the glorious principle of individual greed, although, as this principle requires for its action hypocrisy and fraud, he generally threw in some dash of inconsistent concessions to virtue, as a sop to the vulgar Cerberus. But it is easy to see that the only kind of science this principle would favour would be such as is immediately remunerative with a great preference for such as can be kept secret, like the modern sciences of dyeing and perfumery. Kepler's discovery rendered Newton possible, and Newton rendered modern physics possible, with the steam engine, electricity, and all the other sources of the stupendous fortunes of our age. But Kepler's discovery would not have been possible without the doctrine of conics. Now contemporaries of Kepler—such penetrating minds as Descartes and Pascal—were abandoning the study of geometry (in which they included what we now call the differential calculus, so far as that had at that time any existence) because they said it was so UTTERLY USELESS. There was the future of the human race almost trembling in the balance; for had not the geometry of conic sections already been worked out in large measure, and had their opinion that only sciences apparently useful ought to be pursued [prevailed], the nineteenth century would have had none of those characters which distinguish it from the *ancien régime.*
True science is distinctively the study of useless things. For the useful things will get studied without the aid of scientific men. To employ these rare minds on such work is like running a steam engine by burning diamonds.

The evolutionary theory in general throws great light upon history and especially upon the history of science—both its public history and the account of its development in an individual intellect. As great a light is thrown upon the theory of evolution in general by the evolution of history, especially that of science—whether public or private.

The main theories of the evolution of organic species are three. First, the theory of Darwin, according to which the entire interval from Moner to Man has been traversed by successive purely fortuitous and insensible variations *in reproduction*. The changes on the whole follow a determinate course simply because a certain amount of change in certain directions destroys the species altogether, as the final result of successive weakenings of its reproductive power. Second, the theory of Lamarck, according to which the whole interval has been traversed by a succession of very minute changes. But these have not taken place in reproduction, which has absolutely nothing to do with the business, except to keep the average individuals plastic by their youth. The changes have not been fortuitous but wholly the result of strivings of the individuals. Third, the theory of cataclysmal evolution, according to which the changes have not been small and have not been fortuitous; but they have taken place chiefly in reproduction. According to this view, sudden changes of the environment have taken place from time to time. These changes have put certain organs at a disadvantage, and there has been an effort to use them in new ways. Such organs are particularly apt to sport in reproduction and to change in the way which adapts them better to their recent mode of exercise.

Notwithstanding the teachings of Weismann, it seems altogether probable that all three of these modes of evolution have acted. It is probable that the last has been the most efficient. These three modes of organic evolution have their parallels in other departments of evolution.

Let us consider, for example, the evolution of standards of weights and measures. In order to define the word "pound" in the *Century Dictionary*, I made a list of about four hundred pounds which had been in use in different parts of Europe—undoubtedly a very incomplete list, for it was confined in great measure to certain provinces concerning which I was able to obtain information. Each individual pound or measuring stick is from time to time copied; and at length the old one becomes destroyed. The measure of each copy is imperceptibly larger or smaller than its immediate prototype. If then these variations cannot, by gradual summation, produce a standard much smaller without that standard being destroyed as inconvenient while no such destruction would follow upon an increase of the standard, the average of the standards will slowly grow larger by Darwinian evolution. If there were a disposition on the part of owners of pounds to file them down, so as to make them lighter, though not enough to be noticed, then these filed pounds being copied, and the copies filed, there would be a gradual lightening of the pound by Lamarckian evolution. But it is very unlikely that either of these two modes has been a considerable factor in the actual evolution of weights and measures. As long as their circumstances are unchanged, human communities are exceedingly conservative. Nothing short of the despotism of a modern government with a modern police can cause a change in weights and measures. But from time to time changes occur which cause trade to take new routes. Business has to be adapted to new conditions; and under such influences we find all those habits of communities which are rendered unsuitable by the change become plastic enough. Then it is that a new pound or a new yard may be made which is a compromise between a desire to retain old ways and a desire to please new-comers.

In the evolution of science, a Darwinian mode of evolution might, for example, consist in this, that at every recall of a judgment to the mind—say, for example, a judgment in regard to some such delicate question as the marriage of the clergy—a slight fortuitous modification of the judgment might take place; the modified judgment would cause a corresponding modification of the belief-habit, so that the next recall would be influenced by this fortuitous modification, though it would depart more or less from it by a new fortuitous modification. If, however, by such summation of modifications an opinion quite untenable were reached, it would either be violently changed or would be associationally weak and not apt to be recalled. The effect of this would be in the long run that belief would move away from such untenable positions. It is possible that such a mode of influence may affect our instinctive feelings; but there can be nothing of this sort in science, which is controlled and exact. But another sort of Darwinian evolution undoubtedly does take place. We are studying over phenomena of which we have been unable to acquire any satisfactory account. Various tentative explanations recur to our minds from time to time, and at each occurrence are modified by omission, insertion, or change in the point of view, in an almost fortuitous way. Finally, one of these takes such an aspect that we are led to dismiss it as impossible. Then, all the energy of thought which had previously gone to the consideration of that becomes distributed among the other explanations, until finally one of them becomes greatly strengthened in our minds.

Lamarckian evolution might, for example, take the form of perpetually modifying our opinion in the effort to make that opinion represent the known facts as more and more observations came to be collected. This is all the time going on in regard, for example, to our estimate of the danger of infection of phthisis. Yet, after all, it does not play a prominent part in the evolution of science. The physical journals—say, for example, Poggendorff's [*Annalen der Physik*] and *Beiblätter*—publish each month a great number of new researches. Each of these is a distinct contribution to science. It represents some good, solid, well-trained labour of observation and inference. But as modifying what is already known, the average effect of the ordinary research may be said to be insignificant. Nevertheless, as these modifications are not fortuitous but are for the most part movements toward the truth—could they be rightly understood, all of them would be so—there is no doubt that from decade to decade, even without any splendid discoveries or great studies, science would advance very perceptibly. We see that it is so in branches of physics which remain for a long time without any decisive conquests. It was so, for example, in regard to the classification of the chemical elements in the lapse of time from Berzelius to Mendeléeff, as the valuable history of Venable shows. This is an evolution of the Lamarckian type.

But this is not the way in which science mainly progresses. It advances by leaps; and the impulse for each leap is either some new observational resource, or some novel way of reasoning about the observations. Such novel way of reasoning might, perhaps, be considered as a new observational means, since it draws attention to relations between facts which would previously have been passed by unperceived.

[I] illustrate by the discoveries of Pasteur, who began by applying the microscope to chemistry. He picked out the right- and left-handed crystals of tartaric acid. The two kinds have absolutely the same properties except in regard to direction of rotation of the plane of polarization and in their chemical relations to other "optically active" bodies. Since this method of picking out individual crystals was so slow, Pasteur looked for other means. Ferments of appropriate kinds were found to have the same effect. The microscope showed these were due to living organisms, which Pasteur began studying. At that time the medical world was dominated by Claude Bernard's dictum that a disease is not an entity but merely a sum of symptoms. This was pure metaphysics which only barricaded inquiry in that direction. But that was a generation which attached great value to nominalistic metaphysics. Pasteur began with the phylloxera. He found it influenced the "optical activity" of the sugar. This pointed to a ferment and therefore to an entity. He began to extend the doctrine to other diseases. The medical men, dominated by the metaphysics of Claude Bernard, raised all sorts of sophistical objections. But the method of cultures and inoculation proved the thing, and here we see new ideas connected with new observational methods and a fine example of the usual process of scientific evolution. It is not by insensible steps.

The last fifty years have taught the lesson of not trifling with facts and not trusting to principles and methods which are not logically founded upon facts and which serve only to exclude testimony from consideration.

Such, for example, was the dictum of Claude Bernard that a disease is not an entity—a purely metaphysical doctrine. But the observation of facts has taught us that a disease is in many, if not most, serious cases, just as much an entity as a human family consisting of father, mother, and children.

Such was the dictum of the old psychology which identified the soul with the ego, declared its absolute simplicity, and held that its faculties were mere names for logical divisions of human activity. This was all unadulterated fancy. The observation of facts has now taught us that the ego is a mere wave in the soul, a superficial and small feature, that the soul may contain several personalities and is as complex as the brain itself, and that the faculties, while not exactly definable and not absolutely fixed, are as real as are the different convolutions of the cortex.

Such were the dicta by means of which the internal criticism of historical documents was carried to such a height that it often amounted to the rejection of all the testimony that has come down to us, and the substitution for it of a dream spun out of the critic's brain. But archeological researches have shown that ancient testimony ought to be trusted in the main, with a small allowance for the changes in the meanings of words. When we are told that Pythagoras had a golden thigh, we are to remember that to the ancients gold did not mean a chemical element of atomic weight 197·5 and specific gravity 19·3, melting at 1045° C. and forming saline compounds of the types AuX and AuX_3. It meant something of metallic lustre, warmer in colour than electrum and cooler than copper. Dr. Schliemann's discoveries were the first •

socdolager that "higher criticism" received. It has since got many others.....

Such were the dicta by which everything of the nature of extraordinary powers connected with psychological states of which the hypnotic trance is an example were set down as tricks. At present, while the existence of telepathy cannot be said to be established, all scientific men are obliged by observed facts to admit that it presents at least a very serious problem requiring respectful treatment.

Persons who know science chiefly by its results—that is to say, have no acquaintance with it at all as a living inquiry—are apt to acquire the notion that the universe is now entirely explained in all its leading features; and that it is only here and there that the fabric of scientific knowledge betrays any rents.

But in point of fact, notwithstanding all that has been discovered since Newton's time, his saying that we are little children picking up pretty pebbles on the beach while the whole ocean lies before us unexplored remains substantially as true as ever, and will do so though we shovel up the pebbles by steam shovels and carry them off in carloads. An infinitesimal ratio may be multiplied indefinitely and remain infinitesimal still.

In the first place all that science has done is to study those relations between objects which were brought into prominence and conceiving which we had been endowed with some original knowledge in two instincts—the instinct of *feeding*, which brought with it elementary knowledge of mechanical forces, space, etc., and the instinct of *breeding*, which brought with it elementary knowledge of psychical motives, of time, etc. All the other relations of things concerning which we must suppose there is vast store of truth are for us merely the object of such false sciences as judicial astrology, palmistry, the doctrine of signatures, the doctrine of correspondences, magic, and the like.

In the next place, even within the very bounds to which our science is confined, it is altogether superficial and fragmentary. Want of knowledge of the constitution of matter and of electricity. The conservation of forces, as Helmholtz first enunciated it, untenable; whether it can be universally true in any sense is a difficult problem. To strengthen it Helmholtz greatly insisted on discontinuities—a most objectionable theory from every point of view. Mind quite as little understood as matter, and the relations between the two an enigma. The forces we know can be but a small part of all those that are operative.   Our ignorance of small things and great, of distant times and of very slow operations.   We are equally ignorant of very rapid performances which nevertheless we know to take place.   Our science is altogether middle-sized and mediocre.   Its insignificance compared with the universe cannot be exaggerated.

It is a great mistake to suppose that the mind of the active scientist is filled with propositions which, if not proved beyond all reasonable cavil, are at least extremely probable.   On the contrary, he entertains hypotheses which are almost wildly incredible, and treats them with respect for the time being.   Why does he do this?   Simply because any scientific proposition whatever is always liable to be refuted and dropped at short notice.   A hypothesis is something which looks as if it might be true and were true, and which is capable of verification or refutation by comparison with facts.   The best hypothesis, in the sense of the one most recommending itself to the inquirer, is the one which can be the most readily refuted if it is false.   This far outweighs the trifling merit of being likely.   For after all, what is a *likely* hypothesis?   It is one which falls in with our preconceived ideas.   But these may be wrong.   Their errors are just what the scientific man is out gunning for more particularly.   But if a hypothesis can quickly and easily be cleared away so as to go toward leaving the field free for the main struggle, this is an immense advantage.

II

Upon this first, and in one sense this sole, rule of reason, that in order to learn you must desire to learn, and in so desiring not be satisfied with what you already incline to think, there follows one corollary which itself deserves to be inscribed upon every wall of the city of philosophy:

Do not block the way of inquiry.

Although it is better to be methodical in our investigations, and to consider the economics of research, yet there is no positive sin against logic in *trying* any theory which may come into our heads, so long as it is adopted in such a sense as to permit the investigation to go on unimpeded and undiscouraged.   On the other hand, to set up a philosophy which barricades the road of further advance toward the truth is the one unpardonable offence in reasoning, as it is also the one to which metaphysicians have in all ages shown themselves the most addicted.

Let me call your attention to four familiar shapes in which this venomous error assails our knowledge.

The first is the shape of absolute assertion. That we can be sure of nothing in science is an ancient truth. The Academy taught it. Yet science has been infested with overconfident assertion, especially on the part of the third-rate and fourth-rate men, who have been more concerned with teaching than with learning, at all times. No doubt some of the geometries still teach as a self-evident truth the proposition that if two straight lines in one plane meet a third straight line so as to make the sum of the internal angles on one side less than two right angles those two lines will meet on that side if sufficiently prolonged. Euclid, whose logic was more careful, only reckoned this proposition as a *Postulate*, or arbitrary Hypothesis. Yet even he places among his axioms the proposition that a part is less than its whole, and falls into several conflicts with our most modern geometry in consequence. But why need we stop to consider cases where some subtilty of thought is required to see that the assertion is not warranted when every book which applies philosophy to the conduct of life lays down as positive certainty propositions which it is quite as easy to doubt as to believe?

The second bar which philosophers often set up across the roadway of inquiry lies in maintaining that this, that, and the other never can be known. When Auguste Comte was pressed to specify any matter of positive fact to the knowledge of which no man could by any possibility attain, he instanced the knowledge of the chemical composition of the fixed stars; and you may see his answer set down in the *Philosophie positive*. But the ink was scarcely dry upon the printed page before the spectroscope was discovered and that which he had deemed absolutely unknowable was well on the way of getting ascertained. It is easy enough to mention a question the answer to which is not known to me today. But to aver that that answer will not be known tomorrow is somewhat risky; for oftentimes it is precisely the least expected truth which is turned up under the ploughshare of research. And when it comes to positive assertion that the truth never will be found out, that, in the light of the history of our time, seems to me more hazardous than the venture of Andrée.

The third philosophical stratagem for cutting off inquiry consists in maintaining that this, that, or the other element of science is basic, ultimate, independent of aught else, and utterly inexplicable —not so much from any defect in our knowing as because there is nothing beneath it to know. The only type of reasoning by which such a conclusion could possibly be reached is *retroduction*.[4] Now nothing justifies a retroductive inference except its affording an explanation of the facts. It is, however, no explanation at all of a fact to pronounce it *inexplicable*. That, therefore, is a conclusion which no reasoning can ever justify or excuse.

The last philosophical obstacle to the advance of knowledge which I intend to mention is the holding that this or that law or truth has found its last and perfect formulation—and especially that the ordinary and usual course of nature never can be broken through. "Stones do not fall from heaven," said Laplace, although they had been falling upon inhabited ground every day from the earliest times. But there is no kind of inference which can lend the slightest probability to any such absolute denial of an unusual phenomenon.

All positive reasoning is of the nature of judging the proportion of something in a whole collection by the proportion found in a sample. Accordingly, there are three things to which we can never hope to attain by reasoning, namely, absolute certainty, absolute exactitude, absolute universality. We cannot be absolutely certain that our conclusions are even approximately true; for the sample may be utterly unlike the unsampled part of the collection. We cannot pretend to be even probably exact; because the sample consists of but a finite number of instances and only admits special values of the proportion sought. Finally, even if we could ascertain with absolute certainty and exactness that the ratio of sinful men to all men was as 1 to 1; still among the infinite generations of men there would be room for any finite number of sinless men without violating the proportion. The case is the same with a seven-legged calf.

Now if exactitude, certitude, and universality are not to be attained by reasoning, there is certainly no other means by which they can be reached.

Somebody will suggest *revelation*. There are scientists and people influenced by science who laugh at revelation; and certainly science has taught us to look at testimony in such a light that the whole theological doctrine of the "Evidences" seems pretty weak. However, I do not think it is philosophical to reject the possibility of a revelation. Still, granting that, I declare as a logician that revealed truths—that is, truths which have nothing in their favour but revelations made to a few individuals—constitute by far the most uncertain class of truths there are. There is here no question of universality; for revelation is itself sporadic and miraculous. There is no question of mathematical exactitude; for no revelation makes any pretension to that character. But it does pretend to be *certain*; and against that there are three conclusive objections. First, we never can be absolutely certain that any given deliverance really is inspired; for that can only be established by reasoning. We cannot even prove it with any very high degree of probability. Second, even if it is inspired, we cannot be sure, or nearly sure, that the statement is true. We know that one of the commandments was in one of the Bibles printed with[out] a *not* in it. All inspired matter has been subject to human distortion or colouring. Besides we cannot penetrate the counsels of the most High, or lay down anything as a principle that would govern his conduct. We do not know his inscrutable purposes, nor can we comprehend his plans. We cannot tell but he might see fit to inspire his servants with errors. In the third place, a truth which rests on the authority of inspiration only is of a somewhat incomprehensible nature; and we never can be sure that we rightly comprehend it. As there is no way of evading these difficulties, I say that revelation, far from affording us any certainty, gives results less certain than other sources of information. This would be so even if revelation were much plainer than it is.

But, it will be said, you forget the laws which are known to us *a priori*, the axioms of geometry, the principles of logic, the maxims of *causality*, and the like. Those are absolutely certain, without exception and exact. To this I reply that it seems to me there is the most positive historic proof that innate truths are particularly uncertain and mixed up with error, and therefore *a fortiori* not without exception. This historical proof is, of course, not infallible; but it is very strong. Therefore, I ask *how do you know* that *a priori* truth is certain, exceptionless, and exact? You cannot know it by *reasoning*. For that would be subject to uncertainty and inexactitude. Then, it must amount to this that you know it *a priori*; that is, you take *a priori* judgments at their own valuation, without criticism or credentials. That is barring the gate of inquiry.

Ah! but it will be said, you forget direct experience. Direct experience is neither certain nor uncertain, because it affirms nothing—it just *is*. There are delusions, hallucinations, dreams. But there is no mistake that such things really do appear, and direct experience means simply the appearance. It involves no error, because it testifies to nothing but its own appearance. For the same reason, it affords no certainty. It is not *exact*, because it leaves much vague; though it is not *inexact* either; that is, it has no false exactitude.

All this is true of direct experience at its first presentation. But when it comes up to be criticized it is past, itself, and is represented by *memory*. Now the deceptions and inexactitude of memory are proverbial.

. . . On the whole, then, we cannot in any way reach perfect certitude nor exactitude. We never can be absolutely sure of anything, nor can we with any probability ascertain the exact value of any measure or general ratio.

This is my conclusion, after many years study of the logic of science; and it is the conclusion which others, of very different cast of mind, have come to, likewise. I believe I may say there is no tenable opinion regarding human knowledge which does not legitimately lead to this corollary. Certainly there is nothing new in it; and many of the greatest minds of all time have held it for true.

Indeed, most everybody will admit it until he begins to see what is involved in the admission—and then most people will draw back. It will not be admitted by persons utterly incapable of philosophical reflection. It will not be fully admitted by masterful minds developed exclusively in the direction of action and accustomed to claim practical infallibility in matters of business. These men will admit the incurable fallibility of all opinions readily enough; only, they will always make exception of their own. The doctrine of fallibilism will also be denied by those who fear its consequences for science, for religion, and for morality. But I will take leave to say to these highly conservative gentlemen that however competent they may be to direct the affairs of a church or other corporation, they had better not try to manage science in that way. Conservatism—in the sense of a dread of consequences—is altogether out of place in science—which has on the contrary always been forwarded by radicals and radicalism, in the sense of the eagerness to carry consequences to their extremes. Not the radicalism that is cocksure, however, but the *radicalism that tries experiments*. Indeed, it is precisely among men animated by the spirit of science that the doctrine of fallibilism will find supporters.

Still, even such a man as that may well ask whether I propose to say that it is not quite certain that twice two are four—and that it is even not probably quite exact! But it would be quite misunderstanding the doctrine of fallibilism to suppose that it means that twice two is probably not exactly four. As I have already remarked, it is not my purpose to doubt that people can usually *count* with accuracy. Nor does fallibilism say that men cannot attain a sure knowledge of the creations of their own minds. It neither affirms nor denies that. It only says that people cannot attain absolute certainty concerning questions of fact. Numbers are merely a system of names devised by men for the purpose of counting. It is a matter of real fact to say that in a certain room there are two persons. It is a matter of fact to say that each person has two eyes. It is a matter of fact to say that there are four eyes in the room. But to say that *if* there are two persons and each person has two eyes there *will be* four eyes is not a statement of fact, but a statement about the system of numbers which is our own creation.

5

PHILOSOPHY AND THE SCIENCES: A CLASSIFICATION *

I

THIS classification, which aims to base itself on the principal affinities of the objects classified, is concerned not with all possible sciences, nor with so many branches of knowledge, but with sciences in their present condition, as so many businesses of groups of living men. It borrows its idea from Comte's classification; namely, the idea that one science depends upon another for fundamental principles, but does not furnish such principles to that other. It turns out that in most cases the divisions are trichotomic; the First of the three members relating to universal elements or laws, the Second arranging classes of forms and seeking to bring them under universal laws, the Third going into the utmost detail, describing individual phenomena and endeavouring to explain them. But not all the divisions are of this character.

The classification has been carried into great detail; but only its broader divisions are here given.

All science is either, A. Science of Discovery; B. Science of Review; or C. Practical Science.[5]

By "science of review" is meant the business of those who occupy themselves with arranging the results of discovery, beginning with digests, and going on to endeavour to form a philosophy of science. Such is the nature of Humboldt's *Cosmos*, of Comte's *Philosophie positive*, and of Spencer's *Synthetic Philosophy*. The classification of the sciences belongs to this department.

Science of Discovery is either, I. Mathematics; II. Philosophy; or III. Idioscopy.

Mathematics studies what is and what is not logically possible, without making itself responsible for its actual existence. Philosophy is *positive science*, in the sense of discovering what really is true; but it limits itself to so much of truth as can be inferred from common experience. Idioscopy embraces all the special sciences,

* [I is from *A Syllabus of Certain Topics of Logic* 1903 (*CP* 1.180-92). II consists of selections from the ms. volume "Minute Logic" 1902 (*CP* 1.203, 204, 211, 213-14, 220, 226-7, 239-42, 244-6, 249-50, 273, 278-82). III is from ms. c. 1896 (*CP* 1.176-8).]

which are principally occupied with the accumulation of new facts.

Mathematics may be divided into *a*. the Mathematics of Logic; *b*. the Mathematics of Discrete Series; *c*. the Mathematics of Continua and Pseudo-continua.

I shall not carry this division further. Branch *b* has recourse to branch *a*, and branch *c* to branch *b*.

Philosophy is divided into *a*. Phenomenology; *b*. Normative Science; *c*. Metaphysics.

Phenomenology ascertains and studies the kinds of elements universally present in the phenomenon; meaning by the *phenomenon*, whatever is present at any time to the mind in any way. Normative science distinguishes what ought to be from what ought not to be, and makes many other divisions and arrangements subservient to its primary dualistic distinction. Metaphysics seeks to give an account of the universe of mind and matter. Normative science rests largely on phenomenology and on mathematics; metaphysics on phenomenology and on normative science.

Idioscopy has two wings: α. the Physical Sciences; and β. the Psychical, or Human Sciences.

Psychical science borrows principles continually from the physical sciences; the latter very little from the former.

The physical sciences are: *a*. Nomological, or General, Physics; *b*. Classificatory Physics; *c*. Descriptive Physics.

Nomological physics discovers the ubiquitous phenomena of the physical universe, formulates their laws, and measures their constants. It draws upon metaphysics and upon mathematics for principles. Classificatory physics describes and classifies physical forms and seeks to explain them by the laws discovered by nomological physics with which it ultimately tends to coalesce. Descriptive physics describes individual objects—the earth and the heavens —endeavours to explain their phenomena by the principles of nomological and classificatory physics, and tends ultimately itself to become classificatory.

The Psychical Sciences are: *a*. Nomological Psychics or Psychology; *b*. Classificatory Psychics, or Ethnology; *c*. Descriptive Psychics, or History.

Nomological psychics discovers the general elements and laws of mental phenomena. It is greatly influenced by phenomenology, by logic, by metaphysics, and by biology (a branch of classificatory physics). Classificatory psychics classifies products of mind and endeavours to explain them on psychological principles. At present it is far too much in its infancy (except linguistics, to which reference will be made below) to approach very closely to psychology. It borrows from psychology and from physics. Descriptive psychics endeavours in the first place to describe individual manifestations of mind, whether they be permanent works or actions; and to that task it joins that of endeavouring to explain them on the principles of psychology and ethnology. It borrows from geography (a branch of descriptive physics), from astronomy (another branch) and from other branches of physical and psychical science.

I now consider the subdivisions of these sciences, so far as they are so widely separated as quite to sunder the groups of investigators who today study them.

Phenomenology is, at present, a single study.

Normative science has three widely separated divisions: i. Esthetics; ii. Ethics; iii. Logic.

Esthetics is the science of ideals, or of that which is objectively admirable without any ulterior reason. I am not well acquainted with this science; but it ought to repose on phenomenology. Ethics, or the science of right and wrong, must appeal to Esthetics for aid in determining the *summum bonum*. It is the theory of self-controlled, or deliberate, conduct. Logic is the theory of self-controlled, or deliberate, thought; and as such, must appeal to ethics for its principles. It also depends upon phenomenology and upon mathematics. All thought being performed by means of signs, logic may be regarded as the science of the general laws of signs. It has three branches [6]: 1, Speculative Grammar, or the general theory of the nature and meanings of signs, whether they be icons, indices, or symbols; 2, Critic, which classifies arguments and determines the validity and degree of force of each kind; 3, Methodeutic, which studies the methods that ought to be pursued in the investigation, in the exposition, and in the application of truth. Each division depends on that which precedes it.

Metaphysics may be divided into, i, General Metaphysics, or Ontology; ii, Psychical, or Religious, Metaphysics, concerned chiefly with the questions of 1, God, 2, Freedom, 3, Immortality; and iii, Physical Metaphysics, which discusses the real nature of time, space, laws of nature, matter, etc. The second and third branches appear at present to look upon one another with supreme contempt.

II

Many have been the attempts at a general classification of the sciences. Dr. Richardson's little book upon the subject is quite incomplete, only enumerating one hundred and forty-six systems. They are naturally many, because not only are their purposes various, but their conceptions of a science are divergent, and their notions of what classification is are still more so.   Many of these schemes introduce sciences which nobody ever heard of; so that they seem to aim at classifying, not actually existent sciences, but possible sciences.   A somewhat presumptuous undertaking is that of classifying the science of the remote future.   On the other hand, if classifications are to be restricted to sciences actually existing at the time the classifications are made, the classifications certainly ought to differ from age to age.   If Plato's classification was satisfactory in his day, it cannot be good today; and if it be good now, the inference will be that it was bad when he proposed it.

. . . I am unable to see any need at all in positive science for considering . . . metaphysically real classes.   To my apprehension the business of classification has no concern with them, but only with true and natural classes, in another and a purely experiential sense.   For example, if I were to attempt to classify the arts, which I shall not do, I should have to recognize, as one of them, the art of illumination, and should have occasion to remark that lamps form a true, real, and natural class, because every lamp has been made and has come into being as a result of an aim common and peculiar to all lamps.   A *class*, of course, is the total of whatever objects there may be in the universe which are of a certain description.   What if we try taking the term "natural," or "real, class" to mean a class of which all the members owe their existence as members of the class to a common final cause?   This is somewhat vague; but it is better to allow a term like this to remain vague, until we see our way to rational precision.

It is . . . a widespread error to think that a "final cause" is necessarily a purpose.   A purpose is merely that form of final cause which is most familiar to our experience.   The signification of the phrase "final cause" must be determined by its use in the statement of Aristotle that all causation divides into two grand branches, the efficient, or forceful; and the ideal, or final.   If we are to conserve the truth of that statement, we must understand by final causation that mode of bringing facts about according to which a general description of result is made to come about, quite irrespective of any compulsion for it to come about in this or that particular way; although the means may be adapted to the end.   The general result may be brought about at one time in one way, and at another time in another way. Final causation does not determine in what particular way it is to be brought about, but only that the result shall have a certain general character.

Final causality cannot be imagined without efficient causality; but no whit the less on that account are their modes of action polar contraries. The sheriff would still have his fist, even if there were no court; but an efficient cause, detached from a final cause in the form of a law, would not even possess efficiency: it might exert itself, and something might follow *post hoc*, but not *propter hoc*; for *propter* implies potential regularity. Now without law there is no regularity; and without the influence of ideas there is no potentiality.

The light of these reflections brings out into distinct view characters of our definition of a real class which we might otherwise have overlooked or misinterpreted. Every class has its definition, which is an idea; but it is not every class where the *existence*, that is, the occurrence in the universe of its members is due to the active causality of the defining idea of the class.

I may be asked what I mean by the objects of [a] class *deriving their existence* from an idea. Do I mean that the idea calls new matter into existence? Certainly not. That would be pure intellectualism, which denies that blind force is an element of experience distinct from rationality, or logical force. I believe that to be a great error; but I need not stop to disprove it now, for those who entertain it will be on my side in regard to classification. But it will be urged that if that is not my meaning, then the idea merely confers upon the members of the class its character; and since every class has a defining character, any one class is as "natural" or "real" as another, if that term be taken in the sense I give to it. I cannot, however, quite admit that. Whether or not every class is or is not more or less a natural class is a question which may be worth consideration; but I do not think that the relation of the idea to the members of the natural class is simply that it is applicable to them as a predicate, as it is to every class equally. What I mean by the idea's conferring existence upon the individual members of the class is that it confers upon them the power of working out results in this world, that it confers upon them, that is to say, organic existence, or, in one word, life. The existence of an individual man is a totally different thing from the existence of the matter which at any given instant happens to compose him, and which is incessantly passing in and out.

The sciences are, in part, produced each from others. Thus, spectroscopic astronomy has for its parents, astronomy, chemistry, and optics. But this is not the whole genesis nor the principal part of the genesis of any broad and definite science. It has its own peculiar problem springing from an idea. That geometry derived its birth from land surveying is the tradition, which is borne out by the tradition that it took its origin in Egypt where the yearly floods must have rendered accurate surveying of special importance. Moreover, the wonderful accuracy of the dimensions of the great pyramid exhibit a degree of skill in laying out ground which could only have been attained by great intellectual activity; and this activity could hardly fail to lead to some beginnings of geometry. We may, therefore, accept with considerable confidence the tradition involved in the very name of geometry. Speaking in a broad, rough way, it may be said that the sciences have grown out of the useful arts, or out of arts supposed to be useful. Astronomy out of astrology; physiology, taking medicine as a halfway out of magic; chemistry out of alchemy; thermotics from the steam-engine, etc. Among the theoretical sciences, while some of the most abstract have sprung straight from the concretest arts, there is nevertheless a well-marked tendency for a science to be first descriptive, later classificatory, and lastly to embrace all classes in one law. The classificatory stage may be skipped. Yet in the truer order of development, the generation proceeds quite in the other direction. Men may and do begin to study the different kinds of animals and plants before they know anything of the general laws of physiology. But they cannot attain any true understanding of taxonomic biology until they can be guided by the discoveries of the physiologists. Till then the study of mollusks will be nothing but conchology. On the other hand the physiologist may be aided by a fact or two here and there drawn from taxonomic biology; but he asks but little and that little not very urgently of anything that the taxonomist can tell him and that he could not find out for himself.

All natural classification is then essentially, we may almost say, an attempt to find out the true genesis of the objects classified. But by genesis must be understood, not the efficient action which produces the whole by producing the parts, but the final action which produces the parts because they are needed to make the whole. Genesis is production from ideas. It may be difficult to understand how this is true in the biological world, though there is proof enough that it is so. But in regard to science it is a proposition easily enough intelligible. A science is defined by its problem; and its problem is clearly formulated on the basis of abstracter science.

I recognize two branches of science: Theoretical, whose purpose is simply and solely knowledge of God's truth; and Practical, for the uses of life. In Branch I, I recognize two subbranches, of which, at present, I consider only the first, [the sciences of discovery]. Among the theoretical sciences [of discovery], I distinguish three classes, all resting upon observation, but being observational in very different senses.

The first is mathematics, which does not undertake to ascertain any matter of fact whatever, but merely posits hypotheses, and traces out their consequences. It is observational, in so far as it makes constructions in the imagination according to abstract precepts, and then observes these imaginary objects, finding in them relations of parts not specified in the precept of construction. This is truly observation, yet certainly in a very peculiar sense; and no other kind of observation would at all answer the purpose of mathematics.

Class II is philosophy, which deals with positive truth, indeed, yet contents itself with observations such as come within the range of every man's normal experience, and for the most part in every waking hour of his life. Hence Bentham calls this class, *cœnoscopic*. These observations escape the untrained eye precisely because they permeate our whole lives, just as a man who never takes off his blue spectacles soon ceases to see the blue tinge. Evidently, therefore, no microscope or sensitive film would be of the least use in this class. The observation is observation in a peculiar, yet perfectly legitimate, sense. If philosophy glances now and then at the results of special sciences, it is only as a sort of condiment to excite its own proper observation.

Class III is Bentham's *idioscopic*; that is, the special sciences, depending upon special observation, which travel or other exploration, or some assistance to the senses, either instrumental or given by training, together with unusual diligence, has put within the power of its students. This class manifestly divides itself into two subclasses, the physical and the psychical sciences; or, as I will call them, physiognosy and psychognosy. Under the former is to be included physics, chemistry, biology, astronomy, geognosy, and whatever may be like these sciences; under the latter, psychology, linguistics, ethnology, sociology, history, etc.   Physiognosy sets forth the workings of efficient causation, psychognosy of final causation.   But the two things call for different eyes.   A man will be no whit the worse physiognosist for being utterly blind to facts of mind; and if we sometimes find observation in a psychognosist, it will, unless by exception, be found not to be of a purely physical fact. Thus, a philologist may have a fine ear for language-sounds; but it is by no means pure physical resemblance which determines whether a given sound is or is not "the" Italian close *o*, for example, as it is naïvely called: it is psychical habit.   In any simple physical sense the sounds not distinguished from that differ much more from one another than almost any of them do from sounds which would not be tolerated for "the" close *o*.   So, this fine phonetic observation of the linguist is a knack of understanding a virtual convention. The two kinds of observation are different; but they do not seem to be quite so different as both alike are from the observation of the philosopher and the mathematician; and this is why, though I, at first, was inclined to give each of them equal rank with those classes, it has at length appeared certain that they should be placed a little lower.

Now let us consider the relations of the classes of science to one another.   We have already remarked that relations of generation must always be of the highest concern to natural classification, which is, in fact, no more nor less than an account of the existential, or *natural*, birth concerning relations of things; meaning by birth the relations of a thing to its originating final causes.

Beginning with Class I, mathematics meddles with every other science without exception.   There is no science whatever to which is not attached an application of mathematics.   This is not true of any other science, since pure mathematics has not, as a part of it, any application of any other science, inasmuch as every other science is limited to finding out what is positively true, either as an individual fact, as a class, or as a law; while pure mathematics has no interest in whether a proposition is existentially true or not. In particular, mathematics has such a close intimacy with one of the classes of philosophy, that is, with logic, that no small acumen is required to find the joint between them.

Next, passing to Class II, philosophy, whose business it is to find out all that can be found out from those universal experiences which confront every man in every waking hour of his life, must necessarily have its application in every other science.   For be this science of philosophy that is founded on those universal phenomena as small as you please, as long as it amounts to anything at all, it is evident that every special science ought to take that little into account before it begins work with its microscope, or telescope, or whatever special means of ascertaining truth it may be provided with.

Is physical space hyperbolic, that is, infinite and limited, or is it elliptic, that is, finite and unlimited? Only the exactest measurements upon the stars can decide. Yet even with them the question cannot be answered without recourse to philosophy. But a question at this moment under consideration by physicists is whether matter consists ultimately of minute solids, or whether it consists merely of vortices of an ultimate fluid. The third possibility, which there seems to be reason to suspect is the true one, that it may consist of vortices in a fluid which itself consists of far minuter solids, these, however, being themselves vortices of a fluid, itself consisting of ultimate solids, and so on in endless alternation, has hardly been broached. The question as it stands must evidently depend upon what we ought to conclude from everyday, unspecialized observations, and particularly upon a question of logic. Another still warmer controversy is whether or not it is proper to endeavour to find a mechanical explanation of electricity, or whether it is proper, on the contrary, to leave the differential equations of electrodynamics as the last word of science. This is manifestly only to be decided by a scientific philosophy very different from the amateurish, superficial stuff in which the contestants are now entangling themselves. A third pretty well defended opinion, by the way, is that instead of explaining electricity by molar dynamics, molar dynamics ought to be explained as a special consequence of the laws of electricity. Another appeal to philosophy was not long ago virtually made by the eminent electrician, the lamented Hertz, who wished to explain force, in general, as a consequence of unseen constraints. Philosophy alone can pronounce for or against such a theory. I will not undertake to anticipate questions which have not yet emerged; otherwise, I might suggest that chemists must ere long be making appeal to philosophy to decide whether compounds are held together by force or by some other agency. In biology, besides the old logico-metaphysical dispute about the reality of classifications, the momentous question of evolution has unmistakable dependence on philosophy. Then again, caryocinesis has emboldened some naturalists, having certain philosophical leanings, to rebel against the empire of experimental physiology. The origin of life is another topic where philosophy asserts itself; and with this I close my list, not at all because I have mentioned all the points at which just now the physical sciences are influenced by a philosophy, such as it is, but simply because I have mentioned enough of them for my present purpose.

The dependence of the psychical sciences upon philosophy is no less manifest. A few years ago, indeed, regenerate psychology, in the flush of her first success, not very wisely proposed to do without metaphysics; but I think that today psychologists generally perceive the impossibility of such a thing. It is true that the psychical sciences are not quite so dependent upon metaphysics as are the physical sciences; but, by way of compensation, they must lean more upon logic. The mind works by final causation, and final causation is logical causation. Note, for example, the intimate bearing of logic upon grammatical syntax. Moreover, everything in the psychical sciences is inferential. Not the smallest fact about the mind can be directly perceived as psychical. An emotion is directly felt as a bodily state, or else it is only known inferentially. That a thing is agreeable appears to direct observation as a character of an object, and it is only by inference that it is referred to the mind. If this statement be disputed (and some will dispute it), all the more need is there for the intervention of logic. Very difficult problems of inference are continually emerging in the psychical sciences. In psychology, there are such questions as free-will and innate ideas; in linguistics, there is the question of the origin of language, which must be settled before linguistics takes its final form. The whole business of deriving ancient history from documents that are always insufficient and, even when not conflicting, frequently pretty obviously false, must be carried on under the supervision of logic, or else be badly done.

It is plain that philosophy cannot, like idioscopy, be split from top to bottom into an efficient and a final wing. For, not to mention other reasons, to philosophy must fall the task of comparing the two stems of causation and of exhuming their common root. In another way, however, philosophy falls asunder into two groups of studies to which the appellation of subclasses is alone appropriate, if we are to understand by a subclass a modification of that class-making sense in which philosophy may be said to be observational. For besides what constitutes—in the present stage of the study, at least—the main body of philosophy, resting exclusively upon

universal experience, and imparting to it a tinge of necessity, there
is a department of science which, while it rests, and can only rest,
as to the bulk of it, upon universal experience, yet for certain special
yet obtrusive points is obliged to appeal to the most specialized and
refined observations, in order to ascertain what minute modifications
of everyday experience they may introduce. If in these departments the teachings of ordinary experience took on the true com-
plexion of necessity, as they usually do, it would hardly be in our
power to appeal to special experience to contradict them. But it
is a remarkable fact that though inattentive minds do pronounce
the dicta of ordinary experience in these cases to be necessary, they
do not appear so to those who examine them more critically. For
example, everyday experience is that events occur in time, and that
time has but one dimension. So much appears necessary. For we
should be utterly bewildered by the suggestion that two events
were each anterior to the other or that, happening at different
times, one was not anterior to the other. But a two-dimensional
anteriority is easily shown to involve a self-contradiction. So,
then, that time is one-dimensional is, for the present, necessary;
and we know not how to appeal to special experience to disprove it.
But that space is three-dimensional involves no such necessity.
We can perfectly well suppose that atoms or their corpuscles move
freely in four or more dimensions. So everyday experience seems
to teach us that time flows continuously. But that we are not sure
that it really does so, appears from the fact that many men of
powerful minds who have examined the question are of the opinion
that it is not so. Why may there not be a succession of stationary
states, say a milliasse or so of them or perhaps an infinite multitude
per second, and why may states of things not break abruptly from
one to the next? Here the teachings of ordinary experience are,
at least, difficult of ascertainment. There are cases where they are
decidedly indefinite. Thus, such experience shows that the events
of one day or year are not exactly like those of another, although
in part there is a cyclical repetition.

. . . Every department of idioscopy is based upon special observation, and only resorts to philosophy in order that certain
obstacles to its pursuing its proper special observational inquiries
may be cleared out of the way. The sciences which we are now
considering, on the contrary, are based upon the same sort of
general experience upon which philosophy builds; and they only
resort to special observation to settle some minute details, con-

cerning which the testimony of general experience is possibly insufficient. It is true that they are thus of a nature intermediate between cœnoscopy and idioscopy; but in the main their character is philosophical. They form, therefore, a second subclass of philosophy, to which we may give the name of *theôrics*. As inquiry now stands, this subclass has but two divisions which can hardly rank as orders, but rather as families, *chronotheory* and *topotheory*. This kind of study is in its first infancy. Few men so much as acknowledge that it is anything more than idle speculation. It may be that in the future the subclass will be filled up with other orders.

The first subclass, that of *necessary philosophy*, might be called *epistêmy*, since this alone among the sciences realizes the Platonic and generally Hellenic conception of ἐπιστημη. Under it, three orders stand out clearly.

The first of these is *Phenomenology*, or the Doctrine of Categories, whose business it is to unravel the tangled skein [of] all that in any sense appears and wind it into distinct forms; or in other words, to make the ultimate analysis of all experiences the first task to which philosophy has to apply itself. It is a most difficult, perhaps the most difficult, of its tasks, demanding very peculiar powers of thought, the ability to seize clouds, vast and intangible, to set them in orderly array, to put them through their exercises. The mere reading of this sort of philosophy, the mere understanding of it, is not easy. Anything like a just appreciation of it has not been performed by many of those who have written books. Original work in this department, if it is to be real and hitherto unformulated truth, is—not to speak of whether it is difficult or not—one of those functions of growth which every man, perhaps, in some fashion exercises once, some even twice, but which it would be next to a miracle to perform a third time.

Order II consists of the normative sciences. I wonder how many of those who make use of this term see any particular need of the word "normative." A normative science is one which studies what ought to be. How then does it differ from engineering, medicine, or any other practical science? If, however, logic, ethics, and esthetics, which are the families of normative science, are simply the arts of reasoning, of the conduct of life, and of fine art, they do not belong in the branch of theoretic science which we are alone considering, at all. There is no doubt that they are closely related to three corresponding arts, or practical sciences. But that which renders the word normative needful (and not purely ornamental) is precisely the rather singular fact that, though these sciences do study what ought to be, *i.e.*, ideals, they are the very most purely theoretical of purely theoretical sciences. What was it that Pascal said? "La vraie morale se moque de la morale." It is not worth while, in this corner of the book, to dwell upon so prominent a feature of our subject. The peculiar tinge of mind in these normative sciences has already been much insisted upon. It will come out in stronger and stronger colours as we go on.

Order III consists of metaphysics, whose attitude toward the universe is nearly that of the special sciences (anciently, *physics* was its designation), from which it is mainly distinguished, by its confining itself to such parts of physics and of psychics as can be established without special means of observation. But these are very peculiar parts, extremely unlike the rest.

III

The universally and justly lauded parallel which Kant draws between a philosophical doctrine and a piece of architecture has excellencies which the beginner in philosophy might easily overlook; and not the least of these is its recognition of the cosmic character of philosophy. I use the word "cosmic" because *cosmicus* is Kant's own choice; but I must say I think *secular* or *public* would have approached nearer to the expression of his meaning. Works of sculpture and painting can be executed for a single patron and must be by a single artist. A painting always represents a fragment of a larger whole. It is broken at its edges. It is to be shut up in a room and admired by a few. In such a work individuality of thought and feeling is an element of beauty. But a great building, such as alone can call out the depths of the architect's soul, is meant for the whole people, and is erected by the exertions of an army representative of the whole people. It is the message with which an age is charged, and which it delivers to posterity. Consequently, thought characteristic of an individual—the piquant, the nice, the clever—is too little to play any but the most subordinate *rôle* in architecture. If anybody can doubt whether this be equally true of philosophy, I can but recommend to him that splendid third chapter of the Methodology, in the *Critic of the Pure Reason*.

To the cosmological or secular character of philosophy (to which, as closely connected, Kant with his unfailing discernment joins the circumstance that philosophy is a thing that has to grow by the fission of minute parts and not by accretion) is due the necessity of planning it out from the beginning. Of course, every painting likewise has its composition; but composition is not a very weighty problem, except in that kind of painting which is accessory to architecture, or is, at any rate, very public in its appeal. Indeed historical painting is one of those exceptions which go to prove the rule that in works which aim at being secular, rather than individualistic, the preliminary business of planning is particularly important and onerous.

And the reason is very plain and simple. The instincts of the lower animals answer their purposes much more unerringly than a discursive understanding could do. But for man discourse of reason is requisite, because men are so intensively individualistic and original that the instincts, which are racial ideas, become smothered in them. A deliberate logical faculty, therefore, has in man to take their place; and the sole function of this logical deliberation is to grind off the arbitrary and the individualistic character of thought. Hence, wherever the arbitrary and the individualistic is particularly prejudicial, there logical deliberation, or discourse of reason, must be allowed as much play as possible.

6

THE PRINCIPLES OF PHENOMENOLOGY *

1. The Domain of Phenomenology

PHANEROSCOPY [or Phenomenology] is the description of the *phaneron*; and by the *phaneron* I mean the collective total of all that is in any way or in any sense present to the mind, quite regardless of whether it corresponds to any real thing or not. If you ask present *when*, and to *whose* mind, I reply that I leave these questions unanswered, never having entertained a doubt that those features of the phaneron that I have found in my mind are present at all times and to all minds. So far as I have developed this science of phaneroscopy, it is occupied with the formal elements of the phaneron. I know that there is another series of elements imperfectly represented by Hegel's Categories. But I have been unable to give any satisfactory account of them.

English philosophers have quite commonly used the word *idea* in a sense approaching to that which I give to *phaneron*. But in various ways they have restricted the meaning of it too much to cover my conception (if conception it can be called), besides giving a psychological connotation to their word which I am careful to exclude. The fact that they have the habit of saying that "there is no such idea" as this or that, in the very same breath in which they definitely describe the phaneron in question, renders their term fatally inapt for my purpose.

There is nothing quite so directly open to observation as phanerons; and since I shall have no need of referring to any but those which (or the like of which) are perfectly familiar to everybody, every reader can control the accuracy of what I am going to say about them. Indeed, he must actually repeat my observations and

* [*1* and the first selection in *4* are from mss. 1905 and c. 1904 (*CP* 1.284-7, 304). The first selection in *2* is from ms. 1903 (*CP* 1.23-6). The second in *2*, third in *4*, and fourth in *5* are from ms. c. 1896 (*CP* 1.418-20, 422-8). In *3*, the first selection is from ms. c. 1894 (*CP* 1.302), the second is an unidentified fragment (*CP* 1.325), and the third consists of an unidentified fragment and parts of mss. c. 1875 and 1895 (*CP* 1.337-9, 340). The second selection in *4* is from ms. 1907 (*CP* 1.306-11), the first in *5* from ms. c. 1910 (*CP* 1.321), the second and third in *5* from mss. c. 1905 and c. 1903 respectively (*CP* 1.335-6, 322-3). *6* is from ms. 1903 (*CP* 1.343, 345-7), *7* from mss. c. 1890 and c. 1885 (*CP* 1.374-82), and *8* from ms. c. 1880 (*CP* 1.353).]

74

experiments for himself, or else I shall more utterly fail to convey my meaning than if I were to discourse of effects of chromatic decoration to a man congenitally blind. What I term *phaneroscopy* is that study which, supported by the direct observation of phanerons and generalizing its observations, signalizes several very broad classes of phanerons; describes the features of each; shows that although they are so inextricably mixed together that no one can be isolated, yet it is manifest that their characters are quite disparate; then proves, beyond question, that a certain very short list comprises all of these broadest categories of phanerons there are; and finally proceeds to the laborious and difficult task of enumerating the principal subdivisions of those categories.

It will be plain from what has been said that phaneroscopy has nothing at all to do with the question of how far the phanerons it studies correspond to any realities. It religiously abstains from all speculation as to any relations between its categories and physiological facts, cerebral or other. It does not undertake, but sedulously avoids, hypothetical explanations of any sort. It simply scrutinizes the direct appearances, and endeavours to combine minute accuracy with the broadest possible generalization. The student's great effort is not to be influenced by any tradition, any authority, any reasons for supposing that such and such ought to be the facts, or any fancies of any kind, and to confine himself to honest, single-minded observation of the appearances. The reader, upon his side, must repeat the author's observations for himself, and decide from his own observations whether the author's account of the appearances is correct or not.

2. THE CATEGORIES: FIRSTNESS, SECONDNESS, THIRDNESS

My view is that there are three modes of being. I hold that we can directly observe them in elements of whatever is at any time before the mind in any way. They are the being of positive qualitative possibility, the being of actual fact, and the being of law that will govern facts in the future.

Let us begin with considering actuality, and try to make out just what it consists in. If I ask you what the actuality of an event consists in, you will tell me that it consists in its happening *then* and *there*. The specifications *then* and *there* involve all its relations to other existents. The actuality of the event seems to lie in its relations to the universe of existents. A court may issue *injunctions* and *judgments* against me and I not care a snap of my fingers for them. I may think them idle vapour. But when I feel the sheriff's hand on my shoulder, I shall begin to have a sense of actuality. Actuality is something *brute*. There is no reason in it. I instance putting your shoulder against a door and trying to force it open against an unseen, silent, and unknown resistance. We have a two-sided consciousness of effort and resistance, which seems to me to come tolerably near to a pure sense of actuality. On the whole, I think we have here a mode of being of one thing which consists in how a second object is. I call that Secondness.

Besides this, there are two modes of being that I call Firstness and Thirdness. Firstness is the mode of being which consists in its subject's being positively such as it is regardless of aught else. That can only be a possibility. For as long as things do not act upon one another there is no sense or meaning in saying that they have any being, unless it be that they are such in themselves that they may perhaps come into relation with others. The mode of being a *redness*, before anything in the universe was yet red, was nevertheless a positive qualitative possibility. And redness in itself, even if it be embodied, is something positive and *sui generis*. That I call Firstness. We naturally attribute Firstness to outward objects, that is we suppose they have capacities in themselves which may or may not be already actualized, which may or may not ever be actualized, although we can know nothing of such possibilities [except] so far as they are actualized.

Now for Thirdness. Five minutes of our waking life will hardly pass without our making some kind of prediction; and in the majority of cases these predictions are fulfilled in the event. Yet a prediction is essentially of a general nature, and cannot ever be completely fulfilled. To say that a prediction has a decided tendency to be fulfilled, is to say that the future events are in a measure really governed by a law. If a pair of dice turns up sixes five times running, that is a mere uniformity. The dice might happen for-tuitously to turn up sixes a thousand times running. But that would not afford the slightest security for a prediction that they would turn up sixes the next time. If the prediction has a tendency to be fulfilled, it must be that future events have a tendency to conform to a general rule. "Oh," but say the nominalists, "this general rule is nothing but a mere word or couple of words!" I reply, "Nobody ever dreamed of denying that what is general is of the nature of a general sign; but the question is whether future events will conform to it or not. If they will, your adjective 'mere' seems to be ill-placed." A rule to which future events have a tend-ency to conform is *ipso facto* an important thing, an important element in the happening of those events. This mode of being which *consists*, mind my word if you please, the mode of being which *consists* in the fact that future facts of Secondness will take on a determinate general character, I call a Thirdness.

The first [category] comprises the qualities of phenomena, such as red, bitter, tedious, hard, heartrending, noble; and there are doubtless manifold varieties utterly unknown to us. Beginners in philosophy may object that these are not qualities of things and are not in the world at all, but are mere sensations. Certainly, we only know such as the senses we are furnished with are adapted to reveal; and it can hardly be doubted that the specializing effect of the evolutionary process which has made us what we are has been to blot the greater part of the senses and sensations which were once dimly felt, and to render bright, clear, and separate the rest. But whether we ought to say that it is the senses that make the sensequalities or the sense-qualities to which the senses are adapted, need not be determined in haste. It is sufficient that wherever there is a phenomenon there is a quality; so that it might almost seem that there is nothing else in phenomena. The qualities merge into one another. They have no perfect identities, but only likenesses, or partial identities. Some of them, as the colours and the musical sounds, form well-understood systems. Probably, were our experience of them not so fragmentary, there would be no abrupt demarcations between them at all. Still, each one is what it is in itself without help from the others. They are single but partial determinations.

The second category of elements of phenomena comprises the actual facts. The qualities, in so far as they are general, are somewhat vague and potential. But an occurrence is perfectly individual. It happens here and now. A permanent fact is less purely individual; yet so far as it is actual, its permanence and generality only consist in its being there at every individual instant. Qualities are concerned in facts but they do not make up facts. Facts also concern subjects which are material substances. We do not see them as we see qualities, that is, they are not in the very potentiality and essence of sense. But we feel facts resist our will. That is why facts are proverbially called brutal. Now mere qualities do not resist. It is the matter that resists. Even in actual sensation there is a reaction. Now mere qualities, unmaterialized, cannot actually react. So that, rightly understood, it is correct to say that we immediately, that is, directly perceive matter. To say that we only infer matter from its qualities is to say that we only know the actual through the potential. It would be a little less erroneous to say that we only know the potential through the actual, and only infer qualities by generalization from what we perceive in matter. All that I here insist upon is that quality is one element of phenomena, and fact, action, actuality is another. We shall undertake the analysis of their natures below.

The third category of elements of phenomena consists of what we call laws when we contemplate them from the outside only, but which when we see both sides of the shield we call thoughts. Thoughts are neither qualities nor facts. They are not qualities because they can be produced and grow, while a quality is eternal, independent of time and of any realization. Besides, thoughts may have reasons, and indeed, must have some reasons, good or bad. But to ask why a quality is as it is, why red is red and not green, would be lunacy. If red were green it would not be red; that is all. And any semblance of sanity the question may have is due to its being not exactly a question about quality, but about the relation between two qualities, though even this is absurd. A thought then is not a quality. No more is it a fact. For a thought is general. I had it. I imparted it to you. It is general on that side. It is also general in referring to all possible things, and not merely to those which happen to exist. No collection of facts can constitute a law; for the law goes beyond any accomplished facts and determines how facts that *may be*, but *all* of which never can have happened, shall be characterized. There is no objection to saying that a law is a general fact, provided it be understood that the general has an admixture of potentiality in it, so that no congeries of actions here and now can ever make a general fact. As *general*, the law, or general fact, concerns the potential world of quality, while as *fact*, it concerns the actual world of actuality. Just as action requires a peculiar kind of subject, matter, which is foreign to mere quality, so law requires a peculiar kind of subject, the thought, or, as the phrase in this connection is, the *mind*, as a peculiar kind of subject foreign to mere individual action. Law, then, is something as remote from both quality and action as these are remote from one another.

3. THE MANIFESTATIONS OF THE CATEGORIES

The idea of First is predominant in the ideas of freshness, life, freedom. The free is that which has not another behind it, determining its actions; but so far as the idea of the negation of another enters, the idea of another enters; and such negative idea must be put in the background, or else we cannot say that the Firstness is predominant. Freedom can only manifest itself in unlimited and uncontrolled variety and multiplicity; and thus the first becomes predominant in the ideas of measureless variety and multiplicity. It is the leading idea of Kant's "manifold of sense." But in Kant's synthetic unity the idea of Thirdness is predominant. It is an attained unity; and would better have been called totality; for that is the one of his categories in which it finds a home. In the idea of being, Firstness is predominant, not necessarily on account of the abstractness of that idea, but on account of its self-contained-ness. It is not in being separated from qualities that Firstness is most predominant, but in being something peculiar and idiosyn-cratic. The first is predominant in feeling, as distinct from objective perception, will, and thought.

The idea of second is predominant in the ideas of causation and of statical force. For cause and effect are two; and statical forces always occur between pairs. Constraint is a Secondness. In the flow of time in the mind, the past appears to act directly upon the future, its effect being called memory, while the future only acts upon the past through the medium of thirds. Phenomena of this sort in the outward world shall be considered below. In sense and will, there are reactions of Secondness between the *ego* and the *non-ego* (which non-ego may be an object of direct consciousness). In will, the events leading up to the act are internal, and we say that we are agents more than patients. In sense, the antecedent events are not within us; and besides, the object of which we form a perception (though not that which immediately acts upon the nerves) remains unaffected. Consequently, we say that we are patients, not agents. In the idea of reality, Secondness is pre-dominant; for the real is that which insists upon forcing its way to recognition as something *other* than the mind's creation. (Remember that before the French word, *second*, was adopted into our language, *other* was merely the ordinal numeral corresponding to *two*.) The real is active; we acknowledge it, in calling it the *actual*. (This word is due to Aristotle's use of ἐνέργεια, action, to mean existence, as opposed to a mere germinal state.) Again, the kind of thought of those dualistic philosophers who are fond of laying down propositions as if there were only two alternatives, and no gradual shading off between them, as when they say that in trying to find a law in a phenomenon I commit myself to the proposition that law bears absolute sway in nature, such thought is marked by Secondness.

By the third, I mean the medium or connecting bond between the absolute first and last. The beginning is first, the end second, the middle third. The end is second, the means third. The thread of life is a third; the fate that snips it, its second. A fork in a road is a third, it supposes three ways; a straight road, considered merely as a connection between two places is second, but so far as it implies passing through intermediate places it is third. Position is first, velocity or the relation of two successive positions second, acceleration or the relation of three successive positions third. But velocity in so far as it is continuous also involves a third. Continuity represents Thirdness almost to perfection. Every process comes under that head. Moderation is a kind of Thirdness. The positive degree of an adjective is first, the superlative second, the comparative third. All exaggerated language, "supreme," "utter," "matchless," "root and branch," is the furniture of minds which think of seconds and forget thirds. Action is second, but conduct is third. Law as an active force is second, but order and legislation are third. Sympathy, flesh and blood, that by which I feel my neighbour's feelings, is third.

The ideas in which Thirdness is predominant are, as might be expected, more complicated, and mostly require careful analysis to be clearly apprehended; for ordinary, unenergetic thought slurs over this element as too difficult. There is all the more need of examining some of these ideas.

The easiest of those which are of philosophical interest is the idea of a sign, or representation. A sign stands *for* something *to* the idea which it produces, or modifies. Or, it is a vehicle conveying into the mind something from without. . . . Some of the ideas of prominent Thirdness which, owing to their great importance in philosophy and in science, require attentive study are generality, infinity, continuity, diffusion, growth, and intelligence.

4. FIRSTNESS

. . . Among phanerons there are certain qualities of feeling, such as the colour of magenta, the odour of attar, the sound of a railway whistle, the taste of quinine, the quality of the emotion upon contemplating a fine mathematical demonstration, the quality of feeling of love, etc. I do not mean the sense of actually experiencing these feelings, whether primarily or in any memory or imagination. That is something that involves these qualities as an element of it. But I mean the qualities themselves which, in themselves, are mere may-bes, not necessarily realized. The reader may be inclined to deny that. If so, he has not fully grasped the point that we are not considering what is true, not even what truly appears. I ask him to note that the word *red* means something when I say that the precession of the equinoxes is no more red than it is blue, and that it means just what it means when I say that aniline red is red. That mere *quality*, or suchness, is not in itself an occurrence, as seeing a red object is; it is a mere may-be. Its only being consists in the fact that there *might be* such a peculiar, positive, suchness in a phaneron. When I say it is a quality, I do not mean that it "inheres" in [a] subject. That is a phaneron peculiar to metaphysical thought, not involved in the sensation itself, and therefore not in the quality of feeling, which is entirely contained, or superseded, in the actual sensation. The Germans usually call these qualities feelings, feelings *of pleasure or pain*. To me this seems to be mere repetition of a tradition, never subjected to the test of observation. I can imagine a consciousness whose whole life, alike when wide awake and when drowsy or dreaming, should consist in nothing at all but a violet colour or a stink of rotten cabbage. It is purely a question of what I can imagine and not of what psychological laws permit. The fact that I can imagine this, shows that such a feeling is not *general*, in the sense in which the law of gravitation is general. For nobody can imagine that law to have any being of any kind if it were impossible that there should exist any two masses of matter, or if there were no such things as motion. A true general cannot have any being unless there is to be some prospect of its sometime having occasion to be embodied in a fact, which is itself not a law or anything like a law. A quality of feeling can be imagined to be without any occurrence, as it seems to me. Its mere may-being gets along without any realization at all.

By a feeling, I mean an instance of that kind of consciousness which involves no analysis, comparison or any process whatsoever, nor consists in whole or in part of any act by which one stretch of consciousness is distinguished from another, which has its own positive quality which consists in nothing else, and which is of itself all that it is, however it may have been brought about; so that if this feeling is present during a lapse of time, it is wholly and equally present at every moment of that time. To reduce this description to a simple definition, I will say that by a feeling I mean an instance of that sort of element of consciousness which is all that it is positively, in itself, regardless of anything else.

A feeling, then, is not an event, a happening, a coming to pass, since a coming to pass cannot be such unless there was a time when it had not come to pass; and so it is not in itself all that it is, but is relative to a previous state. A feeling is a *state*, which is in its entirety in every moment of time as long as it endures. But a feeling is not a single state which is other than an exact reproduction of itself. For if that reproduction is in the same mind, it must be at a different time, and then the being of the feeling would be relative to the particular time in which it occurred, which would be something different from the feeling itself, violating the definition which makes the feeling to be all that it is regardless of anything else. Or, if the reproduction were simultaneous with the feeling, it must be in another mind, and thus the identity of the feeling would depend upon the mind in which it was, which is other than the feeling; and again the definition would be violated in the same way. Thus, any feeling must be identical with any exact duplicate of it, which is as much as to say that the feeling is simply a quality of immediate consciousness.

But it must be admitted that a feeling experienced in an outward sensation may be reproduced in memory. For to deny this would be idle nonsense. For instance, you experience, let us say, a certain colour sensation due to red-lead. It has a definite hue, luminosity, and chroma. These [are] three elements—which are not separate in the feeling, it is true, and are not, therefore, in the feeling at all, but are said to be in it, as a way of expressing the results which would follow, according to the principles of chromatics, from certain experiments with a colour disk, colour-box, or other similar apparatus. In that sense, the colour sensation which you derive from looking at the red-lead has a certain hue, luminosity, and chroma which completely define the quality of the colour. The *vividness*, however, is independent of all three of these elements; and it is very different in the memory of the colour a quarter of a second after the actual sensation from what it is in the sensation itself, although this memory is conceivably perfectly true as to hue, luminosity, and chroma, which truth constitutes it an exact reproduction of the entire quality of the feeling.

It follows that the *vividness* of a feeling—which would be more accurately described as the vividness of a consciousness of the feeling—is independent of every component of the quality of that consciousness, and consequently is independent of the resultant of those components, which resultant quality is the feeling itself. We thus learn what vividness is not; and it only remains to ascertain what else it is.

To this end two remarks will be useful. The first is that of whatever is in the mind in any mode of consciousness there is necessarily an immediate consciousness and consequently a feeling. The proof of this proposition is very instructive as to the nature of feeling; for it shows that, if by psychology we mean the positive, or observational, science of the mind or of consciousness, then although the entire consciousness at any one instant is nothing but a feeling, yet psychology can teach us nothing of the nature of feeling, nor can we gain knowledge of any feeling by introspection, the feeling being completely veiled from introspection, for the very reason that it is our immediate consciousness. Possibly this curious truth was what Emerson was trying to grasp—but if so, pretty unsuccessfully—when he wrote the lines,

> The old Sphinx bit her thick lip—
> Said, "Who taught thee me to name?
> I am thy spirit, yoke-fellow,
> Of thine eye I am eyebeam.
>
> "Thou art the unanswered question;
> Couldst see thy proper eye,
> Always it asketh, asketh;
> And each answer is a lie."

But whatever he may have meant, it is plain enough that all that is immediately present to a man is what is in his mind in the present instant. His whole life is in the present. But when he asks what is the content of the present instant, his question always comes too late. The present has gone by, and what remains of it is greatly metamorphosed. He can, it is true, recognize that he was at that time, for example, looking at a specimen of red-lead, and must have seen that colour, which, he perceives, is something positive and *sui generis*, of the nature of feeling. But nobody's immediate consciousness, unless when he was much more than half asleep, ever consisted wholly of a colour-sensation; and since a feeling is absolutely simple and without parts—as it evidently is, since it is whatever it is regardless of anything else, and therefore regardless of any part, which would be something other than the whole—it follows that if the red colour-sensation was not the whole feeling of the instant it has nothing in common with the feeling of the instant.

Indeed, although a feeling is immediate consciousness, that is, is whatever of consciousness there may be that is immediately present, yet there is no consciousness in it because it is instantaneous. For we have seen already that feeling is nothing but a quality, and a quality is not conscious: it is a mere possibility. We can, it is true, see what a feeling in general is like; that, for example, this or that red is a feeling; and it is perfectly conceivable that a being should have that colour for its entire consciousness, throughout a lapse of time, and therefore at every instant of that time. But such a being could never know anything about its own consciousness. It could not think anything that is expressible as a proposition. It could have no idea of such a thing. It would be confined to feeling that colour. Thus, if you perceive that you must at the instant in question have been looking at a given specimen of red-lead, you know that that colour has some resemblance to your feeling at that instant. But this only means that when the feeling gives place to comparison this resemblance appears. But there is no resemblance at all in feeling, since feeling is whatever it is, positively and regardless of anything else, while the resemblance of anything lies in the comparison of that thing with something else. . . .

Every operation of the mind, however complex, has its absolutely simple feeling, the emotion of the *tout ensemble*. This is a secondary feeling or sensation excited from within the mind, just as the qualities of outward sense are excited by something psychic without us. It seems at first glance unaccountable that a mere slight difference in the speed of vibration should make such a difference of quality as that between deep vermillion and violet blue. But then it is to be remembered that it is doubtless our imperfect knowledge of those vibrations which has led us to represent them abstractly as differing only in quantity. There is already a hint in the behaviour of electrons that a lower speed and a greater one have differences which we have not been aware of. People wonder, too, how dead matter can excite feelings in the mind. For my part, instead of wondering how it can be, I feel much disposed to deny downright that it is possible. These new discoveries have reminded us how very little we know of the constitution of matter; and I prefer to guess that it is a psychic feeling of red without us which arouses a sympathetic feeling of red in our senses.

What, then, is a *quality*?

Before answering this, it will be well to say what it is not. It is not anything which is dependent, in its being, upon mind, whether in the form of sense or in that of thought. Nor is it dependent, in its being, upon the fact that some material thing possesses it. That quality is dependent upon sense is the great error of the conceptualists. That it is dependent upon the subject in which it is realized is the great error of all the nominalistic schools. A quality is a mere abstract potentiality; and the error of those schools lies in holding that the potential, or possible, is nothing but what the actual makes it to be. It is the error of maintaining that the whole alone is something, and its components, however essential to it, are nothing. The refutation of the position consists in showing that nobody does, or can, in the light of good sense, consistently retain it. The moment the fusillade of controversy ceases they repose on other conceptions. First, that the quality of red depends on anybody actually seeing it, so that red things are no longer red in the dark, is a denial of common sense. I ask the conceptualist, do you really mean to say that in the dark it is no longer true that red bodies are capable of transmitting the light at the lower end of the spectrum? Do you mean to say that a piece of iron not actually under pressure has lost its power of resisting pressure? If so, you must either hold that those bodies under the circumstances supposed assume the opposite properties, or you must hold that they become indeterminate in those respects. If you hold that the red body in the dark acquires a power of absorbing the long waves of the spectrum, and that the iron acquires a power of condensation under small pressure, then, while you adopt an opinion without any facts to support it, you still admit that qualities exist while they are not actually perceived—only you transfer this belief to qualities which there is no ground for believing in. If, however, you hold that the bodies become indeterminate in regard to the qualities they are not actually perceived to possess, then, since this is the case at any moment in regard to the vast majority of the qualities of all bodies, you must hold that generals exist. In other words, it is concrete things you do not believe in; qualities, that is, generals—which is another word for the same thing—you not only believe in but believe that they alone compose the universe. Consistency, therefore, obliges you to say that the red body is red (or has some colour) in the dark, and that the hard body has some degree of hardness when nothing is pressing upon it. If you attempt to escape the refutation by a distinction between qualities that are real, namely the mechanical qualities, and qualities that are not real, sensible qualities, you may be left there, because you have granted the essential point. At the same time, every modern psychologist will pronounce your distinction untenable. You forget perhaps that a realist fully admits that a sense-quality is only a possibility of sensation; but he thinks a possibility remains possible when it is not actual. The sensation is requisite for its apprehension; but no sensation nor sense-faculty is requisite for the possibility which is the being of the quality. Let us not put the cart before the horse, nor the evolved actuality before the possibility as if the latter *involved* what it only *evolves*. A similar answer may be made to the other nominalists. It is impossible to hold consistently that a quality only exists when it actually inheres in a body. If that were so, nothing but individual facts would be true. Laws would be fictions; and, in fact, the nominalist does object to the word "law," and prefers "uniformity" to express his conviction that so far as the law expresses what only *might* happen, but does not, it is nugatory. If, however, no law subsists other than an expression of actual facts, the future is entirely indeterminate and so is general to the highest degree. Indeed, nothing would exist but the instantaneous state; whereas it is easy to show that if we are going to be so free in calling elements fictions an instant is the first thing to be called fictitious. But I confess I do not take pains accurately to answer a doctrine so monstrous, and just at present out of vogue.

So much for what quality is not. Now what *is* it? We do not care what meaning the usages of language may attach to the word. We have already seen clearly that the elements of phenomena are of three categories, quality, fact, and thought. The question we have to consider is how quality shall be defined so as to preserve the truth of that division. In order to ascertain this, we must consider how qualities are apprehended and from what point of view they become emphatic in thought, and note what it is that will and must be revealed in that mode of apprehension.

There is a point of view from which the whole universe of phenomena appears to be made up of nothing but sensible qualities. What is that point of view? It is that in which we attend to each part as it appears in itself, in its own suchness, while we disregard the connections. Red, sour, toothache are each *sui generis* and indescribable. In themselves, that is all there is to be said about them. Imagine at once a toothache, a splitting headache, a jammed finger, a corn on the foot, a burn, and a colic, not necessarily as existing at once—leave that vague—and attend not to the parts of the imagination but to the resultant impression. That will give an idea of a general quality of pain. We see that the idea of a quality is the idea of a phenomenon or partial phenomenon considered as a monad, without reference to its parts or components and without reference to anything else. We must not consider whether it exists, or is only imaginary, because existence depends on its subject having a place in the general system of the universe. An element separated from everything else and in no world but itself, may be said, when we come to reflect upon its isolation, to be merely potential. But we must not even attend to any determinate absence of other things; we are to consider the total as a unit. We may term this aspect of a phenomenon the *monadic* aspect of it. The quality is what presents itself in the *monadic* aspect.

The phenomenon may be ever so complex and heterogeneous. That circumstance will make no particular difference in the quality. It will make it more general. But one quality is in itself, in its monadic aspect, no more general than another. The resultant effect has no parts. The quality in itself is indecomposable and *sui generis*. When we say that qualities are general, are partial determinations, are mere potentialities, etc., all that is true of qualities reflected upon; but these things do not belong to the quality-element of experience.

Experience is the course of life. The world is that which experience inculcates. Quality is the monadic element of the world. Anything whatever, however complex and heterogeneous, has its quality *sui generis*, its possibility of sensation, would our senses only respond to it.

5. SECONDNESS

We live in two worlds, a world of fact and a world of fancy. Each of us is accustomed to think that he is the creator of his world of fancy; that he has but to pronounce his fiat, and the thing exists, with no resistance and no effort; and although this is so far from the truth that I doubt not that much the greater part of the reader's labour is expended on the world of fancy, yet it is near enough the truth for a first approximation. For this reason we call the world of fancy the internal world, the world of fact the external world. In this latter we are masters, each of us, of his own voluntary muscles, and of nothing more. But man is sly, and contrives to make this little more than he needs. Beyond that, he defends himself from the angles of hard fact by clothing himself with a garment of contentment and of habituation. Were it not for this garment, he would every now and then find his internal world rudely disturbed and his fiats set at naught by brutal inroads of ideas from without. I call such forcible modification of our ways of thinking the influence of the world of fact or *experience*. But he patches up his garment by guessing what those inroads are likely to be and carefully excluding from his internal world every idea which is likely to be so disturbed. Instead of waiting for experience to come at untoward times, he provokes it when it can do no harm and changes the government of his internal world accordingly.

Some writers insist that all experience consists in sense-perception; and I think it is probably true that every element of experience is in the first instance applied to an external object. A man who gets up out of the wrong side of the bed, for example, attributes wrongness to almost every object he perceives. That is the way in which he experiences his bad temper. It cannot, however, be said that he *perceives* the perversity which he wrongly attributes to outward objects.

We perceive objects brought before us; but that which we especially experience—the kind of thing to which the word "experience" is more particularly applied—is an event. We cannot accurately be said to perceive events; for this requires what Kant called the "synthesis of apprehension," not however, by any means, making the needful discriminations. A whistling locomotive passes at high speed close beside me. As it passes the note of the whistle is suddenly lowered from a well-understood cause. I perceive the whistle, if you will. I have, at any rate, a sensation of it. But I cannot be said to have a sensation of the change of note. I have a sensation of the lower note. But the cognition of the change is of a more intellectual kind. That I experience rather than perceive. It is [the] special field of experience to acquaint us with events, with changes of perception. Now that which particularly characterizes sudden changes of perception is a *shock*. A shock is a volitional phenomenon. The long whistle of the approaching locomotive, however disagreeable it may be, has set up in me a certain inertia, so that the sudden lowering of the note meets with a certain resistance. That must be the fact; because if there were no such resistance there could be no shock when the change of note occurs. Now this shock is quite unmistakable. It is more particularly to changes and contrasts of perception that we apply the word "experience." We experience vicissitudes, especially. We cannot experience the vicissitude without experiencing the perception which undergoes the change; but the concept of *experience* is broader than that of *perception*, and includes much that is not, strictly speaking, an object of perception. It is the compulsion, the absolute constraint upon us to think otherwise than we have been thinking that constitutes experience. Now constraint and compulsion cannot exist without resistance, and resistance is effort opposing change. Therefore there must be an element of effort in experience; and it is this which gives it its peculiar character. But we are so disposed to yield to it as soon as we can detect it, that it is extremely difficult to convince ourselves that we have exerted any resistance at all. It may be said that we hardly know it except through the axiom that there can be no force where there is no resistance or inertia. Whoever may be dissatisfied with my statement will do well to sit down and cipher out the matter for himself. He may be able to formulate the nature of the oppositional element in experience, and its relation to ordinary volition, better than I have done; but that there is an oppositional element in it, logically not easily distinguished from volition, will, I make no doubt at all, be his ultimate conclusion.

The second category . . . is the element of struggle.

This is present even in such a rudimentary fragment of experience as a simple feeling. For such a feeling always has a degree of vividness, high or low; and this vividness is a sense of commotion, an action and reaction, between our soul and the stimulus. If, in the endeavour to find some idea which does not involve the element of struggle, we imagine a universe that consists of a single quality that never changes, still there must be some degree of steadiness in this imagination, or else we could not think about and ask whether there was an object having any positive suchness. Now this steadiness of the hypothesis that enables us to think about it—and to mentally manipulate it—which is a perfectly correct expression, because our thinking about the hypothesis really consists in making experiments upon it—this steadiness, I say, consists in this, that if our mental manipulation is delicate enough, the hypothesis will resist being changed. Now there can be no resistance where there is nothing of the nature of struggle or forceful action. By struggle I must explain that I mean mutual action between two things regardless of any sort of third or medium, and in particular regardless of any law of action.

I should not wonder if somebody were to suggest that perhaps the idea of a law is essential to the idea of one thing acting upon another. But surely that would be the most untenable suggestion in the world considering that there is no one of us who after lifelong discipline in looking at things from the necessitarian point of view has ever been able to train himself to dismiss the idea that he can perform any specifiable act of the will. It is one of the most singular instances of how a preconceived theory will blind a man to facts that many necessitarians seem to think that nobody really believes in the freedom of the will, the fact being that he himself believes in it when he is not theorizing. However, I do not think it worth while to quarrel about that. Have your necessitarianism if you approve of it; but still I think you must admit that no law of nature makes a stone fall, or a Leyden jar to discharge, or a steam engine to work.

. . . What is *fact*?

As before, it is not the usage of language which we seek to learn, but what must be the description of fact in order that our division of the elements of phenomena into the categories of quality, fact, and law may not only be true, but also have the utmost possible value, being governed by those same characteristics which really dominate the phenomenal world. It is first requisite to point out something which must be excluded from the category of fact. This is the general, and with it the permanent or eternal (for permanence is a species of generality), and the conditional (which equally involves generality). Generality is either of that negative sort which belongs to the merely potential, as such, and this is peculiar to the category of quality; or it is of that positive kind which belongs to conditional necessity, and this is peculiar to the category of law. These exclusions leave for the category of fact, first, that which the logicians call the *contingent*, that is, the accidentally actual, and second, whatever involves an unconditional necessity, that is, force without law or reason, *brute* force.

It may be said that there is no such phenomenon in the universe as brute force, or freedom of will, and nothing accidental. I do not assent to either opinion; but granting that both are correct, it still remains true that considering a single action by itself, apart from all others and, therefore, apart from the governing uniformity, it is in itself brute, whether it show brute *force* or not. I shall presently point out a sense in which it does display force. That it is possible for a phenomenon in *some* sense to present force to our notice without emphasizing any element of law, is familiar to everybody. We often regard our own exertions of will in that way. In like manner, if we consider any state of an individual thing, putting aside other things, we have a phenomenon which is actual, but *in itself* is not necessitated. It is not pretended that what is here termed fact is the whole phenomenon, but only an element of the phenomenon—so much as belongs to a particular place and time. That when more is taken into account, the observer finds himself in the realm of law in every case, I fully admit.

6. THIRDNESS

. . . It is impossible to resolve everything in our thoughts into those two elements [of Firstness and Secondness]. We may say that the bulk of what is actually done consists of Secondness—or better, Secondness is the predominant character of what *has been* done. The immediate present, could we seize it, would have no character but its Firstness. Not that I mean to say that immediate consciousness (a pure fiction, by the way), would be Firstness, but that the *quality* of what we are immediately conscious of, which is no fiction, is Firstness. But we constantly predict what is to be. Now what is to be, according to our conception of it, can never become wholly past. In general, we may say that *meanings* are inexhaustible. We are too apt to think that what one *means* to do and the *meaning* of a word are quite unrelated meanings of the word "meaning," or that they are only connected by both referring to some actual operation of the mind. Professor Royce especially in his great work *The World and the Individual* has done much to break up this mistake. In truth the only difference is that when a person *means* to do anything he is in some state in consequence of which the brute reactions between things will be moulded [in] to conformity to the form to which the man's mind is itself moulded, while the meaning of a word really lies in the way in which it might, in a proper position in a proposition believed, tend to mould the conduct of a person into conformity to that to which it is itself moulded. Not only will meaning always, more or less, in the long run, mould reactions to itself, but it is only in doing so that its own being consists. For this reason I call this element of the phenomenon or object of thought the element of Thirdness. It is that which is what it is by virtue of imparting a quality to reactions in the future.

I will sketch a proof that the idea of meaning is irreducible to those of quality and reaction. It depends on two main premises. The first is that every genuine triadic relation involves meaning, as meaning is obviously a triadic relation. The second is that a triadic relation is inexpressible by means of dyadic relations alone. Considerable reflection may be required to convince yourself of the first of these premises, that every triadic relation involves meaning. There will be two lines of inquiry. First, all physical forces appear to subsist between pairs of particles. This was assumed by Helmholtz in his original paper, *On the Conservation of Forces*. Take any fact in physics of the triadic kind, by which I mean a fact which can only be defined by simultaneous reference to three things, and you will find there is ample evidence that it never was produced by the action of forces on mere dyadic conditions. Thus, your right hand is that hand which is toward the *east*, when you face the *north* with your head toward the *zenith*. Three things, east, west, and up, are required to define the difference between right and left. Consequently chemists find that those substances which rotate the plane of polarization to the right or left can only be produced from such [similar] active substances. They are all of such complex constitution that they cannot have existed when the earth was very hot, and how the first one was produced is a puzzle. It cannot have been by the action of brute forces. For the second branch of the inquiry, you must train yourself to the analysis of relations, beginning with such as are very markedly triadic, gradually going on to others. In that way, you will convince yourself thoroughly that every genuine triadic relation involves thought or *meaning*. Take, for example, the relation of *giving*. A *gives* B to C. This does not consist in A's throwing B away and its accidentally hitting C, like the date-stone, which hit the Jinnee in the eye. If that were all, it would not be a genuine triadic relation, but merely one dyadic relation followed by another. There need be no motion of the thing given. Giving is a transfer of the right of property. Now right is a matter of law, and law is a matter of thought and meaning. I there leave the matter to your own reflection, merely adding that, though I have inserted the word "genuine," yet I do not really think that necessary. I think even degenerate triadic relations involve something like thought.

The other premise of the argument that genuine triadic relations can never be built of dyadic relations and of qualities is easily shown. In existential graphs, a spot with one tail —X represents a quality, a spot with two tails —R— a dyadic relation. Joining the ends of two tails is also a dyadic relation. But you can never by such joining make a graph with three tails. You may think that a node connecting three lines of identity Y is not a triadic idea. But analysis will show that it is so. I see a man on Monday. On Tuesday I see a man, and I exclaim, "Why, that is the *very* man I saw on Monday." We may say, with sufficient accuracy, that I directly experienced the identity. On Wednesday I see a man and I say, "That is the same man I saw on Tuesday, and consequently is the same I saw on Monday." There is a recognition of triadic identity; but it is only brought about as a conclusion from two premisses, which is itself a triadic relation. If I see two men at once, I cannot by any such direct experience identify both of them with a man I saw before. I can only identify them if I regard them, not as the *very* same, but as two different manifestations of the same man. But the idea of *manifestation* is the idea of a sign. Now a sign is something, A, which denotes some fact or object, B, to some interpretant thought, C.

It is interesting to remark that while a graph with three tails cannot be made out of graphs each with two or one tail, yet combinations of graphs of three tails each will suffice to build graphs with every higher number of tails.

And analysis will show that every relation which is *tetradic, pentadic*, or of any greater number of correlates is nothing but a compound of triadic relations. It is therefore not surprising to find that beyond the three elements of Firstness, Secondness, and Thirdness, there is nothing else to be found in the phenomenon.

7. THE CATEGORIES IN CONSCIOUSNESS

We find the ideas of first, second, third, constant ingredients of our knowledge. It must then either be that they are continually given to us in the presentations of sense, or that it is the peculiar nature of the mind to mix them with our thoughts. Now we certainly cannot think that these ideas are given in sense. First, second, and third are not sensations. They can only be given in sense by things appearing labelled as first, second, and third, and such labels things do not usually bear. They ought therefore to have a psychological origin. A man must be a very uncompromising partisan of the theory of the *tabula rasa* to deny that the ideas of first, second, and third are due to congenital tendencies of the mind. So far there is nothing in my argument to distinguish it from that of many a Kantian. The noticeable thing is that I do not rest here, but seek to put the conclusion to the test by an independent examination of the facts of psychology, to see whether we can find any traces of the existence of three parts or faculties of the soul or modes of consciousness, which might confirm the result just reached.

Now, three departments of the mind have been generally recognized since Kant; they are: Feeling [of pleasure and pain], Knowing, and Willing. The unanimity with which this trisection of the mind has been accepted is, indeed, quite surprising. The division did not have its genesis in the peculiar ideas of Kant. On the contrary, it was borrowed by him from dogmatic philosophers, and his acceptance of it was, as has been well remarked, a concession to dogmatism. It has been allowed even by psychologists to whose general doctrines it seems positively hostile.

The ordinary doctrine is open to a variety of objections from the very point of view from which it was first delineated. First, desire certainly includes an element of pleasure quite as much as of will. Wishing is not willing; it is a speculative variation of willing mingled with a speculative and anticipatory feeling of pleasure. Desire should therefore be struck out of the definition of the third faculty, leaving it mere volition. But volition without desire is not voluntary; it is mere activity. Consequently, all activity, voluntary or not, should be brought under the third faculty. Thus attention is a kind of activity which is sometimes voluntary and sometimes not so. Second, pleasure and pain can only be recognized as such in a judgment; they are general predicates which are attached to feelings rather than true feelings. But mere passive feeling, which does not act and does not judge, which has all sorts of qualities but does not itself recognize these qualities, because it does not analyze nor compare—this is an element of all consciousness to which a distinct title ought to be given. Third, every phenomenon of our mental life is more or less like cognition. Every emotion, every burst of passion, every exercise of will, is like cognition. But modifications of consciousness which are alike have some element in common. Cognition, therefore, has nothing distinctive and cannot be regarded as a fundamental faculty. If, however, we ask whether there be not an element in cognition which is neither feeling, sense, nor activity, we do find something, the faculty of learning, acquisition, memory and inference, synthesis. Fourth, looking once more at activity, we observe that the only consciousness we have of it is the sense of resistance. We are conscious of hitting or of getting hit, of meeting with a *fact*. But whether the activity is within or without we know only by secondary signs and not by our original faculty of recognizing fact.

It seems, then, that the true categories of consciousness are: first, feeling, the consciousness which can be included with an instant of time, passive consciousness of quality, without recognition or analysis; second, consciousness of an interruption into the field of consciousness, sense of resistance, of an external fact, of another something; third, synthetic consciousness, binding time together, sense of learning, thought.

If we accept these [as] the fundamental elementary modes of consciousness, they afford a psychological explanation of the three logical conceptions of quality, relation, and synthesis or mediation. The conception of quality, which is absolutely simple in itself and yet viewed in its relations is seen to be full of variety, would arise whenever feeling or the singular consciousness becomes prominent. The conception of relation comes from the dual consciousness or sense of action and reaction. The conception of mediation springs out of the plural consciousness or sense of learning.

. . . We remember it [sensation]; that is to say, we have another cognition which professes to reproduce it; but we know that there is no resemblance between the memory and the sensation, because, in the first place, nothing can resemble an immediate feeling, for resemblance supposes a dismemberment and recomposition which is totally foreign to the immediate, and in the second place, memory is an articulated complex and worked-over product which differs infinitely and immeasurably from feeling. Look at a red surface, and try to feel what the sensation is, and then shut your eyes and remember it. No doubt different persons are different in this respect; to some the experiment will seem to yield an opposite result, but I have convinced myself that there is nothing in my memory that is in the least like the vision of the red. When red is not before my eyes, I do not see it at all. Some people tell me they see it faintly—a most inconvenient kind of memory, which would lead to remembering bright red as pale or dingy. I remember colours with unusual accuracy, because I have had much training in observing them; but my memory does not consist in any vision but in a habit by virtue of which I can recognize a newly presented colour as like or unlike one I had seen before. But even if the memory of some persons is of the nature of an hallucination, enough arguments remain to show that immediate consciousness or feeling is absolutely unlike anything else.

There are grave objections to making a whole third of the mind of the will alone. One great psychologist has said that the will is nothing but the strongest desire. I cannot grant that; it seems to me to overlook that fact which of all that we observe is quite the most obtrusive, namely, the difference between dreaming and doing. This is not a question of defining, but of noticing what we experience; and surely he who can confound desiring with doing must be a day-dreamer. The evidence, however, seems to be pretty strong that the consciousness of willing does not differ, at least not very much, from a sensation. The sense of hitting and of getting hit are nearly the same, and should be classed together. The common element is the sense of an actual occurrence, of actual action and reaction. There is an intense reality about this kind of experience, a sharp sundering of subject and object. While I am seated calmly in the dark, the lights are suddenly turned on, and at that instant I am conscious, not of a process of change, but yet of something more than can be contained in an instant. I have a sense of a saltus, of there being two sides to that instant. A consciousness of polarity would be a tolerably good phrase to describe what occurs. For will, then, as one of the great types of consciousness, we ought to substitute the polar sense.

But by far the most confused of the three members of the division, in its ordinary statement, is Cognition. In the first place every kind of consciousness enters into cognition. Feelings, in the sense in which alone they can be admitted as a great branch of mental phenomena, form the warp and woof of cognition, and even in the objectionable sense of pleasure and pain, they are constituents of cognition. The will, in the form of attention, constantly enters, and the sense of reality or objectivity, which is what we have found ought to take the place of will, in the division of consciousness, is even more essential yet, if possible. But that element of cognition which is neither feeling nor the polar sense, is the consciousness of a process, and this in the form of the sense of learning, of acquiring, of mental growth is eminently characteristic of cognition. This is a kind of consciousness which cannot be immediate, because it covers a time, and that not merely because it continues through every instant of that time, but because it cannot be contracted into an instant. It differs from immediate consciousness, as a melody does from one prolonged note. Neither can the consciousness of the two sides of an instant, of a sudden occurrence, in its individual reality, possibly embrace the consciousness of a process. This is the consciousness that binds our life together. It is the consciousness of synthesis.

Here then, we have indubitably three radically different elements of consciousness, these and no more. And they are evidently connected with the ideas of one-two-three. Immediate feeling is the consciousness of the first; the polar sense is the consciousness of the second; and synthetical consciousness is the consciousness of a third or medium.

8. THE INTERRELATIONSHIP OF THE CATEGORIES

Perhaps it is not right to call these categories conceptions; they are so intangible that they are rather tones or tints upon conceptions. In my first attempt to deal with them, I made use of three grades of separability of one idea from another. In the first place, two ideas may be so little allied that one of them may be present to the consciousness in an image which does not contain the other at all; in this way we can imagine *red* without imagining blue, and *vice versa*; we can also imagine sound without melody, but not melody without sound. I call this kind of separation *dissociation*. In the second place, even in cases where two conceptions cannot be separated in the imagination, we can often suppose one without the other, that is we can imagine data from which we should be led to believe in a state of things where one was separated from the other. Thus, we can suppose uncoloured space, though we cannot dissociate space from colour. I call this mode of separation *prescission*. In the third place, even when one element cannot even be supposed without another, they may ofttimes be distinguished from one another. Thus we can neither imagine nor suppose a taller without a shorter, yet we can distinguish the taller from the shorter. I call this mode of separation *distinction*. Now, the categories cannot be dissociated in imagination from each other, nor from other ideas. The category of first can be prescinded from second and third, and second can be prescinded from third. But second cannot be prescinded from first, nor third from second. The categories may, I believe, be prescinded from any other one conception, but they cannot be prescinded from some one and indeed many elements. You cannot suppose a first unless that first be something definite and more or less definitely supposed. Finally, though it is easy to distinguish the three categories from one another, it is extremely difficult accurately and sharply to distinguish each from other conceptions so as to hold it in its purity and yet in its full meaning.

7

LOGIC AS SEMIOTIC: THE THEORY OF SIGNS *

1. What is a Sign? Three Divisions of Logic

Logic, in its general sense, is, as I believe I have shown, only another name for *semiotic* (σημειωτική), the quasi-necessary, or formal, doctrine of signs. By describing the doctrine as "quasi-necessary," or formal, I mean that we observe the characters of such signs as we know, and from such an observation, by a process which I will not object to naming Abstraction, we are led to statements, eminently fallible, and therefore in one sense by no means necessary, as to what *must be* the characters of all signs used by a "scientific" intelligence, that is to say, by an intelligence capable of learning by experience. As to that process of abstraction, it is itself a sort of observation. The faculty which I call abstractive observation is one which ordinary people perfectly recognize, but for which the theories of philosophers sometimes hardly leave room. It is a familiar experience to every human being to wish for something quite beyond his present means, and to follow that wish by the question, "Should I wish for that thing just the same, if I had ample means to gratify it?" To answer that question, he searches his heart, and in doing so makes what I term an abstractive observation. He makes in his imagination a sort of skeleton diagram, or outline sketch, of himself, considers what modifications the hypothetical state of things would require to be made in that picture, and then examines it, that is, *observes* what he has imagined, to see whether the same ardent desire is there to be discerned. By such a process, which is at bottom very much like mathematical reasoning, we can reach conclusions as to what *would be* true of signs in all cases, so long as the intelligence using them was scientific. The modes of thought of a God, who should possess an intuitive omniscience superseding reason,

---

* [The first of the three selections in *1* is from ms. c. 1897 (*CP* 2.227-9), the third from ms. c. 1910 (*CP* 2.231-2). The second selection in *1*, *3b*, the second selection in *3c*, and *3d* are from mss. c. 1902, c. 1895, and c. 1893 (*CP* 2.274-302). *2* and *4* are from ms. c. 1903 (*CP* 2.243-52, 254-65). *3a* is from the article "Sign" in Baldwin's *Dictionary of Philosophy and Psychology* 1902 (*CP* 2.304). The first selection in *3c* is from the article "Index" in Baldwin's (*CP* 2.305, 306).]

are put out of the question. Now the whole process of development among the community of students of those formulations by abstractive observation and reasoning of the truths which *must* hold good of all signs used by a scientific intelligence is an observational science, like any other positive science, notwithstanding its strong contrast to all the special sciences which arises from its aiming to find out what *must be* and not merely what *is* in the actual world.

A sign, or *representamen*, is something which stands to somebody for something in some respect or capacity. It addresses somebody, that is, creates in the mind of that person an equivalent sign, or perhaps a more developed sign. That sign which it creates I call the *interpretant* of the first sign. The sign stands for something, its *object*. It stands for that object, not in all respects, but in reference to a sort of idea, which I have sometimes called the *ground* of the representamen. "Idea" is here to be understood in a sort of Platonic sense, very familiar in everyday talk; I mean in that sense in which we say that one man catches another man's idea, in which we say that when a man recalls what he was thinking of at some previous time, he recalls the same idea, and in which when a man continues to think anything, say for a tenth of a second, in so far as the thought continues to agree with itself during that time, that is to have a *like* content, it is the same idea, and is not at each instant of the interval a new idea.

In consequence of every representamen being thus connected with three things, the ground, the object, and the interpretant, the science of semiotic has three branches.[7] The first is called by Duns Scotus *grammatica speculativa*. We may term it *pure grammar*. It has for its task to ascertain what must be true of the representamen used by every scientific intelligence in order that they may embody any *meaning*. The second is logic proper. It is the science of what is quasi-necessarily true of the representamina of any scientific intelligence in order that they may hold good of any *object*, that is, may be true. Or say, logic proper is the formal science of the conditions of the truth of representations. The third, in imitation of Kant's fashion of preserving old associations of words in finding nomenclature for new conceptions, I call *pure rhetoric*. Its task is to ascertain the laws by which in every scientific intelligence one sign gives birth to another, and especially one thought brings forth another.

A *Sign*, or *Representamen*, is a First which stands in such a genuine triadic relation to a Second, called its *Object*, as to be capable of determining a Third, called its *Interpretant*, to assume the same triadic relation to its Object in which it stands itself to the same Object. The triadic relation is *genuine*, that is its three members are bound together by it in a way that does not consist in any complexus of dyadic relations. That is the reason the Interpretant, or Third, cannot stand in a mere dyadic relation to the Object, but must stand in such a relation to it as the Representamen itself does. Nor can the triadic relation in which the Third stands be merely similar to that in which the First stands, for this would make the relation of the Third to the First a degenerate Secondness merely. The Third must indeed stand in such a relation, and thus must be capable of determining a Third of its own; but besides that, it must have a second triadic relation in which the Representamen, or rather the relation thereof to its Object, shall be its own (the Third's) Object, and must be capable of determining a Third to this relation. All this must equally be true of the Third's Thirds and so on endlessly; and this, and more, is involved in the familiar idea of a Sign; and as the term Representamen is here used, nothing more is implied. A *Sign* is a Representamen with a mental Interpretant. Possibly there may be Representamens that are not Signs. Thus, if a sunflower, in turning toward the sun, becomes by that very act fully capable, without further condition, of reproducing a sunflower which turns in precisely corresponding ways toward the sun, and of doing so with the same reproductive power, the sunflower would become a Representamen of the sun. But *thought* is the chief, if not the only, mode of representation.

The Sign can only represent the Object and tell about it. It cannot furnish acquaintance with or recognition of that Object; for that is what is meant in this volume by the Object of a Sign; namely, that with which it presupposes an acquaintance in order to convey some further information concerning it. No doubt there will be readers who will say they cannot comprehend this. They think a Sign need not relate to anything otherwise known, and can make neither head nor tail of the statement that every sign must relate to such an Object. But if there be anything that conveys information and yet has absolutely no relation nor reference to anything with which the person to whom it conveys the information has, when he comprehends that information, the slightest acquaintance, direct or indirect—and a very strange sort of information that would be —the vehicle of that sort of information is not, in this volume, called a Sign.

Two men are standing on the seashore looking out to sea. One of them says to the other, "That vessel there carries no freight at all, but only passengers." Now, if the other, himself, sees no vessel, the first information he derives from the remark has for its Object the part of the sea that he does see, and informs him that a person with sharper eyes than his, or more trained in looking for such things, can see a vessel there; and then, that vessel having been thus introduced to his acquaintance, he is prepared to receive the information about it that it carries passengers exclusively. But the sentence as a whole has, for the person supposed, no other Object than that with which it finds him already acquainted. The Objects—for a Sign may have any number of them—may each be a single known existing thing or thing believed formerly to have existed or expected to exist, or a collection of such things, or a known quality or relation or fact, which single Object may be a collection, or whole of parts, or it may have some other mode of being, such as some act permitted whose being does not prevent its negation from being equally permitted, or something of a general nature desired, required, or invariably found under certain general circumstances.

2. Three Trichotomies of Signs

Signs are divisible by three trichotomies; first, according as the sign in itself is a mere quality, is an actual existent, or is a general law; secondly, according as the relation of the sign to its object consists in the sign's having some character in itself, or in some existential relation to that object, or in its relation to an interpretant; thirdly, according as its Interpretant represents it as a sign of possibility or as a sign of fact or a sign of reason.

i

According to the first division, a Sign may be termed a *Qualisign*, a *Sinsign*, or a *Legisign*.

A *Qualisign* is a quality which is a Sign. It cannot actually act as a sign until it is embodied; but the embodiment has nothing to do with its character as a sign.

A *Sinsign* (where the syllable *sin* is taken as meaning "being only once," as in *single*, *simple*, Latin *semel*, etc.) is an actual existent thing or event which is a sign. It can only be so through its qualities; so that it involves a qualisign, or rather, several qualisigns. But these qualisigns are of a peculiar kind and only form a sign through being actually embodied.

A *Legisign* is a law that is a Sign. This law is usually established by men. Every conventional sign is a legisign [but not conversely]. It is not a single object, but a general type which, it has been agreed, shall be significant. Every legisign signifies through an instance of its application, which may be termed a *Replica* of it. Thus, the word "the" will usually occur from fifteen to twenty-five times on a page. It is in all these occurrences one and the same word, the same legisign. Each single instance of it is a Replica. The Replica is a Sinsign. Thus, every Legisign requires Sinsigns. But these are not ordinary Sinsigns, such as are peculiar occurrences that are regarded as significant. Nor would the Replica be significant if it were not for the law which renders it so.

ii

According to the second trichotomy, a Sign may be termed an *Icon*, an *Index*, or a *Symbol*.

An *Icon* is a sign which refers to the Object that it denotes merely by virtue of characters of its own, and which it possesses, just the same, whether any such Object actually exists or not. It is true that unless there really is such an Object, the Icon does not act as a sign; but this has nothing to do with its character as a sign. Anything whatever, be it quality, existent individual, or law, is an Icon of anything, in so far as it is like that thing and used as a sign of it.

An *Index* is a sign which refers to the Object that it denotes by virtue of being really affected by that Object. It cannot, therefore, be a Qualisign, because qualities are whatever they are independently of anything else. In so far as the Index is affected by the Object, it necessarily has some Quality in common with the Object, and it is in respect to these that it refers to the Object. It does, therefore, involve a sort of Icon, although an Icon of a peculiar kind; and it is not the mere resemblance of its Object, even in these respects which makes it a sign, but it is the actual modification of it by the Object.

A *Symbol* is a sign which refers to the Object that it denotes by virtue of a law, usually an association of general ideas, which operates to cause the Symbol to be interpreted as referring to that Object. It is thus itself a general type or law, that is, is a Legisign. As such it acts through a Replica. Not only is it general itself, but the Object to which it refers is of a general nature. Now that which is general has its being in the instances which it will determine. There must, therefore, be existent instances of what the

Symbol denotes, although we must here understand by "existent," existent in the possibly imaginary universe to which the Symbol refers. The Symbol will indirectly, through the association or other law, be affected by those instances; and thus the Symbol will involve a sort of Index, although an Index of a peculiar kind. It will not, however, be by any means true that the slight effect upon the Symbol of those instances accounts for the significant character of the Symbol.

iii

According to the third trichotomy, a Sign may be termed a *Rheme*, a *Dicisign* or *Dicent Sign* (that is, a proposition or quasi-proposition), or an *Argument*.

A *Rheme* is a Sign which, for its Interpretant, is a Sign of qualitative Possibility, that is, is understood as representing such and such a kind of possible Object. Any Rheme, perhaps, will afford some information; but it is not interpreted as doing so.

A *Dicent Sign* is a Sign, which, for its Interpretant, is a Sign of actual existence. It cannot, therefore, be an Icon, which affords no ground for an interpretation of it as referring to actual existence. A Dicisign necessarily involves, as a part of it, a Rheme, to describe the fact which it is interpreted as indicating. But this is a peculiar kind of Rheme; and while it is essential to the Dicisign, it by no means constitutes it.

An *Argument* is a Sign which, for its Interpretant, is a Sign of law. Or we may say that a Rheme is a sign which is understood to represent its object in its characters merely; that a Dicisign is a sign which is understood to represent its object in respect to actual existence; and that an Argument is a Sign which is understood to represent its Object in its character as Sign. Since these definitions touch upon points at this time much in dispute, a word may be added in defence of them. A question often put is: What is the essence of a Judgment? A judgment is the mental act by which the judger seeks to impress upon himself the truth of a proposition. It is much the same as an act of asserting the proposition, or going before a notary and assuming formal responsibility for its truth, except that those acts are intended to affect others, while the judgment is only intended to affect oneself. However, the logician, as such, cares not what the psychological nature of the act of judging may be. The question for him is: What is the nature of the sort of sign of which a principal variety is called a proposition, which is the matter upon which the act of judging is exercised? The proposition need not be asserted or judged. It may be contemplated as a sign capable of being asserted or denied. This sign itself retains its full meaning whether it be actually asserted or not. The peculiarity of it, therefore, lies in its mode of meaning; and to say this is to say that its peculiarity lies in its relation to its interpretant. The proposition professes to be really affected by the actual existent or real law to which it refers. The argument makes the same pretension, but that is not the principal pretension of the argument. The rheme makes no such pretension.

3. Icon, Index, and Symbol

a. Synopsis

A sign is either an *icon*, an *index*, or a *symbol*. An *icon* is a sign which would possess the character which renders it significant, even though its object had no existence; such as a lead-pencil streak as representing a geometrical line. An *index* is a sign which would, at once, lose the character which makes it a sign if its object were removed, but would not lose that character if there were no interpretant. Such, for instance, is a piece of mould with a bullet-hole in it as sign of a shot; for without the shot there would have been no hole; but there is a hole there, whether anybody has the sense to attribute it to a shot or not. A *symbol* is a sign which would lose the character which renders it a sign if there were no interpretant. Such is any utterance of speech which signifies what it does only by virtue of its being understood to have that signification.

b. Icon

. . . While no Representamen actually functions as such until it actually determines an Interpretant, yet it becomes a Representamen as soon as it is fully capable of doing this; and its Representative Quality is not necessarily dependent upon its ever actually determining an Interpretant, nor even upon its actually having an Object.

An *Icon* is a Representamen whose Representative Quality is a Firstness of it as a First. That is, a quality that it has *qua* thing renders it fit to be a representamen. Thus, anything is fit to be a *Substitute* for anything that it is like. (The conception of "substitute" involves that of a purpose, and thus of genuine thirdness.) Whether there are other kinds of substitutes or not we shall see. A Representamen by Firstness alone can only have a similar

Object. Thus, a Sign by Contrast denotes its object only by virtue of a contrast, or Secondness, between two qualities. A sign by Firstness is an image of its object and, more strictly speaking, can only be an *idea*. For it must produce an Interpretant idea; and an external object excites an idea by a reaction upon the brain. But most strictly speaking, even an idea, except in the sense of a possibility, or Firstness, cannot be an Icon. A possibility alone is an Icon purely by virtue of its quality; and its object can only be a Firstness. But a sign may be *iconic*, that is, may represent its object mainly by its similarity, no matter what its mode of being. If a substantive be wanted, an iconic representamen may be termed a *hypoicon*. Any material image, as a painting, is largely conventional in its mode of representation; but in itself, without legend or label it may be called a *hypoicon*.

Hypoicons may be roughly divided according to the mode of Firstness of which they partake. Those which partake of simple qualities, or First Firstnesses, are *images*; those which represent the relations, mainly dyadic, or so regarded, of the parts of one thing by analogous relations in their own parts, are *diagrams*; those which represent the representative character of a representamen by representing a parallelism in something else, are *metaphors*.

The only way of directly communicating an idea is by means of an icon; and every indirect method of communicating an idea must depend for its establishment upon the use of an icon. Hence, every assertion must contain an icon or set of icons, or else must contain signs whose meaning is only explicable by icons. The idea which the set of icons (or the equivalent of a set of icons) contained in an assertion signifies may be termed the *predicate* of the assertion.

Turning now to the rhetorical evidence, it is a familiar fact that there are such representations as icons. Every picture (however conventional its method) is essentially a representation of that kind. So is every diagram, even although there be no sensuous resemblance between it and its object, but only an analogy between the relations of the parts of each. Particularly deserving of notice are icons in which the likeness is aided by conventional rules. Thus, an algebraic formula is an icon, rendered such by the rules of commutation, association, and distribution of the symbols. It may seem at first glance that it is an arbitrary classification to call an algebraic expression an icon; that it might as well, or better, be regarded as a compound conventional sign. But it is not so. For a great distinguishing property of the icon is that by the direct observation of it other truths concerning its object can be discovered than those which suffice to determine its construction. Thus, by means of two photographs a map can be drawn, etc. Given a conventional or other general sign of an object, to deduce any other truth than that which it explicitly signifies, it is necessary, in all cases, to replace that sign by an icon. This capacity of revealing unexpected truth is precisely that wherein the utility of algebraical formulae consists, so that the iconic character is the prevailing one.

That icons of the algebraic kind, though usually very simple ones, exist in all ordinary grammatical propositions is one of the philosophic truths that the Boolean logic brings to light. In all primitive writing, such as the Egyptian hieroglyphics, there are icons of a non-logical kind, the ideographs. In the earliest form of speech, there probably was a large element of mimicry. But in all languages known, such representations have been replaced by conventional auditory signs. These, however, are such that they can only be explained by icons. But in the syntax of every language there are logical icons of the kind that are aided by conventional rules. . . .

Photographs, especially instantaneous photographs, are very instructive, because we know that they are in certain respects exactly like the objects they represent. But this resemblance is due to the photographs having been produced under such circumstances that they were physically forced to correspond point by point to nature. In that aspect, then, they belong to the second class of signs, those by physical connection. The case is different if I surmise that zebras are likely to be obstinate, or otherwise disagreeable animals, because they seem to have a general resemblance to donkeys, and donkeys are self-willed. Here the donkey serves precisely as a probable likeness of the zebra. It is true we suppose that resemblance has a physical cause in heredity; but then, this hereditary affinity is itself only an inference from the likeness between the two animals, and we have not (as in the case of the photograph) any independent knowledge of the circumstances of the production of the two species. Another example of the use of a likeness is the design an artist draws of a statue, pictorial composition, architectural elevation, or piece of decoration, by the contemplation of which he can ascertain whether what he proposes will be beautiful and satisfactory. The question asked is thus answered almost with certainty because it relates to how the artist will himself be affected. The reasoning of mathematicians will be found to turn chiefly upon the use of likenesses, which are the very hinges of the gates of their science. The utility of likenesses to mathematicians consists in their suggesting in a very precise way, new aspects of supposed states of things. . . .

Many diagrams resemble their objects not at all in looks; it is only in respect to the relations of their parts that their likeness consists. Thus, we may show the relation between the different kinds of signs by a brace, thus:

$$\text{Signs:} \begin{cases} \text{Icons,} \\ \text{Indices,} \\ \text{Symbols.} \end{cases}$$

This is an icon. But the only respect in which it resembles its object is that the brace shows the classes of *icons*, *indices*, and *symbols* to be related to one another and to the general class of signs, as they really are, in a general way. When, in algebra, we write equations under one another in a regular array, especially when we put resembling letters for corresponding coefficients, the array is an icon. Here is an example:

$$a_1 x + b_1 y = n_1,$$
$$a_2 x + b_2 y = n_2.$$

This is an icon,[8] in that it makes quantities look alike which are in analogous relations to the problem. In fact, every algebraical equation is an icon, in so far as it *exhibits*, by means of the algebraical signs (which are not themselves icons), the relations of the quantities concerned.

It may be questioned whether all icons are likenesses or not. For example, if a drunken man is exhibited in order to show, by contrast, the excellence of temperance, this is certainly an icon, but whether it is a likeness or not may be doubted. The question seems somewhat trivial.

c. Index

[An index is] a sign, or representation, which refers to its object not so much because of any similarity or analogy with it, nor because it is associated with general characters which that object happens to possess, as because it is in dynamical (including spatial) connection both with the individual object, on the one hand, and with the senses or memory of the person for whom it serves as a sign, on the other hand. . . . While demonstrative and personal pronouns are, as ordinarily used, "genuine indices," relative pronouns are "degenerate indices"; for though they may, accidentally and indirectly, refer to existing things, they directly refer, and need only refer, to the images in the mind which previous words have created.

Indices may be distinguished from other signs, or representations, by three characteristic marks: first, that they have no significant resemblance to their objects; second, that they refer to individuals, single units, single collections of units, or single continua; third, that they direct the attention to their objects by blind compulsion. But it would be difficult, if not impossible, to instance an absolutely pure index, or to find any sign absolutely devoid of the indexical quality. Psychologically, the action of indices depends upon association by contiguity, and not upon association by resemblance or upon intellectual operations.

An *Index* or *Seme* (σῆμα) is a Representamen whose Representative character consists in its being an individual second. If the Secondness is an existential relation, the Index is *genuine*. If the Secondness is a reference, the Index is *degenerate*. A genuine Index and its Object must be existent individuals (whether things or facts), and its immediate Interpretant must be of the same character. But since every individual must have characters, it follows that a genuine Index may contain a Firstness, and so an Icon as a constituent part of it. Any individual is a degenerate Index of its own characters.

Subindices or *Hyposemes* are signs which are rendered such principally by an actual connection with their objects. Thus a proper name, personal demonstrative, or relative pronoun or the letter attached to a diagram, denotes what it does owing to a real connection with its object, but none of these is an Index, since it is not an individual.

Let us examine some examples of indices. I see a man with a rolling gait. This is a probable indication that he is a sailor. I see a bowlegged man in corduroys, gaiters, and a jacket. These are probable indications that he is a jockey or something of the sort. A sundial or a clock *indicates* the time of day. Geometricians mark letters against the different parts of their diagrams and then use these letters to indicate those parts. Letters are similarly used by lawyers and others. Thus, we may say: If A and B are married to one another and C is their child while D is brother of A, then D is uncle of C. Here A, B, C, and D fulfill the office of relative pronouns, but are more convenient since they require no special collocation of words. A rap on the door is an index. Anything which focusses the attention is an index. Anything which startles us is an index, in so far as it marks the junction between two portions of experience. Thus a tremendous thunderbolt indicates that *something* considerable happened, though we may not know precisely what the event was. But it may be expected to connect itself with some other experience.

. . . A low barometer with a moist air is an index of rain; that is we suppose that the forces of nature establish a probable connection between the low barometer with moist air and coming rain. A weathercock is an index of the direction of the wind; because in the first place it really takes the self-same direction as the wind, so that there is a real connection between them, and in the second place we are so constituted that when we see a weathercock pointing in a certain direction it draws our attention to that direction, and when we see the weathercock veering with the wind, we are forced by the law of mind to think that direction is connected with the wind. The pole star is an index, or pointing finger, to show us which way is north. A spirit-level, or a plumb bob, is an index of the vertical direction. A yard-stick might seem, at first sight, to be an icon of a yard; and so it would be, if it were merely intended to show a yard as near as it can be seen and estimated to be a yard. But the very purpose of a yard-stick is to show a yard nearer than it can be estimated by its appearance. This it does in consequence of an accurate mechanical comparison made with the bar in London called the yard. Thus it is a real connection which gives the yard-stick its value as a representamen; and thus it is an *index*, not a mere *icon*.

When a driver to attract the attention of a foot passenger and cause him to save himself, calls out "Hi!" so far as this is a significant word, it is, as will be seen below, something more than an index; but so far as it is simply intended to act upon the hearer's nervous system and to rouse him to get out of the way, it is an index, because it is meant to put him in real connection with the object, which is his situation relative to the approaching horse. Suppose two men meet upon a country road and one of them says to the other, "The chimney of that house is on fire." The other looks about him and descries a house with green blinds and a verandah having a smoking chimney. He walks on a few miles and meets a second traveller. Like a Simple Simon he says, "The chimney of that house is on fire." "What house?" asks the other. "Oh, a house with green blinds and a verandah," replies the simpleton. "Where is the house?" asks the stranger. He desires some *index* which shall connect his apprehension with the house meant.

Words alone cannot do this. The demonstrative pronouns, "this" and "that," are indices. For they call upon the hearer to use his powers of observation, and so establish a real connection between his mind and the object; and if the demonstrative pronoun does that—without which its meaning is not understood—it goes to establish such a connection; and so is an index. The relative pronouns, *who* and *which*, demand observational activity in much the same way, only with them the observation has to be directed to the words that have gone before. Lawyers use A, B, C, practically as very effective relative pronouns. To show how effective they are, we may note that Messrs. Allen and Greenough, in their admirable (though in the edition of 1877 [?], too small) Latin Grammar, declare that no conceivable syntax could wholly remove the ambiguity of the following sentence, "A replied to B that he thought C (his brother) more unjust to himself than to his own friend." Now, any lawyer would state that with perfect clearness, by using A, B, C, as relatives, thus:

A replied to B that he $\left\{\begin{matrix}A\\B\end{matrix}\right\}$, thought C (his $\left\{\begin{matrix}A's\\B's\end{matrix}\right\}$, brother) more

unjust to himself, $\left\{\begin{matrix}A\\B\\C\end{matrix}\right\}$ than to his $\left\{\begin{matrix}A's\\B's\\C's\end{matrix}\right\}$ own friend. The termina-

tions which in any inflected language are attached to words "governed" by other words, and which serve to show which the governing word is, by repeating what is elsewhere expressed in the same form, are likewise *indices* of the same relative pronoun character. Any bit of Latin poetry illustrates this, such as the twelve-line sentence beginning, "*Jam satis terris.*" Both in these terminations and in the A, B, C, a likeness is relied upon to carry the attention to the right object. But this does not make them icons, in any important way; for it is of no consequence how the letters A, B, C, are shaped or what the terminations are. It is not merely that one occurrence of an A is like a previous occurrence that is the important circumstance, but that *there is an understanding that like letters shall stand for the same thing*, and this acts as a force carrying the attention from one occurrence of A to the previous one. A possessive pronoun is two ways an index: first it indicates the possessor, and, second, it has a modification which syntactically carries the attention to the word denoting the thing possessed.

Some indices are more or less detailed directions for what the hearer is to do in order to place himself in direct experiential or other connection with the thing meant. Thus, the Coast Survey issues

"Notices to Mariners," giving the latitude and longitude, four or five bearings of prominent objects, etc., and saying *there* is a rock, or shoal, or buoy, or lightship. Although there will be other elements in such directions, yet in the main they are indices.

Along with such indexical directions of what to do to find the object meant, ought to be classed those pronouns which should be entitled *selective* pronouns [or quantifiers] because they inform the hearer how he is to pick out one of the objects intended, but which grammarians call by the very indefinite designation of *indefinite* pronouns. Two varieties of these are particularly important in logic, the *universal selectives*, such as *quivis, quilibet, quisquam, ullus, nullus, nemo, quisque, uterque*, and in English, *any, every, all, no, none, whatever, whoever, everybody, anybody, nobody*. These mean that the hearer is at liberty to select any instance he likes within limits expressed or understood, and the assertion is intended to apply to that one. The other logically important variety consists of the *particular selectives, quis, quispiam, nescio quis, aliquis, quidam*, and in English, *some, something, somebody, a, a certain, some or other, a suitable, one*.

Allied to the above pronouns are such expressions as *all but one, one or two, a few, nearly all, every other one*, etc. Along with pronouns are to be classed adverbs of place and time, etc.

Not very unlike these are, *the first, the last, the seventh, two-thirds of, thousands of*, etc.

Other indexical words are prepositions, and prepositional phrases, such as, "on the right (or left) of." Right and left cannot be distinguished by any general description. Other prepositions signify relations which may, perhaps, be described; but when they refer, as they do oftener than would be supposed, to a situation relative to the observed, or assumed to be experientially known, place and attitude of the speaker relatively to that of the hearer, then the indexical element is the dominant element.

Icons and indices assert nothing. If an icon could be interpreted by a sentence, that sentence must be in a "potential mood," that is, it would merely say, "Suppose a figure has three sides," etc. Were an index so interpreted, the mood must be imperative, or exclamatory, as "See there!" or "Look out!" But the kind of signs which we are now coming to consider are, by nature, in the "indicative," or, as it should be called, the *declarative* mood. Of course, they can go to the expression of any other mood, since we may declare assertions to be doubtful, or mere interrogations, or imperatively requisite.

d. Symbol

A Symbol is a Representamen whose Representative character consists precisely in its being a rule that will determine its Interpretant. All words, sentences, books, and other conventional signs are Symbols. We speak of writing or pronouncing the word "man"; but it is only a *replica*, or embodiment of the word, that is pronounced or written. The word itself has no existence although it has a real being, *consisting in* the fact that existents *will* conform to it. It is a general mode of succession of three sounds or representamens of sounds, which becomes a sign only in the fact that a habit, or acquired law, will cause replicas of it to be interpreted as meaning a man or men. The word and its meaning are both general rules; but the word alone of the two prescribes the qualities of its replicas in themselves. Otherwise the "word" and its "meaning" do not differ, unless some special sense be attached to "meaning."

A Symbol is a law, or regularity of the indefinite future. Its Interpretant must be of the same description; and so must be also the complete immediate Object, or meaning. But a law necessarily governs, or "is embodied in" individuals, and prescribes some of their qualities. Consequently, a constituent of a Symbol may be an Index, and a constituent may be an Icon. A man walking with a child points his arm up into the air and says, "There is a balloon." The pointing arm is an essential part of the symbol without which the latter would convey no information. But if the child asks, "What is a balloon," and the man replies, "It is something like a great big soap bubble," he makes the image a part of the symbol. Thus, while the complete object of a symbol, that is to say, its meaning, is of the nature of a law, it must *denote* an individual, and must *signify* a character. A *genuine* symbol is a symbol that has a general meaning. There are two kinds of degenerate symbols, the *Singular Symbol* whose Object is an existent individual, and which signifies only such characters as that individual may realize; and the *Abstract Symbol*, whose only Object is a character.

Although the immediate Interpretant of an Index must be an Index, yet since its Object may be the Object of an Individual [Singular] Symbol, the Index may have such a Symbol for its indirect Interpretant. Even a genuine Symbol may be an imperfect Interpretant of it. So an *icon* may have a degenerate Index, or an Abstract Symbol, for an indirect Interpretant, and a genuine Index or Symbol for an imperfect Interpretant.

A *Symbol* is a sign naturally fit to declare that the set of objects which is denoted by whatever set of indices may be in certain ways attached to it is represented by an icon associated with it. To show what this complicated definition means, let us take as an example of a symbol the word "loveth." Associated with this word is an idea, which is the mental icon of one person loving another. Now we are to understand that "loveth" occurs in a sentence; for what it may mean by itself, if it means anything, is not the question. Let the sentence, then, be "Ezekiel loveth Huldah." Ezekiel and Huldah must, then, be or contain indices; for without indices it is impossible to designate what one is talking about. Any mere description would leave it uncertain whether they were not mere characters in a ballad; but whether they be so or not, indices can designate them. Now the effect of the word "loveth" is that the pair of objects denoted by the pair of indices Ezekiel and Huldah is represented by the icon, or the image we have in our minds of a lover and his beloved.

The same thing is equally true of every verb in the declarative mood; and indeed of every verb, for the other moods are merely declarations of a fact somewhat different from that expressed by the declarative mood. As for a noun, considering the meaning which it has in the sentence, and not as standing by itself, it is most conveniently regarded as a portion of a symbol. Thus the sentence, "every man loves a woman" is equivalent to "whatever is a man loves something that is a woman." Here "whatever" is a universal selective index, "is a man" is a symbol, "loves" is a symbol, "something that" is a particular selective index, and "is a woman" is a symbol. . . .

The word *Symbol* has so many meanings that it would be an injury to the language to add a new one. I do not think that the signification I attach to it, that of a conventional sign, or one depending upon habit (acquired or inborn), is so much a new meaning as a return to the original meaning. Etymologically, it should mean a thing thrown together, just as ἔμβολον (embolum) is a thing thrown into something, a bolt, and παράβολον (parabolum) is a thing thrown besides, collateral security, and ‘πόβολον (hypobolum) is a thing thrown underneath, an antenuptial gift. It is usually said that in the word *symbol* the throwing together is to be understood in the sense of "to conjecture"; but were that the case, we ought to find that *sometimes* at least it meant a conjecture, a meaning for which literature may be searched in vain. But the Greeks used "throw together" (συμβάλλειν) very frequently to signify the making of a contract or convention. Now, we do find symbol (σύμβολον) early and often used to mean a convention or contract. Aristotle calls a noun a "symbol," that is, a conventional sign. In Greek, watch-fire is a "symbol," that is, a signal agreed upon; a standard or ensign is a "symbol," a watchword is a "symbol," a badge is a "symbol"; a church creed is called a "symbol," because it serves as a badge or shibboleth; a theatre ticket is called a "symbol"; any ticket or check entitling one to receive anything is a "symbol." Moreover, any expression of sentiment was called a "symbol." Such were the principal meanings of the word in the original language. The reader will judge whether they suffice to establish my claim that I am not seriously wrenching the word in employing it as I propose to do.

Any ordinary word, as "give," "bird," "marriage," is an example of a symbol. It is *applicable to whatever may be found to realize the idea connected with the word*; it does not, in itself, identify those things. It does not show us a bird, nor enact before our eyes a giving or a marriage, but supposes that we are able to imagine those things, and have associated the word with them.

A regular progression of one, two, three may be remarked in the three orders of signs, Icon, Index, Symbol. The Icon has no dynamical connection with the object it represents; it simply happens that its qualities resemble those of that object, and excite analogous sensations in the mind for which it is a likeness. But it really stands unconnected with them. The index is physically connected with its object; they make an organic pair, but the interpreting mind has nothing to do with this connection, except remarking it, after it is established. The symbol is connected with its object by virtue of the idea of the symbol-using mind, without which no such connection would exist.

Every physical force reacts between a pair of particles, either of which may serve as an index of the other. On the other hand, we shall find that every intellectual operation involves a triad of symbols.

A symbol, as we have seen, cannot indicate any particular thing; it denotes a kind of thing. Not only that, but it is itself a kind and not a single thing. You can write down the word "star," but that does not make you the creator of the word, nor if you erase it have you destroyed the word. The word lives in the minds of those who use it. Even if they are all asleep, it exists in their memory. So we may admit, if there be reason to do so, that generals are mere words without at all saying, as Ockham supposed, that they are really individuals.

Symbols grow. They come into being by development out of other signs, particularly from icons, or from mixed signs partaking of the nature of icons and symbols. We think only in signs. These mental signs are of mixed nature; the symbol-parts of them are called concepts. If a man makes a new symbol, it is by thoughts involving concepts. So it is only out of symbols that a new symbol can grow. *Omne symbolum de symbolo.* A symbol, once in being, spreads among the peoples. In use and in experience, its meaning grows. Such words as *force, law, wealth, marriage,* bear for us very different meanings from those they bore to our barbarous ancestors. The symbol may, with Emerson's sphynx, say to man,

> Of thine eye I am eyebeam.

4. Ten Classes of Signs

The three trichotomies of Signs result together in dividing Signs into TEN CLASSES OF SIGNS, of which numerous subdivisions have to be considered. The ten classes are as follows:

First: A Qualisign [*e.g.,* a feeling of "red"] is any quality in so far as it is a sign. Since a quality is whatever it is positively in itself, a quality can only denote an object by virtue of some common ingredient or similarity; so that a Qualisign is necessarily an Icon. Further, since a quality is a mere logical possibility, it can only be interpreted as a sign of essence, that is, as a Rheme.

Second: An Iconic Sinsign [*e.g.,* an individual diagram] is any object of experience in so far as some quality of it makes it determine the idea of an object. Being an Icon, and thus a sign by likeness purely, of whatever it may be like, it can only be interpreted as a sign of essence, or Rheme. It will embody a Qualisign.

Third: A Rhematic Indexical Sinsign [*e.g.,* a spontaneous cry] is any object of direct experience so far as it directs attention to an Object by which its presence is caused. It necessarily involves an Iconic Sinsign of a peculiar kind, yet is quite different since it brings the attention of the interpreter to the very Object denoted.

Fourth: A Dicent Sinsign [*e.g.,* a weathercock] is any object of direct experience, in so far as it is a sign, and, as such, affords information concerning its Object. This it can only do by being really affected by its Object; so that it is necessarily an Index. The only information it can afford is of actual fact. Such a Sign must involve an Iconic Sinsign to embody the information and a Rhematic Indexical Sinsign to indicate the Object to which the information refers. But the mode of combination, or *Syntax*, of these two must also be significant.

Fifth: An Iconic Legisign [*e.g.*, a diagram, apart from its factual individuality] is any general law or type, in so far as it requires each instance of it to embody a definite quality which renders it fit to call up in the mind the idea of a like object. Being an Icon, it must be a Rheme. Being a Legisign, its mode of being is that of governing single Replicas, each of which will be an Iconic Sinsign of a peculiar kind.

Sixth: A Rhematic Indexical Legisign [*e.g.*, a demonstrative pronoun] is any general type or law, however established, which requires each instance of it to be really affected by its Object in such a manner as merely to draw attention to that Object. Each Replica of it will be a Rhematic Indexical Sinsign of a peculiar kind. The Interpretant of a Rhematic Indexical Legisign represents it as an Iconic Legisign; and so it is, in a measure—but in a very small measure.

Seventh: A Dicent Indexical Legisign [*e.g.*, a street cry] is any general type or law, however established, which requires each instance of it to be really affected by its Object in such a manner as to furnish definite information concerning that Object. It must involve an Iconic Legisign to signify the information and a Rhematic Indexical Legisign to denote the subject of that information. Each Replica of it will be a Dicent Sinsign of a peculiar kind.

Eighth: A Rhematic Symbol or Symbolic Rheme [*e.g.*, a common noun] is a sign connected with its Object by an association of general ideas in such a way that its Replica calls up an image in the mind, which image, owing to certain habits or dispositions of that mind, tends to produce a general concept, and the Replica is interpreted as a Sign of an Object that is an instance of that concept. Thus, the Rhematic Symbol either is, or is very like, what the logicians call a General Term. The Rhematic Symbol, like any Symbol, is necessarily itself of the nature of a general type, and is thus a Legisign. Its Replica, however, is a Rhematic Indexical Sinsign of a peculiar kind, in that the image it suggests to the mind acts upon a Symbol already in that mind to give rise to a General Concept. In this it differs from other Rhematic Indexical Sinsigns, including those which are Replicas of Rhematic Indexical Legisigns. Thus, the demonstrative pronoun "that" is a Legisign, being a general type; but it is not a Symbol, since it does not signify a general concept. Its Replica draws attention to a single Object, and is a Rhematic Indexical Sinsign. A Replica of the word "camel" is likewise a Rhematic Indexical Sinsign, being really affected, through the knowledge of camels, common to the speaker and auditor, by the real camel it denotes, even if this one is not individually known to the auditor; and it is through such real connection that the word "camel" calls up the idea of a camel. The same thing is true of the word "phoenix." For although no phoenix really exists, real descriptions of the phoenix are well known to the speaker and his auditor; and thus the word is really affected by the Object denoted. But not only are the Replicas of Rhematic Symbols very different from ordinary Rhematic Indexical Sinsigns, but so likewise are Replicas of Rhematic Indexical Legisigns. For the thing denoted by "that" has not affected the replica of the word in any such direct and simple manner as that in which, for example, the ring of a telephone-bell is affected by the person at the other end who wants to make a communication. The Interpretant of the Rhematic Symbol often represents it as a Rhematic Indexical Legisign; at other times as an Iconic Legisign; and it does in a small measure partake of the nature of both.

Ninth: A Dicent Symbol, or ordinary Proposition, is a sign connected with its object by an association of general ideas, and acting like a Rhematic Symbol, except that its intended interpretant represents the Dicent Symbol as being, in respect to what it signifies, really affected by its Object, so that the existence or law which it calls to mind must be actually connected with the indicated Object. Thus, the intended Interpretant looks upon the Dicent Symbol as a Dicent Indexical Legisign; and if it be true, it does partake of this nature, although this does not represent its whole nature. Like the Rhematic Symbol, it is necessarily a Legisign. Like the Dicent Sinsign it is composite inasmuch as it necessarily involves a Rhematic Symbol (and thus is for its Interpretant an Iconic Legisign) to express its information and a Rhematic Indexical Legisign to indicate the subject of that information. But its Syntax of these is significant. The Replica of the Dicent Symbol is a Dicent Sinsign of a peculiar kind. This is easily seen to be true when the information the Dicent Symbol conveys is of actual fact. When that information is of a real law, it is not true in the same fullness. For a Dicent Sinsign cannot convey information of law. It is, therefore, true of the Replica of such a Dicent Symbol only in so far as the law has its being in instances.

Tenth: An Argument is a sign whose interpretant represents its object as being an ulterior sign through a law, namely, the law that the passage from all such premisses to such conclusions tends to the truth. Manifestly, then, its object must be general; that is, the Argument must be a Symbol. As a Symbol it must, further, be a Legisign. Its Replica is a Dicent Sinsign.

The affinities of the ten classes are exhibited by arranging their designations in the triangular table here shown, which has heavy boundaries between adjacent squares that are appropriated to classes alike in only one respect. All other adjacent squares pertain to classes alike in two respects. Squares not adjacent pertain to classes alike in one respect only, except that each of the three squares of the vertices of the triangle pertains to a class differing in all three respects from the classes to which the squares along the opposite side of the triangle are appropriated. The lightly printed designations are superfluous.

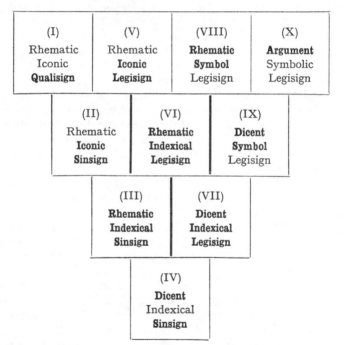

(I) Rhematic Iconic **Qualisign**	(V) Rhematic **Iconic** **Legisign**	(VIII) **Rhematic** **Symbol** Legisign	(X) **Argument** Symbolic Legisign
	(II) Rhematic **Iconic** **Sinsign**	(VI) **Rhematic** **Indexical** **Legisign**	(IX) **Dicent** **Symbol** Legisign
		(III) **Rhematic** **Indexical** **Sinsign**	(VII) **Dicent** **Indexical** **Legisign**
			(IV) **Dicent** Indexical **Sinsign**

In the course of the above descriptions of the classes, certain subdivisions of some of them have been directly or indirectly referred to. Namely, beside the normal varieties of Sinsigns, Indices, and Dicisigns, there are others which are Replicas of Legisigns, Symbols, and Arguments, respectively. Beside the normal

varieties of Qualisigns, Icons, and Rhemes, there are two series of
others; to wit, those which are directly involved in Sinsigns,
Indices, and Dicisigns, respectively, and also those which are
indirectly involved in Legisigns, Symbols, and Arguments, respectively. Thus, the ordinary Dicent Sinsign is exemplified by a
weathercock and its veering and by a photograph. The fact that
the latter is known to be the effect of the radiations from the object
renders it an index and highly informative. A second variety is a
Replica of a Dicent Indexical Legisign. Thus any given street cry,
since its tone and theme identifies the individual, is not a symbol,
but an Indexical Legisign; and any individual instance of it is a
Replica of it which is a Dicent Sinsign. A third variety is a Replica
of a Proposition. A fourth variety is a Replica of an Argument.
Beside the normal variety of the Dicent Indexical Legisign, of
which a street cry is an example, there is a second variety, which
is that sort of proposition which has the name of a well-known
individual as its predicate; as if one is asked, "Whose statue is
this?" the answer may be, "It is Farragut." The meaning of this
answer is a Dicent Indexical Legisign. A third variety may be a
premiss of an argument. A Dicent Symbol, or ordinary proposition,
in so far as it is a premiss of an Argument, takes on a new force,
and becomes a second variety of the Dicent Symbol. It would not
be worth while to go through all the varieties; but it may be well
to consider the varieties of one class more. We may take the
Rhematic Indexical Legisign. *The* shout of "Hullo!" is an example
of the ordinary variety—meaning, not an individual shout, but
this shout "Hullo!" in general—this type of shout. A second
variety is a constituent of a Dicent Indexical Legisign; as the word
"that" in the reply, "that is Farragut." A third variety is a
particular application of a Rhematic Symbol; as the exclamation
"Hark!" A fourth and fifth variety are in the peculiar force a
general word may have in a proposition or argument. It is not
impossible that some varieties are here overlooked. It is a nice
problem to say to what class a given sign belongs; since all the
circumstances of the case have to be considered. But it is seldom
requisite to be very accurate; for if one does not locate the sign
precisely, one will easily come near enough to its character for any
ordinary purpose of logic.

8

THE CRITERION OF VALIDITY IN REASONING *

I

SIGWART, like almost all the stronger logicians of today, present company excepted, makes the fundamental mistake of confounding the logical question with the psychological question. The psychological question is what processes the mind goes through. But the logical question is whether the conclusion that will be reached, by applying this or that maxim, will or will not accord with the *fact*. It may be that the mind is so constituted that that which our intellectual instinct approves will be true to the extent to which that instinct approves of it. If so, that is an interesting fact about the human mind; but it has no relevancy for logic whatsoever. Sigwart says that the question of what is good logic and what bad must in the last resort come down to a question of how we feel; it is a matter of *Gefühl*, that is, a Quality of Feeling. And this he undertakes to demonstrate. For he says if any other criterion be employed, the correctness of this criterion has to be established by reasoning, and in this reasoning antecedent to the establishment of any rational criterion we must rely upon *Gefühl*; so that *Gefühl* is that to which any other criterion must ultimately be referred. Good! This is good intelligent work, such as advances philosophy—a good, square, explicit fallacy that can be squarely met and definitively refuted. It is the more valuable because it is a form of argument of very wide applicability. It is precisely analogous to the reasoning by which the hedonist in ethics, the subjectivist in esthetics, the idealist in metaphysics, attacks the category of reaction. You perceive the analogy between their arguments. The hedonist says that the question of what is good morals and what bad must ultimately come down to a question of pleasure. For, he says, suppose we desire anything but our own pleasure. Then whatever it may be that we desire, we take satisfaction in; and if we did not take satisfaction in it we should not desire it. But this satisfaction is that very

* [In I, the first and fifth selections are from the Lectures on Pragmatism, at Harvard 1903 (*CP* 5.85-6, 87) ; the second, third, and fourth from the ms. volume " Minute Logic " 1902 (*CP* 2.152, 161, 169-73). II is from " Minute Logic " (*CP* 2.186-9).]

Quality of Feeling that we call pleasure; and thus the only thing we ever can desire is pleasure, and all deliberate action must be performed for the sake of our own pleasure.

Every idealist, too, begins with an analogous argument, though he very likely may not remain consistently on the ground it leads to, so far as it leads anywhere. He says: When I perceive anything I am conscious; and when I am conscious of anything, I am immediately conscious, and aught else I may be conscious of, I am conscious of through that immediate consciousness. Consequently whatever I learn from perception is merely that I have a feeling together with whatever I infer from that immediate consciousness.

The answer to all such arguments is that no desire can possibly desire its own satisfaction, no judgment can judge itself to be true, and no reasoning can conclude that it is itself sound. For all these propositions stand on the same footing and must stand or fall together. If any judgment judges itself to be true, all judgments— or at least all assertory judgments—do so likewise; for there is no ground of discrimination between assertory judgments in this respect. Either therefore the judgment, J, and the judgment "I say that J is true" are the same for all judgments or for none. But if they are identical, their denials are identical. But their denials are respectively "J is not true" and "I do not say that J is true," which are very different. Consequently no judgment judges itself to be true. All that J does is to furnish a premiss which is complete evidence warranting my assertion in another judgment that J is true. It is important to draw this distinction. The judgment J may, for example, be that "Sirius is white." That is a judgment about Sirius. To *myself* who perceive myself making this judgment, or to another who hears me assert it and admits my veracity, the evidence is complete that I believe Sirius to be white. But the two propositions "Sirius is white" "I judge that Sirius is white" are two distinct propositions.

In reasoning . . . your opinion is that we have the singular phenomenon of a physiological function which is open to approval and disapproval. In this you are supported by universal common sense, by the traditional logic, and by English logicians as a body. But you are in opposition to German logicians generally, who seldom notice fallacy, conceiving human reason to be an ultimate tribunal which cannot err.

The English logician . . . not only maintains that the proper way of deciding whether a given argument is valid or not is to consider whether there is anything in the constitution of the universe and the nature of things which insures that the facts shall be such as the argument promises that they shall be, but he goes so far as to maintain that our ordinary common sense judgments respecting the validity of arguments are formed in the same way, and differ from the judgments of scientific logic only in resting upon vaguer and less distinct thought. To ask him, therefore, to abandon his method of estimating the validity of arguments in favour of the German method of appeal to natural judgments of good sense, is, in his apprehension, neither more nor less than to ask him to abandon exact thinking for a kind of thinking which differs from it in no respect except that of being loose and confused.

Suppose this case. In the course of a long country ramble, I meet a boy whom I never saw before, and inquire my way of him. I take the turn which he directs me to take, but have not gone many steps further before I am overtaken by a man who informs me that that boy's mother has been arrested upon a charge of perjury and that I am wanted to testify to her veracity. "But," I say, "I never so much as heard of the woman. I did not know she existed." "Oh," says the man, "you must have known the boy had had a mother; and since you took the turn he told you to take, you are bound to acknowledge that the mother tells the truth, for it was she who had told the boy where this road leads to." What should I say to the man? I should say, "My dear sir, if you had asked me to testify that the woman *cannot* lie, for the reason that truth *consists* in her say-so, then I should think that your demand was as unjustifiable as any ever made of me." That would be an exaggeration, since his demand would not be in truth open to all the objections to which the argument of the German logicians is open; but as far as it goes, the analogy would be perfect. Somebody shakes a pair of dice in a dice-box and asks me to guess whether his next throw will be doublets or not. Before replying I make a mental diagram of all possible throws, and relying on that, I reply that I guess the throw will not show doublets. This is unquestionably a probable inference. In making it, the only thing that I am conscious of relying upon is my mental diagram, as representing the probable course of experience. That diagram takes the place of the boy of whom I inquired my way. But now the German logician assures me that the advice to guess against the doublets really originated in an instinct for rationality, of the existence of which I had no assurance, and have not yet;

except that, as he says, the authority of the diagram must have had some origin, just as the boy must have had some mother. Although the dice have not yet been cast, and all I know is that my guess seems reasonable, I am asked to testify to the world and to myself, not only that this unheard-of instinct spoke truly on that occasion, but that it does so invariably: nay, that the truth of reasonings *consists* in that instinct's saying that they are true.   Outside of a German treatise of logic, I never met with so bald a fallacy as that. So this is the sort of reasoning that it is thought not decent to controvert, unless it be with hesitancy, with the utmost humility, and with an implied acknowledgment of the impropriety of a mere American's controverting the opinion of a German.

If I may be allowed to use the word "habit," without any implication as to the time or manner in which it took birth, so as to be equivalent to the corrected phrase "habit or disposition," that is, as some general principle working in a man's nature to determine how he will act, then an instinct, in the proper sense of the word, is an inherited habit, or in more accurate language, an inherited disposition.   But since it is difficult to make sure whether a habit is inherited or is due to infantile training and tradition, I shall ask leave to employ the word "instinct" to cover both cases. Now we certainly have habits of reasoning; and our natural judgments as to what is good reasoning accord with those habits. I am willing to grant that it is probable that some of our judgments of rationality of the very simplest kind have at the bottom instincts in the above broad sense. I am inclined to think that even these have been so often furbished up and painted over by reflection upon the nature of things that they are, in mature life, mostly ordinary habits. In more complicated cases, say for example, in that guess about the pair of dice, I believe that our natural judgments as to what is reasonable are due to thinking over, ordinarily in a more or less confused way, what would happen. We imagine cases, place mental diagrams before our mind's eye, and multiply these cases, until a habit is formed of expecting that always to turn out the case, which has been seen to be the result in all the diagrams. To appeal to such a habit is a very different thing from appealing to any immediate instinct of rationality. That the process of forming a habit of reasoning by the use of diagrams is often performed there is no room for doubt. It is perfectly open to consciousness. Why may not all our natural judgments as to what is good reasoning be founded on habits formed in some such ways? If it be so, the German doctrine falls to the ground; for to form a notion of right reasoning from diagrams showing what will happen, is to form that notion virtually according to the English doctrine of logic, by reasoning from the nature of things. That is to say, a habit is involuntarily formed from the consideration of diagrams, which process when deliberately approved becomes inductive reasoning. Unless there be, in addition, some immediate instinctive feeling of rationality, the German theory cannot be correct. Yet proof of the existence of such an additional instinctive feeling is not forthcoming. Not even so much as a pretended proof of it is offered, nor so much as any likelihood of it, so high do these great German logicians hold themselves above the usual obligations of scientific logic.

On the contrary, pretty strong evidence is at hand that no such instinctive feeling exists. In the first place, our natural judgments as to what is good reasoning are accompanied by a sense of evidence: one thinks one *sees* that the fact is so and *must be* so, not merely that *we* cannot help thinking so. In this respect, these judgments contrast strongly with those of conscience. You and I have a horror of incest. We have been told that there is a reason for it; but that is open to doubt. Reason or no reason, however, our aversion for and horror at the idea is simply felt, without any accompanying sense of evidence. So it is with what offends our taste. "I do not like you, Dr. Fell." I have no accompanying sense of its being a well-founded feeling. In regard to a simple syllogism it is quite otherwise. It is no blind, unaccountable impulse to reason in that way that I feel. I seem to perceive that so the facts must be. This difference between judgments of taste and morals on the one hand and of *rationality* on the other can hardly be accounted for on the German theory.

If, however, as the English suppose, the feeling of rationality is the product of a sort of subconscious reasoning—by which I mean an operation which would be a reasoning if it were fully conscious and deliberate—the accompanying feeling of evidence may well be due to a dim recollection of the experimentation with diagrams. There are many other facts which point in the same way, of which I will only mention one which seems almost conclusive. This is that if we practise logical reflection according to the English method and are thus led to see that a certain method of reasoning promises nothing more than facts must from the nature of things bear out, we do not find that we have two distinct judgments of what is rational. If I am persuaded that incest will have deplorable effects upon off-spring, I feel a distinctly duplex condemnation of the practice, the one of a cool, almost sceptical kind, the other peremptory and without apology. There are some questions about which I, and I suppose it is the same with every thinking man, find these two voices quite at odds, my reason temperately but decidedly asserting that I ought to act in one way, my instincts, whether hereditary or conventional I cannot tell, most emphatically and peremptorily, though with no pretence to rationality, giving reason the lie. That *is* just such a phenomenon as would naturally be anticipated. It is very surprising that I do not find any such discord in my judgments as to what is good reasoning. There are various points in which my present opinions of what is good reasoning differ diametrically from those which I entertained before I had analyzed the matter after the English doctrine. But instead of my old feeling continuing to assert itself beside my new rationalized opinion, to say that it submits with docility is not enough: I cannot detect the least trace of it remaining. If it were an immediate feeling, as the Germans suppose, it certainly would persist. The only possible explanation of its not doing so is that it was merely itself a confused conclusion of subconscious reason which feels itself superseded by clearer analysis of the same kind and along the same line.

I have discussed this matter at some length, because it is a momentous question for logic; and it seemed proper to turn it over upon different sides. But in truth the essence of the matter lies in a nutshell. Facts are hard things which do not consist in my thinking so and so, but stand unmoved by whatever you or I or any man or generations of men may opine about them. It is those facts that I want to know, so that I may avoid disappointments and disasters. Since they are bound to press upon me at last, let me know them as soon as possible, and prepare for them. This is, in the last analysis, my whole motive in reasoning. Plainly, then, I wish to reason in such way that the facts shall not, and cannot, disappoint the promises of my reasoning. Whether such reasoning is agreeable to my intellectual impulses is a matter of no sort of consequence. I do reason not for the sake of my delight in reasoning, but solely to avoid disappointment and surprise. Consequently, I ought to plan out my reasoning so that I evidently shall avoid those surprises. That is the *rationale* of the English doctrine. It is as perfect as it is simple.

To return, then, to Sigwart's argument, I not only deny what he asserts that when I make an inference I can only do so because of a certain *feeling* of logical satisfaction that is connected with doing so, but I maintain that I *never can* draw an inference because of such a feeling. On the contrary, I never know the inference will afford me any such satisfaction except by a subsequent reflection after I have already drawn it. It may be that on recognizing the satisfaction the inference gives me I shall consider that as an additional reason for believing in it. But this is *another* inference which in its turn will afford a new gratification if I stop to reflect about it.

<h1 style="text-align:center">II</h1>

The opinions which you bring to the study of logic comprise among them a system of logic all made, although it is probably a little vague, in places. You know that this is substantially so, presuming that you are a reflective person, as you doubtless are; but you may perhaps be surprised that I should be so confident that it is so. It is simple enough, however. You would certainly not be interested in logic unless you were somewhat given to reasoning; probably not without being more or less addicted to self-observation. Now a person cannot perform the least reasoning without some general ideal of good reasoning; for reasoning involves deliberate approval of one's reasoning; and approval cannot be deliberate unless it is based upon the comparison of the thing approved with some idea of how such a thing ought to appear. Every reasoner, then, has some general idea of what good reasoning is. This constitutes a theory of logic: the scholastics called it the reasoner's *logica utens*. Every reasoner whose attention has been considerably drawn to his inner life must soon become aware of this.

He, therefore, comes to the study of logic handicapped by a conceit that he knows something about it already, but, at the same time, aided by his being able to handle questions of logic with some confidence and familiarity. He ought to endeavour to suppress his conceit while preserving his disposition to think independently.

But the fact that you are sincerely desirous of studying logic shows that you are not altogether satisfied with your *logica utens* nor with your powers of estimating the values of arguments. Of course, there is no good of entering upon any undertaking unless one desires the sole rational purpose of that undertaking, and is consequently more or less dissatisfied with one's present condition in that respect.

It is foolish, therefore, to study logic unless one is persuaded that one's own reasonings are more or less bad. Yet a reasoning is essentially something which one is deliberately convinced is good. There is a slight appearance of contradiction here, which calls for a little logic to remove it. The substance of an opinion is not the whole opinion. It has a mode. That is to say, the opinion has been approved because it has been formed in a certain way, and of opinions formed in that way, we have the opinion that relatively few are much in error. It is for that reason that we have adopted the opinion in question. Still, we attach but a limited degree of confidence to it, being of the opinion that out of a considerable number of opinions formed in the same way, some would probably be grossly erroneous. In this way, it might happen that you should hold that a large minority of your reasonings were bad, although you were inclined to adhere to each one singly. This is the general principle. But logicians are too apt to content themselves with the statement of general principles, and to overlook peculiar effects which may arise from complications of them. The real situation in this case is too complicated to be considered to advantage; but we can illustrate the general way in which complexity may modify the effect of our general principle. Your reasonings are determined by certain general habits of reasoning, each of which has been, in some sense, approved by you. But you may recognize that your habits of reasoning are of two distinct kinds, producing two kinds of reasoning which we may call A-reasonings and B-reasonings. You may think that of the A-reasonings very few are seriously in error, but that none of them much advance your knowledge of the truth. Of your B-reasonings, you may think that so many of them as are good are extremely valuable in teaching a great deal. Yet of these B-reasonings you may think that a large majority are worthless, their error being known by their being subsequently found to come in conflict with A-reasonings. It will be perceived from this description that the B-reasonings are a little more than guesses. You will then be justified in adhering to those habits of reasoning which produced B-reasonings, by the reflection that if you do adhere to them, the evil effects of the bad ones will be mainly eliminated in course of time by opposing A-reasonings, while you will gain the important knowledge brought by the few B-reasonings that are good; whereas, if you were to discard those habits of reasoning which produced B-reasonings you would have nothing left but A-reasonings, and these could never afford you much positive knowledge. This imaginary illustration will serve to show how it might be that you should, with perfect consistency, hold your existing *logica utens* to be excessively unsatisfactory, although you are perfectly justified in adhering to it until you are in possession of a better system. Without knowing anything of your individual case, my general observation of the manner in which men reason leads me to believe it most probable that the above illustration about the A-reasonings and the B-reasonings represents, in a general way, your condition, except that you greatly overrate the value of many of the B-reasonings, which are really little more than guesses at truth, but are, many of them, regarded by you as inductions. If this be the case, a study of logic, while making your whole thought more accurate, will enable you to rate your B-reasonings more accurately, and to substitute for about half of them reasonings that will not often deceive, while greatly improving the quality of those that will still remain more or less conjectural. This improvement will, however, be limited to logical reasonings; and of such you perhaps do not perform a great many. Those acts of the mind which chiefly depend upon instinct will remain unaffected, except that their true character will be recognized.

9

WHAT IS A LEADING PRINCIPLE? *

I

. . . WE ought to begin by considering how logic itself arises.

Thinking, as cerebration, is no doubt subject to the general laws of nervous action.

When a group of nerves are stimulated, the ganglions with which the group is most intimately connected on the whole are thrown into an active state, which in turn usually occasions movements of the body. The stimulation continuing, the irritation spreads from ganglion to ganglion (usually increasing meantime). Soon, too, the parts first excited begin to show fatigue; and thus for a double reason the bodily activity is of a changing kind. When the stimulus is withdrawn, the excitement quickly subsides.

It results from these facts that when a nerve is affected, the reflex action, if it is not at first of the sort to remove the irritation, will change its character again and again until the irritation is removed; and then the action will cease.

Now, all vital processes tend to become easier on repetition. Along whatever path a nervous discharge has once taken place, in that path a new discharge is the more likely to take place.

Accordingly, when an irritation of the nerves is repeated, all the various actions which have taken place on previous similar occasions are the more likely to take place now, and those are most likely to take place which have most frequently taken place on those previous occasions. Now, the various actions which did not remove the irritation may have previously sometimes been performed and some-times not; but the action which removes the irritation must have always been performed, because the action must have every time continued until it was performed. Hence, a strong habit of respond-

---

* [I and the first selection in III are from " On the Algebra of Logic," *American Journal of Mathematics* 1880 (*CP* 3.154-66, 168). II is the article " Leading Principle " in Baldwin's *Dict. of Philos. and Psychol.* 1902 (*CP* 2.588-9). The second selection in III is from " On the Natural Classification of Arguments," *Proc. Amer. Acad. Arts and Sciences* 1867 (*CP* 2.467), the third from the article " Laws of Thought " in Baldwin's (*CP* 2.599).]

ing to the given irritation in this particular way must quickly be established.

A habit so acquired may be transmitted by inheritance.

One of the most important of our habits is that one by virtue of which certain classes of stimuli throw us at first, at least, into a purely cerebral activity.

Very often it is not an outward sensation but only a fancy which starts the train of thought. In other words, the irritation instead of being peripheral is visceral. In such a case the activity has for the most part the same character; an inward action removes the inward excitation. A fancied conjuncture leads us to fancy an appropriate line of action. It is found that such events, though no external action takes place, strongly contribute to the formation of habits of really acting in the fancied way when the fancied occasion really arises.

A cerebral habit of the highest kind, which will determine what we do in fancy as well as what we do in action, is called a *belief*. The representation to ourselves that we have a specified habit of this kind is called a *judgment*. A belief-habit in its development begins by being vague, special, and meagre; it becomes more precise, general, and full, without limit. The process of this development, so far as it takes place in the imagination, is called *thought.* A judgment is formed; and under the influence of a belief-habit this gives rise to a new judgment, indicating an addition to belief. Such a process is called an *inference*; the antecedent judgment is called the *premiss*; the consequent judgment, the *conclusion*; the habit of thought, which determined the passage from the one to the other (when formulated as a proposition), the *leading principle*.

At the same time that this process of inference, or the spontaneous development of belief, is continually going on within us, fresh peripheral excitations are also continually creating new belief-habits. Thus, belief is partly determined by old beliefs and partly by new experience. Is there any law about the mode of the peripheral excitations? The logician maintains that there is, namely, that they are all adapted to an end, that of carrying belief, in the long run, toward certain predestinate conclusions which are the same for all men. This is the faith of the logician. This is the matter of fact, upon which all maxims of reasoning repose. In virtue of this fact, what is to be believed at last is independent of what has been believed hitherto, and therefore has the character of *reality*. Hence, if a given habit, considered as determining an inference, is of such a sort as to tend toward the final result, it is correct; otherwise not. Thus, inferences become divisible into the valid and the invalid; and thus logic takes its reason of existence.

The general type of inference is

$$P$$
$$\therefore C,$$

where $\therefore$ is the sign of illation.

The passage from the premiss (or set of premisses) P to the conclusion C takes place according to a habit or rule active within us. All the inferences which that habit would determine when once the proper premisses were admitted, form a class. The habit is logically good provided it would never (or in the case of a probable inference, seldom) lead from a true premiss to a false conclusion; otherwise it is logically bad. That is, every possible case of the operation of a good habit would either be one in which the premiss was false or one in which the conclusion would be true; whereas, if a habit of inference is bad, there is a possible case in which the premiss would be true, while the conclusion was false. When we speak of a *possible* case, we conceive that from the general description of cases we have struck out all those kinds which we know how to describe in general terms but which we know never will occur; those that then remain, embracing all whose non-occurrence we are not certain of, together with all those whose non-occurrence we cannot explain on any general principle, are called possible.

A habit of inference may be formulated in a proposition which shall state that every proposition c, related in a given general way to any true proposition p, is true. Such a proposition is called the *leading principle* of the class of inferences whose validity it implies. When the inference is first drawn, the leading principle is not present to the mind, but the habit it formulates is active in such a way that, upon contemplating the believed premiss, by a sort of perception the conclusion is judged to be true. Afterwards, when the inference is subjected to logical criticism, we make a new inference, of which one premiss is that leading principle of the former inference, according to which propositions related to one another in a certain way are fit to be premiss and conclusion of a valid inference, while another premiss is a fact of observation, namely, that the given relation does subsist between the premiss and conclusion of the inference under criticism; whence it is concluded that the inference was valid.

Logic supposes inferences not only to be drawn, but also to be subjected to criticism; and therefore we not only require the form

P ∴ C to express an argument, but also a form, $P_i \prec C_i$, to express the truth of its leading principle. Here P_i denotes any one of the class of premisses, and C_i the corresponding conclusion. The symbol $\prec$ is the copula, and signifies primarily that every state of things in which a proposition of the class P_i is true is a state of things in which the corresponding propositions of the class C_i are true. But logic also supposes some inferences to be invalid, and must have a form for denying the leading premiss [? principle]. This we shall write $P_i \overline{\prec} C_i$, *a dash over any symbol signifying in our notation the negative of that symbol.*

Thus, the form $P_i \prec C_i$ implies

either, 1, that it is impossible that a premiss of the class P_i should be true,

or, 2, that every state of things in which P_i is true is a state of things in which the corresponding C_i is true.

The form $P_i \overline{\prec} C_i$ implies

both, 1, that a premiss of the class P_i is possible,
and, 2, that among the possible cases of the truth of a P_i there is one in which the corresponding C_i is not true. . . .

In the form of inference P ∴ C the leading principle is not expressed; and the inference might be justified on several separate principles. One of these, however, $P_i \prec C_i$, is the formulation of the habit which, in point of fact, has governed the inferences. This principle contains all that is necessary besides the premiss P to justify the conclusion. (It will generally assert more than is necessary.) We may, therefore, construct a new argument which shall have for its premisses the two propositions P and $P_i \prec C_i$ taken together, and for its conclusion, C. This argument, no doubt, has, like every other, its leading principle, because the inference is governed by some habit; but yet the substance of the leading principle must already be contained implicitly in the premisses, because the proposition $P_i \prec C_i$ contains by hypothesis all that is requisite to justify the inference of C from P. Such a leading principle, which contains no fact not implied or observable in the premisses, is termed a *logical* principle. . . .

The above will be made clear by an example. Let us begin with the enthymeme,

> Enoch was a man,
> ∴ Enoch died.

The leading principle of this is, "All men die." Stating it, we get the complete argument,

> All men die,
> Enoch was a man;
> ∴ Enoch was to die.

The leading principle of this is *nota notae est nota rei ipsius.* Stating this as a premiss, we have the argument,

> *Nota notae est nota rei ipsius,*
> Mortality is a mark of humanity, which is a mark of Enoch;
> ∴ Mortality is a mark of Enoch.

But this very same principle of the *nota notae* is again active in the drawing of this last inference, so that the last state of the argument is no more complete than the last but one.

II

It is of the essence of reasoning that the reasoner should proceed, and should be conscious of proceeding, according to a general habit, or method, which he holds would either (according to the kind of reasoning) always lead to the truth, provided the premisses were true; or, consistently adhered to, would eventually approximate indefinitely to the truth; or would be generally conducive to the ascertainment of truth, supposing there be any ascertainable truth. The effect of this habit or method could be stated in a proposition of which the antecedent should describe all possible premisses upon which it could operate, while the consequent should describe how the conclusion to which it would lead would be determinately related to those premisses. Such a proposition is called the "leading principle" of the reasoning.

Two different reasoners might infer the same conclusion from the same premisses; and yet their proceeding might be governed by habits which would be formulated in different, or even conflicting, leading principles. Only that man's reasoning would be good whose leading principle was true for all possible cases. It is not essential that the reasoner should have a distinct apprehension of the leading principle of the habit which governs his reasoning; it is sufficient that he should be conscious of proceeding according to a general method, and that he should hold that that method is generally apt to lead to the truth. He may even conceive himself to be following one leading principle when, in reality, he is following another, and may consequently blunder in his conclusion. From the effective leading principle, together with the premises, the propriety of accepting the conclusion in such sense as it is accepted follows necessarily in every case. Suppose that the leading principle involves two propositions, L and L', and suppose that there are three premises, P, P', P''; and let C signify the acceptance of the conclusion, as it is accepted, either as true, or as a legitimate approximation to the truth, or as an assumption conducive to the ascertainment of the truth. Then, from the five premises L, L', P, P', P'', the inference to C would be necessary; but it would not be so from L, L', P', P'' alone, for, if it were, P would not really act as a premiss at all. From P' and P'' as the sole premises, C would follow, if the leading principle consisted of L, L', and P. Or from the four premises L' P, P', P'', the same conclusion would follow if L alone were the leading principle. What, then, could be the leading principle of the inference of C from all five propositions L, L', P, P', P'', taken as premises? It would be something already implied in those premises; and it might be almost any general proposition so implied. Leading principles are, therefore, of two classes; and any leading principle whose truth is implied in the premises of every inference which it governs is called a "logical" (or, less appropriately, a *formal*) leading principle; while a leading principle whose truth is not implied in the premises is called a "factual" (or *material*) leading principle.

III

A logical principle is said to be an *empty* or merely formal proposition, because it can add nothing to the premises of the argument it governs, although it is relevant; so that it implies no fact except such as is presupposed in all discourse. . . .

Since it can never be requisite that a fact stated should also be implied in order to justify a conclusion, every *logical principle* considered as an assertion will be found to be quite empty. The only thing it really enunciates is a rule of inference; considered as expressing truth, it is nothing.

Logical principles of inference are merely rules for the illative transformation of the symbols of the particular system employed. If the system is essentially changed, they will be quite different.

10

THE NATURE OF MATHEMATICS *

I

I WISH I knew with certainty the precise origin of the definition of mathematics as the science of quantity. It certainly cannot be Greek, because the Greeks were advanced in projective geometry, whose problems are such as these: whether or not four points obtained in a given way lie in one plane; whether or not four planes have a point in common; whether or not two rays (or unlimited straight lines) intersect, and the like—problems which have nothing to do with quantity, as such. Aristotle names, as the subjects of mathematical study, quantity and continuity. But though he never gives a formal definition of mathematics, he makes quite clear, in more than a dozen places, his view that mathematics ought not to be defined by the things which it studies but by its peculiar mode and degree of abstractness. Precisely what he conceives this to be it would require me to go too far into the technicalities of his philosophy to explain; and I do not suppose anybody would today regard the details of his opinion as important for my purpose. Geometry, arithmetic, astronomy, and music were, in the Roman schools of the fifth century and earlier, recognized as the four branches of mathematics. And we find Boëthius (A.D. 500) defining them as the arts which relate, not to quantity, but to *quantities*, or *quanta*. What this would seem to imply is, that mathematics is the foundation of the minutely exact sciences; but really it is not worth our while, for the present purpose, to ascertain what the schoolmasters of that degenerate age conceived mathematics to be.

In modern times projective geometry was, until the middle of this century, almost forgotten, the extraordinary book of Desargues

* [I is from "The Logic of Mathematics in Relation to Education," *Educational Review* 1898 (*CP* 3.554-60). II consists of three selections from the ms. volume "Minute Logic" 1902 (*CP* 4.232, 238-43, 246). III consists of two selections from "The Logic of Relatives," *The Monist* 1897 (*CP* 3.527-8, 531). The first two selections in IV are from the ms. volume "Grand Logic" 1893 (*CP* 4.86, 88-91), the third from "Reply to the Necessitarians," *The Monist* 1893 (*CP* 6.595).]

having been completely lost until, in 1845, Chasles came across a MS. copy of it; and, especially before imaginaries became very prominent, the definition of mathematics as the science of quantity suited well enough such mathematics as existed in the seventeenth and eighteenth centuries.

Kant, in the *Critique of Pure Reason* (Methodology, chapter 1, section 1), distinctly rejects the definition of mathematics as the science of quantity. What really distinguishes mathematics, according to him, is not the subject of which it treats, but its method, which consists in studying constructions, or diagrams. That such is its method is unquestionably correct; for, even in algebra, the great purpose which the symbolism subserves is to bring a skeleton representation of the relations concerned in the problem before the mind's eye in a schematic shape, which can be studied much as a geometrical figure is studied.

But Rowan Hamilton and De Morgan, having a superficial acquaintance with Kant, were just enough influenced by the *Critique* to be led, when they found reason for rejecting the definition as the science of quantity, to conclude that mathematics was the science of pure time and pure space. Notwithstanding the profound deference which every mathematician must pay to Hamilton's opinions and my own admiration for De Morgan, I must say that it is rare to meet with a careful definition of a science so extremely objectionable as this. If Hamilton and De Morgan had attentively read what Kant himself has to say about number, in the first chapter of the *Analytic of principles* and elsewhere, they would have seen that it has no more to do with time and space than has every conception. Hamilton's intention probably was, by means of this definition, to throw a slur upon the introduction of imaginaries into geometry, as a false science; but what De Morgan, who was a student of multiple algebra, and whose own formal logic is plainly mathematical, could have had in view, it is hard to comprehend, unless he wished to oppose Boole's theory of logic. Not only do mathematicians study hypotheses which, both in truth and according to the Kantian epistemology, no otherwise relate to time and space than do all hypotheses whatsoever, but we now all clearly see, since the non-Euclidean geometry has become familiar to us, that there *is* a real science of space and a real science of time, and that these sciences are positive and experiential—branches of physics, and so not mathematical except in the sense in which thermotics and electricity are mathematical; that is, as calling in the aid of mathematics. But the gravest objection of all to the definition is that it altogether ignores the veritable characteristics of this science, as they were pointed out by Aristotle and by Kant.

Of late decades philosophical mathematicians have come to a pretty just understanding of the nature of their own pursuit. I do not know that anybody struck the true note before Benjamin Peirce, who, in 1870, declared mathematics to be "the science which draws necessary conclusions," adding that it must be defined "subjectively" and not "objectively." A view substantially in accord with his, though needlessly complicated, is given in the article "Mathematics," in the ninth edition of the *Encyclopædia Britannica*. The author, Professor George Chrystal, holds that the essence of mathematics lies in its making pure hypotheses, and in the character of the hypotheses which it makes. What the mathematicians mean by a "hypothesis" is a proposition imagined to be strictly true of an ideal state of things. In this sense, it is only about hypotheses that necessary reasoning has any application; for, in regard to the real world, we have no right to presume that any given intelligible proposition is true in absolute strictness. On the other hand, probable reasoning deals with the ordinary course of experience; now, nothing like *a course of experience* exists for ideal hypotheses. Hence to say that mathematics busies itself in drawing necessary conclusions, and to say that it busies itself with hypotheses, are two statements which the logician perceives come to the same thing.

A simple way of arriving at a true conception of the mathematician's business is to consider what service it is which he is called in to render in the course of any scientific or other inquiry. Mathematics has always been more or less a trade. An engineer, or a business company (say, an insurance company), or a buyer (say, of land), or a physicist, finds it suits his purpose to ascertain what the necessary consequences of possible facts would be; but the facts are so complicated that he cannot deal with them in his usual way. He calls upon a mathematician and states the question. Now the mathematician does not conceive it to be any part of his duty to verify the facts stated. He accepts them absolutely without question. He does not in the least care whether they are correct or not. He finds, however, in almost every case that the statement has one inconvenience, and in many cases that it has a second. The first inconvenience is that, though the statement may not at first sound very complicated, yet, when it is accurately analyzed, it is found to imply so intricate a condition of things that it far surpasses the power of the mathematician to say with exactitude what its consequence would be. At the same time, it frequently happens that the facts, as stated, are insufficient to answer the question that is put. Accordingly, the first business of the mathematician, often a most difficult task, is to frame another simpler but quite fictitious problem (supplemented, perhaps, by some supposition), which shall be within his powers, while at the same time it is sufficiently like the problem set before him to answer, well or ill, as a substitute for it. This substituted problem differs also from that which was first set before the mathematician in another respect: namely, that it is highly abstract. All features that have no bearing upon the relations of the premisses to the conclusion are effaced and obliterated. The skeletonization or diagrammatization of the problem serves more purposes than one; but its principal purpose is to strip the significant relations of all disguise. Only one kind of concrete clothing is permitted—namely, such as, whether from habit or from the constitution of the mind, has become so familiar that it decidedly aids in tracing the consequences of the hypothesis. Thus, the mathematician does two very different things: namely, he first frames a pure hypothesis stripped of all features which do not concern the drawing of consequences from it, and this he does without inquiring or caring whether it agrees with the actual facts or not; and, secondly, he proceeds to draw necessary consequences from that hypothesis.

Kant is entirely right in saying that, in drawing those consequences, the mathematician uses what, in geometry, is called a "construction," or in general a diagram, or visual array of characters or lines. Such a construction is formed according to a precept furnished by the hypothesis. Being formed, the construction is submitted to the scrutiny of observation, and new relations are discovered among its parts, not stated in the precept by which it was formed, and are found, by a little mental experimentation, to be such that they will always be present in such a construction. Thus, the necessary reasoning of mathematics is performed by means of observation and experiment, and its necessary character is due simply to the circumstance that the subject of this observation and experiment is a diagram of our own creation, the conditions of whose being we know all about.

But Kant, owing to the slight development which formal logic had received in his time, and especially owing to his total ignorance of the logic of relatives, which throws a brilliant light upon the whole of logic, fell into error in supposing that mathematical and philosophical necessary reasoning are distinguished by the circumstance that the former uses constructions. This is not true. All necessary reasoning whatsoever proceeds by constructions; and the only difference between mathematical and philosophical necessary deductions is that the latter are so excessively simple that the construction attracts no attention and is overlooked. The construction exists in the simplest syllogism in Barbara. Why do the logicians like to state a syllogism by writing the major premiss on one line and the minor below it, with letters substituted for the subject and predicates? It is merely because the reasoner has to notice that relation between the parts of those premisses which such a diagram brings into prominence. If the reasoner makes use of syllogistic in drawing his conclusion, he has such a diagram or construction in his mind's eye, and observes the result of eliminating the middle term. If, however, he trusts to his unaided reason, he still uses some kind of a diagram which is familiar to him personally. The true difference between the necessary logic of philosophy and mathematics is merely one of degree. It is that, in mathematics, the reasoning is frightfully intricate, while the elementary conceptions are of the last degree of familiarity; in contrast to philosophy, where the reasonings are as simple as they can be, while the elementary conceptions are abstruse and hard to get clearly apprehended. But there is another much deeper line of demarcation between the two sciences. It is that mathematics studies nothing but pure hypotheses, and is the only science which never inquires what the actual facts are; while philosophy, although it uses no microscopes or other apparatus of special observation, is really an experimental science, resting on that experience which is common to us all; so that its principal reasonings are not mathematically necessary at all, but are only necessary in the sense that all the world knows beyond all doubt those truths of experience upon which philosophy is founded. This is why the mathematician holds the reasoning of the metaphysician in supreme contempt, while he himself, when he ventures into philosophy, is apt to reason fantastically and not solidly, because he does not recognize that he is upon ground where elaborate deduction is of no more avail than it is in chemistry or biology.

II

Kant regarded mathematical propositions as synthetical judgments *a priori*; wherein there is this much truth, that they are not, for the most part, what he called analytical judgments; that is, the predicate is not, in the sense he intended, contained in the definition of the subject. But if the propositions of arithmetic, for example, are true cognitions, or even forms of cognition, this circumstance is quite aside from their mathematical truth. For all modern mathematicians agree with Plato and Aristotle that mathematics deals exclusively with hypothetical states of things, and asserts no matter of fact whatever; and further, that it is thus alone that the necessity of its conclusions is to be explained. This is the true essence of mathematics; and my father's definition is in so far correct that it is impossible to reason necessarily concerning anything else than a pure hypothesis. Of course, I do not mean that if such pure hypothesis happened to be true of an actual state of things, the reasoning would thereby cease to be necessary. Only, it never would be known apodictically to be true of an actual state of things. Suppose a state of things of a perfectly definite, general description. That is, there must be no room for doubt as to whether anything, itself determinate, would or would not come under that description. And suppose, further, that this description refers to nothing occult—nothing that cannot be summoned up fully into the imagination. Assume, then, a range of possibilities equally definite and equally subject to the imagination; so that, so far as the given description of the supposed state of things is general, the different ways in which it might be made determinate could never introduce doubtful or occult features. The assumption, for example, must not refer to any matter of fact. For questions of fact are not within the purview of the imagination. Nor must it be such that, for example, it could lead us to ask whether the vowel *OO* can be imagined to be sounded on as high a pitch as the vowel *EE*. Perhaps it would have to be restricted to pure spatial, temporal, and logical relations. Be that as it may, the question whether in such a state of things, a certain other similarly definite state of things, equally a matter of the imagination, could or could not, in the assumed range of possibility, ever occur, would be one in reference to which one of the two answers, *Yes* and *No*, would be true, but never both. But all pertinent facts would be within the beck and call of the imagination; and consequently nothing but the operation of thought would be necessary to render the true answer. Nor, supposing the answer to cover the whole range of possibility assumed, could this be rendered otherwise than by reasoning that would be apodictic, general, and exact. No knowledge of what actually is, no *positive* knowledge, as we say, could result. On the other hand, to assert that any source of information that is restricted to actual facts could afford us a necessary knowledge, that is, knowledge relating to a whole general range of possibility, would be a flat contradiction in terms.

It is difficult to decide between the two definitions of mathematics; the one by its method, that of drawing necessary conclusions; the other by its aim and subject matter, as the study of hypothetical states of things. The former makes or seems to make the deduction of the consequences of hypotheses the sole business of the mathematician as such. But it cannot be denied that immense genius has been exercised in the mere framing of such general hypotheses as the field of imaginary quantity and the allied idea of Riemann's surface, in imagining non-Euclidean measurement, ideal numbers, the perfect liquid. Even the framing of the particular hypotheses of special problems almost always calls for good judgment and knowledge, and sometimes for great intellectual power, as in the case of Boole's logical algebra. Shall we exclude this work from the domain of mathematics? Perhaps the answer should be that, in the first place, whatever exercise of intellect may be called for in applying mathematics to a question not propounded in mathematical form [it] is certainly not pure mathematical thought; and in the second place, that the mere creation of a hypothesis may be a grand work of poietic genius, but cannot be said to be scientific, inasmuch as that which it produces is neither true nor false, and therefore is not knowledge. This reply suggests the further remark that if mathematics is the study of purely imaginary states of things, poets must be great mathematicians, especially that class of poets who write novels of intricate and enigmatical plots. Even the reply, which is obvious, that by *studying* imaginary states of things we mean *studying* what is true of them, perhaps does not fully meet the objection. . . .

The philosophical mathematician, Dr. Richard Dedekind, holds mathematics to be a branch of logic. This would not result from my father's definition, which runs, not that mathematics is the science of *drawing* necessary conclusions—which would be deductive logic —but that it is the science which *draws* necessary conclusions. It is evident, and I know as a fact, that he had this distinction in view. At the time when he thought out this definition, he, a mathematician, and I, a logician, held daily discussions about a large subject which interested us both; and he was struck, as I was, with the contrary nature of his interest and mine in the same propositions. The logician does not care particularly about this or that hypothesis or its consequences, except so far as these things may throw a light upon the nature of reasoning. The mathematician is intensely interested in efficient methods of reasoning, with a view to their possible extension to new problems; but he does not, *qua* mathematician, trouble himself minutely to dissect those parts of this method whose correctness is a matter of course. The different aspects which the algebra of logic will assume for the two men is instructive in this respect. The mathematician asks what value this algebra has as a calculus. Can it be applied to unravelling a complicated question? Will it, at one stroke, produce a remote consequence? The logician does not wish the algebra to have that character. On the contrary, the greater number of distinct logical steps, into which the algebra breaks up an inference, will for him constitute a superiority of it over another which moves more swiftly to its conclusions. He demands that the algebra shall analyze a reasoning into its last elementary steps. Thus, that which is a merit in a logical algebra for one of these students is a demerit in the eyes of the other. The one studies the science of drawing conclusions, the other the science which draws necessary conclusions.

But, indeed, the difference between the two sciences is far more than that between two points of view. Mathematics is purely hypothetical: it produces nothing but conditional propositions. Logic, on the contrary, is categorical in its assertions. True, it is not merely, or even mainly, a mere discovery of what really is, like metaphysics. It is a normative science. It thus has a strongly mathematical character, at least in its methodeutic division; for here it analyzes the problem of how, with given means, a required end is to be pursued. This is, at most, to say that it has to call in the aid of mathematics; that it has a mathematical branch. But so much may be said of every science. There is a mathematical logic, just as there is a mathematical optics and a mathematical economics. Mathematical logic is formal logic. Formal logic, however developed, is mathematics. Formal logic, however, is by no means the whole of logic, or even its principal part. It is hardly to be reckoned as a part of logic proper. Logic has to define its aim; and in doing so is even more dependent upon ethics, or the philosophy of aims, by far, than it is, in the methodeutic branch, upon mathematics. We shall soon come to understand how a student of ethics might well be tempted to make his science a branch of logic; as, indeed, it pretty nearly was in the mind of Socrates. But this would be no truer a view than the other. Logic depends upon mathematics; still more intimately upon ethics; but its proper concern is with truths beyond the purview of either.

There are two characters of mathematics which have not yet been mentioned, because they are not exclusive characteristics of it. One of these, which need not detain us, is that mathematics is distinguished from all other sciences except only ethics, in standing in no need of ethics. Every other science, even logic—logic, especially —is in its early stages in danger of evaporating into airy nothingness, degenerating, as the Germans say, into an anachrioid [?] film, spun from the stuff that dreams are made of. There is no such danger for pure mathematics; for that is precisely what mathematics ought to be.

The other character—and of particular interest it is to us just now—is that mathematics, along with ethics and logic alone of the sciences, has no need of any appeal to logic. No doubt, some reader may exclaim in dissent to this, on first hearing it said. Mathematics, they may say, is preëminently a science of reasoning. So it is; preëminently a science that reasons. But just as it is not necessary, in order to talk, to understand the theory of the formation of vowel sounds, so it is not necessary, in order to reason, to be in possession of the theory of reasoning. Otherwise, plainly, the science of logic could never be developed. The contrary objection would have more excuse, that no science stands in need of logic, since our natural power of reason is enough. Make of logic what the majority of treatises in the past have made of it, and a very common class of English and French books still make of it—that is to say, mainly formal logic, and that formal logic represented as an art of reasoning —and in my opinion this objection is more than sound, for such logic is a great hindrance to right reasoning. It would, however, be aside from our present purpose to examine this objection minutely. I will content myself with saying that undoubtedly our natural power of reasoning is enough, in the same sense that it is enough, in order to obtain a wireless transatlantic telegraph, that men should be born. That is to say, it is bound to come sooner or later. But that does not make research into the nature of electricity needless for gaining such a telegraph. So likewise if the study of electricity had been pursued resolutely, even if no special attention had ever been paid to mathematics, the requisite mathematical ideas would surely have been evolved. Faraday, indeed, did evolve them without any acquaintance with mathematics. Still it would be far more economical to postpone electrical researches, to study mathematics by itself, and then to apply it to electricity, which was Maxwell's way. In this same manner, the various logical difficulties which arise in the course of every science except mathematics, ethics, and logic, will, no doubt, get worked out after a time, even though no special study of logic be made. But it would be far more economical to make first a systematic study of logic. If anybody should ask what are these logical difficulties which arise in all the sciences, he must have read the history of science very irreflectively. What was the famous controversy concerning the measure of force but a logical difficulty? What was the controversy between the uniformitarians and the catastrophists but a question of whether or not a given conclusion followed from acknowledged premisses? . . .

But it may be asked whether mathematics, ethics, and logic have not encountered similar difficulties. Are the doctrines of logic at all settled?. Is the history of ethics anything but a history of controversy? Have no logical errors been committed by mathematicians? To that I reply, first, as to logic, that not only have the rank and file of writers on the subject been, as an eminent psychiatrist, Maudsley, declares, men of arrested brain-development, and not only have they generally lacked the most essential qualification for the study, namely mathematical training, but the main reason why logic is unsettled is that thirteen different opinions are current as to the true aim of the science. Now this is not a logical difficulty but an ethical difficulty; for ethics is the science of aims. Secondly, it is true that pure ethics has been, and always must be, a theatre of discussion, for the reason that its study consists in the gradual development of a distinct recognition of a satisfactory aim. It is a science of subtleties, no doubt; but it is not logic, but the development of the ideal, which really creates and resolves the problems of ethics. Thirdly, in mathematics errors of reasoning have occurred, nay, have passed unchallenged for thousands of years. This, however, was simply because they escaped notice. Never, in the whole history of the science, has a question whether a given conclusion followed *mathematically* from given premises, when once started, failed to receive a speedy and unanimous reply. Very few have been even the apparent exceptions; and those few have been due to the fact that it is only within the last half century that mathematicians have come to have a perfectly clear recognition of what is mathematical soil and what foreign to mathematics. Perhaps the nearest approximation to an exception was the dispute about the use of divergent series. Here neither party was in possession of sufficient pure mathematical reasons covering the whole ground; and such reasons as they had were not only of an extra-mathematical kind, but were used to support more or less vague positions. It appeared then, as we all know now, that divergent series are of the utmost utility.

Struck by this circumstance, and making an inference, of which it is sufficient to say that it was not mathematical, many of the old mathematicians pushed the use of divergent series beyond all reason. This was a case of mathematicians disputing about the validity of a kind of inference that is not mathematical. No doubt, a sound logic (such as has not hitherto been developed) would have shown clearly that that non-mathematical inference was not a sound one. But this is, I believe, the only instance in which any large party in the mathematical world ever proposed to rely, in mathematics, upon unmathematical reasoning. My proposition is that true mathematical reasoning is so much more evident than it is possible to render any doctrine of logic proper—without just such reasoning— that an appeal in mathematics to logic could only embroil a situation. On the contrary, such difficulties as may arise concerning necessary reasoning have to be solved by the logician by reducing them to questions of mathematics. Upon those mathematical dicta, as we shall come clearly to see, the logician has ultimately to repose.

Each branch of mathematics sets out from a general hypothesis of its own. I mean by its general hypothesis the substance of its postulates and axioms, and even of its definitions, should they be contaminated with any substance, instead of being the pure verbiage they ought to be. We have to make choice, then, between a division of mathematics according to the matter of its hypotheses, or according to the forms of the schemata of which it avails itself. These latter are either geometrical or algebraical. Geometrical schemata are linear figures with letters attached; the perfect imaginability, on the one hand, and the extreme familiarity, on the other hand, of spatial relations are taken advantage of, to enable us to see what will necessarily be true under supposed conditions. The algebraical schemata are arrays of characters, sometimes in series, sometimes in blocks, with which are associated certain rules of permissible transformation. With these rules the algebraist has perfectly to familiarize himself. By virtue of these rules, become habits of association, when one array has been written or assumed to be permissibly scriptible, the mathematician just as directly perceives that another array is permissibly scriptible, as he perceives that a person talking in a certain tone is angry, or [is] using certain words in such and such a sense.

III

I formerly defined the possible as that which in a given state of information (real or feigned) we do not know not to be true. But this definition today seems to me only a twisted phrase which, by means of two negatives, conceals an anacoluthon. We know in advance of experience that certain things are not true, because we see they are impossible. Thus, if a chemist tests the contents of a hundred bottles for fluorine, and finds it present in the majority, and if another chemist tests them for oxygen and finds it in the majority, and if each of them reports his result to me, it will be useless for them to come to me together and say that they know infallibly that fluorine and oxygen cannot be present in the same bottle; for I see that such infallibility is *impossible*. I know it is not true, because I satisfy myself that there is no room for it even in that ideal world of which the real world is but a fragment. I need no sensible experimentation, because ideal experimentation establishes a much broader answer to the question than sensible experimentation could give. It has come about through the agencies of development that man is endowed with intelligence of such a nature that he can by ideal experiments ascertain that in a certain universe of logical possibility certain combinations occur while others do not occur. Of those which occur in the ideal world some do and some do not occur in the real world; but all that occur in the real world occur also in the ideal world. For the real world is the world of sensible experience, and it is a part of the process of sensible experience to locate its facts in the world of ideas. This is what I mean by saying that the sensible world is but a fragment of the ideal world. In respect to the ideal world we are virtually omniscient; that is to say, there is nothing but lack of time, of perseverance, and of activity of mind to prevent our making the requisite experiments to ascertain positively whether a given combination occurs or not. Thus, every proposition about the ideal world can be ascertained to be either true or false. A description of thing which occurs in that world is *possible, in the substantive logical sense*. Very many writers assert that everything is logically possible which involves no contradiction. Let us call that sort of logical possibility, *essential*, or *formal*, logical possibility. It is not the only logical possibility; for in this sense, two propositions contradictory of one another may both be severally possible, although their combination is not possible. But in the *substantive* sense, the contradictory of a possible proposition is impossible, because we are virtually omniscient in regard to the ideal world. For example, there is no contradiction in supposing that only four, or any other number, of independent atoms exist. But it is made clear to us by ideal experimentation, that five atoms are to be found in the ideal world. Whether all five are to be found in the sensible world or not, to say that there are only four in the ideal world is a proposition absolutely to be rejected, notwithstanding its involving no contradiction.

It would be a great mistake to suppose that ideal experimentation can be performed without danger of error; but by the exercise of care and industry this danger may be reduced indefinitely. In sensible experimentation, no care can always avoid error. The results of induction from sensible experimentation are to afford some ratio of frequency with which a given consequence follows given conditions in the existing order of experience. In induction from ideal experimentation, no particular order of experience is forced upon us; and consequently no such numerical ratio is deducible. We are confined to a dichotomy: the result either is that some description of thing occurs or that it does not occur. For example, we cannot say that one number in every three is divisible by three and one in every five is divisible by five. This is, indeed, so if we choose to arrange the numbers in the order of counting; but if we arrange them with reference to their prime factors, just as many are divisible by one prime as by another. I mean, for instance, when they are arranged [in blocks] as follows:

1,	2,	4,	8, etc.		5,	10,	20,	40, etc.
3,	6,	12,	24, etc.		15,	30,	60,	120, etc.
9,	18,	36,	72, etc.		45,	90,	180,	360, etc.
27,	54,	108,	216, etc.		135,	270,	540,	1080, etc.
		etc.					etc.	

7,	14,	28,	56, etc.		35,	70, etc.
21,	42,	84,	168, etc.		105,	210, etc.
		etc.				etc.

Every result of an ideal induction clothes itself, in our modes of thinking, in the dress of a *contradiction*. It is an anacoluthon to say that a proposition is impossible *because* it is self-contradictory. It rather is thought so as to appear self-contradictory because the ideal induction has shown it to be impossible. But the result is that in the absence of any interfering contradiction every particular proposition is possible in the substantive logical sense, and its contradictory universal proposition is impossible. But where contradiction interferes this is reversed.

IV

[Kant] says we necessarily think the explicatory proposition although confusedly, whenever we think its subject. This is monstrous! The question whether a given thing is consistent with a hypothesis, is the question of whether they are logically compossible or not. I can easily throw all the axioms of number, which are neither numerous nor complicated, into the antecedent of a proposition—or into its *subject*, if that be insisted upon—so that the question of whether every number is the sum of three cubes, is simply a question of whether that is *involved* in the conception of the subject and nothing more. But to say that because the answer is *involved* in the conception of the subject, it is confusedly *thought* in it, is a great error. To be *involved*, is a phrase to which nobody before Kant ever gave such a psychological meaning.

[From]
Some A is B,
Some not-A is B,

it follows that there are at least two B's. This inference is strictly logical, depending on the principle of contradiction, that is, on the non-identity of A and not-A. By the same principle, from

Some A is B,
Some not-A is B,
Any B is C,
Some not-B is C,

taken together it follows that there are at least three C's.

Hamilton admits that the arithmetical proposition, "Some B is not some-B," is so urgently called for in logic, that a special propositional form must be made for it. So, if a distributive meaning be given to "every," Every A is every A, implies that there is but one A, at most. This is what this proposition must mean, if it is to be the precise contradiction of the other. If a proposition is infralogical in form, its denial must be admitted to be so.

It clearly belongs to logic to evolve the consequences of its own forms. Hence, the whole of the theory of numbers belongs to logic; or rather, it would do so, were it not, as pure mathematics, *pre-logical*, that is, even more abstract than logic.

These considerations are sufficient of themselves to refute Kant's doctrine that the propositions of arithmetic are "synthetical." As for the argument of J. S. Mill, or what is usually attributed to him, for what this elusive writer really meant, if he precisely meant anything, about any difficult point, it is utterly impossible to determine—I mean the argument that because we can conceive of a world in which when two things were put together, a third should spring up, therefore arithmetical propositions are experiential, this argument proves too much. For, in the existing world, this often happens; and the fact that nobody dreams of its constituting any infringement of the truths of arithmetic shows that arithmetical propositions are not understood in any experiential sense.

But Mill is wrong in supposing that those who maintain that arithmetical propositions are logically necessary, are therein *ipso facto* saying that they are verbal in their nature. This is only the same old idea that Barbara in all its simplicity represents all there is to necessary reasoning, utterly overlooking the construction of a diagram, the mental experimentation, and the surprising novelty of many deductive discoveries.

If Mill wishes me to admit that *experience* is the only source of any kind of knowledge, I grant it at once, provided only that by experience he means *personal history*, life. But if he wants me to admit that inner experience is nothing, and that nothing of moment is found out by diagrams, he asks what cannot be granted.

. . . The propositions of arithmetic, which Dr. Carus usually adduces as examples of formal law, are, in fact, only corollaries from definitions. They are certain only as applied to ideal constructions and, in such application, they are merely analytical. . . . An analytical proposition is a definition or a proposition *deducible* from definitions; a synthetical proposition is a proposition not analytical.

II

ABDUCTION AND INDUCTION *

I

ALL our knowledge may be said to rest upon *observed facts*. It is
true that there are psychological states which antecede our observing
facts as such. Thus, it is a fact that I see an inkstand before me;
but before I can say that I am obliged to have impressions of sense
into which no idea of an inkstand, or of any separate object, or of
an "I," or of seeing, enter at all; and it is true that my judging
that I see an inkstand before me is the product of mental operations
upon these impressions of sense. But it is only when the cognition
has become worked up into a proposition, or judgment of a fact,
that I can exercise any direct control over the process; and it is idle
to discuss the "legitimacy" of that which cannot be controlled.
Observations of fact have, therefore, to be accepted as they occur.

But observed facts relate exclusively to the particular circumstances that happened to exist when they were observed. They do
not relate to any future occasions upon which we may be in doubt
how we ought to act. They, therefore, do not, in themselves, contain
any practical knowledge.

Such knowledge must involve additions to the facts observed.
The making of those additions is an operation which we can control;
and it is evidently a process during which error is liable to creep in.

Any proposition added to observed facts, tending to make them
applicable in any way to other circumstances than those under
which they were observed, may be called a hypothesis. A hypothesis ought, at first, to be entertained interrogatively. Thereupon,
it ought to be tested by experiment so far as practicable. There are
two distinct processes, both of which may be performed rightly or
wrongly. We may go wrong and be wasting time in so much as
entertaining a hypothesis, even as a question. That is a subject
for criticism in every case. There are some hypotheses which are of
such a nature that they never can be tested at all. Whether such

* [In I, the first and third selections are from ms. c. 1901 (*CP* 6.522-8),
the second from the Lectures on Pragmatism, at Harvard 1903 (*CP* 5.189).
II is from ms. of notes c. 1896 (*CP* 1.71-4), III from " A Neglected Argument
for the Reality of God," *Hibbert Journal* 1908 (*CP* 6.477).]

hypotheses ought to be entertained at all, and if so in what sense, is a serious question; but it hardly concerns our present inquiry. The hypotheses with which we shall have in this paper to deal are capable of being put to the test. How this is to be done is a question of extreme importance; but my intention is to consider it only in a very cursory manner, at present. There are, moreover, many hypotheses in regard to which knowledge already in our possession may, at once, quite justifiably either raise them to the rank of opinions, or even positive beliefs, or cause their immediate rejection. This also is a matter to be considered. But it is the first process, that of entertaining the question, which will here be of foremost importance.

Before we go further, let us get the points stated above quite clear. By a *hypothesis*, I mean, not merely a supposition about an observed object, as when I suppose that a man is a Catholic priest because that would explain his dress, expression of countenance, and bearing, but also any other supposed truth from which would result such facts as have been observed, as when van't Hoff, having remarked that the osmotic pressure of one per cent solutions of a number of chemical substances was inversely proportional to their atomic weights, thought that perhaps the same relation would be found to exist between the same properties of any other chemical substance. The first starting of a hypothesis and the entertaining of it, whether as a simple interrogation or with any degree of confidence, is an inferential step which I propose to call *abduction* [or *retroduction*]. This will include a preference for any one hypothesis over others which would equally explain the facts, so long as this preference is not based upon any previous knowledge bearing upon the truth of the hypotheses, nor on any testing of any of the hypotheses, after having admitted them on probation. I call all such inference by the peculiar name, *abduction*, because its legitimacy depends upon altogether different principles from those of other kinds of inference.

Long before I first classed abduction as an inference it was recognized by logicians that the operation of adopting an explanatory hypothesis—which is just what abduction is—was subject to certain conditions. Namely, the hypothesis cannot be admitted, even as a hypothesis, unless it be supposed that it would account for the facts or some of them. The form of inference, therefore, is this:

> The surprising fact, C, is observed;
> But if A were true, C would be a matter of course,
> Hence, there is reason to suspect that A is true.

Thus, A cannot be abductively inferred, or if you prefer the expression, cannot be abductively conjectured until its entire content is already present in the premiss, "If A were true, C would be a matter of course."

The operation of testing a hypothesis by experiment, which consists in remarking that, if it is true, observations made under certain conditions ought to have certain results, and then causing those conditions to be fulfilled, and noting the results, and, if they are favourable, extending a certain confidence to the hypothesis, I call *induction*. For example, suppose that I have been led to surmise that among our coloured population there is a greater tendency toward female births than among our whites. I say, if that be so, the last census must show it. I examine the last census report and find that, sure enough, there was a somewhat greater proportion of female births among coloured births than among white births in that census year. To accord a certain faith to my hypothesis on that account is legitimate. It is a strong induction. I have taken all the births of that year as a sample of all the births of years in general, so long as general conditions remain as they were then. It is a very large sample, quite unnecessarily so, were it not that the excess of the one ratio over the other is quite small. All induction whatever may be regarded as the inference that throughout a whole class a ratio will have about the same value that it has in a random sample of that class, provided the nature of the ratio for which the sample is to be examined is specified (or virtually specified) in advance of the examination. So long as the class sampled consists of units, and the ratio in question is a ratio between counts of occurrences, induction is a comparatively simple affair. But suppose we wish to test the hypothesis that a man is a Catholic priest, that is, has all the characters that are common to Catholic priests and peculiar to them. Now characters are not units, nor do they consist of units, nor can they be counted, in such a sense that one count is right and every other wrong. Characters have to be estimated according to their significance. The consequence is that there will be a certain element of guess-work in such an induction; so that I call it an *abductory induction*. I might say to myself, let me think of some other character that belongs to Catholic priests, beside those that I have remarked in this man, a character which I can ascertain whether he possesses or not. All Catholic priests are more or less familiar with Latin pronounced in the Italian manner. If, then, this man is a Catholic priest, and I make some remark in Latin which a person not accustomed to the Italian pronunciation would not at once understand, and I pronounce it in that way, then if that man is a Catholic priest he will be so surprised that he cannot but betray his understanding of it. I make such a remark; and I notice that he does understand it. But how much weight am I to attach to that test? After all, it does not touch an essential characteristic of a priest or even of a Catholic. It must be acknowledged that it is but a weak confirmation, and all the more so, because it is quite uncertain how much weight should be attached to it. Nevertheless, it does and ought to incline me to believe that the man is a Catholic priest. It is an induction, because it is a test of the hypothesis by means of a prediction, which has been verified. But it is only an abductory induction, because it was a sampling of the characters of priests to see what proportion of them this man possessed, when characters cannot be counted, nor even weighed, except by guess-work. It also partakes of the nature of abduction in involving an original suggestion; while typical induction has no originality in it, but only tests a suggestion already made.

In induction, it is not the fact predicted that in any degree necessitates the truth of the hypothesis or even renders it probable. It is the fact that it has been predicted successfully and that it is a haphazard specimen of all the predictions which might be based on the hypothesis and which constitute its practical truth. But it frequently happens that there are facts which, merely as facts, apart from the manner in which they have presented themselves, necessitate the truth, or the falsity, or the probability in some definite degree, of the hypothesis. For example, suppose the hypothesis to be that a man believes in the infallibility of the Pope. Then, if we ascertain in any way that he believes in the immaculate conception, in the confessional, and in prayers for the dead, or on the other hand that he disbelieves all or some of these things, either fact will be almost decisive of the truth or falsity of the proposition. Such inference is *deduction*. So if we ascertain that the man in question is a violent partisan in politics and in many other subjects. If, then, we find that he has given money toward a Catholic institution, we may fairly reason that such a man would not do that unless he believed in the Pope's infallibility. Or again, we might learn that he is one of five brothers whose opinions are identical on almost all subjects. If, then, we find that the other four all believe in the Pope's infallibility or all disbelieve it, this will affect our confidence in the hypothesis. This consideration will be strengthened by our general experience that while different members of a large family usually differ about most subjects, yet it mostly happens that they are either all Catholics or all Protestants. Those are four different varieties of deductive considerations which may legitimately influence our belief in a hypothesis.

These distinctions are perfectly clear in principle, which is all that is necessary, although it might sometimes be a nice question to say to which class a given inference belongs. It is to be remarked that, in pure abduction, it can never be justifiable to accept the hypothesis otherwise than as an interrogation. But as long as that condition is observed, no positive falsity is to be feared; and therefore the whole question of what one out of a number of possible hypotheses ought to be entertained becomes purely a question of economy.

II

Mill denies that there was any reasoning in Kepler's procedure. He says it is merely a description of the facts. He seems to imagine that Kepler had all the places of Mars in space given him by Tycho's observations; and that all he did was to generalize and so obtain a general expression for them. Even had that been all, it would certainly have been inference. Had Mill had even so much practical acquaintance with astronomy as to have practised discussions of the motions of double stars, he would have seen that. But so to characterize Kepler's work is to betray total ignorance of it. Mill certainly never read the *De Motu [Motibus] Stellae Martis*, which is not easy reading. The reason it is not easy is that it calls for the most vigorous exercise of all the powers of reasoning from beginning to end.

What Kepler had given was a large collection of observations of the apparent places of Mars at different times. He also knew that, in a general way, the Ptolemaic theory agrees with the appearances, although there were various difficulties in making it fit exactly. He was furthermore convinced that the hypothesis of Copernicus ought to be accepted. Now this hypothesis, as Copernicus himself understood its first outline, merely modifies the theory of Ptolemy so far as [to] impart to all the bodies of the solar system one common motion, just what is required to annul the mean motion of the sun. It would seem, therefore, at first sight, that it ought not to affect the appearances at all. If Mill had called the work of Copernicus mere description he would not have been *so very far* from the truth as he was. But Kepler did not understand the matter quite as Copernicus did. Because the sun was so near the centre of the system, and was of vast size (even Kepler knew its diameter must be at least fifteen times that of the earth), Kepler, looking at the matter dynamically, thought it must have something to do with causing the planets to move in their orbits. This retroduction, vague as it was, cost great intellectual labour, and was most important in its bearings upon all. Kepler's work. Now Kepler remarked that the lines of apsides of the orbits of Mars and of the earth are not parallel; and he utilized various observations most ingeniously to infer that they probably intersected in the sun. Consequently, it must be supposed that a general description of the motion would be simpler when referred to the sun as a fixed point of reference than when referred to any other point. Thence it followed that the proper times at which to take the observations of Mars for determining its orbit were when it appeared just opposite the sun—the true sun—instead of when it was opposite the *mean* sun, as had been the practice. Carrying out this idea, he obtained a theory of Mars which satisfied the longitudes at all the oppositions observed by Tycho and himself, thirteen in number, to perfection. But unfortunately, it did not satisfy the latitudes at all and was totally irreconcilable with observations of Mars when far from opposition.

At each stage of his long investigation, Kepler has a theory which is approximately true, since it approximately satisfies the observations (that is, within 8', which is less than any but Tycho's observations could decisively pronounce an error), and he proceeds to modify this theory, after the most careful and judicious reflection, in such a way as to render it more rational or closer to the observed fact. Thus, having found that the centre of the orbit bisects the eccentricity, he finds in this an indication of the falsity of the theory of the equant and substitutes, for this artificial device, the principle of the equable description of areas. Subsequently, finding that the planet moves faster at ninety degrees from its apsides than it ought to do, the question is whether this is owing to an error in the law of areas or to a compression of the orbit. He ingeniously proves that the latter is the case.

Thus, never modifying his theory capriciously, but always with a sound and rational motive for just the modification he makes, it follows that when he finally reaches a modification—of most striking simplicity and rationality—which exactly satisfies the observations, it stands upon a totally different logical footing from what it would if it had been struck out at random, or the reader knows not how, and had been found to satisfy the observation. Kepler shows his keen logical sense in detailing the whole process by which he finally arrived at the true orbit.   This is the greatest piece of Retroductive reasoning ever performed.

III

Modern science has been builded after the model of Galileo, who founded it, on *il lume naturale*.   That truly inspired prophet had said that, of two hypotheses, the *simpler* is to be preferred; but I was formerly one of those who, in our dull self-conceit fancying ourselves more sly than he, twisted the maxim to mean the *logically* simpler, the one that adds the least to what has been observed, in spite of three obvious objections: first, that so there was no support for any hypothesis; secondly, that by the same token we ought to content ourselves with simply formulating the special observations actually made; and thirdly, that every advance of science that further opens the truth to our view discloses a world of unexpected complications.   It was not until long experience forced me to realize that subsequent discoveries were every time showing I had been wrong, while those who understood the maxim as Galileo had done, early unlocked the secret, that the scales fell from my eyes and my mind awoke to the broad and flaming daylight that it is the simpler Hypothesis in the sense of the more facile and natural, the one that instinct suggests, that must be preferred; for the reason that, unless man have a natural bent in accordance with nature's, he has no chance of understanding nature at all.

12

ON THE DOCTRINE OF CHANCES, WITH LATER
REFLECTIONS *

I

THE theory of probabilities is simply the science of logic quantita-
tively treated. There are two conceivable certainties with reference
to any hypothesis, the certainty of its truth and the certainty of its
falsity. The numbers *one* and *zero* are appropriated, in this calculus,
to marking these extremes of knowledge; while fractions having
values intermediate between them indicate, as we may vaguely say,
the degrees in which the evidence leans toward one or the other.
The general problem of probabilities is, from a given state of facts, to
determine the numerical probability of a possible fact. This is the
same as to inquire how much the given facts are worth, considered
as evidence to prove the possible fact. Thus the problem of probabilities is simply the general problem of logic.

Probability is a continuous quantity, so that great advantages
may be expected from this mode of studying logic. Some writers
have gone so far as to maintain that, by means of the calculus of
chances, every solid inference may be represented by legitimate
arithmetical operations upon the numbers given in the premisses.
If this be, indeed, true, the great problem of logic, how it is that the
observation of one fact can give us knowledge of another independent fact, is reduced to a mere question of arithmetic. It seems
proper to examine this pretension before undertaking any more
recondite solution of the paradox.

But, unfortunately, writers on probabilities are not agreed in
regard to this result. This branch of mathematics is the only one,
I believe, in which good writers frequently get results entirely
erroneous. In elementary geometry the reasoning is frequently
fallacious, but erroneous conclusions are avoided; but it may be
doubted if there is a single extensive treatise on probabilities in

* [The three selections in I are from "The Doctrine of Chances," the third
paper of a series (cf. ch. 2), *Popular Science Monthly* 1878 (*CP* 2.647-57, 658).
In II, the first selection is a note of 1910 on the preceding article (*CP* 2.661-8),
the second is from ms. c. 1905 (*CP* 2.758).]

existence which does not contain solutions absolutely indefensible. This is partly owing to the want of any regular method of procedure; for the subject involves too many subtilities to make it easy to put its problems into equations without such an aid. But, beyond this, the fundamental principles of its calculus are more or less in dispute. In regard to that class of questions to which it is chiefly applied for practical purposes, there is comparatively little doubt; but in regard to others to which it has been sought to extend it, opinion is somewhat unsettled.

This last class of difficulties can only be entirely overcome by making the idea of probability perfectly clear in our minds in the way set forth in our last paper.[9]

To get a clear idea of what we mean by probability, we have to consider what real and sensible difference there is between one degree of probability and another.

The character of probability belongs primarily, without doubt, to certain inferences. Locke explains it as follows: After remarking that the mathematician positively knows that the sum of the three angles of a triangle is equal to two right angles because he apprehends the geometrical proof, he thus continues: "But another man who never took the pains to observe the demonstration, hearing a mathematician, a man of credit, affirm the three angles of a triangle to be equal to two right ones, *assents* to it; *i.e.*, receives it for true. In which case the foundation of his assent is the probability of the thing, the proof being such as, for the most part, carries truth with it; the man on whose testimony he receives it not being wont to affirm anything contrary to, or besides his knowledge, especially in matters of this kind." The celebrated *Essay Concerning Humane Understanding* contains many passages which, like this one, make the first steps in profound analyses which are not further developed. It was shown in the first of these papers [1] that the validity of an inference does not depend on any tendency of the mind to accept it, however strong such tendency may be; but consists in the real fact that, when premises like those of the argument in question are true, conclusions related to them like that of this argument are also true. It was remarked that in a logical mind an argument is always conceived as a member of a *genus* of arguments all constructed in the same way, and such that, when their premises are real facts, their conclusions are so also. If the argument is demonstrative, then this is always so; if it is only probable, then it is for the most part so. As Locke says, the probable argument is "*such as* for the most part carries truth with it."

According to this, that real and sensible difference between one degree of probability and another, in which the meaning of the distinction lies, is that in the frequent employment of two different modes of inference, one will carry truth with it oftener than the other. It is evident that this is the only difference there is in the existing fact. Having certain premisses, a man draws a certain conclusion, and as far as this inference alone is concerned the only possible practical question is whether that conclusion is true or not, and between existence and non-existence there is no middle term. "Being only is and nothing is altogether not," said Parmenides; and this is in strict accordance with the analysis of the conception of reality given in the last paper.[9] For we found that the distinction of reality and fiction depends on the supposition that sufficient investigation would cause one opinion to be universally received and all others to be rejected. That presupposition, involved in the very conceptions of reality and figment, involves a complete sundering of the two. It is the heaven-and-hell idea in the domain of thought. But, in the long run, there is a real fact which corresponds to the idea of probability, and it is that a given mode of inference sometimes proves successful and sometimes not, and that in a ratio ultimately fixed. As we go on drawing inference after inference of the given kind, during the first ten or hundred cases the ratio of successes may be expected to show considerable fluctuations; but when we come into the thousands and millions, these fluctuations become less and less; and if we continue long enough, the ratio will approximate toward a fixed limit. We may, therefore, define the probability of a mode of argument as the proportion of cases in which it carries truth with it.

The inference from the premiss, A, to the conclusion, B, depends, as we have seen, on the guiding principle, that if a fact of the class A is true, a fact of the class B is true. The probability consists of the fraction whose numerator is the number of times in which both A and B are true, and whose denominator is the total number of times in which A is true, whether B is so or not. Instead of speaking of this as the probability of the inference, there is not the slightest objection to calling it the probability that, if A happens, B happens. But to speak of the probability of the event B, without naming the condition, really has no meaning at all. It is true that when it is perfectly obvious what condition is meant, the ellipsis may be permitted. But we should avoid contracting the habit of using language in this way (universal as the habit is), because it gives rise to a vague way of thinking, as if the action of causation might either determine an event to happen or determine it not to happen, or leave it more or less free to happen or not, so as to give rise to an *inherent* chance in regard to its occurrence. It is quite clear to me that some of the worst and most persistent errors in the use of the doctrine of chances have arisen from this vicious mode of expression.†

But there remains an important point to be cleared up. According to what has been said, the idea of probability essentially belongs to a kind of inference which is repeated indefinitely. An individual inference must be either true or false, and can show no effect of probability; and, therefore, in reference to a single case considered in itself, probability can have no meaning. Yet if a man had to choose between drawing a card from a pack containing twenty-five red cards and a black one, or from a pack containing twenty-five black cards and a red one, and if the drawing of a red card were destined to transport him to eternal felicity, and that of a black one to consign him to everlasting woe, it would be folly to deny that he ought to prefer the pack containing the larger proportion of red cards, although, from the nature of the risk, it could not be repeated. It is not easy to reconcile this with our analysis of the conception of chance. But suppose he should choose the red pack, and should draw the wrong card, what consolation would he have? He might say that he had acted in accordance with reason, but that would only show that his reason was absolutely worthless. And if he should choose the right card, how could he regard it as anything but a happy accident? He could not say that if he had drawn from the other pack, he might have drawn the wrong one, because an hypothetical proposition such as, "if A, then B," means nothing with reference to a single case. Truth consists in the existence of a real fact corresponding to the true proposition. Corresponding to the proposition, "if A, then B," there may be the fact that *whenever* such an event as A happens such an event as B happens. But in the case supposed, which has no parallel as far as this man is concerned, there would be no real fact whose existence could give any truth to the statement that, if he had drawn from the other pack, he might have drawn a black card. Indeed, since the validity of an inference consists in the truth of the hypothetical proposition that *if* the premises be true the conclusion will also be true, and since

† The conception of probability here set forth is substantially that first developed by Mr. Venn, in his *Logic of Chance*. Of course, a vague apprehension of the idea had always existed, but the problem was to make it perfectly clear, and to him belongs the credit of first doing this.

the only real fact which can correspond to such a proposition is that whenever the antecedent is true the consequent is so also, it follows that there can be no sense in reasoning in an isolated case, at all.

These considerations appear, at first sight, to dispose of the difficulty mentioned. Yet the case of the other side is not yet exhausted. Although probability will probably manifest its effect in, say, a thousand risks, by a certain proportion between the numbers of successes and failures, yet this, as we have seen, is only to say that it certainly will, at length, do so. Now the number of risks, the number of probable inferences, which a man draws in his whole life, is a finite one, and he cannot be absolutely *certain* that the mean result will accord with the probabilities at all. Taking all his risks collectively, then, it cannot be certain that they will not fail, and his case does not differ, except in degree, from the one last supposed. It is an indubitable result of the theory of probabilities that every gambler, if he continues long enough, must ultimately be ruined. Suppose he tries the martingale, which some believe infallible, and which is, as I am informed, disallowed in the gambling-houses. In this method of playing, he first bets say $1; if he loses it he bets $2; if he loses that he bets $4; if he loses that he bets $8; if he then gains he has lost 1+2+4=7, and he has gained $1 more; and no matter how many bets he loses, the first one he gains will make him $1 richer than he was in the beginning. In that way, he will probably gain at first; but, at last, the time will come when the run of luck is so against him that he will not have money enough to double, and must, therefore, let his bet go. This will *probably* happen before he has won as much as he had in the first place, so that this run against him will leave him poorer than he began; some time or other it will be sure to happen. It is true that there is always a possibility of his winning any sum the bank can pay, and we thus come upon a celebrated paradox that, though he is certain to be ruined, the value of his expectation calculated according to the usual rules (which omit this consideration) is large. But, whether a gambler plays in this way or any other, the same thing is true, namely, that if [he] plays long enough he will be sure some time to have such a run against him as to exhaust his entire fortune. The same thing is true of an insurance company. Let the directors take the utmost pains to be independent of great conflagrations and pestilences, their actuaries can tell them that, according to the doctrine of chances, the time must come, at last, when their losses will bring them to a stop. They may tide over such a crisis by extraordinary means, but then they will start again in a weakened state, and the same thing will happen again all the sooner. An actuary might be inclined to deny this, because he knows that the expectation of his company is large, or perhaps (neglecting the interest upon money) is infinite. But calculations of expectations leave out of account the circumstance now under consideration, which reverses the whole thing. However, I must not be understood as saying that insurance is on this account unsound, more than other kinds of business. All human affairs rest upon probabilities, and the same thing is true everywhere. If man were immortal he could be perfectly sure of seeing the day when everything in which he had trusted should betray his trust, and, in short, of coming eventually to hopeless misery. He would break down, at last, as every great fortune, as every dynasty, as every civilization does. In place of this we have death.

But what, without death, would happen to every man, with death must happen to some man. At the same time, death makes the number of our risks, of our inferences, finite, and so makes their mean result uncertain. The very idea of probability and of reasoning rests on the assumption that this number is indefinitely great. We are thus landed in the same difficulty as before, and I can see but one solution of it. It seems to me that we are driven to this, that logicality inexorably requires that our interests shall *not* be limited. They must not stop at our own fate, but must embrace the whole community. This community, again, must not be limited, but must extend to all races of beings with whom we can come into immediate or mediate intellectual relation. It must reach, however vaguely, beyond this geological epoch, beyond all bounds. He who would not sacrifice his own soul to save the whole world, is, as it seems to me, illogical in all his inferences, collectively. Logic is rooted in the social principle.

To be logical men should not be selfish; and, in point of fact, they are not so selfish as they are thought. The willful prosecution of one's desires is a different thing from selfishness. The miser is not selfish; his money does him no good, and he cares for what shall become of it after his death. We are constantly speaking of *our* possessions on the Pacific, and of *our* destiny as a republic, where no personal interests are involved, in a way which shows that we have wider ones. We discuss with anxiety the possible exhaustion of coal in some hundreds of years, or the cooling-off of the sun in some millions, and show in the most popular of all religious tenets that we can conceive the possibility of a man's descending into hell for the salvation of his fellows.

Now, it is not necessary for logicality that a man should himself be capable of the heroism of self-sacrifice. It is sufficient that he should recognize the possibility of it, should perceive that only that man's inferences who has it are really logical, and should consequently regard his own as being only so far valid as they would be accepted by the hero. So far as he thus refers his inferences to that standard, he becomes identified with such a mind.

This makes logicality attainable enough. Sometimes we can personally attain to heroism. The soldier who runs to scale a wall knows that he will probably be shot, but that is not all he cares for. He also knows that if all the regiment, with whom in feeling he identifies himself, rush forward at once, the fort will be taken. In other cases we can only imitate the virtue. The man whom we have supposed as having to draw from the two packs, who if he is not a logician will draw from the red pack from mere habit, will see, if he is logician enough, that he cannot be logical so long as he is concerned only with his own fate, but that that man who should care equally for what was to happen in all possible cases of the sort could act logically, and would draw from the pack with the most red cards, and thus, though incapable himself of such sublimity, our logician would imitate the effect of that man's courage in order to share his logicality.

But all this requires a conceived identification of one's interests with those of an unlimited community. Now, there exist no reasons, and a later discussion will show that there can be no reasons, for thinking that the human race, or any intellectual race, will exist forever. On the other hand, there can be no reason against it; and, fortunately, as the whole requirement is that we should have certain sentiments, there is nothing in the facts to forbid our having a *hope*, or calm and cheerful wish, that the community may last beyond any assignable date.

It may seem strange that I should put forward three sentiments, namely, interest in an indefinite community, recognition of the possibility of this interest being made supreme, and hope in the unlimited continuance of intellectual activity, as indispensable requirements of logic. Yet, when we consider that logic depends on a mere struggle to escape doubt, which, as it terminates in action, must begin in emotion, and that, furthermore, the only cause of our planting ourselves on reason is that other methods of escaping doubt fail on account of the social impulse, why should we wonder to find social sentiment presupposed in reasoning? As for the other two sentiments which I find necessary, they are so only as supports and accessories of that. It interests me to notice that these three sentiments seem to be pretty much the same as that famous trio of Charity, Faith, and Hope, which, in the estimation of St. Paul, are the finest and greatest of spiritual gifts. Neither Old nor New Testament is a textbook of the logic of science, but the latter is certainly the highest existing authority in regard to the dispositions of heart which a man ought to have.

Such average statistical numbers as the number of inhabitants per square mile, the average number of deaths per week, the number of convictions per indictment, or, generally speaking, the number of x's per y, where the x's are a class of things some or all of which are connected with another class of things, their y's, I term *relative numbers*. Of the two classes of things to which a relative number refers, that one of which it is a number may be called its *relate*, and that one *per* which the numeration is made may be called its *correlate*.

Probability is a kind of relative number; namely, it is the ratio of the number of arguments of a certain genus which carry truth with them to the total number of arguments of that genus, and the rules for the calculation of probabilities are very easily derived from this consideration.

To find the probability that from a given class of premisses, A, a given class of conclusions, B, follows, it is simply necessary to ascertain what proportion of the times in which premisses of that class are true, the appropriate conclusions are also true. In other words, it is the number of cases of the occurrence of both the events A and B, divided by the total number of cases of the occurrence of the event A.

II

On reperusing this article after the lapse of a full generation, it strikes me as making two points that were worth making. The better made of the two . . . is that no man can be logical whose supreme desire is the well-being of himself or of any other existing person or collection of persons. The other good point is that probability never properly refers immediately to a single event, but exclusively to the happening of a given kind of event on any occasion of a given kind. So far all is well. But when I come to define probability, I repeatedly say that it is the quotient of the *number* of occurrences of the event divided by the *number* of occurrences of the occasion. Now this is manifestly wrong, for probability relates to the future; and how can I say how many times a given die will be thrown in the future? To be sure I might, immediately after my throw, put the die in strong nitric acid, and dissolve it, but this suggestion only puts the preposterous character of the definition in a still stronger light. For it is plain that, if probability be the ratio of the occurrences of the specific event to the occurrences of the generic occasion, it is the ratio that there *would be* in the long run, and has nothing to do with any supposed cessation of the occasions. This long run can be nothing but an endlessly long run; and even if it be correct to speak of an infinite "number," yet $\frac{\infty}{\infty}$ (infinity divided by infinity) has certainly, *in itself*, no definite value.

But we have not yet come to the end of the flaws in the definition, since no notice whatever has been taken of two conditions which require the strictest precautions in all experiments to determine the probability of a specific event on a generic occasion. Namely, in the first place we must limit our endeavours strictly to counting occurrences of the right genus of occasion and carefully resist all other motives for counting them, and strive to take them just as they would ordinarily occur. In the next place, it must be known that the occurrence of the specific event on one occasion will have no tendency to produce or to prevent the occurrence of the same event upon any other of the occurrences of the generic occasion. In the third place, after the probability has been ascertained, we must remember that this probability cannot be relied upon at any future time unless we have adequate grounds for believing that it has not too much changed in the interval.

I will now give over jeering at my former inaccuracies, committed when I had been a student of logic for only about a quarter of a century, and was naturally not so well-versed in it as now, and will proceed to define probability. I must premiss that we, all of us, use this word with a degree of laxity which corrupts and rots our reasoning to a degree that very few of us are at all awake to. When I say our "reasoning," I mean not formal reasonings only but our thoughts in general, so far as they are concerned with any of those approaches toward knowledge which we confound with probability. The result is that we not only fall into the falsest ways of thinking, but, what is often still worse, we give up sundry problems as beyond our powers—problems of gravest concern, too—when, in fact, we should find they were not a bit so, if we only rightly discriminated between the different kinds of imperfection of certitude, and if we had only once acquainted ourselves with their different natures. I shall in these notes endeavour to mark the three ways of falling short of certainty by the three terms *probability, verisimilitude* or *likelihood,* and *plausibility.* Just at present I propose to deal only with Probability; but I will so far characterize *verisimilitude* and *plausibility* as to mark them off as being entirely different from Probability. Beginning with Plausibility, I will first endeavour to give an example of an idea which shall be strikingly marked by its very low degree of this quality. Suppose a particularly symmetrical larch tree near the house of a great lover of such trees had been struck by lightning and badly broken, and that as he was looking sorrowfully out of the window at it, he should have happened to say, "I wonder why that particular tree should have been struck, when there are so many about the place that seem more exposed!" Suppose, then, his wife should reply, "Perhaps there may be an eagle's eyrie on some of the hills in the neighbourhood, and perhaps the male bird in building it may have used some stick that had a nail in it; and one of the eaglets may have scratched itself against the nail; so that the mother may have reproached the male for using such a dangerous stick; and he, being vexed with her teasing, may have determined to carry the piece to a great distance; it may have been while he was doing this that the explosion of lightning took place, and the electricity may have been deflected by the iron in such a way as to strike this tree. Mind, I do not say that this is what did happen; but if you want to find out why that tree was struck, I think you had better search for an eyrie, and see whether any of the eaglets have been scratched." This is an example of as unplausible a theory as I can think of. We should commonly say it was highly improbable; and I suppose it would be so. But were it ever so probable in all its elements, it would still deserve no attention, because it is perfectly gratuitous to suppose that the lightning was deflected at all; and this supposition does not help to explain the phenomenon.

Eusapia Palladino had been proved to be a very clever prestigiateuse and cheat, and was visited by a Mr. Carrington, whom I suppose to be so clever in finding out how tricks are done, that it is highly improbable that any given trick should long baffle him. In point of fact he has often caught the Palladino creature in acts of fraud. Some of her performances, however, he cannot explain; and thereupon he urges the theory that these are supernatural, or, as he prefers to phrase it, "supernormal." Well, I know how it is that when a man has been long intensely exercised and overfatigued by an enigma, his common-sense will sometimes desert him; but it seems to me that the Palladino has simply been too clever for him, as no doubt she would be for me. The theory that there is anything "supernormal," or *super* anything but *superchérie* in the case, seems to me as needless as any theory I ever came across. That is to say, granted that it is not yet *proved* that women who deceive for gain receive aid from the spiritual world, I think it more plausible that there are tricks that can deceive Mr. Carrington than that the Palladino woman has received such aid. By Plausible, I mean that a theory that has not yet been subjected to any test, although more or less surprising phenomena have occurred which it would explain if it were true, is in itself of such a character as to recommend it for further examination or, if it be *highly* plausible, justify us in seriously inclining toward belief in it, as long as the phenomena be inexplicable otherwise.

I will now give an idea of what I mean by *likely* or *verisimilar*. It is to be understood that I am only endeavouring so far to explain the meanings I attach to "plausible" and to "likely," as this may be an assistance to the reader in understanding the meaning I attach to *probable*. I call that theory *likely* which is not yet proved but is supported by such evidence that if the rest of the conceivably possible evidence should turn out upon examination to be of a *similar* character, the theory would be conclusively proved. Strictly speaking, matters of fact never can be demonstrably proved, since it will always remain conceivable that there should be some mistake about it. For instance, I regard it as *sufficiently* proved that my name is Charles Peirce and that I was born in Cambridge, Massachusetts, in a stone-coloured wooden house in Mason Street. But even of the part of this of which I am most assured—of my name—there is a certain small probability that I am in an abnormal condition and have got it wrong. I am conscious myself of occasional lapses of memory about other things; and though I well remember —or think I do—living in that house at a tender age, I do not in the least remember being born there, impressive as such a first experience might be expected to be. Indeed, I cannot specify any date on which any certain person informed me I had been born there; and it certainly would have been easy to deceive me in the matter had there been any serious reason for doing so; and how can I be so sure as I surely am that no such reason did exist? It would be a theory without plausibility; that is all.

The history of science, particularly physical science, in contradistinction to natural science—or, as I usually, though inadequately, phrase the distinction, the history of nomological in contradistinction to classificatory sciences—this history ever since I first seriously set myself, at the age of thirteen, in 1852, to the study of logic, shows only too grievously how great a boon would be any way [of] determining and expressing by numbers the degree of likelihood that a theory had attained—any general recognition, even among leading men of science, of the true degree of significance of a given fact, and of the proper method of determining it. I hope my writings may, at any rate, awaken a few to the enormous waste of effort it would save. But any numerical determination of likelihood is more than I can expect.

The only kind of reasoning which can render our conclusions certain—and even this kind can do so only under the proviso that no blunder has been committed in the process—attains this certainty by limiting the conclusion (as Kant virtually said, and others before him), to facts already expressed and accepted in the premisses. This is called necessary, or syllogistic reasoning. Syllogism, not confined to the kind that Aristotle and Theophrastus studied, is merely an artificial form in which it may be expressed, and it is not its best form, from any point of view. But the kind of reasoning which creates likelihoods by virtue of observations may render a likelihood *practically* certain—as certain as that a stone let loose from the clutch will, under circumstances not obviously exceptional, fall to the ground—and this conclusion may be that under a certain general condition, easily verified, a certain actuality will be *probable*, that is to say, will come to pass once in so often in the long run. One such familiar conclusion, for example, is that a die thrown from a dice box will with a *probability* of one-third, that is, once in three times in the long run, turn up a number (either *tray* or *size*) that is divisible by three. But this can be affirmed with practical certainty only if by a "long run" be meant an endless series of trials, and (as just said) infinity divided by infinity gives of itself an entirely indefinite quotient. It is therefore necessary to define the phrase. I might give the definition with reference to the probability, p, where p is any vulgar fraction, and in reference to a generic condition, m, and a specific kind of event n. But I think the reader will follow me more readily, if in place of the letter, m (which in itself is but a certain letter, to which is attached a peculiar meaning, that of the fulfillment of some generic condition) I put instead the supposition that a die is thrown from a dice box; and this special supposition will be as readily understood by the reader to be replaceable by any other general condition along with a simultaneous replacement of the *event*, that a number divisible by three is turned up, and at the same time with the replacement of one-third by whatever other vulgar fraction may be called for when some different example of a probability is before us. I am, then, to define the meanings of the statement that the *probability*, that if a die be thrown from a dice box it will turn up a number divisible by three, is one-third. The statement means that the die has a certain "would-be"; and to say that a die has a "would-be" is to say that it has a property, quite analogous to any *habit* that a man might have. Only the "would-be" of the die is presumably as much simpler and more definite than the man's habit as the die's homogeneous composition and cubical shape is simpler than the nature of the man's nervous system and soul; and just as it would be necessary, in order to define a man's habit, to describe how it would lead him to behave and upon what sort of occasion—albeit this statement would by no means imply that the habit *consists* in that action—so to define the die's "would-be," it is necessary to say how it would lead the die to behave on an occasion that would bring out the full consequence of the "would be"; and this statement will not of itself imply that the "would-be" of the die *consists* in such behaviour.

Now in order that the full effect of the die's "would-be" may find expression, it is necessary that the die should undergo an endless series of throws from the dice box, the result of no throw having the slightest influence upon the result of any other throw, or, as we express it, the throws must be *independent* each of every other.

It will be no objection to our considering the consequences of the supposition that the die is thrown an endless succession of times, and that with a finite pause after each throw, that such an endless series of events is impossible, for the reason that the impossibility is merely a physical, and not a logical, impossibility, as was well illustrated in that famous sporting event in which Achilles succeeded in overtaking the champion tortoise, in spite of his giving the latter the start of a whole *stadion*. For it having been ascertained, by delicate measurements between a mathematical point between the shoulder-blades of Achilles (marked [by] a limit between a red, a green, and a violet sector of a stained disk) and a similar point on the carapace of the tortoise, that when Achilles arrived where the tortoise started, the latter was just 60 feet 8 inches and $\frac{1}{10}$ inch further on, which is just one-tenth of a stadion, and that when Achilles reached that point the tortoise was still 6 feet and $8\frac{1}{100}$

inch in advance of him, and finally that, both advancing at a perfectly uniform rate, the tortoise had run just 67 feet 5 inches when he was overtaken by Achilles, it follows that the tortoise progressed at just one-tenth the speed of Achilles, the latter running a distance in *stadia* of 1·11111111, so that he had to traverse the sum of an infinite multitude of finite distances, each in a finite time, and yet covered the *stadion* and one-ninth in a finite time. No contradiction, therefore, is involved in the idea of an endless series of finite times or spaces having but a finite sum, provided there is no *fixed* finite quality which every member of an endless part of that series must each and every one *exceed*.

The reader must pardon me for occupying any of his time with such puerile stuff as that $0·1111=\frac{1}{9}$; for astounding as it seems, it has more than once happened to me that men have come to me—every one of them not merely educated men, but highly accomplished —men who might well enough be famous over the civilized world, if fame were anything to the purpose, but men whose studies had been such that one would have expected to find each of them an adept in the accurate statement of arguments, and yet each has come and has undertaken to prove to me that the old catch of Achilles and the tortoise is a sound argument. If I tell you what after listening to them by the hour, I have always ended by saying —it may serve your turn on a similar occasion—I have said, "I suppose you do not mean to say that you really believe that a fast runner cannot, as a matter of fact, overtake a slow one. I therefore conclude that the argument which you have been unable to state, either syllogistically or in any other intelligible form, is intended to show that Zeno's reasoning about Achilles and the tortoise is sound according to some system of logic which admits that sound necessary reasoning may lead from true premisses to a false conclusion. But in my system of logic what I mean by bad necessary reasoning is precisely an argument which might lead from true premisses to a false conclusion—just that and nothing else. If you prefer to call such reasoning a sound necessary argument, I have no objection in the world to your doing so; and you will kindly allow me to employ my different nomenclature. For I am such a plain, un-cultured soul that when I reason I aim at nothing else than just to find out the truth." To get back, then, to the die and its habit— its "would-be"—I really know no other way of defining a habit than by describing the kind of behaviour in which the habit becomes actualized. So I am obliged to define the statement that there is a probability of one-third that the die when thrown will turn up either a three or a six by stating how the numbers will run when the die is thrown.

But my purpose in doing so is to explain what *probability*, as I use the word, consists in. Now it would be no explanation at all to say that it consists in something being *probable*. So I must avoid using that word or any synonym of it. If I were to use such an expression, you would very properly turn upon me and say, "I either know what it is to be *probable*, in your sense of the term, or I do not. If I don't, how can I be expected to understand you until you have explained yourself; and if I do, what is the use of the explanation?" But the fact [is] that the probability of the die turning up a three or a six is not *sure* to produce any determination [of] the run of the numbers thrown in any *finite* series of throws. It is only when the series is endless that we can be *sure* that it will have a particular character. Even when there is an endless series of throws, there is no syllogistic certainty, no "mathematical" certainty (if you are more familiar with this latter phrase)—that the die will not turn up a six obstinately at every single throw. It might be that if in the course of the endless series, some friends should borrow the die to make a pair for a game of backgammon, there might be nothing unusual in the behaviour of the lent die, and yet when it was returned and our experimental series was resumed where it had been interrupted, the die might return to turning up nothing but six every time. I say it *might*, in the sense that it would not violate the principle of contradiction if it did. It sanely *would not*, however, unless a miracle were performed; and moreover if such miracle *were* worked, I should say (since it is my use of the term "probability" that we have supposed to be in question) that during this experimental series of throws, the die took on an abnormal, a miraculous, habit. For I should think that the performance of a certain line of behaviour, throughout an endless succession of occasions, without exception, very decidedly *constituted* a habit. There may be some doubt about this, for owing to our not being accustomed to reason in this way about successions of events which are endless *in the sequence* and yet are completed *in time*, it is hard for me quite to satisfy myself what I ought to say in such a case. But I have reflected seriously on it, and though I am not perfectly sure of my ground (and I am a cautious reasoner), yet I am more than what you would understand by "pretty confident," that supposing one to be in a condition to assert what *would surely be* the behaviour, *in any single determinate respect*, of any subject throughout an endless series of occasions of a stated kind, he *ipso facto* knows a "would-be," or habit, of that subject. It is very true, mind you, that *no* collection whatever of single acts, though it were ever so many grades greater than a simple endless series, can constitute a would-be, nor can the knowledge of single acts, whatever their multitude, tell us for *sure* of a would-be. But there are two remarks to be made; first, that in the case under consideration a person is supposed to be in a condition to assert what surely *would be* the behaviour of the subject throughout the endless series of occasions—a knowledge which cannot have been derived from reasoning from its behaviour on the single occasions; and second, that that which in our case renders it true, as stated, that the person supposed "*ipso facto* knows a would-be of that subject," is not the occurrence of the single acts, but the fact that the person supposed "was in condition to assert what *would surely be* the behaviour of the subject throughout an endless series of occasions."

I will now describe the behaviour of the die during the endless series of throws, in respect to turning up numbers divisible by three. It would be perfectly possible to construct a machine that would automatically throw the die and pick it up, and continue doing so as long as it was supplied with energy. It would further be still easier to design the plan of an arrangement whereby a hand should after each throw move over an arc graduated so as to indicate the value of the quotient of the number of throws of three or six that had been known since the beginning of the experiment, divided by the total number of throws since the beginning. It is true that the mechanical difficulties would become quite insuperable before the die had been thrown many times; but fortunately a general description of the way the hand would move will answer our purpose much better than would the actual machine, were it ever so perfect.

After the first throw, the hand will go either to $0=\frac{0}{1}$ or $1=\frac{1}{1}$; and there it may stay for several throws. But when it once moves, it will move after every throw, without exception, since the denominator of the fraction at whose value it points will always increase by 1, and consequently the value of the fraction will be diminished if the numerator remains unchanged, as it will be increased in case the numerator is increased by 1, these two being the only possible cases. The behaviour of the hand may be described as an excessively irregular oscillation, back and forth, from one side of $\frac{1}{3}$ to the other. . . .

. . . When we say that a certain ratio will have a certain value in "the long run," we refer to the *probability-limit* of an endless succession of fractional values; that is, to the only possible value from 0 to ∞, inclusive, about which the values of the endless succession will never cease to oscillate; so that, no matter what place in the succession you may choose, there will follow both values above the probability-limit and values below it; while if V be any *other* possible value from 0 to ∞, but *not* the probability-limit there will be some place in the succession beyond which all the values of the succession will agree, either in all being greater than V, or else in all being less.

13

THE PROBABILITY OF INDUCTION *

WE have found [10] that every argument derives its force from the general truth of the class of inferences to which it belongs; and that probability is the proportion of arguments carrying truth with them among those of any *genus*. This is most conveniently expressed in the nomenclature of the medieval logicians. They called the fact expressed by a premiss an *antecedent*, and that which follows from it its *consequent*; while the leading principle, that every (or almost every) such antecedent is followed by such a consequent, they termed the *consequence*. Using this language, we may say that probability belongs exclusively to *consequences*, and the probability of any consequence is the number of times in which antecedent and consequent both occur divided by the number of all the times in which the antecedent occurs. From this definition are deduced the following rules for the addition and multiplication of probabilities:

Rule for the Addition of Probabilities.—Given the separate probabilities of two consequences having the same antecedent and incompatible consequents. Then the sum of these two numbers is the probability of the consequence, that from the same antecedent one or other of those consequents follows.

Rule for the Multiplication of Probabilities.—Given the separate probabilities of the two consequences, "If A, then B," and "If both A and B, then C." Then the product of these two numbers is the probability of the consequence, "If A, then both B and C."

Special Rule for the Multiplication of Independent Probabilities.—Given the separate probabilities of two consequences having the same antecedents, "If A, then B," and "If A, then C." Suppose that these consequences are such that the probability of the second is equal to the probability of the consequence, "If both A and B, then C." Then the product of the two given numbers is equal to the probability of the consequence, "If A, then both B and C."

To show the working of these rules we may examine the prob-

* [This chapter, with Peirce's title, is the entire fourth paper of a series (cf. ch. 2), *Popular Science Monthly* 1878 (*CP* 2.669-93).]

abilities in regard to throwing dice. What is the probability of throwing a six with one die? The antecedent here is the event of throwing a die; the consequent, its turning up a six. As the die has six sides, all of which are turned up with equal frequency, the probability of turning up any one is $\frac{1}{6}$. Suppose two dice are thrown, what is the probability of throwing sixes? The probability of either coming up six is obviously the same when both are thrown as when one is thrown—namely, $\frac{1}{6}$. The probability that either will come up six when the other does is also the same as that of its coming up six whether the other does or not. The probabilities are, therefore, independent; and, by our rule, the probability that both events will happen together is the product of their several probabilities, or $\frac{1}{6} \times \frac{1}{6}$. What is the probability of throwing deuce-ace? The probability that the first die will turn up ace and the second deuce is the same as the probability that both will turn up sixes—namely, $\frac{1}{36}$; the probability that the *second* will turn up ace and the *first* deuce is likewise $\frac{1}{36}$; these two events—first, ace; second, deuce; and, second, ace; first, deuce—are incompatible. Hence the rule for addition holds, and the probability that either will come up ace and the other deuce is $\frac{1}{36} + \frac{1}{36}$, or $\frac{1}{18}$.

In this way all problems about dice, etc., may be solved. When the number of dice thrown is supposed very large, mathematics (which may be defined as the art of making groups to facilitate numeration) comes to our aid with certain devices to reduce the difficulties.

The conception of probability as a matter of *fact*, *i.e.*, as the proportion of times in which an occurrence of one kind is accompanied by an occurrence of another kind, is termed by Mr. Venn the materialistic view of the subject. But probability has often been regarded as being simply the degree of belief which ought to attach to a proposition; and this mode of explaining the idea is termed by Venn the conceptualistic view. Most writers have mixed the two conceptions together. They, first, define the probability of an event as the reason we have to believe that it has taken place, which is conceptualistic; but shortly after they state that it is the ratio of the number of cases favourable to the event to the total number of cases favourable or contrary, and all equally possible. Except that this introduces the thoroughly unclear idea of cases equally possible in place of cases equally frequent, this is a tolerable statement of the materialistic view. The pure conceptualistic theory has been best expounded by Mr. De Morgan in his *Formal Logic : or, the Calculus of Inference, Necessary and Probable.*

The great difference between the two analyses is, that the conceptualists refer probability to an event, while the materialists make it the ratio of frequency of events of a *species* to those of a *genus* over that *species*, thus *giving it two terms instead of one*. The opposition may be made to appear as follows:

Suppose that we have two rules of inference, such that, of all the questions to the solution of which both can be applied, the first yields correct answers to $\frac{81}{100}$, and incorrect answers to the remaining $\frac{19}{100}$; while the second yields correct answers to $\frac{93}{100}$, and incorrect answers to the remaining $\frac{7}{100}$. Suppose, further, that the two rules are entirely independent as to their truth, so that the second answers correctly $\frac{93}{100}$ of the questions which the first answers correctly, and also $\frac{93}{100}$ of the questions which the first answers incorrectly, and answers incorrectly the remaining $\frac{7}{100}$ of the questions which the first answers correctly, and also the remaining $\frac{7}{100}$ of the questions which the first answers incorrectly. Then, of all the questions to the solution of which both rules can be applied—

both answer correctly . . . . $\frac{93}{100}$ of $\frac{81}{100}$, or $\frac{93 \times 81}{100 \times 100}$;

the second answers correctly and the first incorrectly $\frac{93}{100}$ of $\frac{19}{100}$, or $\frac{93 \times 19}{100 \times 100}$;

the second answers incorrectly and the first correctly $\frac{7}{100}$ of $\frac{81}{100}$, or $\frac{7 \times 81}{100 \times 100}$;

and both answer incorrectly . . . $\frac{7}{100}$ of $\frac{19}{100}$, or $\frac{7 \times 19}{100 \times 100}$;

Suppose, now, that, in reference to any question, both give the same answer. Then (the questions being always such as are to be answered by *yes* or *no*), those in reference to which their answers agree are the same as those which both answer correctly together with those which both answer falsely, or

$$\frac{93 \times 81}{100 \times 100} + \frac{7 \times 19}{100 \times 100}$$

of all. The proportion of those which both answer correctly out of those their answers to which agree is, therefore—

$$\frac{\frac{93 \times 81}{100 \times 100}}{\frac{93 \times 81}{100 \times 100} + \frac{7 \times 19}{100 \times 100}} \text{ or } \frac{93 \times 81}{(93 \times 81) + (7 \times 19)}.$$

This is, therefore, the probability that, if both modes of inference yield the same result, that result is correct. We may here conveniently make use of another mode of expression. *Probability* is the ratio of the favourable cases to all the cases. Instead of expressing our result in terms of this ratio, we may make use of another—the ratio of favourable to unfavourable cases. This last ratio may be called the *chance* of an event. Then the chance of a true answer by the first mode of inference is $\frac{81}{19}$ and by the second is $\frac{93}{7}$; and the chance of a correct answer from both, when they agree, is—

$$\frac{81 \times 93}{19 \times 7} \text{ or } \frac{81}{19} \times \frac{93}{7},$$

or the product of the chances of each singly yielding a true answer.

It will be seen that a chance is a quantity which may have any magnitude, however great. An event in whose favour there is an even chance, or $\frac{1}{1}$, has a probability of $\frac{1}{2}$. An argument having an even chance can do nothing toward reënforcing others, since according to the rule its combination with another would only multiply the chance of the latter by 1.

Probability and chance undoubtedly belong primarily to consequences, and are relative to premises; but we may, nevertheless, speak of the chance of an event absolutely, meaning by that the chance of the combination of all arguments in reference to it which exist for us in the given state of our knowledge. Taken in this sense it is incontestable that the chance of an event has an intimate connection with the degree of our belief in it. Belief is certainly something more than a mere feeling; yet there is a feeling of believing, and this feeling does and ought to vary with the chance of the thing believed, as deduced from all the arguments. Any quantity which varies with the chance might, therefore, it would seem, serve as a thermometer for the proper intensity of belief. Among all such quantities there is one which is peculiarly appropriate. When there is a very great chance, the feeling of belief ought to be very intense. Absolute certainty, or an infinite chance, can never be attained by mortals, and this may be represented appropriately by an infinite belief. As the chance diminishes the feeling of believing should diminish, until an even chance is reached, where it should completely vanish and not incline either toward or away from the proposition. When the chance becomes less, then a contrary belief should spring up and should increase in intensity as the chance diminishes, and as the chance almost vanishes (which it can never quite do) the contrary belief should tend toward an infinite intensity. Now, there is one quantity which, more simply than any other, fulfills these conditions; it is the *logarithm* of the chance. But there is another consideration which must, if admitted, fix us to this choice for our thermometer. It is that our belief ought to be proportional to the weight of evidence, in this sense, that two arguments which are entirely independent, neither weakening nor strengthening each other, ought, when they concur, to produce a belief equal to the sum of the intensities of belief which either would produce separately. Now, we have seen that the chances of independent concurrent arguments are to be multiplied together to get the chance of their combination, and therefore the quantities which best express the intensities of belief should be such that they are to be *added* when the *chances* are multiplied in order to produce the quantity which corresponds to the combined chance. Now, the logarithm is the only quantity which fulfills this condition. There is a general law of sensibility, called Fechner's psycho-physical law. It is that the intensity of any sensation is proportional to the logarithm of the external force which produces it. It is entirely in harmony with this law that the feeling of belief should be as the logarithm of the chance, this latter being the expression of the state of facts which produces the belief.

The rule for the combination of independent concurrent arguments takes a very simple form when expressed in terms of the intensity of belief, measured in the proposed way. It is this: Take the sum of all the feelings of belief which would be produced separately by all the arguments *pro*, subtract from that the similar sum for arguments *con*, and the remainder is the feeling of belief which we ought to have on the whole. This is a proceeding which men often resort to, under the name of *balancing reasons*.

These considerations constitute an argument in favour of the conceptualistic view. The kernel of it is that the conjoint probability of all the arguments in our possession, with reference to any fact, must be intimately connected with the just degree of our belief in that fact; and this point is supplemented by various others showing the consistency of the theory with itself and with the rest of our knowledge.

But probability, to have any value at all, must express a fact. It is, therefore, a thing to be inferred upon evidence. Let us, then, consider for a moment the formation of a belief of probability. Suppose we have a large bag of beans from which one has been secretly taken at random and hidden under a thimble. We are now to form a probable judgment of the colour of that bean, by drawing others singly from the bag and looking at them, each one to be thrown back, and the whole well mixed up after each drawing. Suppose the first drawing is white and the next black. We conclude that there is not an immense preponderance of either colour, and that there is something like an even chance that the bean under the thimble is black. But this judgment may be altered by the next few drawings. When we have drawn ten times, if 4, 5, or 6, are white, we have more confidence that the chance is even. When we have drawn a thousand times, if about half have been white, we have great confidence in this result. We now feel pretty sure that, if we were to make a large number of bets upon the colour of single beans drawn from the bag, we could approximately insure ourselves in the long run by betting each time upon the white, a confidence which would be entirely wanting if, instead of sampling the bag by 1,000 drawings, we had done so by only two. Now, as the whole utility of probability is to insure us in the long run, and as that assurance depends, not merely on the value of the chance, but also on the accuracy of the evaluation, it follows that we ought not to have the same feeling of belief in reference to all events of which the chance is even. In short, to express the proper state of our belief, not *one* number but *two* are requisite, the first depending on the inferred probability, the second on the amount of knowledge on which that probability is based. It is true that when our knowledge is very precise, when we have made many drawings from the bag, or, as in most of the examples in the books, when the total contents of the bag are absolutely known, the number which expresses the uncertainty of the assumed probability and its liability to be changed by further experience may become insignificant, or utterly vanish. But, when our knowledge is very slight, this number may be even more important than the probability itself; and when we have no knowledge at all this completely overwhelms the other, so that there is no sense in saying that the chance of the totally unknown event is even (for what expresses absolutely no fact has absolutely no meaning), and what ought to be said is that the chance is entirely indefinite. We thus perceive that the conceptualistic view, though answering well enough in some cases, is quite inadequate.

Suppose that the first bean which we drew from our bag were black. That would constitute an argument, no matter how slender, that the bean under the thimble was also black. If the second bean were also to turn out black, that would be a second independent argument reënforcing the first. If the whole of the first twenty beans drawn should prove black, our confidence that the hidden bean was black would justly attain considerable strength. But suppose the twenty-first bean were to be white and that we were to go on drawing until we found that we had drawn 1,010 black beans and 990 white ones. We should conclude that our first twenty beans being black was simply an extraordinary accident, and that in fact the proportion of white beans to black was sensibly equal, and that it was an even chance that the hidden bean was black. Yet according to the rule of *balancing reasons*, since all the drawings of black beans are so many independent arguments in favour of the one under the thimble being black, and all the white drawings so many against it, an excess of twenty black beans ought to produce the same degree of belief that the hidden bean was black, whatever the total number drawn.

In the conceptualistic view of probability, complete ignorance, where the judgment ought not to swerve either toward or away from the hypothesis, is represented by the probability $\frac{1}{2}$.

But let us suppose that we are totally ignorant what coloured hair the inhabitants of Saturn have. Let us, then, take a colour-chart in which all possible colours are shown shading into one another by imperceptible degrees. In such a chart the relative areas occupied by different classes of colours are perfectly arbitrary. Let us inclose such an area with a closed line, and ask what is the chance on conceptualistic principles that the colour of the hair of the inhabitants of Saturn falls within that area? The answer cannot be indeterminate because we must be in some state of belief; and, indeed, conceptualistic writers do not admit indeterminate prob-abilities. As there is no certainty in the matter, the answer lies between *zero* and *unity*. As no numerical value is afforded by the data, the number must be determined by the nature of the scale of probability itself, and not by calculation from the data. The answer can, therefore, only be one-half, since the judgment should neither favour nor oppose the hypothesis. What is true of this area is true of any other one; and it will equally be true of a third area which embraces the other two. But the probability for each of the smaller areas being one-half, that for the larger should be at least unity, which is absurd.

All our reasonings are of two kinds: 1. *Explicative, analytic*, or *deductive* ; 2. *Amplifiative, synthetic*, or (loosely speaking) *inductive*. In explicative reasoning, certain facts are first laid down in the premisses. These facts are, in every case, an inexhaustible multi-tude, but they may often be summed up in one simple proposition by means of some regularity which runs through them all. Thus, take the proposition that Socrates was a man; this implies (to go no further) that during every fraction of a second of his whole life (or, if you please, during the greater part of them) he was a man. He did not at one instant appear as a tree and at another as a dog; he did not flow into water, or appear in two places at once; you could not put your finger through him as if he were an optical image, etc. Now, the facts being thus laid down, some order among some of them, not particularly made use of for the purpose of stating them, may perhaps be discovered; and this will enable us to throw part or all of them into a new statement, the possibility of which might have escaped attention. Such a statement will be the conclusion of an analytic inference. Of this sort are all mathematical demonstrations. But synthetic reasoning is of another kind. In this case the facts summed up in the conclusion are not among those stated in the premises. They are different facts, as when one sees that the tide rises m times and concludes that it will rise the next time. These are the only inferences which increase our real knowledge, however useful the others may be.

In any problem in probabilities, we have given the relative frequency of certain events, and we perceive that in these facts the relative frequency of another event is given in a hidden way. This being stated makes the solution. This is therefore mere explicative reasoning, and is evidently entirely inadequate to the representation of synthetic reasoning, which goes out beyond the facts given in the premises. There is, therefore, a manifest impossibility in so tracing out any probability for a synthetic conclusion.

Most treatises on probability contain a very different doctrine. They state, for example, that if one of the ancient denizens of the shores of the Mediterranean, who had never heard of tides, had gone to the bay of Biscay, and had there seen the tide rise, say m times, he could know that there was a probability equal to

$$\frac{m+1}{m+2}$$

that it would rise the next time. In a well-known work by Quetelet, much stress is laid on this, and it is made the foundation of a theory of inductive reasoning.

But this solution betrays its origin if we apply it to the case in which the man has never seen the tide rise at all; that is, if we put $m=0$. In this case, the probability that it will rise the next time comes out $\frac{1}{2}$, or, in other words, the solution involves the conceptualistic principle that there is an even chance of a totally unknown event. The manner in which it has been reached has been by considering a number of urns all containing the same number of balls, part white and part black. One urn contains all white balls, another one black and the rest white, a third two black and the rest white, and so on, one urn for each proportion, until an urn is reached containing only black balls. But the only possible reason for drawing any analogy between such an arrangement and that of Nature is the principle that alternatives of which we know nothing must be considered as equally probable. But this principle is absurd. There is an indefinite variety of ways of enumerating the different possibilities, which, on the application of this principle, would give different results. If there be any way of enumerating the possibilities so as to make them all equal, it is not that from which this solution is derived, but is the following: Suppose we had an immense granary filled with black and white balls well mixed up; and suppose each urn were filled by taking a fixed number of balls from this granary quite at random. The relative number of white balls in the granary might be anything, say one in three. Then in one-third of the urns the first ball would be white, and in two-thirds black. In one-third of those urns of which the first ball was white, and also in one-third of those in which the first ball was black, the second ball would be white. In this way, we should have a distribution like that shown in the following table, where w stands for a white ball and b for a black one. The reader can, if he chooses, verify the table for himself.

wwww.

| wwwb. | wwbw. | wbww. | bwww. |
| wwwb. | wwbw. | wbww. | bwww. |

wwbb.	wbwb.	bwwb.	wbbw.	bwbw.	bbww.
wwbb.	wbwb.	bwwb.	wbbw.	bwbw.	bbww.
wwbb.	wbwb.	bwwb.	wbbw.	bwbw.	bbww.
wwbb.	wbwb.	bwwb.	wbbw.	bwbw.	bbww.

wbbb.	bwbb.	bbwb.	bbbw.
wbbb.	bwbb.	bbwb.	bbbw.
wbbb.	bwbb.	bbwb.	bbbw.
wbbb.	bwbb.	bbwb.	bbbw.
wbbb.	bwbb.	bbwb.	bbbw.
wbbb.	bwbb.	bbwb.	bbbw.
wbbb.	bwbb.	bbwb.	bbbw.
wbbb.	bwbb.	bbwb.	bbbw.

bbbb. In the second group, where there is one b, there are two
bbbb. sets just alike; in the third there are 4, in the fourth 8, and
bbbb. in the fifth 16, doubling every time. This is because we
bbbb. have supposed twice as many black balls in the granary as
bbbb. white ones; had we supposed 10 times as many, instead of
bbbb.
bbbb.   1, 2, 4, 8, ᛚ 16
bbbb.
bbbb. sets we should have had
bbbb.
bbbb.   1, 10, 100, 1000, 10000
bbbb.
bbbb. sets; on the other hand, had the numbers of black and
bbbb. white balls in the granary been even, there would have been
bbbb. but one set in each group. Now suppose two balls were
bbbb. drawn from one of these urns and were found to be both
white, what would be the probability of the next one being white?
If the two drawn out were the first two put into the urns, and the
next to be drawn out were the third put in, then the probability
of this third being white would be the same whatever the colours
of the first two, for it has been supposed that just the same proportion of urns has the third ball white among those which have the
first two *white-white, white-black, black-white,* and *black-black.* Thus,
in this case, the chance of the third ball being white would be the
same whatever the first two were. But, by inspecting the table,
the reader can see that in each group all orders of the balls occur
with equal frequency, so that it makes no difference whether they
are drawn out in the order they were put in or not. Hence the
colours of the balls already drawn have no influence on the probability of any other being white or black.

Now, if there be any way of enumerating the possibilities of
Nature so as to make them equally probable, it is clearly one which
should make one arrangement or combination of the elements of
Nature as probable as another, that is, a distribution like that we
have supposed, and it, therefore, appears that the assumption that
any such thing can be done, leads simply to the conclusion that
reasoning from past to future experience is absolutely worthless.
In fact, the moment that you assume that the chances in favour
of that of which we are totally ignorant are even, the problem about
the tides does not differ, in any arithmetical particular, from the
case in which a penny (known to be equally likely to come up heads
and tails) should turn up heads m times successively. In short, it

would be to assume that Nature is a pure chaos, or chance combination of independent elements, in which reasoning from one fact to another would be impossible; and since, as we shall hereafter see, there is no judgment of pure observation without reasoning, it would be to suppose all human cognition illusory and no real knowledge possible. It would be to suppose that if we have found the order of Nature more or less regular in the past, this has been by a pure run of luck which we may expect is now at an end. Now, it may be we have no scintilla of proof to the contrary, but reason is unnecessary in reference to that belief which is of all the most settled, which nobody doubts or can doubt, and which he who should deny would stultify himself in so doing.

The relative probability of this or that arrangement of Nature is something which we should have a right to talk about if universes were as plenty as blackberries, if we could put a quantity of them in a bag, shake them well up, draw out a sample, and examine them to see what proportion of them had one arrangement and what proportion another. But, even in that case, a higher universe would contain us, in regard to whose arrangements the conception of probability could have no applicability.

We have examined the problem proposed by the conceptualists, which, translated into clear language, is this: Given a synthetic conclusion; required to know out of all possible states of things how many will accord, to any assigned extent, with this conclusion; and we have found that it is only an absurd attempt to reduce synthetic to analytic reason, and that no definite solution is possible.

But there is another problem in connection with this subject. It is this: Given a certain state of things, required to know what proportion of all synthetic inferences relating to it will be true within a given degree of approximation. Now, there is no difficulty about this problem (except for its mathematical complication); it has been much studied, and the answer is perfectly well known. And is not this, after all, what we want to know much rather than the other? Why should we want to know the probability that the fact will accord with our conclusion? That implies that we are interested in all possible worlds, and not merely the one in which we find ourselves placed. Why is it not much more to the purpose to know the probability that our conclusion will accord with the fact? One of these questions is the first above stated and the other the second, and I ask the reader whether, if people, instead of using the word probability without any clear apprehension of their own meaning, had always spoken of relative frequency, they could have failed to see that what they wanted was not to follow along the synthetic procedure with an analytic one, in order to find the probability of the conclusion; but, on the contrary, to begin with the fact at which the synthetic inference aims, and follow back to the facts it uses for premisses in order to see the probability of their being such as will yield the truth.

As we cannot have an urn with an infinite number of balls to represent the inexhaustibleness of Nature, let us suppose one with a finite number, each ball being thrown back into the urn after being drawn out, so that there is no exhaustion of them. Suppose one ball out of three is white and the rest black, and that four balls are drawn. Then the table on pp. 182-3 represents the relative frequency of the different ways in which these balls might be drawn. It will be seen that if we should judge by these four balls of the proportion in the urn, 32 times out of 81 we should find it $\frac{1}{4}$, and 24 times out of 81 we should find it $\frac{1}{2}$, the truth being $\frac{1}{3}$. To extend this table to high numbers would be great labour, but the mathematicians have found some ingenious ways of reckoning what the numbers would be. It is found that, if the true proportion of white balls is p, and s balls are drawn, then the error of the proportion obtained by the induction will be—

half the time within	$0 \cdot 477 \sqrt{\dfrac{2p(1-p)}{s}}$
9 times out of 10 within	$1 \cdot 163 \sqrt{\dfrac{2p(1-p)}{s}}$
99 times out of 100 within	$1 \cdot 821 \sqrt{\dfrac{2p(1-p)}{s}}$
999 times out of 1,000 within	$2 \cdot 328 \sqrt{\dfrac{2p(1-p)}{s}}$
9,999 times out of 10,000 within	$2 \cdot 751 \sqrt{\dfrac{2p(1-p)}{s}}$
9,999,999,999 times out of 10,000,000,000 within	$4 \cdot 77 \sqrt{\dfrac{2p(1-p)}{s}}$

The use of this may be illustrated by an example. By the census of 1870, it appears that the proportion of males among native white children under one year old was 0·5082, while among coloured children of the same age the proportion was only 0·4977. The difference between these is 0·0105, or about one in 100. Can this be attributed to chance, or would the difference always exist among a great number of white and coloured children under like circumstances? Here p may be taken at $\frac{1}{2}$; hence $2p(1-p)$ is also $\frac{1}{2}$. The number of white children counted was near 1,000,000; hence the fraction whose square-root is to be taken is about $\frac{1}{2000000}$. The root is about $\frac{1}{1400}$, and this multiplied by 0·477 gives about 0·0003 as the probable error in the ratio of males among the whites as obtained from the induction. The number of black children was about 150,000, which gives 0·0008 for the probable error. We see that the actual discrepancy is ten times the sum of these, and such a result would happen, according to our table, only once out of 10,000,000,000 censuses, in the long run.

It may be remarked that when the real value of the probability sought inductively is either very large or very small, the reasoning is more secure. Thus, suppose there were in reality one white ball in 100 in a certain urn, and we were to judge of the number by 100 drawings. The probability of drawing no white ball would be $\frac{366}{1000}$; that of drawing one white ball would be $\frac{370}{1000}$; that of drawing two would be $\frac{185}{1000}$; that of drawing three would be $\frac{61}{1000}$; that of drawing four would be $\frac{15}{1000}$; that of drawing five would be only $\frac{3}{1000}$, etc. Thus we should be tolerably certain of not being in error by more than one ball in 100.

It appears, then, that in one sense we can, and in another we cannot, determine the probability of synthetic inference. When I reason in this way:

> Ninety-nine Cretans in a hundred are liars;
> But Epimenides is a Cretan;
> Therefore, Epimenides is a liar;

I know that reasoning similar to that would carry truth 99 times in 100. But when I reason in the opposite direction:

> Minos, Sarpedon, Rhadamanthus, Deucalion, and Epimenides, are all the Cretans I can think of;
> But these were all atrocious liars;
> Therefore, pretty much all Cretans must have been liars;

I do not in the least know how often such reasoning would carry me right. On the other hand, what I do know is that some definite proportion of Cretans must have been liars, and that this proportion can be probably approximated to by an induction from five or six instances. Even in the worst case for the probability of such an inference, that in which about half the Cretans are liars, the ratio so obtained would probably not be in error by more than $\frac{1}{6}$. So much I know; but, then, in the present case the inference is that pretty much all Cretans are liars, and whether there may not be a special improbability in that I do not know.

Late in the last century, Immanuel Kant asked the question, "How are synthetical judgments *a priori* possible?" By synthetical judgments he meant such as assert positive fact and are not mere affairs of arrangement; in short, judgments of the kind which synthetical reasoning produces, and which analytic reasoning cannot yield. By *a priori* judgments he meant such as that all outward objects are in space, every event has a cause, etc., propositions which according to him can never be inferred from experience. Not so much by his answer to this question as by the mere asking of it, the current philosophy of that time was shattered and destroyed, and a new epoch in its history was begun. But before asking *that* question he ought to have asked the more general one, "How are any synthetical judgments at all possible?" How is it that a man can observe one fact and straightway pronounce judgment concerning another different fact not involved in the first? Such reasoning, as we have seen, has, at least in the usual sense of the phrase, no definite probability; how, then, can it add to our knowledge? This is a strange paradox; the Abbé Gratry says it is a miracle, and that every true induction is an immediate inspiration from on high. I respect this explanation far more than many a pedantic attempt to solve the question by some juggle with probabilities, with the forms of syllogism, or what not. I respect it because it shows an appreciation of the depth of the problem, because it assigns an adequate cause, and because it is intimately connected—as the true account should be—with a general philosophy of the universe. At the same time, I do not accept this explanation, because an explanation should tell *how* a thing is done, and to assert a perpetual miracle seems to be an abandonment of all hope of doing that, without sufficient justification.

It will be interesting to see how the answer which Kant gave to his question about synthetical judgments *a priori* will appear if extended to the question of synthetical judgments in general. That answer is, that synthetical judgments *a priori* are possible because whatever is universally true is involved in the conditions of experience. Let us apply this to a general synthetical reasoning. I take from a bag a handful of beans; they are all purple, and I infer that all the beans in the bag are purple. How can I do that? Why, upon the principle that whatever is universally true of my experience (which is here the appearance of these different beans) is involved in the condition of experience. The condition of this special experience is that all these beans were taken from that bag. According to Kant's principle, then, whatever is found true of all the beans drawn from the bag must find its explanation in some peculiarity of the contents of the bag. This is a satisfactory statement of the principle of induction.

When we draw a deductive or analytic conclusion, our rule of inference is that facts of a certain general character are either invariably or in a certain proportion of cases accompanied by facts of another general character. Then our premiss being a fact of the former class, we infer with certainty or with the appropriate degree of probability the existence of a fact of the second class. But the rule for synthetic inference is of a different kind. When we sample a bag of beans we do not in the least assume that the fact of some beans being purple involves the necessity or even the probability of other beans being so. On the contrary, the conceptualistic method of treating probabilities, which really amounts simply to the deductive treatment of them, when rightly carried out leads to the result that a synthetic inference has just an even chance in its favour, or in other words is absolutely worthless. The colour of one bean is entirely independent of that of another. But synthetic inference is founded upon a classification of facts, not according to their characters, but according to the manner of obtaining them. Its rule is, that a number of facts obtained in a given way will in general more or less resemble other facts obtained in the same way; or, *experiences whose conditions are the same will have the same general characters.*

In the former case, we know that premisses precisely similar in form to those of the given ones will yield true conclusions, just once in a calculable number of times. In the latter case, we only know that premisses obtained under circumstances similar to the given ones (though perhaps themselves very different) will yield true conclusions, at least once in a calculable number of times. We may express this by saying that in the case of analytic inference we know the probability of our conclusion (if the premisses are true), but in the case of synthetic inferences we only know the degree of trustworthiness of our proceeding. As all knowledge comes from synthetic inference, we must equally infer that all human certainty consists merely in our knowing that the processes by which our knowledge has been derived are such as must generally have led to true conclusions.

Though a synthetic inference cannot by any means be reduced

to deduction, yet that the rule of induction will hold good in the long run may be deduced from the principle that reality is only the object of the final opinion to which sufficient investigation would lead. That belief gradually tends to fix itself under the influence of inquiry is, indeed, one of the facts with which logic sets out.

14

THE GENERAL THEORY OF PROBABLE INFERENCE *

I

THE following is an example of the simplest kind of probable inference:

> About two per cent of persons wounded in the liver recover,
> This man has been wounded in the liver;
> Therefore, there are two chances out of a hundred that he will recover.

Compare this with the simplest of syllogisms, say the following:

> Every man dies,
> Enoch was a man;
> Hence, Enoch must have died.

The latter argument consists in the application of a general rule to a particular case. The former applies to a particular case a rule not absolutely universal, but subject to a known proportion of exceptions. Both may alike be termed deductions, because they bring information about the uniform or usual course of things to bear upon the solution of special questions; and the probable argument may approximate indefinitely to demonstration as the ratio named in the first premiss approaches to unity or to zero.

Let us set forth the general formulae of the two kinds of inference in the manner of formal logic.

Form I.

Singular Syllogism in Barbara.

> Every M is a P,
> S is an M;
> Hence, S is a P.

---

* [I is an abridgement of " A Theory of Probable Inference " in the Johns Hopkins *Studies in Logic*, edited by Peirce 1883 (*CP* 2.694-7, 700-1, 702-3, 706-9, 710-18, 719-23, 725-32, 735-40, 748-54). II is (with a sentence omitted) the article " Validity " in Baldwin's *Dict. of Philos. and Psychol.* 1902 (*CP* 2.780-1).]

Form II.

Simple Probable Deduction.

The proportion ρ of the M's are P's;
S is an M;
It follows, with probability ρ, that S is a P.

It is to be observed that the ratio ρ need not be exactly specified. We may reason from the premiss that not more than two per cent of persons wounded in the liver recover, or from "not less than a certain proportion of the M's are P's," or from "no very large nor very small proportion," etc. In short, ρ is subject to every kind of indeterminacy; it simply excludes some ratios and admits the possibility of the rest.

The analogy between syllogism and what is here called probable deduction is certainly genuine and important; yet how wide the differences between the two modes of inference are, will appear from the following considerations:

(1) The logic of probability is related to ordinary syllogistic as the quantitative to the qualitative branch of the same science. Necessary syllogism recognizes only the inclusion or non-inclusion of one class under another; but probable inference takes account of the proportion of one class which is contained under a second. It is like the distinction between projective geometry, which asks whether points coincide or not, and metric geometry, which determines their distances.

(2) For the existence of ordinary syllogism, all that is requisite is that we should be able to say, in some sense, that one term is contained in another, or that one object stands to a second in one of those relations: "better than," "equivalent to," etc., which are termed *transitive* because if A is in any such relation to B, and B is in the same relation to C, then A is in that relation to C. The universe might be all so fluid and variable that nothing should preserve its individual identity, and that no measurement should be conceivable; and still one portion might remain inclosed within a second, itself inclosed within a third, so that a syllogism would be possible. But probable inference could not be made in such a universe, because no signification would attach to the words "quantitative ratio." For that there must be counting; and consequently units must exist, preserving their identity and variously grouped together.

(3) A cardinal distinction between the two kinds of inference is, that in demonstrative reasoning the conclusion follows from the

existence of the objective facts laid down in the premisses; while in probable reasoning these facts in themselves do not even render the conclusion probable, but account has to be taken of various subjective circumstances—of the manner in which the premisses have been obtained, of there being no countervailing considerations, etc.; in short, good faith and honesty are essential to good logic in probable reasoning.

When the partial rule that the proportion p of the M's are P's is applied to show with probability p that S is a P, it is requisite, not merely that S should *be* an M, but also that it should be an instance drawn *at random* from among the M's. Thus, there being four aces in a piquet pack of thirty-two cards, the chance is one-eighth that a given card not looked at is an ace; but this is only on the supposition that the card has been drawn at random from the whole pack. If, for instance, it had been drawn from the cards discarded by the players at piquet or euchre, the probability would be quite different. The instance must be drawn at random. Here is a maxim of conduct. The volition of the reasoner (using what machinery it may) has to choose S so that it shall be an M; but he ought to restrain himself from all further preference, and not allow his will to act in any way that might tend to settle what particular M is taken, but should leave that to the operation of chance. Willing and wishing, like other operations of the mind, are *general* and imperfectly determinate. I wish for a horse—for some particular kind of horse perhaps, but not usually for any individual one. I will to act in a way of which I have a general conception; but so long as my action conforms to that general description, how it is further determined I do not care. Now in choosing the instance S, the general intention (including the whole plan of action) should be to select an M, but beyond that there should be no preference; and the act of choice should be such that if it were repeated many enough times with the same intention, the result would be that among the totality of selections the different sorts of M's would occur with the same relative frequencies as in experiences in which volition does not intermeddle at all. In cases in which it is found difficult thus to restrain the will by a direct effort, the apparatus of games of chance—a lottery-wheel, a roulette, cards, or dice—may be called to our aid. Usually, however, in making a simple probable deduction, we take that instance in which we happen at the time to be interested. In such a case, it is our interest that fulfills the function of an apparatus for random selection; and no better need be desired, so long as we have reason to deem the premiss "the proportion ρ of the M's are P's" to be equally true in regard to that part of the M's which are alone likely ever to excite our interest.

Nor is it a matter of indifference in what manner the other premiss has been obtained. A card being drawn at random from a piquet pack, the chance is one-eighth that it is an ace, if we have no other knowledge of it. But after we have looked at the card, we can no longer reason in that way. That the conclusion must be drawn in advance of any other knowledge on the subject is a rule that, however elementary, will be found in the sequel to have great importance.

(4) The conclusions of the two modes of inference likewise differ. One is necessary; the other only probable. . . . The difference between necessary and probable reasoning is that in the one case we conceive that such facts as are expressed by the premisses are never, in the whole range of possibility, true, without another fact, related to them as our conclusion is to our premisses, being true likewise; while in the other case we merely conceive that, in reasoning as we do, we are following a general maxim that will usually lead us to the truth.

So long as there are exceptions to the rule that all men wounded in the liver die, it does not necessarily follow that because a given man is wounded in the liver he cannot recover. Still, we know that if we were to reason in that way, we should be following a mode of inference which would only lead us wrong, in the long run, once in fifty times; and this is what we mean when we say that the probability is one out of fifty that the man will recover. To say, then, that a proposition has the probability ρ means that to infer it to be true would be to follow an argument such as would carry truth with it in the ratio of frequency ρ.

[There is] another form of inference to which I give the name of statistical deduction. Its general formula is as follows:

Form III.

Statistical Deduction.

The proportion r of the M's are P's,
  ', S'', S''', etc. are a *numerous* set, taken at random from among the M's;
Hence, *probably* and *approximately*, the proportion r of the S's are P's.

As an example, take this:

> A little more than half of all human births are males;
> Hence, probably a little over half of all the births in New York
> during any one year are males.

We have now no longer to deal with a mere probable inference, but with a *probable approximate* inference. This conception is a somewhat complicated one, meaning that the probability is greater according as the limits of approximation are wider. . . . This conclusion has no meaning at all unless there be more than one instance; and it has hardly any meaning unless the instances are somewhat numerous.

The principle of statistical deduction is that these two proportions—namely, that of the P's among the M's, and that of the P's among the S's—are probably and approximately equal. If, then, this principle justifies our inferring the value of the second proportion from the known value of the first, it equally justifies our inferring the value of the first from that of the second, if the first is unknown but the second has been observed. We thus obtain the following form of inference:

Form IV.

Induction.

S', S'', S''', etc. form a numerous set taken at random from
    among the M's,
S', S'', S''', etc. are found to be—the proportion ρ of them—P's;
Hence, *probably* and *approximately* the same proportion, ρ, of
    the M's are P's.

The following are examples. From a bag of coffee a handful is taken out, and found to have nine-tenths of the beans perfect; whence it is inferred that about nine-tenths of all the beans in the bag are probably perfect. The United States Census of 1870 shows that of native white children under one year old, there were 478,774 males to 463,320 females; while of coloured children of the same age there were 75,985 males to 76,637 females. We infer that generally there is a larger proportion of female births among negroes than among whites.

When the ratio ρ is *unity* or *zero*, the inference is an ordinary induction; and I ask leave to extend the term "induction" to all such inference, whatever be the value of ρ. It is, in fact, inferring from a sample to the whole lot sampled. These two forms of inference, statistical deduction and induction, plainly depend upon the same principle of equality of ratios, so that their validity is the same. Yet the nature of the probability in the two cases is very different. In the statistical deduction, we know that among the whole body of M's the proportion of P's is ρ; we say, then, that the S's being random drawings of M's are probably P's in about the same proportion—and though this may happen not to be so, yet at any rate, on continuing the drawing sufficiently, our prediction of the ratio will be vindicated at last. On the other hand, in induction we say that the proportion ρ of the sample being P's, probably there is about the same proportion in the whole lot; or at least, if this happens not to be so, then on continuing the drawings the inference will be, not *vindicated* as in the other case, but *modified* so as to become true. The deduction, then, is probable in this sense, that though its conclusion may in a particular case be falsified, yet similar conclusions (with the same ratio ρ) would generally prove approximately true; while the induction is probable in this sense, that though it may happen to give a false conclusion, yet in most cases in which the same precept of inference was followed, a different and approximately true inference (with the right value of ρ) would be drawn.

Corresponding to induction, we have the following mode of inference:

Form IV (*bis*).

Hypothesis.

M has, for example, the numerous marks P', P'', P''', etc.,
S has the proportion r of the marks P', P'', P''', etc.;
Hence, probably and approximately, S has an r-likeness to M.

Thus, we know, that the ancient Mound-builders of North America present, in all those respects in which we have been able to make the comparison, a limited degree of resemblance with the Pueblo Indians. The inference is, then, that in all respects there is about the same degree of resemblance between these races.

If I am permitted the extended sense which I have given to the word "induction," this argument is simply an induction respecting qualities instead of respecting things. In point of fact P', P'', P''', etc., constitute a random sample of the characters of M, and the ratio r of them being found to belong to S, the same ratio of all the characters of M are concluded to belong to S. This kind of argument, however, as it actually occurs, differs very much from induction, owing to the impossibility of simply counting qualities as individual things are counted. Characters have to be weighed rather than counted. Thus, antimony is bluish-grey: that is a character. Bismuth is a sort of rose-grey; it is decidedly different from antimony in colour, and yet not so very different as gold, silver, copper, and tin are.

I call this induction of characters *hypothetic inference*, or, briefly, *hypothesis*.[11] This is perhaps not a very happy designation, yet it is difficult to find a better. The term "hypothesis" has many well established and distinct meanings. Among these is that of a proposition believed in because its consequences agree with experience. This is the sense in which Newton used the word when he said, *Hypotheses non fingo*. He meant that he was merely giving a general formula for the motions of the heavenly bodies, but was not undertaking to mount to the causes of the acceleration they exhibit. The inferences of Kepler, on the other hand, were hypotheses in this sense; for he traced out the miscellaneous consequences of the supposition that Mars moved in an ellipse, with the sun at the focus, and showed that both the longitudes and the latitudes resulting from this theory were such as agreed with observation. These two components of the motion were observed; the third, that of approach to or regression from the earth, was supposed. Now, if in Form IV (*bis*) we put $r=1$, the inference is the drawing of a hypothesis in this sense. I take the liberty of extending the use of the word by permitting r to have any value from zero to unity. The term is certainly not all that could be desired; for the word hypothesis, as ordinarily used, carries with it a suggestion of uncertainty, and of something to be superseded, which does not belong at all to my use of it. But we must use existing language as best we may, balancing the reasons for and against any mode of expression, for none is perfect; at least the term is not so utterly misleading as "analogy" would be, and with proper explanation it will, I hope, be understood.

The following examples will illustrate the distinction between statistical deduction, induction, and hypothesis. If I wished to order a font of type expressly for the printing of this book, knowing, as I do, that in all English writing the letter e occurs oftener than any other letter, I should want more e's in my font than other letters. For what is true of all other English writing is no doubt true of these papers. This is a statistical deduction. But then the words used in logical writings are rather peculiar, and a good deal of use is made of single letters. I might, then, count the number of occurrences of the different letters upon a dozen or so pages of the manuscript, and thence conclude the relative amounts of the different kinds of type required in the font. That would be inductive inference. If now I were to order the font, and if, after some days, I were to receive a box containing a large number of little paper parcels of very different sizes, I should naturally infer that this was the font of types I had ordered; and this would be hypothetic inference. Again, if a dispatch in cipher is captured, and it is found to be written with twenty-six characters, one of which occurs much more frequently than any of the others, we are at once led to suppose that each character represents a letter, and that the one occurring so frequently stands for *e*. This is also hypothetic inference.

We are thus led to divide all probable reasoning into deductive and ampliative, and further to divide ampliative reasoning into induction and hypothesis. In deductive reasoning, though the predicted ratio may be wrong in a limited number of drawings, yet it will be approximately verified in a larger number. In ampliative reasoning the ratio may be wrong, because the inference is based on but a limited number of instances; but on enlarging the sample the ratio will be changed till it becomes approximately correct. In induction, the instances drawn at random are numerable things; in hypothesis they are characters, which are not capable of strict enumeration, but have to be otherwise estimated.

. . . In *Barbara* we have a *Rule*, a *Case* under the *Rule*, and the inference of the *Result* of that rule in that case. For example:

> *Rule.* All men are mortal,
> *Case.* Enoch was a man;
> *Result.* ∴ Enoch was mortal.

The cognition of a rule is not necessarily conscious, but is of the nature of a habit, acquired or congenital. The cognition of a case is of the general nature of a sensation; that is to say, it is something which comes up into present consciousness. The cognition of a result is of the nature of a decision to act in a particular way on a given occasion. In point of fact, a syllogism in *Barbara* virtually takes place when we irritate the foot of a decapitated frog. The connection between the afferent and efferent nerve, whatever it may be, constitutes a nervous habit, a rule of action, which is the physiological analogue of the major premiss. The disturbance of the ganglionic equilibrium, owing to the irritation, is the physiological form of that which, psychologically considered, is a sensation; and, logically considered, is the occurrence of a case. The explosion through the efferent nerve is the physiological form of that which psychologically is a volition, and logically the inference of a result. When we pass from the lowest to the highest forms of inervation, the physiological equivalents escape our observation; but, psychologically, we still have, first, habit—which in its highest form is understanding, and which corresponds to the major premiss of *Barbara*; we have, second, feeling, or present consciousness, corresponding to the minor premiss of *Barbara*; and we have, third, volition, corresponding to the conclusion of the same mode of syllogism. Although these analogies, like all very broad generalizations, may seem very fanciful at first sight, yet the more the reader reflects upon them the more profoundly true I am confident they will appear. They give a significance to the ancient system of formal logic which no other can at all share.

Deduction proceeds from Rule and Case to Result; it is the formula of Volition. Induction proceeds from Case and Result to Rule; it is the formula of the formation of a habit or general conception—a process which, psychologically as well as logically, depends on the repetition of instances or sensations. Hypothesis proceeds from Rule and Result to Case; it is the formula of the acquirement of secondary sensation—a process by which a confused concatenation of predicates is brought into order under a synthetizing predicate.

We usually conceive Nature to be perpetually making deductions in *Barbara*. This is our natural and anthropomorphic metaphysics. We conceive that there are Laws of Nature, which are her Rules or major premisses. We conceive that Cases arise under these laws; these cases consist in the predication, or occurrence, of *causes*, which are the middle terms of the syllogisms. And, finally, we conceive that the occurrence of these causes, by virtue of the laws of Nature, results in effects which are the conclusions of the syllogisms. Conceiving of nature in this way, we naturally conceive of science as having three tasks—(1) the discovery of Laws, which is accomplished by induction; (2) the discovery of Causes, which is accomplished by hypothetic inference; and (3) the prediction of Effects, which is accomplished by Deduction. It appears to me to be highly useful to select a system of logic which shall preserve all these natural conceptions.

It may be added that, generally speaking, the conclusions of Hypothetic Inference cannot be arrived at inductively, because their truth is not susceptible of direct observation in single cases. Nor can the conclusions of Inductions, on account of their generality, be reached by hypothetic inference. For instance, any historical fact, as that Napoleon Bonaparte once lived, is a hypothesis; we believe the fact, because its effects—I mean current tradition, the histories, the monuments, etc.—are observed. But no mere generalization of observed facts could ever teach us that Napoleon lived. So we inductively infer that every particle of matter gravitates toward every other. Hypothesis might lead to this result for any given pair of particles, but it never could show that the law was universal.

We now come to the consideration of the Rules which have to be followed in order to make valid and strong Inductions and Hypotheses. These rules can all be reduced to a single one; namely, that the statistical deduction of which the Induction or Hypothesis is the inversion, must be valid and strong.

. . . Inductions and Hypotheses are inferences from the conclusion and one premiss of a statistical syllogism to the other premiss. In the case of hypothesis, this syllogism is called the *explanation*. Thus in one of the examples used above, we suppose the cryptograph to be an English cipher, because, as we say, this *explains* the observed phenomena that there are about two dozen characters, that one occurs more frequently than the rest, especially at the end of words, etc. The explanation is—

> Simple English ciphers have certain peculiarities,
> This is a simple English cipher;
> Hence, this necessarily has these peculiarities.

This explanation is present to the mind of the reasoner, too; so much so, that we commonly say that the hypothesis is adopted *for the sake of* the explanation. Of induction we do not, in ordinary language, say that it explains phenomena; still, the statistical deduction, of which it is the inversion, plays, in a general way, the same part as the explanation in hypothesis. From a barrel of apples, that I am thinking of buying, I draw out three or four as a sample. If I find the sample somewhat decayed, I ask myself, in ordinary language, not "Why is this?" but "How is this?" And I answer that it probably comes from nearly all the apples in the barrel being in bad condition. The distinction between the "Why" of hypothesis and the "How" of induction is not very great; both ask for a statistical syllogism, of which the observed fact shall be the conclusion, the known conditions of the observation one premiss, and the inductive or hypothetic inference the other. This statistical syllogism may be conveniently termed the explanatory syllogism.

In order that an induction or hypothesis should have any validity at all, it is requisite that the explanatory syllogism should be a valid statistical deduction. Its conclusion must not merely follow from the premisses, but follow from them upon the principle of probability. The inversion of *ordinary* syllogism does not give rise to an induction or hypothesis. The statistical syllogism of Form III is invertible, because it proceeds upon the principle of an approximate *equality* between the ratio of P's in the whole class and the ratio in a well-drawn sample, and because equality is a convertible relation. But ordinary syllogism is based upon the property of the relation of containing and contained, and that is not a convertible relation. There is, however, a way in which ordinary syllogism may be inverted; namely, the conclusion and either of the premisses may be interchanged by negativing each of them. . . .

Now suppose we ask ourselves what would be the result of thus apagogically inverting a statistical deduction. Let us take, for example, Form III:

> The S's are a numerous random sample of the M's,
> The proportion r of the M's are P's;
> Hence, probably about the proportion r of the S's are P's.

The ratio r, as we have already noticed, is not necessarily perfectly definite; it may be only known to have a certain maximum or minimum; in fact, it may have any kind of indeterminacy. Of all possible values between 0 and 1, it admits of some and excludes others. The logical negative of the ratio r is, therefore, itself a ratio, which we may name ρ; it admits of every value which r excludes, and excludes every value of which r admits. Transposing, then, the major premiss and conclusion of our statistical deduction, and at the same time denying both, we obtain the following inverted form:

> The S's are a numerous random sample of the M's,
> The proportion ρ of the S's are P's;
> Hence, probably about the proportion ρ of the M's are P's.†

---

† The conclusion of the statistical deduction is here regarded as being " the proportion r of the S's are P's," and the words " probably about " as indicating

But this coincides with the formula of Induction. . . . Thus we see that Induction and Hypothesis are nothing but the apagogical inversions of statistical deductions. Accordingly, when r is taken as 1, so that ρ is "less than 1," or when r is taken as 0, so that ρ is "more than 0," the induction degenerates into a syllogism of the third figure and the hypothesis into a syllogism of the second figure. In these special cases, there is no very essential difference between the mode of reasoning in the direct and in the apagogical form. But, in general, while the probability of the two forms is precisely the same—in this sense, that for any fixed proportion of P's among the M's (or of marks of S's among the marks of the M's) the probability of any given error in the concluded value is precisely the same in the indirect as it is in the direct form—yet there is this striking difference, that a multiplication of instances will in the one case *confirm*, and in the other *modify*, the concluded value of the ratio.

We are thus led to another form for our rule of validity of ampliative inference; namely, instead of saying that the *explanatory* syllogism must be a good probable deduction, we may say that the syllogism of which the induction or hypothesis is the apagogical modification (in the traditional language of logic, the *reduction*) must be valid.

Although the rule given above really contains all the conditions to which Inductions and Hypotheses need to conform, yet inasmuch as there are many delicate questions in regard to the application of it, and particularly since it is of that nature that a violation of it, if not too gross, may not absolutely destroy the virtue of the reasoning, a somewhat detailed study of its requirements in regard to each of the premisses of the argument is still needed.

The first premiss of a scientific inference is that certain things (in the case of induction) or certain characters (in the case of hypothesis) constitute a fairly chosen *sample* of the class of things or the run of characters from which they have been drawn.

The rule requires that the sample should be drawn at random and independently from the whole lot sampled. That is to say, the sample must be taken according to a precept or method which, being applied over and over again indefinitely, would in the long

the modality with which this conclusion is drawn and held for true. It would be equally true to consider the "probably about" as forming part of the contents of the conclusion ; only from that point of view the inference ceases to be probable, and becomes rigidly necessary, and its apagogical inversion is also a necessary inference presenting no particular interest.

run result in the drawing of any one set of instances as often as any other set of the same number.

The needfulness of this rule is obvious; the difficulty is to know how we are to carry it out. The usual method is mentally to run over the lot of objects or characters to be sampled, abstracting our attention from their peculiarities, and arresting ourselves at this one or that one from motives wholly unconnected with those peculiarities. But this abstention from a further determination of our choice often demands an effort of the will that is beyond our strength; and in that case a mechanical contrivance may be called to our aid. We may, for example, number all the objects of the lot, and then draw numbers by means of a roulette, or other such instrument. We may even go so far as to say that this method is the type of all random drawing; for when we abstract our attention from the peculiarities of objects, the psychologists tell us that what we do is to substitute for the images of sense certain mental signs, and when we proceed to a random and arbitrary choice among these abstract objects we are governed by fortuitous determinations of the nervous system, which in this case serves the purpose of a roulette.

The drawing of objects at random is an act in which honesty is called for; and it is often hard enough to be sure that we have dealt honestly with ourselves in the matter, and still more hard to be satisfied of the honesty of another. Accordingly, one method of sampling has come to be preferred in argumentation; namely, to take of the class to be sampled all the objects of which we have a sufficient knowledge. Sampling is, however, a real art, well deserving an extended study by itself: to enlarge upon it here would lead us aside from our main purpose.

Let us rather ask what will be the effect upon inductive inference of an imperfection in the strictly random character of the sampling. Suppose that, instead of using such a precept of selection that any one M would in the long run be chosen as often as any other, we used a precept which would give a preference to a certain half of the M's, so that they would be drawn twice as often as the rest. If we were to draw a numerous sample by such a precept, and if we were to find that the proportion ρ of the sample consisted of P's, the inference that we should be regularly entitled to make would be, that among all the M's, counting the preferred half for two each, the proportion ρ would be P's. But this regular inductive inference being granted, from it we could deduce by arithmetic the further conclusion that, counting the M's for one each, the proportion of P's among them must (ρ being over $\frac{2}{3}$) lie between $\frac{3}{4}\rho+\frac{1}{4}$ and $\frac{3}{2}\rho-\frac{1}{2}$. Hence, if more than two-thirds of the instances drawn by the use of the false precept were found to be P's, we should be entitled to conclude that more than half of all the M's were P's. Thus, without allowing ourselves to be led away into a mathematical discussion, we can easily see that, in general, an imperfection of that kind in the random character of the sampling will only weaken the inductive conclusion, and render the concluded ratio less determinate, but will not necessarily destroy the force of the argument completely. In particular, when ρ approximates towards 1 or 0, the effect of the imperfect sampling will be but slight.

Nor must we lose sight of the constant tendency of the inductive process to correct itself. This is of its essence. This is the marvel of it. The probability of its conclusion only consists in the fact that if the true value of the ratio sought has not been reached, an extension of the inductive process will lead to a closer approximation. Thus, even though doubts may be entertained whether one selection of instances is a random one, yet a different selection, made by a different method, will be likely to vary from the normal in a different way, and if the ratios derived from such different selections are nearly equal, they may be presumed to be near the truth. This consideration makes it extremely advantageous in all ampliative reasoning to fortify one method of investigation by another.† Still we must not allow ourselves to trust so much to this virtue of induction as to relax our efforts towards making our drawings of instances as random and independent as we can. For if we infer a ratio from a number of different inductions, the magnitude of its probable error will depend very much more on the worst than on the best inductions used.

We have, thus far, supposed that although the selection of instances is not exactly regular, yet the precept followed is such that every unit of the lot would eventually get drawn. But very often it is impracticable so to draw our instances, for the reason

---

† This I conceive to be all the truth there is in the doctrine of Bacon and Mill regarding different Methods of Experimental Inquiry. The main proposition of Bacon's and Mill's doctrine is, that in order to prove that all M's are P's, we should not only take random instances of the M's and examine them to see that they are P's, but we should also take instances of not-P's and examine them to see that they are not-M's. This is an excellent way of fortifying one induction by another, when it is applicable ; but it is entirely inapplicable when r has any other value than 1 or 0. For, in general, there is no connection between the proportion of M's that are P's and the proportion of non-P's that are non-M's. A very small proportion of calves may be monstrosities, and yet a very large proportion of monstrosities may be calves.

that a part of the lot to be sampled is absolutely inaccessible to our powers of observation. If we want to know whether it will be profitable to open a mine, we sample the ore; but in advance of our mining operations, we can obtain only what ore lies near the surface. Then, simple induction becomes worthless, and another method must be resorted to. Suppose we wish to make an induction regarding a series of events extending from the distant past to the distant future; only those events of the series which occur within the period of time over which available history extends can be taken as instances. Within this period we may find that the events of the class in question present some uniform character; yet how do we know but this uniformity was suddenly established a little while before the history commenced, or will suddenly break up a little while after it terminates? Now, whether the uniformity observed consists (1) in a mere resemblance between all the phenomena, or (2) in their consisting of a disorderly mixture of two kinds in a certain constant proportion, or (3) in the character of the events being a mathematical function of the time of occurrence—in any of these cases we can make use of an apagoge from the following probable deduction:

> Within the period of time M, a certain event P occurs,
> S is a period of time taken at random from M, and more than half as long;
> Hence, probably the event P will occur within the time S.

Inverting this deduction, we have the following ampliative inference:

> S is a period of time taken at random from M, and more than half as long,
> The event P does not happen in the time S;
> Hence, probably the event P does not happen in the period M.

The probability of the conclusion consists in this, that we here follow a precept of inference, which, if it is very often applied will more than half the time lead us right. Analogous reasoning would obviously apply to any portion of an unidimensional continuum, which might be similar to periods of time. This is a sort of logic which is often applied by physicists in what is called *extrapolation* of an empirical law. As compared with a typical induction, it is obviously an excessively weak kind of inference. Although indispensable in almost every branch of science, it can lead to no solid conclusions in regard to what is remote from the field of direct perception, unless it be bolstered up in certain ways to which we shall have occasion to refer further on.

Let us now consider another class of difficulties in regard to the rule that the samples must be drawn at random and independently. In the first place, what if the lot to be sampled be infinite in number? In what sense could a random sample be taken from a lot like that? A random sample is one taken according to a method that would, in the long run, draw any one object as often as any other. In what sense can such drawing be made from an infinite class? The answer is not far to seek. Conceive a cardboard disk revolving in its own plane about its centre, and pretty accurately balanced, so that when put into rotation it shall be about as likely to come to rest in any one position as in any other; and let a fixed pointer indicate a position on the disk: the number of points on the circumference is infinite, and on rotating the disk repeatedly the pointer enables us to make a selection from this infinite number. This means merely that although the points are innumerable, yet there is a certain order among them that enables us to run them through and pick from them as from a very numerous collection. In such a case, and in no other, can an infinite lot be sampled. But it would be equally true to say that a finite lot can be sampled only on condition that it can be regarded as equivalent to an infinite lot. For the random sampling of a finite class supposes the possibility of drawing out an object, throwing it back, and continuing this process indefinitely; so that what is really sampled is not the finite collection of things, but the unlimited number of possible drawings.

But though there is thus no insuperable difficulty in sampling an infinite lot, yet it must be remembered that the conclusion of inductive reasoning only consists in the approximate evaluation of a *ratio*, so that it never can authorize us to conclude that in an infinite lot sampled there exists no single exception to a rule. Although all the planets are found to gravitate toward one another, this affords not the slightest direct reason for denying that among the innumerable orbs of heaven there may be some which exert no such force. Although at no point of space where we have yet been have we found any possibility of motion in a fourth dimension, yet this does not tend to show (by simple induction, at least) that space has absolutely but three dimensions. Although all the bodies we have had the opportunity of examining appear to obey the law of inertia, this does not prove that atoms and atomicules are subject to the same law. Such conclusions must be reached, if at all, in some other way than by simple induction. The latter may show that it is unlikely that, in my lifetime or yours, things so extra-ordinary should be found, but [does] not warrant extending the prediction into the indefinite future. And experience shows it is not safe to predict that such and such a fact will *never* be met with.

Take any human being, at random—say Queen Elizabeth. Now a little more than half of all the human beings who have ever existed have been males; but it does not follow that it is a little more likely than not that Queen Elizabeth was a male, since we know she was a woman. Nor, if we had selected Julius Caesar, would it be only a little more likely than not that he was a male. It is true that if we were to go on drawing at random an indefinite number of instances of human beings, a slight excess over one-half would be males. But that which constitutes the probability of an inference is the proportion of true conclusions among all those which could be derived *from the same precept.* Now a precept of inference, being a rule which the mind is to follow, changes its character and becomes different when the case presented to the mind is essentially different. When, knowing that the proportion r of all M's are P's, I draw an instance, S, of an M, without any other knowledge of whether it is a P or not, and infer with proba-bility, r, that it is P, the case presented to my mind is very different from what it is if I have such other knowledge. In short, I cannot make a valid probable inference without taking into account whatever knowledge I have (or, at least, whatever occurs to my mind) that bears upon the question.

The same principle may be applied to the statistical deduction of Form III. If the major premiss, that the proportion r of the M's are P's be laid down first, before the instances of M's are drawn, we really draw our inference concerning those instances (that the proportion r of them will be P's) in advance of the draw-ing, and therefore before we know whether they are P's or not. But if we draw the instances of the M's first, and after the examina-tion of them decide what we will select for the predicate of our major premiss, the inference will generally be completely fallacious. In short, we have the rule that the major term P must be decided upon in advance of the examination of the sample. . . .

The same rule follows us into the logic of induction and hypo-thesis. If in sampling any class, say the M's, we first decide what the character P is for which we propose to sample that class, and also how many instances we propose to draw, our inference is really made before these latter are drawn, that the proportion of P's in the whole class is probably about the same as among the instances that are to be drawn, and the only thing we have to do is to draw them and observe the ratio. But suppose we were to draw our inferences without the predesignation of the character P; then we might in every case find some recondite character in which those instances would all agree. That, by the exercise of sufficient ingenuity, we should be sure to be able to do this, even if not a single other object of the class M possessed that character, is a matter of demonstration. For in geometry a curve may be drawn through any given series of points, without passing through any one of another given series of points, and this irrespective of the number of dimensions. Now, all the qualities of objects may be conceived to result from variations of a number of continuous variables; hence any lot of objects possesses some character in common, not possessed by any other. It is true that if the universe of quality is limited, this is not altogether true; but it remains true that unless we have some special premiss from which to infer the contrary, it always *may* be possible to assign some common character of the instances S', S'', S''', etc., drawn at random from among the M's, which does not belong to the M's generally. So that if the character P were not predesignate, the deduction of which our induction is the apagogical inversion would not be valid; that is to say, we could not reason that if the M's did not generally possess the character P, it would not be likely that the S's should all possess this character.

I take from a biographical dictionary the first five names of poets, with their ages at death. They are,

Aagard,	died at 48
Abeille,	died at 76
Abulola,	died at 84
Abunowas,	died at 48
Accords,	died at 45

These five ages have the following characters in common:

1. The difference of the two digits composing the number, divided by three, leaves a remainder of *one*.

2. The first digit raised to the power indicated by the second, and then divided by three, leaves a remainder of *one*.

3. The sum of the prime factors of each age, including *one* as a prime factor, is divisible by *three*.

Yet there is not the smallest reason to believe that the next poet's age would possess these characters.

Here we have a *conditio sine qua non* of valid induction which has been singularly overlooked by those who have treated of the logic of the subject, and is very frequently violated by those who draw inductions. So accomplished a reasoner as Dr. Lyon Playfair, for instance, has written a paper of which the following is an abstract. He first takes the specific gravities of the three allotropic forms of carbon, as follows:

$$\begin{array}{ll} \text{Diamond,} & 3\cdot48 \\ \text{Graphite,} & 2\cdot29 \\ \text{Charcoal,} & 1\cdot88 \end{array}$$

He now seeks to find a uniformity connecting these three instances; and he discovers that the atomic weight of carbon, being 12,

$$\begin{array}{l} \text{Sp. gr. diamond nearly} = 3\cdot46 = \sqrt[2]{12} \\ \text{Sp. gr. graphite nearly} = 2\cdot29 = \sqrt[3]{12} \\ \text{Sp. gr. charcoal nearly} = 1\cdot86 = \sqrt[4]{12} \end{array}$$

This, he thinks, renders it probable that the specific gravities of the allotropic forms of other elements would, if we knew them, be found to equal the different roots of their atomic weight. But so far, the character in which the instances agree not having been predesignated, the induction can serve only to suggest a question, and ought not to create any belief. To test the proposed law, he selects the instance of silicon, which like carbon exists in a diamond and in a graphitoidal condition. He finds for the specific gravities—

$$\begin{array}{ll} \text{Diamond silicon,} & 2\cdot47 \\ \text{Graphite silicon,} & 2\cdot33 \end{array}$$

Now, the atomic weight of silicon, that of carbon being 12, can only be taken as 28. But 2·47 does not approximate to any root of 28. It is, however, nearly the cube root of 14 ($\sqrt[3]{\frac{1}{2} \times 28} = 2\cdot41$), while 2·33 is nearly the fourth root of 28 ($\sqrt[4]{28} = 2\cdot30$). Dr. Playfair claims that silicon is an instance satisfying his formula. But in fact this instance requires the formula to be modified; and the modification not being predesignate, the instance cannot count. Boron also exists in a diamond and a graphitoidal form; and accordingly Dr. Playfair takes this as his next example. Its atomic weight is 10·9, and its specific gravity is 2·68; which is the square root of $\frac{2}{3} \times 10\cdot9$. There seems to be here a further modification of the formula not predesignated, and therefore this instance can hardly be reckoned as confirmatory. The next instances which would occur to the mind of any chemist would be phosphorus and sulphur, which exist in familiarly known allotropic forms. Dr. Playfair admits that the specific gravities of phosphorus have no relations to its atomic weight at all analogous to those of carbon. The different forms of sulphur have nearly the same specific gravity, being approximately the fifth root of the atomic weight 32. Selenium also has two allotropic forms, whose specific gravities are 4·8 and 4·3; one of these follows the law, while the other does not. For tellurium the law fails altogether; but for bromine and iodine it holds. Thus the number of specific gravities for which the law was predesignate are 8; namely, 2 for phosphorus, 1 for sulphur, 2 for selenium, 1 for tellurium, 1 for bromine, and 1 for iodine. The law holds for 4 of these, and the proper inference is that about half the specific gravities of metalloids are roots of some simple ratio of their atomic weights.

Having thus determined this ratio, we proceed to inquire whether an agreement half the time with the formula constitutes any special connection between the specific gravity and the atomic weight of a metalloid. As a test of this, let us arrange the elements in the order of their atomic weights, and compare the specific gravity of the first with the atomic weight of the last, that of the second with the atomic weight of the last but one, and so on. The atomic weights are—

Boron,	10·9	Tellurium,	128·1
Carbon,	12·0	Iodine,	126·9
Silicon,	28·0	Bromine,	80·0
Phosphorus,	31·0	Selenium,	79·1
	Sulphur, 32		

There are three specific gravities given for carbon, and two each for silicon, phosphorus, and selenium. The question, therefore, is, whether of the fourteen specific gravities as many as seven are in Playfair's relation with the atomic weights, not of the same element, but of the one paired with it. Now, taking the original formula of Playfair we find

	Sp. gr. boron	=2·68	$\sqrt[5]{Te}$	=2·64
3d	Sp. gr. carbon	=1·88	$\sqrt[5]{I}$	=1·84
2d	Sp. gr. carbon	=2·29	$\sqrt[6]{I}$	=2·24
1st	Sp. gr. phosphorus	=1·83	$\sqrt[7]{Se}$	=1·87
2d	Sp. gr. phosphorus	=2·10	$\sqrt[6]{Se}$	=2·07

or five such relations without counting that of sulphur to itself.

Next, with the modification introduced by Playfair, we have

1st Sp. gr. silicon	$=2\cdot47$	$\sqrt[4]{\frac{1}{2}\times Br}$	$=2\cdot51$
2d Sp. gr. silicon	$=2\cdot33$	$\sqrt[6]{2\times Br}$	$=2\cdot33$
Sp. gr. iodine	$=4\cdot95$	$\sqrt[2]{2\times C}$	$=4\cdot90$
1st Sp. gr. carbon	$=3\cdot48$	$\sqrt[3]{\frac{1}{4}\times I}$	$=3\cdot48$

It thus appears that there is no more frequent agreement with Playfair's proposed law than what is due to chance.

Another example of this fallacy was "Bode's law" of the relative distances of the planets, which was shattered by the first discovery of a true planet after its enunciation. In fact, this false kind of induction is extremely common in science and in medicine. In the case of hypothesis, the correct rule has often been laid down; namely, that a hypothesis can only be received upon the ground of its having been *verified* by successful *prediction*. The term *predesignation* used in this paper appears to be more exact, inasmuch as it is not at all requisite that the ratio ρ should be given in advance of the examination of the samples. Still, since ρ is equal to 1 in all ordinary hypotheses, there can be no doubt that the rule of prediction, so far as it goes, coincides with that here laid down.

We have now to consider an important modification of the rule. Suppose that, before sampling a class of objects, we have predesignated not a single character but n characters, for which we propose to examine the samples. This is equivalent to making n different inductions from the same instances. The probable error in this case is that error whose probability for a simple induction is only $(\frac{1}{2})^n$, and the theory of probabilities shows that it increases but slowly with n; in fact, for $n=1,000$ it is only about five times as great as for $n=1$, so that with only 25 times as many instances the inference would be as secure for the former value of n as with the latter; with 100 times as many instances an induction in which $n=10,000,000,000$ would be equally secure. Now the whole universe of characters will never contain such a number as the last; and the same may be said of the universe of objects in the case of hypothesis. So that, without any voluntary predesignation, the limitation of our imagination and experience amounts to a predesignation far within those limits; and we thus see that if the number of instances be very great indeed, the failure to predesignate is not an important fault. Of characters at all striking, or of objects at all familiar, the number will seldom reach 1,000; and of very striking characters or very familiar objects the number is still less. So that if a large number of samples of a class are found to have some very striking character in common, or if a large number of characters of one object are found to be possessed by a very familiar object, we need not hesitate to infer, in the first case, that the same characters belong to the whole class, or, in the second case, that the two objects are practically identical; remembering only that the inference is less to be relied upon than it would be had a deliberate predesignation been made. This is no doubt the precise significance of the rule sometimes laid down, that a hypothesis ought to be *simple*—simple here being taken in the sense of familiar.

This modification of the rule shows that, even in the absence of voluntary predesignation, *some* slight weight is to be attached to an induction or hypothesis. And perhaps when the number of instances is not very small, it is enough to make it worth while to subject the inference to a regular test. But our natural tendency will be to attach too much importance to such suggestions, and we shall avoid waste of time in passing them by without notice until some stronger plausibility presents itself.

The theory here proposed does not assign any probability to the inductive or hypothetic conclusion, in the sense of undertaking to say how frequently *that conclusion* would be found true. It does not propose to look through all the possible universes, and say in what proportion of them a certain uniformity occurs; such a proceeding, were it possible, would be quite idle. The theory here presented only says how frequently, in this universe, the special form of induction or hypothesis would lead us right. The probability given by this theory is in every way different—in meaning, numerical value, and form—from that of those who would apply to ampli- ative inference the doctrine of inverse chances.[12]

Other logicians hold that if inductive and hypothetic premisses lead to true oftener than to false conclusions, it is only because the universe happens to have a certain constitution. Mill and his followers maintain that there is a general tendency toward uni- formity in the universe. . , . The Abbé Gratry believes that the tendency toward the truth in induction is due to a miraculous intervention of Almighty God. . . . Others have supposed that there is a special adaptation of the mind to the universe, so that we are more apt to make true theories than we otherwise should be. Now, to say that a theory such as these is *necessary* to explain- ing the validity of induction and hypothesis is to say that these modes of inference are not in themselves valid, but that their conclusions are rendered probable by being probable deductive inferences from a suppressed (and originally unknown) premiss. But I maintain that it has been shown that the modes of inference in question are necessarily valid, whatever the constitution of the universe, so long as it admits of the premisses being true. Yet I am willing to concede, in order to concede as much as possible, that when a man draws instances at random, all that he knows is that he *tries* to follow a certain precept; so that the sampling process might be rendered generally fallacious by the existence of a mysterious and malign connection between the mind and the universe, such that the possession by an object of an *unperceived* character might influence the will toward choosing it or rejecting it. Such a circumstance would, however, be as fatal to deductive as to ampliative inference. Suppose, for example, that I were to enter a great hall where people were playing *rouge et noir* at many tables; and suppose that I knew that the red and black were turned up with equal frequency. Then, if I were to make a large number of mental bets with myself, at this table and at that, I might, by statistical deduction, expect to win about half of them—precisely as I might expect, from the results of these samples, to infer by induction the probable ratio of frequency of the turnings of red and black in the long run, if I did not know it. But could some devil look at each card before it was turned, and then influence me mentally to bet upon it or to refrain therefrom, the observed ratio in the cases upon which I had bet might be quite different from the observed ratio in those cases upon which I had not bet. I grant, then, that even upon my theory some fact has to be supposed to make induction and hypothesis valid processes; namely, it is supposed that the supernal powers withhold their hands and let me alone, and that no mysterious uniformity or adaptation interferes with the action of chance. But then this negative fact supposed by my theory plays a totally different part from the facts supposed to be requisite by the logicians of whom I have been speaking. So far as facts like those they suppose can have any bearing, they serve as major premisses from which the fact inferred by induction or hypothesis might be deduced; while the negative fact supposed by me is merely the denial of any major premiss from which the falsity of the inductive or hypothetic conclusion could in general be deduced. Nor is it necessary to deny altogether the existence of mysterious influences adverse to the validity of the inductive and hypothetic processes. So long as their influence were not too overwhelming, the wonderful self-correcting nature of the ampliative inference would enable us, even if they did exist, to detect and make allowance for them.

Although the universe need have no peculiar constitution to render ampliative inference valid, yet it is worth while to inquire whether or not it has such a constitution;[13] for if it has, that circumstance must have its effect upon all our inferences. It cannot any longer be denied that the human intellect is peculiarly adapted to the comprehension of the laws and facts of nature, or at least of some of them; and the effect of this adaptation upon our reasoning will be briefly considered in the next section. Of any miraculous interference by the higher powers, we know absolutely nothing; and it seems in the present state of science altogether improbable. The effect of a knowledge of special uniformities upon ampliative inferences has already been touched upon.[13] That there is a general tendency toward uniformity in nature is not merely an unfounded, it is an absolutely absurd, idea in any other sense than that man is adapted to his surroundings. For the universe of marks is only limited by the limitation of human interests and powers of observation. Except for that limitation, every lot of objects in the universe would have (as I have elsewhere shown)[13] some character in common and peculiar to it. Consequently, there is but one possible arrangement of characters among objects as they exist, and there is no room for a greater or less degree of uniformity in nature. If nature seems highly uniform to us, it is only because our powers are adapted to our desires.

The questions discussed in this essay relate to but a small part of the Logic of Scientific Investigation. Let us just glance at a few of the others.

Suppose a being from some remote part of the universe, where the conditions of existence are inconceivably different from ours, to be presented with a United States Census Report—which is for us a mine of valuable inductions, so vast as almost to give that epithet a new signification. He begins, perhaps, by comparing the ratio of indebtedness to deaths by consumption in counties whose names begin with the different letters of the alphabet. It is safe to say that he would find the ratio everywhere the same, and thus his inquiry would lead to nothing. For an induction is wholly unimportant unless the proportions of P's among the M's and among the non-M's differ; and a hypothetic inference is unimportant unless it be found that S has either a greater or a less proportion of the characters of M than it has of other characters.

The stranger to this planet might go on for some time asking inductive questions that the Census would faithfully answer, without learning anything except that certain conditions were independent of others. At length, it might occur to him to compare the January rainfall with the illiteracy. What he would find is given in the following table:

Region.	January Rainfall.	Illiteracy.
	Inches.	Per cent.
Atlantic seacoast, Portland to Washington .	0·92	11
Vermont, Northern and Western New York	0·78	7
Upper Mississippi River	0·52	3
Ohio River Valley	0·74	8
Lower Mississippi, Red River, and Kentucky	1·08	50
Mississippi Delta and Northern Gulf Coast .	1·09	57
Southeastern Coast	0·68	40

He would infer that in places that are drier in January there is, not always but generally, less illiteracy than in wetter places. A detailed comparison between Mr. Schott's map of the winter rainfall with the map of illiteracy in the general census, would confirm the result that these two conditions have a partial connection. This is a very good example of an induction in which the proportion of P's among the M's is different, but not very different, from the proportion among the non-M's. It is unsatisfactory; it provokes further inquiry; we desire to replace the M by some different class, so that the two proportions may be more widely separated. Now we, knowing as much as we do of the effects of winter rainfall upon agriculture, upon wealth, etc., and of the causes of illiteracy, should come to such an inquiry furnished with a large number of appropriate conceptions; so that we should be able to ask intelligent questions not unlikely to furnish the desired key to the problem. But the strange being we have imagined could only make his inquiries haphazard, and could hardly hope ever to find the induction of which he was in search.

Nature is a far vaster and less clearly arranged repertory of facts than a census report; and if men had not come to it with special aptitudes for guessing right, it may well be doubted whether in the ten or twenty thousand years that they may have existed their greatest mind would have attained the amount of knowledge which is actually possessed by the lowest idiot. But, in point of fact, not man merely, but all animals derive by inheritance (presumably by natural selection) two classes of ideas which adapt them to their environment.   In the first place, they all have from birth some notions, however crude and concrete, of force, matter, space, and time; and, in the next place, they have some notion of what sort of objects their fellow-beings are, and of how they will act on given occasions.   Our innate mechanical ideas were so nearly correct that they needed but slight correction.   The fundamental principles of statics were made out by Archimedes.   Centuries later Galileo began to understand the laws of dynamics, which in our times have been at length, perhaps, completely mastered.   The other physical sciences are the results of inquiry based on guesses suggested by the ideas of mechanics.   The moral sciences, so far as they can be called sciences, are equally developed out of our instinctive ideas about human nature.   Man has thus far not attained to any knowledge that is not in a wide sense either mechanical or anthropological in its nature, and it may be reasonably presumed that he never will.

Side by side, then, with the well established proposition that all knowledge is based on experience, and that science is only advanced by the experimental verifications of theories, we have to place this other equally important truth, that all human knowledge, up to the highest flights of science, is but the development of our inborn animal instincts.

II

Every argument or inference professes to conform to a general method or type of reasoning, which method, it is held, has one kind of virtue or another in producing truth.   In order to be valid the argument or inference must really pursue the method it professes to pursue, and furthermore, that method must have the kind of truth-producing virtue which it is supposed to have.   For example, an induction may conform to the formula of induction; but it may be conceived, and often is conceived, that induction lends a probability to its conclusion.   Now that is not the way in which induction leads to the truth.   It lends no definite probability to its conclusion.   It is nonsense to talk of the probability of a law, as if we could pick universes out of a grab-bag and find in what proportion of them the law held good.   Therefore, such an induction is not valid; for it does not do what it professes to do, namely, to make its conclusion probable.   But yet if it had only professed to do what induction does (namely, to commence a proceeding which must in the long run approximate to the truth), which is infinitely more to the purpose than what it professes, it would have been valid. Validity must not be confounded with *strength*. For an argument may be perfectly valid and yet excessively weak. I wish to know whether a given coin is so accurately made that it will turn up heads and tails in approximately equal proportions. I therefore pitch it five times and note the results, say three heads and two tails; and from this I conclude that the coin is approximately correct in its form. Now this is a valid induction; but it is contemptibly weak. All simple arguments about matters of fact are weak. The strength of an argument might be theoretically defined as the number of *independent* equal standard unit arguments upon the other side which would balance it. But since it is next to impossible to imagine independent arguments upon any question, or to compare them with accuracy, and since moreover the "other side" is a vague expression, this definition only serves to convey a rough idea of what is meant by the strength of an argument. It is doubtful whether the idea of strength can be made less vague. But we may say that an induction from more instances is, other things being equal, stronger than an induction from fewer instances. Of probable deductions the more probable conclusion is the stronger. In the case of hypotheses adopted presumptively on probation, one of the very elements of their strength lies in the absence of any other hypothesis; so that the above definition of strength cannot be applied, even in imagination, without imagining the strength of the presumption to be considerably reduced. Perhaps we might conceive the strength, or urgency, of a hypothesis as measured by the amount of wealth, in time, thought, money, etc., that we ought to have at our disposal before it would be worth while to take up that hypothesis for examination. In that case it would be a quantity dependent upon many factors. Thus a strong instinctive inclination toward it must be allowed to be a favouring circumstance, and a disinclination an unfavourable one. Yet the fact that it would throw a great light upon many things, if it were established, would be in its favour; and the more surprising and unexpected it would be to find it true, the more light it would generally throw. The expense which the examination of it would involve must be one of the main factors of its urgency.

Returning to the matter of validity, an argument professing to be necessary is valid in case the premisses could not under any hypothesis, not involving contradiction, be true, without the conclusion being also true. If this is so in fact, while the argument fails to make it evident, it is a bad argument rhetorically, and yet is valid; for it absolutely leads to the truth if the premisses are true. It is thus possible for an argument to be valid and yet bad. Yet an argument ought not to be called bad because it does not elucidate steps with which readers may be assumed to be familiar. A probable deductive argument is valid, if the conclusions of precisely such arguments (from true premisses) would be true, in the long run, in a proportion of times equal to the probability which this argument assigns to its conclusion; for that is all that is pretended. Thus, an argument that out of a certain set of sixty throws of a pair of dice about to be thrown, about ten will probably be doublets, is rendered valid by the fact that if a great number of just such arguments were made, the immense majority of the conclusions would be true, and indeed ten would be indefinitely near the actual average number in the long run. The validity of induction is entirely different; for it is by no means certain that the conclusion actually drawn in any given case would turn out true in the majority of cases where precisely such a method was followed; but what is certain is that, in the majority of cases, the method would lead to *some* conclusion that was true, and that in the individual case in hand, if there is any error in the conclusion, that error will get corrected by simply persisting in the employment of the same method. The validity of an inductive argument consists, then, in the fact that it pursues a method which, if duly persisted in, must, in the very nature of things, lead to a result indefinitely approximating to the truth in the long run. The validity of a presumptive adoption of a hypothesis for examination consists in this, that the hypothesis being such that its consequences are capable of being tested by experimentation, and being such that the observed facts would follow from it as necessary conclusions, that hypothesis is selected according to a method which must ultimately lead to the discovery of the truth, so far as the truth is capable of being discovered, with an indefinite approximation to accuracy.

15

UNIFORMITY *

I

(1) [UNIFORMITY is] a fact consisting in this: that, of a certain genus of facts, a proportion approaching unity (the whole) belongs, in the course of experience, to a certain species; so that, though of itself the knowledge of this uniformity gives no information concerning a certain thing or character, yet it will strengthen any inductive conclusion of a certain kind.

It is, therefore, a high objective probability concerning an objective probability. There are, in particular, four classes of uniformities, the knowledge of any of which, or of its falsity, may deductively strengthen or weaken an inductive conclusion. These four kinds of uniformity are as follows:

i. The members of a class may present an extraordinary resemblance to one another in regard to a certain line of characters. Thus, the Icelanders are said to resemble one another most strikingly in their opinions about general subjects. Knowing this, we should not need to question many Icelanders, if we found that the first few whom we met all shared a common superstition, in order to conclude with considerable confidence that nearly all Icelanders were of the same way of thinking. Philodemus insists strongly upon this kind of uniformity as a support of induction.

ii. A character may be such that, in whatever genus it occurs at all, it almost always belongs to all the species of that genus; or this uniformity may be lacking. Thus, when only white swans were known, it would have been hazardous to assert that all swans were white, because whiteness is not usually a generic character. It is considerably more safe to assert that all crows are black, because blackness is oftener a generic character. This kind of uniformity is especially emphasized by J. S. Mill as important in inductive inquiries.

iii. A certain set of characters may be intimately connected so as to be usually all present or all absent from certain kinds of objects. Thus, the different chemical reactions of gold are so inseparable that a chemist need only to succeed in getting, say, the

* [I is from the article " Uniformity " in Baldwin's *Dict. of Philos. and Psychol.* 1902 (*CP* 6.98-100). II is from " The Order of Nature," the fourth paper of a series (cf. ch. 2), *Popular Science Monthly* 1878 (*CP* 6.399-406).]

purple of Cassius to be confident that the body under examination will show every reaction of gold.

iv. Of a certain object it may be known that its characteristic is that when it possesses one of a set of characters within a certain group of such sets, it possesses the rest. Thus, it may be known of a certain man that to whatever party he belongs, he is apt to embrace without reserve the entire creed of that party. We shall not, then, need to know many of his opinions, say in regard to politics, in order to infer with great confidence his position upon other political questions.

(2) The word "uniformity" plays such a singular and prominent rôle in the logic of J. S. Mill that it is proper to note it. He was apt to be greatly influenced by Ockham's razor in forming theories which he defended with great logical acumen; but he differed from other men of that way of thinking in that his natural candour led to his making many admissions without perceiving how fatal they were to his negative theories. In addition to that, perhaps more than other philosophers, in endeavouring to embrace several ideas under a common term, he often leaves us at a loss to find any other character common and peculiar to those notions except that of their having received from him that common designation. In one passage of his *System of Logic* (1842), he declares, in reference to the difference in strength between two inductive conclusions, that whoever shall discover the cause of that difference will have discovered the secret of inductive reasoning. When, therefore, he shortly afterwards points out that the distinction between those two inductions is that one of them is supported by a uniformity of the second of the above four classes, while the other is met by a distinct diversity of the same kind, and when he himself gives to that uniformity this designation when he afterwards declares that the validity of induction depends upon uniformity, his reader naturally supposes he means uniformity in that sense. But we find that he employs the word for quite another purpose. Namely, he does not like the word *law*, as applied to an inductive generalization of natural facts—such as the "law" of gravitation—because it implies an element in nature, the reality of a general, which no nominalist can admit. He, therefore, desires to call the reality to which a true universal proposition about natural phenomena corresponds a "uniformity."

The implication of the word, thus used, is that the facts are, in themselves, entirely disconnected, and that it is the mind alone which unites them. One stone dropping to the earth has no real connection with another stone dropping to the earth. It is, surely, not difficult to see that this theory of uniformities, far from helping to establish the validity of induction, would be, if consistently admitted, an insuperable objection to such validity. For if two facts, A and B, are entirely independent in their real nature, then the truth of B cannot follow, either necessarily or probably, from the truth of A. If I have tried the experiment with a million stones and have found that every one of them fell when allowed to drop, it may be very natural for me to believe that almost any stone will act in the same way. But if it can be proved that there is no real connection between the behaviour of different stones, then there is nothing for it but to say that it was a chance coincidence that those million stones all behaved in the same way; for if there was any *reason* for it, and they *really* dropped, there was a *real reason*, that is, a real general. Now, if it is mere chance that they all dropped, that affords no more reason for supposing that the next will drop than my throwing three double sixes successively with a pair of dice is a reason for thinking that the next throw will be double sixes.

(3) But now we find that Mill's good sense and candour will not allow him to take the course which a Hobbes would have taken, and utterly deny the validity of induction; and this leads to a new use of the word *uniformity*, in which he speaks of the "uniformity of nature." Before asking exactly what this phrase means, it may be noted that, whatever it means, the assertion of it is an assent to scholastic realism, except for a difference of emphasis. For to say that throughout the whole course of experience, events always, or even only usually, happen alike under the same conditions (what is usually called the "invariability" of nature) is to assert an agreement (complete or partial) which could not be ascribed to chance without self-contradiction. For chance is merely the possible discrepancy between the character of the limited experience to which it belongs and the whole course of experience. Hence, to say that of the *real*, objective facts some *general* character can be predicated, is to assert the reality of a general. It only differs from scholastic realism in that Mill and his followers treat this aspect of the matter lightly—that is to say, the objective reality of the general—while the Scholastics regarded it as a great and vital feature of the universe. Instead of "uniformity" now importing that what others call "laws" are fabrications of the human mind, this "uniformity of nature" is erected by Mill into the greatest of laws and absolutely objective and real.

Let us now inquire what the "uniformity of nature," with its

synonymous expressions that "the future resembles the past," and
so forth, can mean. Mill says that it means that if all the circumstances attending two phenomena are the same, they will be alike.
But taken strictly this means absolutely nothing, since no two
phenomena ever can happen in circumstances precisely alike, nor
are two phenomena precisely alike. It is, therefore, necessary to
modify the statement in order to give it any meaning at all; and
it will be found that, however it may be so modified, the moment
it begins to carry a definite meaning, one of three things results:
it becomes either, first, grossly false, or, second, an assertion which
there is really no good reason to believe even approximately true,
or, thirdly, it becomes a quasi-subjective truth, not lending any
colour of validity to induction proper. If, for example, we were
to say that, under any given species of circumstances presenting
any similarity, phenomena of any given genus would be found to
have a specific general resemblance in contrast with the specific
character of phenomena of the same genus occurring under a
different species of circumstances of the same genus, this would
be monstrously false, whether intended as an absolutely universal
proposition or merely as one approximately true. Let, for example,
the genus of phenomena be the values of the throws of a pair of
dice in a given series of successive throws indefinitely continued.
Let the first species of circumstances be that the ordinal number
of a throw in the series is *prime*. It is pretty certain that there
would be no general character in the corresponding values of throws
to distinguish them from those which would result when the ordinal
number is divisible by 2, or by 3, or by any other prime. It thus
appears that when we take *any* genus of circumstances, the law
turns out false. Suppose, then, that we modify it by saying that,
taking any genus of phenomena and separating this into two species,
there will be found in the discoverable circumstances *some* general
resemblance for all those attending phenomena of the same species
in contrast to those attending phenomena of the other species.
This is a proposition which there is not the slightest reason to believe. Take, for example, as the genus of phenomena, the many
thousands of Latin descriptions of American species of plants by
Asa Gray and his scholars. Now consider the species of this genus
of phenomena which agree in this respect, that the two first words
of the description have their first vowels the same. There is no
reason to suppose that there was any general respect in which the
circumstances of that species of the genus of phenomena agree
with one another and differ from others, either universally or usually.

It is a mere chance result. It is true that some persons will not be inclined to assent to this judgment; but they cannot prove it otherwise. It can afford no adequate basis for induction. We see, then, that when we consider *all* phenomena, there is no way of making the statement sufficiently definite and certain. Suppose, then, that we attempt still another modification of the law, that, of *interesting* resemblances and differences between phenomena, some considerable proportion are accompanied by corresponding resemblances and differences between those of the circumstances which appear to us to be *pertinent*. The proposition is now rather psychological than metaphysical. It would be impossible, with any evidentiary basis, to strengthen the expression "some considerable proportion"; and in other respects the statement is vague enough. Still, there is sufficient truth in it, perhaps, to warrant the presumptive adoption of hypotheses, provided this adoption merely means that they are taken as sufficiently reasonable to justify some expense in experimentation to test their truth by induction; but it gives no warrant at all to induction itself. For, in the first place, induction needs no such dubious support, since it is mathematically certain that the general character of a limited experience will, as that experience is prolonged, approximate to the character of what will be true in the long run, if anything is true in the long run. Now all that induction infers is what would be found true in the usual course of experience, if it were indefinitely prolonged. Since the method of induction must generally approximate to that truth, that is a sufficient justification for the use of that method, although no definite probability attaches to the inductive conclusion. In the second place, the law, as now formulated, neither helps nor hinders the validity of induction proper; for induction proper consists in judging of the relative frequency of a character among all the individuals of a class by the relative frequency of that character among the individuals of a random sample of that class. Now the law, as thus formulated, may tend to make our hypothesis approximately true; but that advantage has been gained before the operation of induction, which merely tests the hypothesis, begins. This inductive operation is just as valid when the hypothesis is bad as when it is good, when the character dealt with is trivial as when it is interesting. The ratio which induction ascertains may be nearer $\frac{1}{2}$, and more remote from 1 or 0, when the characters are uninteresting; and in that case a larger number of instances will usually be requisite for obtaining the ratio with any given degree of precision (for if the ratio is really 1 or 0, it will be almost a miracle if in the sample it is far from that ratio, although this will not be impossible, if the whole class is infinite), but the essential validity of the process of induction remains unaffected by that circumstance.

What is usually meant by the uniformity of nature probably is that in proportion as the circumstances are alike or unlike, so are any phenomena connected with them alike or unlike. It may be asked to what degree nature is uniform in that sense. The only tenable answer is that it is as little uniform as it possibly could be imagined to be; for were any considerable proportion of existing uniformities, or laws, of nature destroyed, others would necessarily thereby result.

In fact, the great characteristic of nature is its diversity. For every uniformity known, there would be no difficulty in pointing out thousands of non-uniformities; but the diversities are usually of small use to us, and attract the attention of poets mainly, while the uniformities are the very staff of life. Hence, the higher and wider are our desires the greater will be the general impression of uniformity produced upon us by the contemplation of nature as it interests us.

II

If anyone has ever maintained that the universe is a pure throw of the dice, the theologians have abundantly refuted him. "How often," says Archbishop Tillotson, "might a man, after he had jumbled a set of letters in a bag, fling them out upon the ground before they would fall into an exact poem, yea, or so much as make a good discourse in prose! And may not a little book be as easily made by chance as this great volume of the world?" The chance-world, here shown to be so different from that in which we live, would be one in which there were no laws, the characters of different things being entirely independent; so that, should a sample of any kind of objects ever show a prevalent character, it could only be by accident, and no general proposition could ever be established. Whatever further conclusions we may come to in regard to the order of the universe, this much may be regarded as solidly established, that the world is not a mere chance-medley.

But whether the world makes an exact poem or not, is another question. When we look up at the heavens at night, we readily perceive that the stars are not simply splashed onto the celestial vault; but there does not seem to be any precise system in their arrangement either. It will be worth our while, then, to inquire into the degree of orderliness in the universe; and, to begin, let us ask whether the world we live in is any more orderly than a purely chance-world would be.

Any uniformity, or law of Nature, may be stated in the form, "Every A is B"; as, every ray of light is a non-curved line, every body is accelerated toward the earth's centre, etc. This is the same as to say, "There does not exist any A which is not B"; there is no curved ray; there is no body not accelerated toward the earth; so that the uniformity consists in the non-occurrence in Nature of a certain combination of characters (in this case, the combination of being A with being non-B). And, conversely, every case of the non-occurrence of a combination of characters would constitute a uniformity in Nature. Thus, suppose the quality A is never found in combination with the quality C: for example, suppose the quality of idiocy is never found in combination with that of having a well-developed brain. Then nothing of the sort A is of the sort C, or everything of the sort A is of the sort non-C (or say, every idiot has an ill-developed brain), which, being something universally true of the A's, is a uniformity in the world. Thus we see that, in a world where there were no uniformities, no logically possible combination of characters would be excluded, but every combination would exist in some object. But two objects not identical must differ in some of their characters, though it be only in the character of being in such and such a place. Hence, precisely the same combination of characters could not be found in two different objects; and, consequently, in a chance-world every combination involving either the positive or negative of every character would belong to just one thing. Thus, if there were but five simple characters in such a world, we might denote them by A, B, C, D, E, and their negatives by a, b, c, d, e; and then, as there would be 2^5 or 32 different combinations of these characters, completely determinate in reference to each of them, that world would have just 32 objects in it, their characters being as in the following table:

TABLE I.

ABCDE	AbCDE	aBCDE	abCDE
ABCDe	AbCDe	aBCDe	abCDe
ABCdE	AbCdE	aBCdE	abCdE
ABCde	AbCde	aBCde	abCde
ABcDE	AbcDE	aBcDE	abcDE
ABcDe	AbcDe	aBcDe	abcDe
ABcdE	AbcdE	aBcdE	abcdE
ABcde	Abcde	aBcde	abcde

For example, if the five primary characters were *hard, sweet, fragrant, green, bright*, there would be one object which re-united all these qualities, one which was hard, sweet, fragrant, and green, but not bright; one which was hard, sweet, fragrant, and bright, but not green; one which was hard, sweet, and fragrant, but neither green nor bright; and so on through all the combinations.

This is what a thoroughly chance-world would be like, and certainly nothing could be imagined more systematic. When a quantity of letters are poured out of a bag, the appearance of disorder is due to the circumstance that the phenomena are only partly fortuitous. The laws of space are supposed, in that case, to be rigidly preserved, and there is also a certain amount of regularity in the formation of the letters. The result is that some elements are orderly and some are disorderly, which is precisely what we observe in the actual world. Tillotson, in the passage of which a part has been quoted, goes on to ask, "How long might 20,000 blind men which should be sent out from the several remote parts of England, wander up and down before they would all meet upon Salisbury Plains, and fall into rank and file in the exact order of an army? And yet this is much more easy to be imagined than how the innumerable blind parts of matter should rendezvous themselves into a world." This is very true, but in the actual world the *blind men* are, as far as we can see, *not* drawn up in any particular order at all. And, in short, while a certain amount of order exists in the world, it would seem that the world is not so orderly as it might be, and, for instance, not so much so as a world of pure chance would be.

But we can never get to the bottom of this question until we take account of a highly-important logical principle which I now proceed to enounce. This principle is that any plurality or lot of objects whatever have some character in common (no matter how insignificant) which is peculiar to them and not shared by anything else. The word "character" here is taken in such a sense as to include negative characters, such as incivility, inequality, etc., as well as their positives, civility, equality, etc. To prove the theorem, I will show what character any two things, A and B, have in common, not shared by anything else. The things, A and B, are each distinguished from all other things by the possession of certain characters which may be named A-ness and B-ness. Corresponding to these positive characters are the negative characters un-A-ness, which is possessed by everything except A, and un-B-ness, which is possessed by everything except B. These two characters are united in everything except A and B; and this union of the characters un-*A*-ness and un-*B*-ness makes a compound character which may be termed *A*-*B*-lessness. This is not possessed by either *A* or *B*, but it is possessed by everything else. This character, like every other, has its corresponding negative un-*A*-*B*-lessness, and this last is the character possessed by both *A* and *B*, and by nothing else. It is obvious that what has thus been shown true of two things is *mutatis mutandis*, true of any number of things.—Q.E.D.

In any world whatever, then, there must be a character peculiar to each possible group of objects. If, as a matter of nomenclature, characters peculiar to the same group be regarded as only different aspects of the same character, then we may say that there will be precisely one character for each possible group of objects. Thus, suppose a world to contain five things, α, β, γ, δ, ϵ. Then it will have a separate character for each of the 31 groups (with *non-existence* making up 32 or 2^5) shown in the following table:

TABLE II.

	$\alpha\beta$	$\alpha\beta\gamma$	$\alpha\beta\gamma\delta$	$\alpha\beta\gamma\delta\epsilon$
α	$\alpha\gamma$	$\alpha\beta\delta$	$\alpha\beta\gamma\epsilon$	
β	$\alpha\delta$	$\alpha\beta\epsilon$	$\alpha\beta\delta\epsilon$	
γ	$\alpha\epsilon$	$\alpha\gamma\delta$	$\alpha\gamma\delta\epsilon$	
δ	$\beta\gamma$	$\alpha\gamma\epsilon$	$\beta\gamma\delta\epsilon$	
ϵ	$\beta\delta$	$\alpha\delta\epsilon$		
	$\beta\epsilon$	$\beta\gamma\delta$		
	$\gamma\delta$	$\beta\gamma\epsilon$		
	$\gamma\epsilon$	$\beta\delta\epsilon$		
	$\delta\epsilon$	$\gamma\delta\epsilon$		

This shows that a contradiction is involved in the very idea of a chance-world, for in a world of 32 things, instead of there being only 3^5 or 243 characters, as we have seen that the notion of a chance-world requires, there would, in fact, be no less than 2^{32}, or 4,294,967,296 characters, which would not be all independent, but would have all possible relations with one another.

We further see that so long as we regard characters abstractly, without regard to their relative importance, etc., there is no possibility of a more or less degree of orderliness in the world, the whole system of relationship between the different characters being given by mere logic; that is, being implied in those facts which are tacitly admitted as soon as we admit that there is any such thing as reasoning.

In order to descend from this abstract point of view, it is requisite to consider the characters of things as relative to the perceptions and active powers of living beings. Instead, then, of attempting to imagine a world in which there should be no uniformities, let us suppose one in which none of the uniformities should have reference to characters interesting or important to us. In the first place, there would be nothing to puzzle us in such a world. The small number of qualities which would directly meet the senses would be the ones which would afford the key to everything which could possibly interest us. The whole universe would have such an air of system and perfect regularity that there would be nothing to ask. In the next place, no action of ours, and no event of Nature, would have important consequences in such a world. We should be perfectly free from all responsibility, and there would be nothing to do but to enjoy or suffer whatever happened to come along. Thus there would be nothing to stimulate or develop either the mind or the will, and we consequently should neither act nor think. We should have no memory, because that depends on a law of our organization. Even if we had any senses, we should be situated toward such a world precisely as inanimate objects are toward the present one, provided we suppose that these objects have an absolutely transitory and instantaneous consciousness without memory—a supposition which is a mere mode of speech, for that would be no consciousness at all. We may, therefore, say that a world of chance is simply our actual world viewed from the standpoint of an animal at the very vanishing-point of intelligence. The actual world is almost a chance-medley to the mind of a polyp. The interest which the uniformities of Nature have for an animal measures his place in the scale of intelligence.

16

SOME CONSEQUENCES OF FOUR INCAPACITIES *

DESCARTES is the father of modern philosophy, and the spirit of Cartesianism—that which principally distinguishes it from the scholasticism which it displaced—may be compendiously stated as follows:

1. It teaches that philosophy must begin with universal doubt; whereas scholasticism had never questioned fundamentals.

2. It teaches that the ultimate test of certainty is to be found in the individual consciousness; whereas scholasticism had rested on the testimony of sages and of the Catholic Church.

3. The multiform argumentation of the middle ages is replaced by a single thread of inference depending often upon inconspicuous premisses.

4. Scholasticism had its mysteries of faith, but undertook to explain all created things. But there are many facts which Cartesianism not only does not explain, but renders absolutely inexplicable, unless to say that "God makes them so" is to be regarded as an explanation.

In some, or all of these respects, most modern philosophers have been, in effect, Cartesians. Now without wishing to return to scholasticism, it seems to me that modern science and modern logic require us to stand upon a very different platform from this.

1. We cannot begin with complete doubt. We must begin with all the prejudices which we actually have when we enter upon the study of philosophy. These prejudices are not to be dispelled by a maxim, for they are things which it does not occur to us *can* be questioned. Hence this initial scepticism will be a mere self-deception, and not real doubt; and no one who follows the Cartesian method will ever be satisfied until he has formally recovered all those beliefs which in form he has given up. It is, therefore, as useless a preliminary as going to the North Pole would be in order to get to Constantinople by coming down regularly upon a meridian.

---

* [This chapter, with Peirce's title, and omitting several paragraphs where the spatial division occurs, is the greater part of a paper in the *Journal of Speculative Philosophy* 1868 (*CP* 5.264-8, 280-317).]

A person may, it is true, in the course of his studies, find reason to doubt what he began by believing; but in that case he doubts because he has a positive reason for it, and not on account of the Cartesian maxim. Let us not pretend to doubt in philosophy what we do not doubt in our hearts.

2. The same formalism appears in the Cartesian criterion, which amounts to this: "Whatever I am clearly convinced of, is true." If I were really convinced, I should have done with reasoning, and should require no test of certainty. But thus to make single individuals absolute judges of truth is most pernicious. The result is that metaphysicians will all agree that metaphysics has reached a pitch of certainty far beyond that of the physical sciences;—only they can agree upon nothing else. In sciences in which men come to agreement, when a theory has been broached, it is considered to be on probation until this agreement is reached. After it is reached, the question of certainty becomes an idle one, because there is no one left who doubts it. We individually cannot reasonably hope to attain the ultimate philosophy which we pursue; we can only seek it, therefore, for the *community* of philosophers. Hence, if disciplined and candid minds carefully examine a theory and refuse to accept it, this ought to create doubts in the mind of the author of the theory himself.

3. Philosophy ought to imitate the successful sciences in its methods, so far as to proceed only from tangible premises which can be subjected to careful scrutiny, and to trust rather to the multitude and variety of its arguments than to the conclusiveness of any one. Its reasoning should not form a chain which is no stronger than its weakest link, but a cable whose fibres may be ever so slender, provided they are sufficiently numerous and intimately connected.

4. Every unidealistic philosophy supposes some absolutely inexplicable, unanalyzable ultimate; in short, something resulting from mediation itself not susceptible of mediation. Now that anything *is* thus inexplicable can only be known by reasoning from signs. But the only justification of an inference from signs is that the conclusion explains the fact. To suppose the fact absolutely inexplicable, is not to explain it, and hence this supposition is never allowable.

In the last number of this journal will be found a piece entitled "Questions concerning certain Faculties claimed for Man," which has been written in this spirit of opposition to Cartesianism. That criticism of certain faculties resulted in four denials, which for convenience may here be repeated:

1. We have no power of Introspection, but all knowledge of the internal world is derived by hypothetical reasoning from our knowledge of external facts.

2. We have no power of Intuition, but every cognition is determined logically by previous cognitions.

3. We have no power of thinking without signs.

4. We have no conception of the absolutely incognizable.

These propositions cannot be regarded as certain; and, in order to bring them to a further test, it is now proposed to trace them out to their consequences. We may first consider the first alone; then trace the consequences of the first and second; then see what else will result from assuming the third also; and, finally, add the fourth to our hypothetical premises.

In accepting the first proposition, we must put aside all prejudices derived from a philosophy which bases our knowledge of the external world on our self-consciousness. We can admit no statement concerning what passes within us except as a hypothesis necessary to explain what takes place in what we commonly call the external world. Moreover when we have upon such grounds assumed one faculty or mode of action of the mind, we cannot, of course, adopt any other hypothesis for the purpose of explaining any fact which can be explained by our first supposition, but must carry the latter as far as it will go. In other words, we must, as far as we can do so without additional hypotheses, reduce all kinds of mental action to one general type.

The class of modifications of consciousness with which we must commence our inquiry must be one whose existence is indubitable, and whose laws are best known, and, therefore (since this knowledge comes from the outside), which most closely follows external facts; that is, it must be some kind of cognition. Here we may hypothetically admit the second proposition of the former paper, according to which there is no absolutely first cognition of any object, but cognition arises by a continuous process. We must begin, then, with a *process* of cognition, and with that process whose laws are best understood and most closely follow external facts. This is no other than the process of valid inference, which proceeds from its premiss, A, to its conclusion, B, only if, as a matter of fact, such a proposition as B is always or usually true when such a proposition as A is true. It is a consequence, then, of the first two principles whose results we are to trace out, that we must, as far as we can, without any other supposition than that the mind reasons, reduce all mental action to the formula of valid reasoning.

But does the mind in fact go through the syllogistic process? It is certainly very doubtful whether a conclusion—as something existing in the mind independently, like an image—suddenly displaces two premises existing in the mind in a similar way. But it is a matter of constant experience, that if a man is made to believe in the premises, in the sense that he will act from them and will say that they are true, under favourable conditions he will also be ready to act from the conclusion and to say that that is true. Something, therefore, takes place within the organism which is equivalent to the syllogistic process.

An apparent obstacle to the reduction of all mental action to the type of valid inferences is the existence of fallacious reasoning. Every argument implies the truth of a general principle of inferential procedure (whether involving some matter of fact concerning the subject of argument, or merely a maxim relating to a system of signs), according to which it is a valid argument. If this principle is false, the argument is a fallacy; but neither a valid argument from false premises, nor an exceedingly weak, but not altogether illegitimate, induction or hypothesis, however its force may be overestimated, however false its conclusion, is a fallacy.

Now words, taken just as they stand, if in the form of an argument, thereby do imply whatever fact may be necessary to make the argument conclusive; so that to the formal logician, who has to do only with the meaning of the words according to the proper principles of interpretation, and not with the intention of the speaker as guessed at from other indications, the only fallacies should be such as are simply absurd and contradictory, either because their conclusions are absolutely inconsistent with their premises, or because they connect propositions by a species of illative conjunction, by which they cannot under any circumstances be validly connected.

But to the psychologist an argument is valid only if the premises from which the mental conclusion is derived would be sufficient, if true, to justify it, either by themselves, or by the aid of other propositions which had previously been held for true. But it is easy to show that all inferences made by man, which are not valid in this sense, belong to four classes, viz.: 1. Those whose premises are false; 2. Those which have some little force, though only a little; 3. Those which result from confusion of one proposition

with another; 4. Those which result from the indistinct apprehension, wrong application, or falsity, of a rule of inference. For,
if a man were to commit a fallacy not of either of these classes, he
would, from true premisses conceived with perfect distinctness,
without being led astray by any prejudice or other judgment serving
as a rule of inference, draw a conclusion which had really not the
least relevancy. If this could happen, calm consideration and care
could be of little use in thinking, for caution only serves to insure
our taking all the facts into account, and to make those which we
do take account of, distinct; nor can coolness do anything more
than to enable us to be cautious, and also to prevent our being
affected by a passion in inferring that to be true which we wish
were true, or which we fear may be true, or in following some other
wrong rule of inference. But experience shows that the calm and
careful consideration of the same distinctly conceived premisses
(including prejudices) will insure the pronouncement of the same
judgment by all men. Now if a fallacy belongs to the first of these
four classes and its premisses are false, it is to be presumed that the
procedure of the mind from these premisses to the conclusion is
either correct, or errs in one of the other three ways; for it cannot
be supposed that the mere falsity of the premisses should affect the
procedure of reason when that falsity is not known to reason. If
the fallacy belongs to the second class and has some force, however
little, it is a legitimate probable argument, and belongs to the type
of valid inference. If it is of the third class and results from the
confusion of one proposition with another, this confusion must be
owing to a resemblance between the two propositions; that is to
say, the person reasoning, seeing that one proposition has some of
the characters which belong to the other, concludes that it has all
the essential characters of the other, and is equivalent to it. Now
this is a hypothetic inference, which though it may be weak, and
though its conclusion happens to be false, belongs to the type of
valid inferences; and, therefore, as the *nodus* of the fallacy lies in
this confusion, the procedure of the mind in these fallacies of the
third class conforms to the formula of valid inference. If the fallacy
belongs to the fourth class, it either results from wrongly applying
or misapprehending a rule of inference, and so is a fallacy of confusion, or it results from adopting a wrong rule of inference. In
this latter case, this rule is in fact taken as a premiss, and therefore
the false conclusion is owing merely to the falsity of a premiss. In
every fallacy, therefore, possible to the mind of man, the procedure
of the mind conforms to the formula of valid inference.

The third principle whose consequences we have to deduce is, that, whenever we think, we have present to the consciousness some feeling, image, conception, or other representation, which serves as a sign. But it follows from our own existence (which is proved by the occurrence of ignorance and error) that everything which is present to us is a phenomenal manifestation of ourselves. This does not prevent its being a phenomenon of something without us, just as a rainbow is at once a manifestation both of the sun and of the rain. When we think, then, we ourselves, as we are at that moment, appear as a sign. Now a sign has, as such, three references: 1st, it is a sign *to* some thought which interprets it; 2d, it is a sign *for* some object to which in that thought it is equivalent; 3d, it is a sign, *in* some respect or quality, which brings it into connection with its object. Let us ask what the three correlates are to which a thought-sign refers.

1. When we think, to what thought does that thought-sign which is ourself address itself? It may, through the medium of outward expression, which it reaches perhaps only after considerable internal development, come to address itself to thought of another person. But whether this happens or not, it is always interpreted by a subsequent thought of our own. If, after any thought, the current of ideas flows on freely, it follows the law of mental association. In that case, each former thought suggests something to the thought which follows it, *i.e.* is the sign of something to this latter. Our train of thought may, it is true, be interrupted. But we must remember that, in addition to the principal element of thought at any moment, there are a hundred things in our mind to which but a small fraction of attention or consciousness is conceded. It does not, therefore, follow, because a new constituent of thought gets the uppermost, that the train of thought which it displaces is broken off altogether. On the contrary, from our second principle, that there is no intuition or cognition not determined by previous cognitions, it follows that the striking in of a new experience is never an instantaneous affair, but is an *event* occupying time, and coming to pass by a continuous process. Its prominence in consciousness, therefore, must probably be the consummation of a growing process; and if so, there is no sufficient cause for the thought which had been the leading one just before, to cease abruptly and instantaneously. But if a train of thought ceases by gradually dying out, it freely follows its own law of association as long as it lasts, and there is no moment at which there is a thought belonging to this series, subsequently to which there is not a thought

which interprets or repeats it.   There is no exception, therefore, to the law that every thought-sign is translated or interpreted in a subsequent one, unless it be that all thought comes to an abrupt and final end in death.

2. The next question is: For what does the thought-sign stand —what does it name—what is its *suppositum*? The outward thing, undoubtedly, when a real outward thing is thought of. But still, as the thought is determined by a previous thought of the same object, it only refers to the thing through denoting this previous thought. Let us suppose, for example, that Toussaint is thought of, and first thought of as a *negro*, but not distinctly as a man. If this distinctness is afterwards added, it is through the thought that a *negro* is a *man*; that is to say, the subsequent thought, *man*, refers to the outward thing by being predicated of that previous thought, *negro*, which has been had of that thing. If we afterwards think of Toussaint as a general, then we think that this negro, this man, was a general. And so in every case the subsequent thought denotes what was thought in the previous thought.

3. The thought-sign stands for its object in the respect which is thought; that is to say, this respect is the immediate object of consciousness in the thought, or, in other words, it is the thought itself, or at least what the thought is thought to be in the subsequent thought to which it is a sign.

We must now consider two other properties of signs which are of great importance in the theory of cognition. Since a sign is not identical with the thing signified, but differs from the latter in some respects, it must plainly have some characters which belong to it in itself, and have nothing to do with its representative function. These I call the *material* qualities of the sign. As examples of such qualities, take in the word "man" its consisting of three letters— in a picture, its being flat and without relief. In the second place, a sign must be capable of being connected (not in the reason but really) with another sign of the same object, or with the object itself. Thus, words would be of no value at all unless they could be connected into sentences by means of a real copula which joins signs of the same thing. The usefulness of some signs—as a weather-cock, a tally, etc.—consists wholly in their being really connected with the very things they signify. In the case of a picture such a connection is not evident, but it exists in the power of association which connects the picture with the brain-sign which labels it. This real, physical connection of a sign with its object, either immediately or by its connection with another sign, I call the *pure demonstrative application* of the sign. Now the representative function of a sign lies neither in its material quality nor in its pure demonstrative application; because it is something which the sign is, not in itself or in a real relation to its object, but which it is *to a thought*, while both of the characters just defined belong to the sign independently of its addressing any thought. And yet if I take all the things which have certain qualities and physically connect them with another series of things, each to each, they become fit to be signs. If they are not regarded as such they are not actually signs, but they are so in the same sense, for example, in which an unseen flower can be said to be *red*, this being also a term relative to a mental affection.

Consider a state of mind which is a conception. It is a conception by virtue of having a *meaning*, a logical comprehension; and if it is applicable to any object, it is because that object has the characters contained in the comprehension of this conception. Now the logical comprehension of a thought is usually said to consist of the thoughts contained in it; but thoughts are events, acts of the mind. Two thoughts are two events separated in time, and one cannot literally be contained in the other. It may be said that all thoughts exactly similar are regarded as one; and that to say that one thought contains another, means that it contains one exactly similar to that other. But how can two thoughts be similar? Two objects can only be *regarded* as similar if they are compared and brought together in the mind. Thoughts have no existence except in the mind; only as they are regarded do they exist. Hence, two thoughts cannot *be* similar unless they are brought together in the mind. But, as to their existence, two thoughts are separated by an interval of time. We are too apt to imagine that we can frame a thought similar to a past thought, by matching it with the latter, as though this past thought were still present to us. But it is plain that the knowledge that one thought is similar to or in any way truly representative of another, cannot be derived from immediate perception, but must be an hypothesis (unquestionably fully justifiable by facts), and that therefore the formation of such a representing thought must be dependent upon a real effective force behind consciousness, and not merely upon a mental comparison. What we must mean, therefore, by saying that one concept is contained in another, is that we normally represent one to be in the other; that is, that we form a particular kind of judgment, of which the subject signifies one concept and the predicate the other.

No thought in itself, then, no feeling in itself, contains any others, but is absolutely simple and unanalyzable; and to say that it is composed of other thoughts and feelings, is like saying that a movement upon a straight line is composed of the two movements of which it is the resultant; that is to say, it is a metaphor, or fiction, parallel to the truth. Every thought, however artificial and complex, is, so far as it is immediately present, a mere sensation without parts, and therefore, in itself, without similarity to any other, but incomparable with any other and absolutely *sui generis*. Whatever is wholly incomparable with anything else is wholly inexplicable, because explanation consists in bringing things under general laws or under natural classes. Hence every thought, in so far as it is a feeling of a peculiar sort, is simply an ultimate, inexplicable fact. Yet this does not conflict with my postulate that that fact should be allowed to stand as inexplicable; for, on the one hand, we never can think, "This is present to me," since, before we have time to make the reflection, the sensation is past, and, on the other hand, when once past, we can never bring back the quality of the feeling as it was *in and for itself*, or know what it was like *in itself*, or even discover the existence of this quality except by a corollary from our general theory of ourselves, and then not in its idiosyncrasy, but only as something present. But, as something present, feelings are all alike and require no explanation, since they contain only what is universal. So that nothing which we can truly predicate of feelings is left inexplicable, but only something which we cannot reflectively know. So that we do not fall into the contradiction of making the Mediate immediate. Finally, no present actual thought (which is a mere feeling) has any meaning, any intellectual value; for this lies not in what is actually thought, but in what this thought may be connected with in representation by subsequent thoughts; so that the meaning of a thought is altogether something virtual. It may be objected, that if no thought has any meaning, all thought is without meaning. But this is a fallacy similar to saying, that, if in no one of the successive spaces which a body fills there is room for motion, there is no room for motion throughout the whole. At no one instant in my state of mind is there cognition or representation, but in the relation of my states of mind at different instants there is.† In short, the Immediate (and therefore in itself unsusceptible of

† Accordingly, just as we say that a body is in motion, and not that motion is in a body we ought to say that we are in thought, and not that thoughts are in us.

mediation—the Unanalyzable, the Inexplicable, the Unintellectual) runs in a continuous stream through our lives; it is the sum total of consciousness, whose mediation, which is the continuity of it, is brought about by a real effective force behind consciousness.

Thus, we have in thought three elements: 1st, the representative function which makes it a *representation*; 2d, the pure denotative application, or real connection, which brings one thought into *relation* with another; and 3d, the material quality, or how it feels, which gives thought its *quality*.

That a sensation is not necessarily an intuition, or first impression of sense, is very evident in the case of the sense of beauty. . . . When the sensation beautiful is determined by previous cognitions, it always arises as a predicate; that is, we think that something is beautiful. Whenever a sensation thus arises in consequence of others, induction shows that those others are more or less complicated. Thus, the sensation of a particular kind of sound arises in consequence of impressions upon the various nerves of the ear being combined in a particular way, and following one another with a certain rapidity. A sensation of colour depends upon impressions upon the eye following one another in a regular manner, and with a certain rapidity. The sensation of beauty arises upon a manifold of other impressions. And this will be found to hold good in all cases. Secondly, all these sensations are in themselves simple, or more so than the sensations which give rise to them. Accordingly, a sensation is a simple predicate taken in place of a complex predicate; in other words, it fulfills the function of an hypothesis. But the general principle that every thing to which such and such a sensation belongs, has such and such a complicated series of predicates, is not one determined by reason (as we have seen), but is of an arbitrary nature. Hence, the class of hypothetic inferences which the arising of a sensation resembles, is that of reasoning from definition to definitum, in which the major premiss is of an arbitrary nature. Only in this mode of reasoning, this premiss is determined by the conventions of language, and expresses the occasion upon which a word is to be used; and in the formation of a sensation, it is determined by the constitution of our nature, and expresses the occasions upon which sensation, or a natural mental sign, arises. Thus, the sensation, so far as it represents something, is determined, according to a logical law, by previous cognitions; that is to say, these cognitions determine that there shall be a sensation. But so far as the sensation is a mere feeling of a particular sort, it is determined only by an inexplicable, occult power; and so far, it is not a representation, but only the material quality of a representation. For just as in reasoning from definition to definitum, it is indifferent to the logician how the defined word shall sound, or how many letters it shall contain, so in the case of this constitutional word, it is not determined by an inward law how it shall feel in itself. A feeling, therefore, as a feeling, is merely the *material quality* of a mental sign.

But there is no feeling which is not also a representation, a predicate of something determined logically by the feelings which precede it. For if there are any such feelings not predicates, they are the emotions. Now every emotion has a subject. If a man is angry, he is saying to himself that this or that is vile and outrageous. If he is in joy, he is saying "this is delicious." If he is wondering, he is saying "this is strange." In short, whenever a man feels, he is thinking of *something*. Even those passions which have no definite object—as melancholy—only come to consciousness through tinging the *objects of thought*. That which makes us look upon the emotions more as affections of self than other cognitions, is that we have found them more dependent upon our accidental situation at the moment than other cognitions; but that is only to say that they are cognitions too narrow to be useful. The emotions, as a little observation will show, arise when our attention is strongly drawn to complex and inconceivable circumstances. Fear arises when we cannot predict our fate; joy, in the case of certain indescribable and peculiarly complex sensations. If there are some indications that something greatly for my interest, and which I have anticipated would happen, may not happen; and if, after weighing probabilities, and inventing safeguards, and straining for further information, I find myself unable to come to any fixed conclusion in reference to the future, in the place of that intellectual hypothetic inference which I seek, the feeling of *anxiety* arises. When something happens for which I cannot account, I *wonder*. When I endeavour to realize to myself what I never can do, a pleasure in the future, I *hope*. "I do not understand you," is the phrase of an angry man. The indescribable, the ineffable, the incomprehensible, commonly excite emotion; but nothing is so chilling as a scientific explanation. Thus an emotion is always a simple predicate substituted by an operation of the mind for a highly complicated predicate. Now if we consider that a very complex predicate demands explanation by means of an hypothesis, that that hypothesis must be a simpler predicate substituted for that complex one; and that when we have an emotion, an hypothesis, strictly speaking, is hardly possible—the analogy of the parts played by emotion and hypothesis is very striking. There is, it is true, this difference between an emotion and an intellectual hypothesis, that we have reason to say in the case of the latter, that to whatever the simple hypothetic predicate can be applied, of that the complex predicate is true; whereas, in the case of an emotion this is a proposition for which no reason can be given, but which is determined merely by our emotional constitution. But this corresponds precisely to the difference between hypothesis and reasoning from definition to definitum, and thus it would appear that emotion is nothing but sensation. There appears to be a difference, however, between emotion and sensation, and I would state it as follows:

There is some reason to think that, corresponding to every feeling within us, some motion takes place in our bodies. This property of the thought-sign, since it has no rational dependence upon the meaning of the sign, may be compared with what I have called the material quality of the sign; but it differs from the latter inasmuch as it is not essentially necessary that it should be felt in order that there should be any thought-sign. In the case of a sensation, the manifold of impressions which precede and determine it are not of a kind, the bodily motion corresponding to which comes from any large ganglion or from the brain, and probably for this reason the sensation produces no great commotion in the bodily organism; and the sensation itself is not a thought which has a very strong influence upon the current of thought except by virtue of the information it may serve to afford. An emotion, on the other hand, comes much later in the development of thought—I mean, further from the first beginning of the cognition of its object—and the thoughts which determine it already have motions corresponding to them in the brain, or the chief ganglion; consequently, it produces large movements in the body, and, independently of its representative value, strongly affects the current of thought. The animal motions to which I allude, are, in the first place and obviously, blushing, blenching, staring, smiling, scowling, pouting, laughing, weeping, sobbing, wriggling, flinching, trembling, being petrified, sighing, sniffing, shrugging, groaning, heartsinking, trepidation, swelling of the heart, etc. etc. To these may, perhaps, be added, in the second place, other more complicated actions, which nevertheless spring from a direct impulse and not from deliberation.

That which distinguishes both sensations proper and emotions from the feeling of a thought, is that in the case of the two former the material quality is made prominent, because the thought has no relation of reason to the thoughts which determine it, which exists in the last case and detracts from the attention given to the mere feeling. By there being no relation of reason to the determining thoughts, I mean that there is nothing in the content of the thought which explains why it should arise only on occasion of these determining thoughts. If there is such a relation of reason, if the thought is essentially limited in its application to these objects, then the thought comprehends a thought other than itself; in other words, it is then a complex thought. An incomplex thought can, therefore, be nothing but a sensation or emotion, having no rational character. This is very different from the ordinary doctrine, according to which the very highest and most metaphysical conceptions are absolutely simple. I shall be asked how such a conception of a *being* is to be analyzed, or whether I can ever define *one*, *two*, and *three*, without a diallelon. Now I shall admit at once that neither of these conceptions can be separated into two others higher than itself; and in that sense, therefore, I fully admit that certain very metaphysical and eminently intellectual notions are absolutely simple. But though these concepts cannot be defined by genus and difference, there is another way in which they can be defined. All determination is by negation; we can first recognize any character only by putting an object which possesses it into comparison with an object which possesses it not. A conception, therefore, which was quite universal in every respect would be unrecognizable and impossible. We do not obtain the conception of Being, in the sense implied in the copula, by observing that all the things which we can think of have something in common, for there is no such thing to be observed. We get it by reflecting upon signs—words or thoughts;—we observe that different predicates may be attached to the same subject, and that each makes some conception applicable to the subject; then we imagine that a subject has something true of it merely because a predicate (no matter what) is attached to it,—and that we call Being. The conception of being is, therefore, a conception about a sign—a thought, or word;—and since it is not applicable to every sign, it is not primarily universal, although it is so in its mediate application to things. Being, therefore, may be defined; it may be defined, for example, as that which is common to the objects included in any class, and to the objects not included in the same class. But it is nothing new to say that metaphysical conceptions are primarily and at bottom thoughts about words, or thoughts about thoughts;

it is the doctrine both of Aristotle (whose categories are parts of speech) and of Kant (whose categories are the characters of different kinds of propositions).

Sensation and the power of abstraction or attention may be regarded as, in one sense, the sole constituents of all thought. Having considered the former, let us now attempt some analysis of the latter. By the force of attention, an emphasis is put upon one of the objective elements of consciousness. This emphasis is, therefore, not itself an object of immediate consciousness; and in this respect it differs entirely from a feeling. Therefore, since the emphasis, nevertheless, consists in some effect upon consciousness, and so can exist only so far as it affects our knowledge; and since an act cannot be supposed to determine that which precedes it in time, this act can consist only in the capacity which the cognition emphasized has for producing an effect upon memory, or otherwise influencing subsequent thought. This is confirmed by the fact that attention is a matter of continuous quantity; for continuous quantity, so far as we know it, reduces itself in the last analysis to time. Accordingly, we find that attention does, in fact, produce a very great effect upon subsequent thought. In the first place, it strongly affects memory, a thought being remembered for a longer time the greater the attention originally paid to it. In the second place, the greater the attention, the closer the connection and the more accurate the logical sequence of thought. In the third place, by attention a thought may be recovered which has been forgotten. From these facts, we gather that attention is the power by which thought at one time is connected with and made to relate to thought at another time; or, to apply the conception of thought as a sign, that it is the *pure demonstrative application* of a thought-sign.

Attention is roused when the same phenomenon presents itself repeatedly on different occasions, or the same predicate in different subjects. We see that A has a certain character, that B has the same, C has the same; and this excites our attention, so that we say, "*These* have this character." Thus attention is an act of induction; but it is an induction which does not increase our knowledge, because our "these" covers nothing but the instances experienced. It is, in short, an argument from enumeration.

Attention produces effects upon the nervous system. These effects are habits, or nervous associations. A habit arises, when, having had the sensation of performing a certain act, m, on several occasions a, b, c, we come to do it upon every occurrence of the general event, l, of which a, b and c are special cases. That is to say, by the cognition that

Every case of a, b, or c, is a case of m,

is determined the cognition that

Every case of l is a case of m.

Thus the formation of a habit is an induction, and is therefore necessarily connected with attention or abstraction. Voluntary actions result from the sensations produced by habits, as instinctive actions result from our original nature.

We have thus seen that every sort of modification of consciousness—Attention, Sensation, and Understanding—is an inference. But the objection may be made that inference deals only with general terms, and that an image, or absolutely singular representation, cannot therefore be inferred.

"Singular" and "individual" are equivocal terms. A singular may mean that which can be but in one place at one time. In this sense it is not opposed to general. *The sun* is a singular in this sense, but, as is explained in every good treatise on logic, it is a general term. I may have a very general conception of Hermolaus Barbarus, but still I conceive him only as able to be in one place at one time. When an image is said to be singular, it is meant that it is absolutely determinate in all respects. Every possible character, or the negative thereof, must be true of such an image. In the words of the most eminent expounder of the doctrine, the image of a man "must be either of a white, or a black, or a tawny; a straight, or a crooked; a tall, or a low, or a middle-sized man." It must be of a man with his mouth open or his mouth shut, whose hair is precisely of such and such a shade, and whose figure has precisely such and such proportions. No statement of Locke has been so scouted by all friends of images as his denial that the "idea" of a triangle must be either of an obtuse-angled, right-angled, or acute-angled triangle. In fact, the image of a triangle must be of one, each of whose angles is of a certain number of degrees, minutes, and seconds.

This being so, it is apparent that no man has a *true* image of the road to his office, or of any other real thing. Indeed he has no image of it at all unless he can not only recognize it, but imagines it (truly or falsely) in all its infinite details. This being the case, it becomes very doubtful whether we ever have any such thing as an image in our imagination. Please, reader, to look at a bright red book, or other brightly coloured object, and then to shut your eyes and say whether you *see* that colour, whether brightly or faintly

—whether, indeed, there is anything like sight there. Hume and the other followers of Berkeley maintain that there is no difference between the sight and the memory of the red book except in "their different degrees of force and vivacity." "The colours which the memory employs," says Hume, "are faint and dull compared with those in which our original perceptions are clothed." If this were a correct statement of the difference, we should remember the book as being less red than it is; whereas, in fact, we remember the colour with very great precision for a few moments (please to test this point, reader), although we do not see any thing like it. We carry away absolutely nothing of the colour except the *consciousness that we could recognize it*. As a further proof of this, I will request the reader to try a little experiment. Let him call up, if he can, the image of a horse—not of one which he has ever seen, but of an imaginary one,—and before reading further let him by contemplation fix the image in his memory. . . [sic]. Has the reader done as requested? for I protest that it is not fair play to read further without doing so.——Now, the reader can say in general of what colour that horse was, whether grey, bay, or black. But he probably cannot say *precisely* of what shade it was. He cannot state this as exactly as he could just after having *seen* such a horse. But why, if he had an image in his mind which no more had the general colour than it had the particular shade, has the latter vanished so instantaneously from his memory while the former still remains? It may be replied, that we always forget the details before we do the more general characters; but that this answer is insufficient is, I think, shown by the extreme disproportion between the length of time that the exact shade of something looked at is remembered as compared with that instantaneous oblivion to the exact shade of the thing imagined, and the but slightly superior vividness of the memory of the thing seen as compared with the memory of the thing imagined.

The nominalists, I suspect, confound together thinking a triangle without thinking that it is either equilateral, isosceles, or scalene, and thinking a triangle without thinking whether it is equilateral, isosceles, or scalene.

It is important to remember that we have no intuitive power of distinguishing between one subjective mode of cognition and another; and hence often think that something is presented to us as a picture, while it is really constructed from slight data by the understanding. This is the case with dreams, as is shown by the frequent impossibility of giving an intelligible account of one without adding something which we feel was not in the dream itself. Many dreams, of which the waking memory makes elaborate and consistent stories, must probably have been in fact mere jumbles of these feelings of the ability to recognize this and that which I have just alluded to.

I will now go so far as to say that we have no images even in actual perception. It will be sufficient to prove this in the case of vision; for if no picture is seen when we look at an object, it will not be claimed that hearing, touch, and the other senses, are superior to sight in this respect. That the picture is not painted on the nerves of the retina is absolutely certain, if, as physiologists inform us, these nerves are needle-points pointing to the light and at distances considerably greater than the *minimum visibile*. The same thing is shown by our not being able to perceive that there is a large blind spot near the middle of the retina. If, then, we have a picture before us when we see, it is one constructed by the mind at the suggestion of previous sensations. Supposing these sensations to be signs, the understanding by reasoning from them could attain all the knowledge of outward things which we derive from sight, while the sensations are quite inadequate to forming an image or representation absolutely determinate. If we have such an image or picture, we must have in our minds a representation of a surface which is only a part of every surface we see, and we must see that each part, however small, has such and such a colour. If we look from some distance at a speckled surface, it seems as if we did not see whether it were speckled or not; but if we have an image before us, it must appear to us either as speckled, or as not speckled. Again, the eye by education comes to distinguish minute differences of colour; but if we see only absolutely determinate images, we must, no less before our eyes are trained than afterwards, see each colour as particularly such and such a shade. Thus to suppose that we have an image before us when we see, is not only a hypothesis which explains nothing whatever, but is one which actually creates difficulties which require new hypotheses in order to explain them away.

One of these difficulties arises from the fact that the details are less easily distinguished than, and forgotten before, the general circumstances. Upon this theory, the general features exist in the details: the details are, in fact, the whole picture. It seems, then, very strange that that which exists only secondarily in the picture should make more impression than the picture itself. It is true that in an old painting the details are not easily made out; but this is because we know that the blackness is the result of time, and is no part of the picture itself. There is no difficulty in making out the details of the picture as it looks at present; the only difficulty is in guessing what it used to be. But if we have a picture on the retina, the minutest details are there as much as, nay, more than, the general outline and significancy of it. Yet that which must actually be seen, it is extremely difficult to recognize; while that which is only abstracted from what is seen is very obvious.

But the conclusive argument against our having any images, or absolutely determinate representations in perception, is that in that case we have the materials in each such representation for an infinite amount of conscious cognition, which we yet never become aware of. Now there is no meaning in saying that we have something in our minds which never has the least effect on what we are conscious of knowing. The most that can be said is, that when we see we are put in a condition in which we are able to get a very large and perhaps indefinitely great amount of knowledge of the visible qualities of objects.

Moreover, that perceptions are not absolutely determinate and singular is obvious from the fact that each sense is an abstracting mechanism. Sight by itself informs us only of colours and forms. No one can pretend that the images of sight are determinate in reference to taste. They are, therefore, so far general that they are neither sweet nor non-sweet, bitter nor non-bitter, having savour nor insipid.

The next question is whether we have any general conceptions except in judgments. In perception, where we know a thing as existing, it is plain that there is a judgment that the thing exists, since a mere general concept of a thing is in no case a cognition of it as existing. It has usually been said, however, that we can call up any concept without making any judgment; but it seems that in this case we only arbitrarily suppose ourselves to have an experience. In order to conceive the number 7, I suppose, that is, I arbitrarily make the hypothesis or judgment, that there are certain points before my eyes, and I judge that these are seven. This seems to be the most simple and rational view of the matter, and I may add that it is the one which has been adopted by the best logicians. If this be the case, what goes by the name of the association of images is in reality an association of judgments. The association of ideas is said to proceed according to three principles —those of resemblance, of contiguity, and of causality. But it would be equally true to say that signs denote what they do on the three principles of resemblance, contiguity, and causality. There can be no question that anything *is* a sign of whatever is associated with it by resemblance, by contiguity, or by causality: nor can there be any doubt that any sign recalls the thing signified. So, then, the association of ideas consists in this, that a judgment occasions another judgment, of which it is the sign. Now this is nothing less nor more than inference.

Everything in which we take the least interest creates in us its own particular emotion, however slight this may be. This emotion is a sign and a predicate of the thing. Now, when a thing resembling this thing is presented to us, a similar emotion arises; hence, we immediately infer that the latter is like the former. A formal logician of the old school may say, that in logic no term can enter into the conclusion which had not been contained in the premisses, and that therefore the suggestion of something new must be essentially different from inference. But I reply that that rule of logic applies only to those arguments which are technically called completed. We can and do reason—

> Elias was a man;
> ∴ He was mortal.

And this argument is just as valid as the full syllogism, although it is so only because the major premiss of the latter happens to be true. If to pass from the judgment "Elias was a man" to the judgment "Elias was mortal," without actually saying to one's self that "All men are mortal," is not inference, then the term "inference" is used in so restricted a sense that inferences hardly occur outside of a logic-book.

What is here said of association by resemblance is true of all association. All association is by signs. Everything has its subjective or emotional qualities, which are attributed either absolutely or relatively, or by conventional imputation to anything which is a sign of it. And so we reason,

> The sign is such and such;
> ∴ The sign is that thing.

This conclusion receiving, however, a modification, owing to other considerations, so as to become—

> The sign is almost (is representative of) that thing.

We come now to the consideration of the last of the four principles whose consequences we were to trace; namely, that the absolutely incognizable is absolutely inconceivable. That upon Cartesian principles the very realities of things can never be known in the least, most competent persons must long ago have been convinced. Hence the breaking forth of idealism, which is essentially anti-Cartesian, in every direction, whether among empiricists (Berkeley, Hume), or among noölogists (Hegel, Fichte). The principle now brought under discussion is directly idealistic; for, since the meaning of a word is the conception it conveys, the absolutely incognizable has no meaning because no conception attaches to it. It is, therefore, a meaningless word; and, consequently, whatever is meant by any term as "the real" is cognizable in some degree, and so is of the nature of a cognition, in the objective sense of that term.

At any moment we are in possession of certain information, that is, of cognitions which have been logically derived by induction and hypothesis from previous cognitions which are less general, less distinct, and of which we have a less lively consciousness. These in their turn have been derived from others still less general, less distinct, and less vivid; and so on back to the ideal first, which is quite singular, and quite out of consciousness. This ideal first is the particular thing-in-itself. It does not exist *as such*. That is, there is no thing which is in-itself in the sense of not being relative to the mind, though things which are relative to the mind doubtless are, apart from that relation. The cognitions which thus reach us by this infinite series of inductions and hypotheses (which though infinite *a parte ante logice*, is yet as one continuous process not without a beginning *in time*) are of two kinds, the true and the untrue, or cognitions whose objects are *real* and those whose objects are *unreal*. And what do we mean by the real? It is a conception which we must first have had when we discovered that there was an unreal, an illusion; that is, when we first corrected ourselves. Now the distinction for which alone this fact logically called, was between an *ens* relative to private inward determinations, to the negations belonging to idiosyncrasy, and an *ens* such as would stand in the long run. The real, then, is that which, sooner or later, information and reasoning would finally result in, and which is therefore independent of the vagaries of me and you. Thus, the very origin of the conception of reality shows that this conception essentially involves the notion of a COMMUNITY, without definite limits, and capable of a definite increase of knowledge. And so those two series of cognitions—the real and the unreal—consist of those which, at a time sufficiently future, the community will always continue to re-affirm; and of those which, under the same conditions, will ever after be denied. Now, a proposition whose falsity can never be discovered, and the error of which therefore is absolutely incognizable, contains, upon our principle, absolutely no error. Consequently, that which is thought in these cognitions is the real, as it really is. There is nothing, then, to prevent our knowing outward things as they really are, and it is most likely that we do thus know them in numberless cases, although we can never be absolutely certain of doing so in any special case.

But it follows that since no cognition of ours is absolutely determinate, generals must have a real existence. Now this scholastic realism is usually set down as a belief in metaphysical fictions. But, in fact, a realist is simply one who knows no more recondite reality than that which is represented in a true representation. Since, therefore, the word "man" is true of something, that which "man" means is real. The nominalist must admit that man is truly applicable to something; but he believes that there is beneath this a thing in itself, an incognizable reality. His is the metaphysical figment. Modern nominalists are mostly superficial men, who do not know, as the more thorough Roscellinus and Ockham did, that a reality which has no representation is one which has no relation and no quality. The great argument for nominalism is that there is no man unless there is some particular man. That, however, does not affect the realism of Scotus; for although there is no man of whom all further determination can be denied, yet there is a man, abstraction being made of all further determination. There is a real difference between man irrespective of what the other determinations may be, and man with this or that particular series of determinations, although undoubtedly this difference is only relative to the mind and not *in re*. Such is the position of Scotus. Ockham's great objection is, there can be no real distinction which is not *in re*, in the thing-in-itself; but this begs the question, for it is itself based only on the notion that reality is something independent of representative relation.

Such being the nature of reality in general, in what does the reality of the mind consist? We have seen that the content of consciousness, the entire phenomenal manifestation of mind, is a sign resulting from inference. Upon our principle, therefore, that the absolutely incognizable does not exist, so that the phenomenal manifestation of a substance is the substance, we must conclude that the mind is a sign developing according to the laws of inference. What distinguishes a man from a word? There is a distinction doubtless. The material qualities, the forces which constitute the pure denotative application, and the meaning of the human sign, are all exceedingly complicated in comparison with those of the word. But these differences are only relative. What other is there? It may be said that man is conscious, while a word is not. But consciousness is a very vague term. It may mean that emotion which accompanies the reflection that we have animal life. This is a consciousness which is dimmed when animal life is at its ebb in old age, or sleep, but which is not dimmed when the spiritual life is at its ebb; which is the more lively the better *animal* a man is, but which is not so, the better *man* he is. We do not attribute this sensation to words, because we have reason to believe that it is dependent upon the possession of an animal body. But this consciousness, being a mere sensation, is only a part of the *material quality* of the man-sign. Again, consciousness is sometimes used to signify the *I think*, or unity in thought; but the unity is nothing but consistency, or the recognition of it. Consistency belongs to every sign, so far as it is a sign; and therefore every sign, since it signifies primarily that it is a sign, signifies its own consistency. The man-sign acquires information, and comes to mean more than he did before. But so do words. Does not electricity mean more now than it did in the days of Franklin? Man makes the word, and the word means nothing which the man has not made it mean, and that only to some man. But since man can think only by means of words or other external symbols, these might turn round and say: "You mean nothing which we have not taught you, and then only so far as you address some word as the interpretant of your thought." In fact, therefore, men and words reciprocally educate each other; each increase of a man's information involves and is involved by, a corresponding increase of a word's information.

Without fatiguing the reader by stretching this parallelism too far, it is sufficient to say that there is no element whatever of man's consciousness which has not something corresponding to it in the word; and the reason is obvious. It is that the word or sign which man uses *is* the man himself. For, as the fact that every thought is a sign, taken in conjunction with the fact that life is a train of thought, proves that man is a sign; so, that every thought is an *external* sign, proves that man is an external sign. That is to say, the man and the external sign are identical, in the same sense in which the words *homo* and *man* are identical. Thus my language is the sum total of myself; for the man is the thought.

It is hard for man to understand this, because he persists in identifying himself with his will, his power over the animal organism, with brute force.   Now the organism is only an instrument of thought.   But the identity of a man consists in the *consistency* of what he does and thinks, and consistency is the intellectual character of a thing; that is, is its expressing something.

Finally, as what anything really is, is what it may finally come to be known to be in the ideal state of complete information, so that reality depends on the ultimate decision of the community; so thought is what it is, only by virtue of its addressing a future thought which is in its value as thought identical with it, though more developed.   In this way, the existence of thought now, depends on what is to be hereafter; so that it has only a potential existence, dependent on the future thought of the community.

The individual man, since his separate existence is manifested only by ignorance and error, so far as he is anything apart from his fellows, and from what he and they are to be, is only a negation. This is man,

> . . . proud man,
> Most ignorant of what he's most assured,
> His glassy essence.

17

THE ESSENTIALS OF PRAGMATISM *

I

THE writer of this article has been led by much experience to believe that every physicist, and every chemist, and, in short, every master in any department of experimental science, has had his mind moulded by his life in the laboratory to a degree ·that is little suspected. The experimentalist himself can hardly be fully aware of it, for the reason that the men whose intellects he really knows about are much like himself in this respect. With intellects of widely different training from his own, whose education has largely been a thing learned out of books, he will never become inwardly intimate, be he on ever so familiar terms with them; for he and they are as oil and water, and though they be shaken up together, it is remarkable how quickly they will go their several mental ways, without having gained more than a faint flavour from the association. Were those other men only to take skillful soundings of the experimentalist's mind—which is just what they are unqualified to do, for the most part—they would soon discover that, excepting perhaps upon topics where his mind is trammelled by personal feeling or by his bringing up, his disposition is to think of everything just as everything is thought of in the laboratory, that is, as a question of experimentation. Of course, no living man possesses in their fullness all the attributes characteristic of his type: it is not the typical doctor whom you will see every day driven in buggy or coupé, nor is it the typical pedagogue that will be met with in the first schoolroom you enter. But when you have found, or ideally constructed upon a basis of observation, the typical experimentalist, you will find that whatever assertion you may make to him, he will either understand as meaning that if a given prescription for an experiment ever can be and ever is carried out in act, an experience of a given description will result, or else he will see no sense at all in what you

---

* [I is (with a paragraph omitted where the spatial division occurs) the paper "What Pragmatism Is," *The Monist* 1905 (*CP* 5.411-34, 436). In II, the first selection is from the Lectures on Pragmatism, at Harvard 1903 (*CP* 5.197), the second from ms. 1903 (*CP* 5.597), and the third from ms. c. 1902 (*CP* 5.541).]

say. If you talk to him as Mr. Balfour talked not long ago to the British Association saying that "the physicist . . . seeks for something deeper than the laws connecting possible objects of experience," that "his object is physical reality" unrevealed in experiments, and that the existence of such non-experiential reality "is the unalterable faith of science," to all such ontological meaning you will find the experimentalist mind to be colour-blind. What adds to that confidence in this, which the writer owes to his conversations with experimentalists, is that he himself may almost be said to have inhabited a laboratory from the age of six until long past maturity; and having all his life associated mostly with experimentalists, it has always been with a confident sense of understanding them and of being understood by them.

That laboratory life did not prevent the writer (who here and in what follows simply exemplifies the experimentalist type) from becoming interested in methods of thinking; and when he came to read metaphysics, although much of it seemed to him loosely reasoned and determined by accidental prepossessions, yet in the writings of some philosophers, especially Kant, Berkeley, and Spinoza, he sometimes came upon strains of thought that recalled the ways of thinking of the laboratory, so that he felt he might trust to them; all of which has been true of other laboratory-men.

Endeavouring, as a man of that type naturally would, to formulate what he so approved, he framed the theory that a *conception*, that is, the rational purport of a word or other expression, lies exclusively in its conceivable bearing upon the conduct of life; so that, since obviously nothing that might not result from experiment can have any direct bearing upon conduct, if one can define accurately all the conceivable experimental phenomena which the affirmation or denial of a concept could imply, one will have therein a complete definition of the concept, and *there is absolutely nothing more in it*. For this doctrine he invented the name *pragmatism*. Some of his friends wished him to call it *practicism* or *practicalism* (perhaps on the ground that πρακτικός is better Greek than πραγματικός). But for one who had learned philosophy out of Kant, as the writer, along with nineteen out of every twenty experimentalists who have turned to philosophy, had done, and who still thought in Kantian terms most readily, *praktisch* and *pragmatisch* were as far apart as the two poles, the former belonging in a region of thought where no mind of the experimentalist type can ever make sure of solid ground under his feet, the latter expressing relation to some definite human purpose. Now quite the most striking feature of the new theory was its recognition of an inseparable connection between rational cognition and rational purpose; and that consideration it was which determined the preference for the name *pragmatism*.

Concerning the matter of philosophical nomenclature, there are a few plain considerations, which the writer has for many years longed to submit to the deliberate judgment of those few fellow-students of philosophy, who deplore the present state of that study, and who are intent upon rescuing it therefrom and bringing it to a condition like that of the natural sciences, where investigators, instead of contemning each the work of most of the others as misdirected from beginning to end, coöperate, stand upon one another's shoulders, and multiply incontestable results; where every observation is repeated, and isolated observations go for little; where every hypothesis that merits attention is subjected to severe but fair examination, and only after the predictions to which it leads have been remarkably borne out by experience is trusted at all, and even then only provisionally; where a radically false step is rarely taken, even the most faulty of those theories which gain wide credence being true in their main experiential predictions. To those students, it is submitted that no study can become scientific in the sense described, until it provides itself with a suitable technical nomenclature, whose every term has a single definite meaning universally accepted among students of the subject, and whose vocables have no such sweetness or charms as might tempt loose writers to abuse them—which is a virtue of scientific nomenclature too little appreciated. It is submitted that the experience of those sciences which have conquered the greatest difficulties of terminology, which are unquestionably the taxonomic sciences, chemistry, mineralogy, botany, zoölogy, has conclusively shown that the one only way in which the requisite unanimity and requisite ruptures with individual habits and preferences can be brought about is so to shape the canons of terminology that they shall gain the support of *moral principle* and of every man's sense of decency; and that, in particular (under defined restrictions), the general feeling shall be that he who introduces a new conception into philosophy is under an obligation to invent acceptable terms to express it, and that when he has done so, the duty of his fellow-students is to accept those terms, and to resent any wresting of them from their original meanings, as not only a gross discourtesy to him to whom philosophy was indebted for each conception, but also as an injury to philosophy itself; and furthermore, that once a conception has been supplied with suitable and sufficient words for its expression, no other *technical* terms denoting the same things, considered in the same relations, should be countenanced. Should this suggestion find favour, it might be deemed needful that the philosophians in congress assembled should adopt, after due deliberation, convenient canons to limit the application of the principle. Thus, just as is done in chemistry, it might be wise to assign fixed meanings to certain prefixes and suffixes. For example, it might be agreed, perhaps, that the prefix *prope-* should mark a broad and rather indefinite extension of the meaning of the term to which it was prefixed; the name of a doctrine would naturally end in *-ism*, while *-icism* might mark a more strictly defined acception of that doctrine, etc. Then again, just as in biology no account is taken of terms antedating Linnaeus, so in philosophy it might be found best not to go back of the scholastic terminology. To illustrate another sort of limitation, it has probably never happened that any philosopher has attempted to give a general name to his own doctrine without that name's soon acquiring in common philosophical usage, a signification much broader than was originally intended. Thus, special systems go by the names Kantianism, Benthamism, Comteanism, Spencerianism, etc., while transcendentalism, utilitarianism, positivism, evolutionism, synthetic philosophy, etc., have irrevocably and very conveniently been elevated to broader governments.

After awaiting in vain, for a good many years, some particularly opportune conjuncture of circumstances that might serve to recommend his notions of the ethics of terminology, the writer has now, at last, dragged them in over head and shoulders, on an occasion when he has no specific proposal to offer nor any feeling but satisfaction at the course usage has run without any canons or resolutions of a congress. His word "pragmatism" has gained general recognition in a generalized sense that seems to argue power of growth and vitality. The famed psychologist, James, first took it up, seeing that his "radical empiricism" substantially answered to the writer's definition of pragmatism, albeit with a certain difference in the point of view. Next, the admirably clear and brilliant thinker, Mr. Ferdinand C. S. Schiller, casting about for a more attractive name for the "anthropomorphism" of his *Riddle of the Sphinx*, lit, in that most remarkable paper of his on *Axioms as Postulates*, upon the same designation "pragmatism," which in its original sense was in generic agreement with his own doctrine, for which he has since found the more appropriate specification "humanism," while he still retains "pragmatism" in a somewhat wider sense. So far all went happily. But at present, the word begins to be met with occasionally in the literary journals, where it gets abused in the merciless way that words have to expect when they fall into literary clutches. Sometimes the manners of the British have effloresced in scolding at the word as ill-chosen— ill-chosen, that is, to express some meaning that it was rather designed to exclude. So then, the writer, finding his bantling "pragmatism" so promoted, feels that it is time to kiss his child good-by and relinquish it to its higher destiny; while to serve the precise purpose of expressing the original definition, he begs to announce the birth of the word "pragmaticism," which is ugly enough to be safe from kidnappers.

Much as the writer has gained from the perusal of what other pragmatists have written, he still thinks there is a decisive advantage in his original conception of the doctrine.[9] From this original form every truth that follows from any of the other forms can be deduced, while some errors can be avoided into which other pragmatists have fallen. The original view appears, too, to be a more compact and unitary conception than the others. But its capital merit, in the writer's eyes, is that it more readily connects itself with a critical proof of its truth. Quite in accord with the logical order of investigation, it usually happens that one first forms an hypothesis that seems more and more reasonable the further one examines into it, but that only a good deal later gets crowned with an adequate proof. The present writer having had the pragmatist theory under consideration for many years longer than most of its adherents, would naturally have given more attention to the proof of it. At any rate, in endeavouring to explain pragmatism, he may be excused for confining himself to that form of it that he knows best. In the present article there will be space only to explain just what this doctrine (which, in such hands as it has now fallen into, may probably play a pretty prominent part in the philosophical discussions of the next coming years), really consists in. Should the exposition be found to interest readers of *The Monist*, they would certainly be much more interested in a second article which would give some samples of the manifold applications of pragmaticism (assuming it to be true) to the solution of problems of different kinds. After that, readers might be prepared to take an interest in a proof that the doctrine is true—a proof which seems to the writer to leave no reasonable doubt on the subject, and to be the one contribution of value that he has to make to philosophy.

For it would essentially involve the establishment of the truth of synechism.[14]

The bare definition of pragmaticism could convey no satisfactory comprehension of it to the most apprehensive of minds, but requires the commentary to be given below. Moreover, this definition takes no notice of one or two other doctrines without the previous acceptance (or virtual acceptance) of which pragmaticism itself would be a nullity. They are included as a part of the pragmatism of Schiller, but the present writer prefers not to mingle different propositions. The preliminary propositions had better be stated forthwith.

The difficulty in doing this is that no formal list of them has ever been made. They might all be included under the vague maxim, "Dismiss make-believes." Philosophers of very diverse stripes propose that philosophy shall take its start from one or another state of mind in which no man, least of all a beginner in philosophy, actually is. One proposes that you shall begin by doubting everything, and says that there is only one thing that you cannot doubt, as if doubting were "as easy as lying." Another proposes that we should begin by observing "the first impressions of sense," forgetting that our very percepts are the results of cognitive elaboration. But in truth, there is but one state of mind from which you can "set out," namely, the very state of mind in which you actually find yourself at the time you do "set out"—a state in which you are laden with an immense mass of cognition already formed, of which you cannot divest yourself if you would; and who knows whether, if you could, you would not have made all knowledge impossible to yourself? Do you call it *doubting* to write down on a piece of paper that you doubt? If so, doubt has nothing to do with any serious business. But do not make believe; if pedantry has not eaten all the reality out of you, recognize, as you must, that there is much that you do not doubt, in the least. Now that which you do not at all doubt, you must and do regard as infallible, absolute truth. Here breaks in Mr. Make Believe: "What! Do you mean to say that one is to believe what is not true, or that what a man does not doubt is *ipso facto* true?" No, but unless he can make a thing white and black at once, *he* has to regard what he does not doubt as absolutely true. Now you, *per hypothesiu*, are that man. "But you tell me there are scores of things I do not doubt. I really cannot persuade myself that there is not some one of them about which I am mistaken." You are adducing one of your make-believe facts, which, even if it were established, would only go to show that doubt has a *limen*, that is, is only called into being by a certain finite stimulus. You only puzzle yourself by talking of this metaphysical "truth" and metaphysical "falsity," that you know nothing about. All you have any dealings with are your doubts and beliefs, with the course of life that forces new beliefs upon you and gives you power to doubt old beliefs. If your terms "truth" and "falsity" are taken in such senses as to be definable in terms of doubt and belief and the course of experience (as for example they would be, if you were to define the "truth" as that to a belief in which belief would tend if it were to tend indefinitely toward absolute fixity), well and good: in that case, you are only talking about doubt and belief. But if by truth and falsity you mean something not definable in terms of doubt and belief in any way, then you are talking of entities of whose existence you can know nothing, and which Ockham's razor would clean shave off. Your problems would be greatly simplified, if, instead of saying that you want to know the "Truth," you were simply to say that you want to attain a state of belief unassailable by doubt.

Belief is not a momentary mode of consciousness; it is a habit of mind essentially enduring for some time, and mostly (at least) unconscious; and like other habits, it is (until it meets with some surprise that begins its dissolution) perfectly self-satisfied. Doubt is of an altogether contrary genus. It is not a habit, but the privation of a habit. Now a privation of a habit, in order to be anything at all, must be a condition of erratic activity that in some way must get superseded by a habit.

Among the things which the reader, as a rational person, does not doubt, is that he not merely has habits, but also can exert a measure of self-control over his future actions; which means, however, *not* that he can impart to them any arbitrarily assignable character, but, on the contrary, that a process of self-preparation will tend to impart to action (when the occasion for it shall arise), one fixed character, which is indicated and perhaps roughly measured by the absence (or slightness) of the feeling of self-reproach, which subsequent reflection will induce. Now, this subsequent reflection is part of the self-preparation for action on the next occasion. Consequently, there is a tendency, as action is repeated again and again, for the action to approximate indefinitely toward the perfection of that fixed character, which would be marked by entire absence of self-reproach. The more closely this is approached, the less room for self-control there will be; and where no self-control is possible there will be no self-reproach.

These phenomena seem to be the fundamental characteristics which distinguish a rational being. Blame, in every case, appears to be a modification, often accomplished by a transference, or "projection," of the primary feeling of self-reproach. Accordingly, we never blame anybody for what had been beyond his power of previous self-control. Now, thinking is a species of conduct which is largely subject to self-control. In all their features (which there is no room to describe here), logical self-control is a perfect mirror of ethical self-control—unless it be rather a species under that genus. In accordance with this, what you cannot in the least help believing is not, justly speaking, wrong belief. In other words, for you it is the absolute truth. True, it is conceivable that what you cannot help believing today, you might find you thoroughly disbelieve tomorrow. But then there is a certain distinction between things you "cannot" do, merely in the sense that nothing stimulates you to the great effort and endeavours that would be required, and things you cannot do because in their own nature they are insusceptible of being put into practice. In every stage of your excogitations, there is something of which you can only say, "I cannot think otherwise," and your experientially based hypothesis is that the impossibility is of the second kind.

There is no reason why "thought," in what has just been said, should be taken in that narrow sense in which silence and darkness are favourable to thought. It should rather be understood as covering all rational life, so that an experiment shall be an operation of thought. Of course, that ultimate state of habit to which the action of self-control ultimately tends, where no room is left for further self-control, is, in the case of thought, the state of fixed belief, or perfect knowledge.

Two things here are all-important to assure oneself of and to remember. The first is that a person is not absolutely an individual. His thoughts are what he is "saying to himself," that is, is saying to that other self that is just coming into life in the flow of time. When one reasons, it is that critical self that one is trying to persuade; and all thought whatsoever is a sign, and is mostly of the nature of language. The second thing to remember is that the man's circle of society (however widely or narrowly this phrase may be understood), is a sort of loosely compacted person, in some respects of higher rank than the person of an individual organism. It is these two things alone that render it possible for you—but only in the abstract, and in a Pickwickian sense—to distinguish between absolute truth and what you do not doubt.

Let us now hasten to the exposition of pragmaticism itself. Here it will be convenient to imagine that somebody to whom the doctrine is new, but of rather preternatural perspicacity, asks questions of a pragmaticist. Everything that might give a dramatic illusion must be stripped off, so that the result will be a sort of cross between a dialogue and a catechism, but a good deal liker the latter—something rather painfully reminiscent of Mangnall's *Historical Questions*.

Questioner: I am astounded at your definition of your pragmatism, because only last year I was assured by a person above all suspicion of warping the truth—himself a pragmatist—that your doctrine precisely was "that a conception is to be tested by its practical effects." You must surely, then, have entirely changed your definition very recently.

Pragmatist: If you will turn to Vols. VI and VII of the *Revue Philosophique*, or to the *Popular Science Monthly* for November 1877 and January 1878,[15] you will be able to judge for yourself whether the interpretation you mention was not then clearly excluded. The exact wording of the English enunciation (changing only the first person into the second) was: "Consider what effects that might conceivably have practical bearing you conceive the object of your conception to have. Then your conception of those effects is the WHOLE of your conception of the object."

Questioner: Well, what reason have you for asserting that this is so?

Pragmatist: That is what I specially desire to tell you. But the question had better be postponed until you clearly understand what those reasons profess to prove.

Questioner: What, then, is the *raison d'être* of the doctrine? What advantage is expected from it?

Pragmatist: It will serve to show that almost every proposition of ontological metaphysics is either meaningless gibberish—one word being defined by other words, and they by still others, without any real conception ever being reached—or else is downright absurd; so that all such rubbish being swept away, what will remain of philosophy will be a series of problems capable of investigation by the observational methods of the true sciences—the truth about which can be reached without those interminable misunderstandings and disputes which have made the highest of the positive sciences a mere amusement for idle intellects, a sort of chess—idle pleasure its purpose, and reading out of a book its method. In this regard, pragmaticism is a species of prope-positivism. But what distinguishes it from other species is, first, its retention of a purified philosophy; secondly, its full acceptance of the main body of our instinctive beliefs; and thirdly, its strenuous insistence upon the truth of scholastic realism (or a close approximation to that, well-stated by the late Dr. Francis Ellingwood Abbot in the Introduction to his *Scientific Theism*). So, instead of merely jeering at metaphysics, like other prope-positivists, whether by long-drawn-out parodies or otherwise, the pragmaticist extracts from it a precious essence, which will serve to give life and light to cosmology and physics. At the same time, the moral applications of the doctrine are positive and potent; and there are many other uses of it not easily classed. On another occasion, instances may be given to show that it really has these effects.

Questioner: I hardly need to be convinced that your doctrine would wipe out metaphysics. Is it not as obvious that it must wipe out every proposition of science and everything that bears on the conduct of life? For you say that the only meaning that, for you, any assertion bears is that a certain experiment has resulted in a certain way: Nothing else but an experiment enters into the meaning. Tell me, then, how can an experiment, in itself, reveal anything more than that something once happened to an individual object and that subsequently some other individual event occurred?

Pragmatist: That question is, indeed, to the purpose—the purpose being to correct any misapprehensions of pragmaticism. You speak of an experiment in itself, emphasizing *"in itself."* You evidently think of each experiment as isolated from every other. It has not, for example, occurred to you, one might venture to surmise, that every connected series of experiments constitutes a single collective experiment. What are the essential ingredients of an experiment? First, of course, an experimenter of flesh and blood. Secondly, a verifiable hypothesis. This is a proposition relating to the universe environing the experimenter, or to some well-known part of it and affirming or denying of this only some experimental possibility or impossibility. The third indispensable ingredient is a sincere doubt in the experimenter's mind as to the truth of that hypothesis.

Passing over several ingredients on which we need not dwell, the purpose, the plan, and the resolve, we come to the act of choice by which the experimenter singles out certain identifiable objects to be operated upon. The next is the external (or quasi-external) ACT by which he modifies those objects. Next, comes the subsequent *reaction* of the world upon the experimenter in a perception; and finally, his recognition of the teaching of the experiment. While the two chief parts of the event itself are the action and the reaction, yet the unity of essence of the experiment lies in its purpose and plan, the ingredients passed over in the enumeration.

Another thing: in representing the pragmaticist as making rational meaning to consist in an experiment (which you speak of as an event in the past), you strikingly fail to catch his attitude of mind. Indeed, it is not in an experiment, but in *experimental phenomena*, that rational meaning is said to consist. When an experimentalist speaks of a *phenomenon*, such as "Hall's phenomenon," "Zeemann's phenomenon" and its modification, "Michelson's phenomenon," or "the chessboard phenomenon," he does not mean any particular event that did happen to somebody in the dead past, but what *surely will* happen to everybody in the living future who shall fulfill certain conditions. The phenomenon consists in the fact that when an experimentalist shall come to *act* according to a certain scheme that he has in mind, then will something else happen, and shatter the doubts of sceptics, like the celestial fire upon the altar of Elijah.

And do not overlook the fact that the pragmaticist maxim says nothing of single experiments or of single experimental phenomena (for what is conditionally true *in futuro* can hardly be singular), but only speaks of *general kinds* of experimental phenomena. Its adherent does not shrink from speaking of general objects as real, since whatever is true represents a real. Now the laws of nature are true.

The rational meaning of every proposition lies in the future. How so? The meaning of a proposition is itself a proposition. Indeed, it is no other than the very proposition of which it is the meaning: it is a translation of it. But of the myriads of forms into which a proposition may be translated, what is that one which is to be called its very meaning? It is, according to the pragmaticist, that form in which the proposition becomes applicable to human conduct, not in these or those special circumstances, nor when one entertains this or that special design, but that form which is most directly applicable to self-control under every situation, and to every purpose. This is why he locates the meaning in future time; for future conduct is the only conduct that is subject to self-control. But in order that that form of the proposition which is to be taken as its meaning should be applicable to every situation and to every purpose upon which the proposition has any bearing, it must be simply the general description of all the experimental phenomena which the assertion of the proposition virtually predicts. For an experimental phenomenon is the fact asserted by the proposition that action of a certain description will have a certain kind of experimental result; and experimental results are the only results that can affect human conduct. No doubt, some unchanging idea may come to influence a man more than it had done; but only because some experience equivalent to an experiment has brought its truth home to him more intimately than before. Whenever a man acts purposively, he acts under a belief in some experimental phenomenon. Consequently, the sum of the experimental phenomena that a proposition implies makes up its entire bearing upon human conduct. Your question, then, of how a pragmaticist can attribute any meaning to any assertion other than that of a single occurrence is substantially answered.

Questioner: I see that pragmaticism is a thorough-going phenomenalism. Only why should you limit yourself to the phenomena of experimental science rather than embrace all observational science? Experiment, after all, is an uncommunicative informant. It never expatiates: it only answers "yes" or "no"; or rather it usually snaps out "No!", or at best only utters an inarticulate grunt for the negation of its "no." The typical experimentalist is not much of an observer. It is the student of natural history to whom nature opens the treasury of her confidence, while she treats the cross-examining experimentalist with the reserve he merits. Why should your phenomenalism sound the meagre jew's-harp of experiment rather than the glorious organ of observation?

Pragmaticist: Because pragmaticism is not definable as "thorough-going phenomenalism," although the latter doctrine may be a kind of pragmatism. The *richness* of phenomena lies in their sensuous quality. Pragmaticism does not intend to define the phenomenal equivalents of words and general ideas, but, on the contrary, eliminates their sential element, and endeavours to define the rational purport, and this it finds in the purposive bearing of the word or proposition in question.

Questioner: Well, if you choose so to make Doing the Be-all and the End-all of human life, why do you not make meaning to consist simply in doing? Doing has to be done at a certain time upon a certain object. Individual objects and single events cover all reality, as everybody knows, and as a practicalist ought to be the first to insist. Yet, your meaning, as you have described it, is *general.* Thus, it is of the nature of a mere word and not a reality. You say yourself that your meaning of a proposition is only the same proposition in another dress. But a practical man's meaning is the very thing he means. What do you make to be the meaning of "George Washington"?

Pragmaticist: Forcibly put! A good half dozen of your points must certainly be admitted. It must be admitted, in the first place, that if pragmaticism really made Doing to be the Be-all and the End-all of life, that would be its death. For to say that we live for the mere sake of action, as action, regardless of the thought it carries out, would be to say that there is no such thing as rational purport. Secondly, it must be admitted that every proposition professes to be true of a certain real individual object, often the environing universe. Thirdly, it must be admitted that pragmaticism fails to furnish any translation or meaning of a proper name, or other designation of an individual object. Fourthly, the pragmaticistic meaning is undoubtedly general; and it is equally indisputable that the general is of the nature of a word or sign. Fifthly, it must be admitted that individuals alone exist; and sixthly, it may be admitted that the very meaning of a word or significant object ought to be the very essence of reality of what it signifies. But when those admissions have been unreservedly made, you find the pragmaticist still constrained most earnestly to deny the force of your objection, you ought to infer that there is some consideration that has escaped you. Putting the admissions together, you will perceive that the pragmaticist grants that a proper name (although it is not customary to say that it has a *meaning*) has a certain denotative function peculiar, in each case, to that name and its equivalents; and that he grants that every assertion contains such a denotative or pointing-out function. In its peculiar individuality, the pragmaticist excludes this from the rational purport of the assertion, although *the like* of it, being common to all assertions, and so, being general and not individual, may enter into the pragmaticistic purport. Whatever exists, *ex-sists*, that is, really acts upon other existents, so obtains a self-identity, and is definitely individual. As to the general, it will be a help to thought to notice that there are two ways of being general. A statue of a soldier on some village monument, in his overcoat and with his musket, is for each of a hundred families the image of its uncle, its sacrifice to the Union. That statue, then, though it is itself single, represents any one man of whom a certain predicate may be true. It is *objectively* general. The word "soldier," whether spoken or written, is general in the same way; while the name, "George Washington," is not so. But each of these two terms remains one and the same noun, whether it be spoken or written, and whenever and wherever it be spoken or written. This noun is not an existent thing: it is a *type*, or *form*, to which objects, both those that are externally existent and those which are imagined, may *conform*, but which none of them can exactly be. This is subjective generality. The pragmaticistic purport is general in both ways.

As to reality, one finds it defined in various ways; but if that principle of terminological ethics that was proposed be accepted, the equivocal language will soon disappear. For *realis* and *realitas* are not ancient words. They were invented to be terms of philosophy in the thirteenth century, and the meaning they were intended to express is perfectly clear. That is *real* which has such and such characters, whether anybody thinks it to have those characters or not. At any rate, that is the sense in which the pragmaticist uses the word. Now, just as conduct controlled by ethical reason tends toward fixing certain habits of conduct, the nature of which (as to illustrate the meaning, peaceable habits and not quarrelsome habits) does not depend upon any accidental circumstances, and *in that sense* may be said to be *destined*; so, thought, controlled by a rational experimental logic, tends to the fixation of certain opinions, equally destined, the nature of which will be the same in the end, however the perversity of thought of whole generations may cause the postponement of the ultimate fixation. If this be so, as every man of us virtually assumes that it is, in regard to each matter the truth of which he seriously discusses, then, according to the adopted definition of "real," the state of things which will be believed in that ultimate opinion is real. But, for the most part, such opinions will be general. Consequently, *some* general objects are real. (Of course, nobody ever thought that *all* generals were real; but the scholastics used to assume that generals were real when they had hardly any, or quite no, experiential evidence to support their assumption; and their fault lay just there, and not in holding that generals could be real.) One is struck with the inexactitude of thought even of analysts of power, when they touch upon modes of being. One will meet, for example, the virtual assumption that what is relative to thought cannot be real. But why not, exactly? *Red* is relative to sight, but the fact that this or that is in that relation to vision that we call being red is not *itself* relative to sight; it is a real fact.

Not only may generals be real, but they may also be *physically efficient*, not in every metaphysical sense, but in the common-sense acception in which human purposes are physically efficient. Aside from metaphysical nonsense, no sane man doubts that if I feel the air in my study to be stuffy, that thought may cause the window to be opened. My thought, be it granted, was an individual event. But what determined it to take the particular determination it did, was in part the general fact that stuffy air is unwholesome, and in part other *Forms*, concerning which Dr. Carus has caused so many men to reflect to advantage—or rather, *by* which, and the general truth concerning which Dr. Carus's mind was determined to the forcible enunciation of so much truth. For truths, on the average, have a greater tendency to get believed than falsities have. Were it otherwise, considering that there are myriads of false hypotheses to account for any given phenomenon, against one sole true one (or if you will have it so, against every true one), the first step toward genuine knowledge must have been next door to a miracle. So, then, when my window was opened, because of the truth that stuffy air is *malsain*, a physical effort was brought into existence by the efficiency of a general and non-existent truth. This has a droll sound because it is unfamiliar; but exact analysis is with it and not against it; and it has besides, the immense advantage of not blinding us to great facts—such as that the ideas "justice" and "truth" are, notwithstanding the iniquity of the world, the mightiest of the forces that move it. Generality is, indeed, an indispensable ingredient of reality; for mere individual existence or actuality without any regularity whatever is a nullity. Chaos is pure nothing.

That which any true proposition asserts is *real*, in the sense of being as it is regardless of what you or I may think about it. Let this proposition be a general conditional proposition as to the future, and it is a real general such as is calculated really to influence human conduct; and such the pragmaticist holds to be the rational purport of every concept.

Accordingly, the pragmaticist does not make the *summum bonum* to consist in action, but makes it to consist in that process of evolution whereby the existent comes more and more to embody those generals which were just now said to be *destined*, which is what we strive to express in calling them *reasonable*. In its higher stages, evolution takes place more and more largely through self-control, and this gives the pragmaticist a sort of justification for making the rational purport to be general.

There is much more in elucidation of pragmaticism that might be said to advantage, were it not for the dread of fatiguing the reader. It might, for example, have been well to show clearly that the pragmaticist does not attribute any different essential mode of being to an event in the future from that which he would attribute to a similar event in the past, but only that the practical attitude of the thinker toward the two is different. It would also have been well to show that the pragmaticist does not make Forms to be the *only* realities in the world, any more than he makes the reasonable purport of a word to be the only kind of meaning there is. These things are, however, implicitly involved in what has been said.

Suffer me to add one word more on this point. For if one cares at all to know what the pragmaticist theory consists in, one must understand that there is no other part of it to which the pragmaticist attaches quite as much importance as he does to the recognition in his doctrine of the utter inadequacy of action or volition or even of resolve or actual purpose, as materials out of which to construct a conditional purpose or the concept of conditional purpose. Had a purposed article concerning the principle of continuity and synthetizing the ideas of the other articles of a series [16] in the early volumes of *The Monist* ever been written, it would have appeared how, with thorough consistency, that theory involved the recognition that continuity is an indispensable element of reality, and that continuity is simply what generality becomes in the logic of relatives, and thus, like generality, and more than generality, is an affair of thought, and is the essence of thought. Yet even in its truncated condition, an extra-intelligent reader might discern that the theory of those cosmological articles made reality to consist in something more than feeling and action could supply, inasmuch as the primeval chaos, where those two elements were present, was explicitly shown to be pure nothing. Now, the motive for alluding to that theory just here is, that in this way one can put in a strong light a position which the pragmaticist holds and must hold, whether that cosmological theory be ultimately sustained or exploded, namely, that the third category—the category of thought, representation, triadic relation, mediation, genuine thirdness, thirdness as such—is an essential ingredient of reality, yet does not by itself constitute reality, since this category (which in that cosmology appears as the element of habit) can have no concrete being without action, as a separate object on which to work its government, just as action cannot exist without the immediate being of feeling on which to act. The truth is that pragmaticism is closely allied to the Hegelian absolute idealism, from which, however, it is sundered by its vigorous denial that the third category (which Hegel degrades to a mere stage of thinking) suffices to make the world, or is even so much as self-sufficient. Had Hegel, instead of regarding the first two stages with his smile of contempt, held on to them as independent or distinct elements of the triune Reality, pragmaticists might have looked up to him as the great vindicator of their truth. (Of course, the external trappings of his doctrine are only here and there of much significance.) For pragmaticism belongs essentially to the triadic class of philosophical doctrines, and is much more essentially so than Hegelianism is. (Indeed, in one passage, at least, Hegel alludes to the triadic form of his exposition as to a mere fashion of dress.)

II

What . . . is the end of an explanatory hypothesis? Its end is, through subjection to the test of experiment, to lead to the avoidance of all surprise and to the establishment of a habit of positive expectation that shall not be disappointed. Any hypothesis, therefore, may be admissible, in the absence of any special reasons to the contrary, provided it be capable of experimental verification, and only in so far as it is capable of such verification. This is approximately the doctrine of pragmatism. But just here a broad question opens out before us. What are we to understand by experimental verification?

Auguste Comte . . . would condemn every theory that was not "verifiable." Like the majority of Comte's ideas, this is a bad interpretation of a *truth*. An explanatory hypothesis, that is to say, a conception which does not limit its purpose to enabling the mind to grasp into one a variety of facts, but which seeks to connect those facts with our general conceptions of the universe, ought, in one sense, to be *verifiable*; that is to say, it ought to be little more than a ligament of numberless possible predictions concerning future experience, so that if they fail, it fails. Thus, when Schliemann entertained the hypothesis that there really had been a city of Troy and a Trojan War, this meant to his mind among other things that when he should come to make excavations at Hissarlik he would probably find remains of a city with evidences of a civilization more or less answering to the descriptions of the Iliad, and which would correspond with other probable finds at Mycenae, Ithaca, and elsewhere. So understood, Comte's maxim is sound.

Nothing but that *is* an explanatory hypothesis. But Comte's own notion of a *verifiable* hypothesis was that it must not suppose anything that you are not able directly to observe. From such a rule it would be fair to infer that he would permit Mr. Schliemann to suppose he was going to find arms and utensils at Hissarlik, but would forbid him to suppose that they were either made or used by any human being, since no such beings could ever be detected by direct percept. . . . Comte, Poincaré, and Karl Pearson take what they consider to be the first impressions of sense, but which are really nothing of the sort, but are percepts that are products of psychical operations, and they separate these from all the intellectual part of our knowledge, and arbitrarily call the first *real* and the second *fictions*. These two words *real* and *fictive* bear no significations whatever except as marks of *good* and *bad*. But the truth is that what they call *bad* or *fictitious*, or *subjective*, the intellectual part of our knowledge, comprises all that is valuable on its own account, while what they mark *good*, or *real*, or *objective*, is nothing but the pretty vessel that carries the precious thought.

A theory which should be capable of being absolutely demonstrated in its entirety by future events, would be no scientific theory but a mere piece of fortune telling. On the other hand, a theory which goes beyond what may be verified to any degree of approximation by future discoveries is, in so far, metaphysical gabble.

18

PRAGMATISM IN RETROSPECT: A LAST FORMULATION *

... ANY philosophical doctrine that should be completely new could hardly fail to prove completely false; but the rivulets at the head of the river of pragmatism are easily traced back to almost any desired antiquity.

Socrates bathed in these waters. Aristotle rejoices when he can find them. They run, where least one would suspect them, beneath the dry rubbish-heaps of Spinoza. Those clean definitions that strew the pages of the *Essay concerning Humane Understanding* (I refuse to reform the spelling) had been washed out in these same pure springs. It was this medium, and not tar-water, that gave health and strength to Berkeley's earlier works, his *Theory of Vision* and what remains of his *Principles*. From it the general views of Kant derive such clearness as they have. Auguste Comte made still more—much more—use of this element; as much as he saw his way to using. Unfortunately, however, both he and Kant, in their rather opposite ways, were in the habit of mingling these sparkling waters with a certain mental sedative to which many men are addicted—and the burly business men very likely to their benefit, but which plays sad havoc with the philosophical constitution. I refer to the habit of cherishing contempt for the close study of logic.

So much for the past. The ancestry of pragmatism is respectable enough; but the more conscious adoption of it as *lanterna pedibus* in the discussion of dark questions, and the elaboration of it into a method in aid of philosophic inquiry came, in the first instance, from the humblest *souche* imaginable. It was in the earliest seventies that a knot of us young men in Old Cambridge, calling ourselves, half-ironically, half-defiantly, "The Metaphysical Club,"—for agnosticism was then riding its high horse, and was frowning superbly upon all metaphysics—used to meet, sometimes in my study, sometimes in that of William James. It may be that some of our old-time confederates would today not care to have such

* [From ms. c. 1906, the two spatial divisions each indicating an omission of some paragraphs (*CP* 5.11-13, 464-8, 470-90, 491-6).]

wild-oats-sowings made public, though there was nothing but boiled oats, milk, and sugar in the mess. Mr. Justice Holmes, however, will not, I believe, take it ill that we are proud to remember his membership; nor will Joseph Warner, Esq. Nicholas St. John Green was one of the most interested fellows, a skillful lawyer and a learned one, a disciple of Jeremy Bentham. His extraordinary power of disrobing warm and breathing truth of the draperies of long worn formulas was what attracted attention to him everywhere. In particular, he often urged the importance of applying Bain's definition of belief, as "that upon which a man is prepared to act." From this definition, pragmatism is scarce more than a corollary; so that I am disposed to think of him as the grandfather of pragmatism. Chauncey Wright, something of a philosophical celebrity in those days, was never absent from our meetings. I was about to call him our corypheus; but he will better be described as our boxing-master whom we—I particularly—used to face to be severely pummelled. He had abandoned a former attachment to Hamiltonianism to take up with the doctrines of Mill, to which and to its cognate agnosticism he was trying to weld the really incongruous ideas of Darwin. John Fiske and, more rarely, Francis Ellingwood Abbot, were sometimes present, lending their countenances to the spirit of our endeavours, while holding aloof from any assent to their success. Wright, James, and I were men of science, rather scrutinizing the doctrines of the metaphysicians on their scientific side than regarding them as very momentous spiritually. The type of our thought was decidedly British. I, alone of our number, had come upon the threshing-floor of philosophy through the doorway of Kant, and even my ideas were acquiring the English accent.

Our metaphysical proceedings had all been in winged words (and swift ones, at that, for the most part), until at length, lest the club should be dissolved, without leaving any material *souvenir* behind, I drew up a little paper expressing some of the opinions that I had been urging all along under the name of pragmatism. This paper was received with such unlooked-for kindness, that I was encouraged, some half dozen years later, on the invitation of the great publisher, Mr. W. H. Appleton, to insert it, somewhat expanded, in the *Popular Science Monthly* for November 1877 and January 1878,[15] not with the warmest possible approval of the Spencerian editor, Dr. Edward Youmans. The same paper appeared the next year in a French redaction in the *Revue Philosophique* (Vol. VI, 1878, p. 553; Vol. VII, 1879, p. 39). In those medieval times, I dared not in type use an English word to express an idea unrelated to its received meaning. The authority of Mr. Principal Campbell weighed too heavily upon my conscience. I had not yet come to perceive, what is so plain today, that if philosophy is ever to stand in the ranks of the sciences, literary elegance must be sacrificed— like the soldier's old brilliant uniforms—to the stern requirements of efficiency, and the philosophist must be encouraged—yea, and required—to coin new terms to express such new scientific concepts as he may discover, just as his chemical and biological brethren are expected to do. Indeed, in those days, such brotherhood was scorned, alike on the one side and on the other—a lamentable but not surprising state of scientific feeling. As late as 1893, when I might have procured the insertion of the word pragmatism in the *Century Dictionary*, it did not seem to me that its vogue was sufficient to warrant that step.

It is now high time to explain what pragmatism is. I must, however, preface the explanation by a statement of what it is not, since many writers, especially of the starry host of Kant's progeny, in spite of pragmatists' declarations, unanimous, reiterated, and most explicit, still remain unable to "catch on" to what we are driving at, and persist in twisting our purpose and purport all awry. I was long enough, myself, within the Kantian fold to comprehend their difficulty; but let it go. Suffice it to say once more that pragmatism is, in itself, no doctrine of metaphysics, no attempt to determine any truth of things. It is merely a method of ascertaining the meanings of hard words and of abstract concepts. All pragmatists of whatsoever stripe will cordially assent to that statement. As to the ulterior and indirect effects of practising the pragmatistic method, that is quite another affair.

All pragmatists will further agree that their method of ascertaining the meanings of words and concepts is no other than that experimental method by which all the successful sciences (in which number nobody in his senses would include metaphysics) have reached the degrees of certainty that are severally proper to them today; this experimental method being itself nothing but a particular application of an older logical rule, "By their fruits ye shall know them."

Beyond these two propositions to which pragmatists assent *nem. con.*, we find such slight discrepancies between the views of one and another declared adherent as are to be found in every healthy and vigorous school of thought in every department of inquiry. The most prominent of all our school and the most respected, William

James, defines pragmatism as the doctrine that the whole "meaning" of a concept expresses itself either in the shape of conduct to be recommended or of experience to be expected. Between this definition and mine there certainly appears to be no slight theoretical divergence, which, for the most part, becomes evanescent in practice; and though we may differ on important questions of philosophy—especially as regards the infinite and the absolute—I am inclined to think that the discrepancies reside in other than the pragmatistic ingredients of our thought. If pragmatism had never been heard of, I believe the opinion of James on one side, of me on the other would have developed substantially as they have; notwithstanding our respective connecting them at present with our conception of that method. The brilliant and marvellously human thinker, Mr. F. C. S. Schiller, who extends to the philosophic world a cup of nectar stimulant in his beautiful *Humanism*, seems to occupy ground of his own, intermediate, as to this question, between those of James and mine.

I understand pragmatism to be a method of ascertaining the meanings, not of all ideas, but only of what I call "intellectual concepts," that is to say, of those upon the structure of which, arguments concerning objective fact may hinge. Had the light which, as things are, excites in us the sensation of blue, always excited the sensation of red, and *vice versa*, however great a difference that might have made in our feelings, it could have made none in the force of any argument. In this respect, the qualities of hard and soft strikingly contrast with those of red and blue; because while red and blue name mere subjective feelings only, hard and soft express the factual behaviour of the thing under the pressure of a knife-edge. (I use the word "hard" in its strict mineralogical sense, "would resist a knife-edge.") My pragmatism, having nothing to do with qualities of feeling, permits me to hold that the predication of such a quality is just what it seems, and has nothing to do with anything else. Hence, could two qualities of feeling everywhere be interchanged, nothing but feelings could be affected. Those qualities have no intrinsic significations beyond themselves. Intellectual concepts, however—the only sign-burdens that are properly denominated "concepts"—essentially carry some implication concerning the general behaviour either of some conscious being or of some inanimate object, and so convey more, not merely than any feeling, but more, too, than any existential fact, namely, the "would-acts," "would-dos" of habitual behaviour; and no agglomeration of actual happenings can ever completely fill up the meaning of a "would-be." But [pragmatism asserts], that the *total* meaning of the predication of an intellectual concept is contained in an affirmation that, under all conceivable circumstances of a given kind (or under this or that more or less indefinite part of the cases of their fulfillment, should the predication be modal) the subject of the predication would behave in a certain general way—that is, it would be true under given experiential circumstances (or under a more or less definitely stated proportion of them, *taken as they would occur*, that is in the same order of succession, *in experience*).

A most pregnant principle, quite undeniably, will this "kernel of pragmatism" prove to be, that the *whole* meaning of an intellectual predicate is that certain kinds of events would happen, once in so often, in the course of experience, under certain kinds of existential conditions—provided it can be proved to be true. But how is this to be done in the teeth of Messrs. Bradley, Taylor, and other high metaphysicians, on the one hand, and of the entire nominalistic nation, with its Wundts, its Haeckels, its Karl Pearsons, and many other regiments, in their divers uniforms, on the other?

At this difficulty I have halted for weeks and weeks. It has not been that I could not furnish forth an ample supply of seductive persuasions to pragmatism, or even two or three scientific proofs of its truth. Without a recognition of the chief moments, or points, of these latter it is quite impossible that the power and heart's blood of any variety of doctrine or tendency that ought to be classed among the different species of pragmatism should be really comprehended. A man may very well feel advantages in applications of pragmatism without anything of that. He may even make new applications of the method, himself—with much risk of blundering, however; but it appears very plain, both to reason and to observation of experience, that he cannot know in what interior eye, what pineal gland its soul and power reside, unless he clearly understands the chief conditions of its truth. Unfortunately, however, all the real proofs of pragmatism that I know—and, I hardly doubt, all there are to be known—require just as close and laborious exertion of attention as any but the very most difficult of mathematical theorems, while they add to that all those difficulties of logical analysis which force the mathematician to creep with exceeding caution, if not timorously. But mature consideration has brought me to see that, while those circumstances would render a task quite hopeless that I had never dreamed of undertaking, that of convincing the readers of a literary journal by any honest argument, of the truth of pragmatism, and consequently must prevent communicating to them quite the idea of this method that an accomplished pragmatist has, yet an idea perfectly fulfilling the reader's desire, that of enabling him to place pragmatism and its concepts in the area of his own thought, and of showing roughly how its concepts are related to familiar concepts [may be given].

The next moment of the argument for pragmatism is the view that every thought is a sign. This is the doctrine of Leibniz, Berkeley, and the thinkers of the years about 1700. They were all extreme nominalists; but it is a great mistake to suppose that this doctrine is peculiarly nominalistic. I am myself a scholastic realist of a somewhat extreme stripe. Every realist must, as such, admit that a general is a term and therefore a sign. If, in addition, he holds that it is an absolute exemplar, this Platonism passes quite beyond the question of nominalism and realism; and indeed the doctrine of Platonic ideas has been held by the extremest nominalists. There is some reason to suspect that it was shared by Roscellinus himself.

The next point is still less novel; for not to mention references to it by the Greek commentators upon Aristotle, it was between six and seven centuries ago that John of Salisbury spoke of it as "fere in omnium ore celebre." It is the distinction, to use that author's phrases, between that which a term *nominat*—its logical breadth—and that which it *significat*—its logical depth. In the case of a proposition, it is the distinction between that which its subject denotes and that which its predicate asserts. In the case of an argument, it is the distinction between the state of things in which its premisses are true and the state of things which is defined by the truth of its conclusion.

The action of a sign calls for a little closer attention. Let me remind you of the distinction referred to above [17] between dynamical, or dyadic, action; and intelligent, or triadic, action. An event, A, may, by brute force, produce an event, B; and then the event, B, may in its turn produce a third event, C. The fact that the event, C, is about to be produced by B has no influence at all upon the production of B by A. It is impossible that it should, since the action of B in producing C is a contingent future event at the time B is produced. Such is dyadic action, which is so called because each step of it concerns a pair of objects.

But now when a microscopist is in doubt whether a motion of an animalcule is guided by intelligence, of however low an order, the test he always used to apply when I went to school, and I suppose he does so still, is to ascertain whether event, A, produces a second event, B, *as a means* to the production of a third event, C, or not. That is, he asks whether B will be produced if it will produce or is likely to produce C in its turn, but will not be produced if it will not produce C in its turn nor is likely to do so. Suppose, for example, an officer of a squad or company of infantry gives the word of command, "Ground arms!" This order is, of course, a sign. That thing which causes a sign as such is called the *object* (according to the usage of speech, the "real;" but more accurately, the *existent* object) represented by the sign: the sign is determined to some species of correspondence with that object. In the present case, the object the command represents is the will of the officer that the butts of the muskets be brought down to the ground. Nevertheless, the action of his will upon the sign is not simply dyadic; for if he thought the soldiers were deaf mutes, or did not know a word of English, or were raw recruits utterly undrilled, or were indisposed to obedience, his will probably would not produce the word of command. However, although this condition is most usually fulfilled, it is not essential to the action of a sign. For the acceleration of the pulse is a probable *symptom* of fever and the rise of the mercury in an ordinary thermometer or the bending of the double strip of metal in a metallic thermometer is an indication, or, to use the technical term, is an *index*, of an increase of atmospheric temperature, which, nevertheless, acts upon it in a purely brute and dyadic way. In these cases, however, a mental representation of the index is produced, which mental representation is called the *immediate object* of the sign; and this object does triadically produce the intended, or proper, effect of the sign strictly by means of another mental sign; and that this triadic character of the action is regarded as essential is shown by the fact that if the thermometer is dynamically connected with the heating and cooling apparatus, so as to check either effect, we do not, in ordinary parlance, speak of there being any *semeiosy*, or action of a sign, but, on the contrary, say that there is an "automatic regulation," an idea opposed, in our minds, to that of semeiosy. For the proper significate outcome of a sign, I propose the name, the *interpretant* of the sign. The example of the imperative command shows that it need not be of a mental mode of being. Whether the interpretant be necessarily a triadic result is a question of words, that is, of how we limit the extension of the term "sign"; but it seems to me convenient to make the triadic production of the interpretant essential to a "sign," calling the wider concept like a Jacquard loom, for example, a "quasi-sign." On these terms, it is very easy (not descending to niceties with which I will not annoy your readers) to see what the interpretant of a sign is: it is all that is explicit in the sign itself apart from its context and circumstances of utterance. Still, there is a possible doubt as to where the line should be drawn between the interpretant and the object. It will be convenient to give the mere glance, which is all that can be afforded, to this question as it applies to propositions. The interpretant of a proposition is its predicate; its object is the things denoted by its subject or subjects (including its grammatical objects, direct and indirect, etc.). Take the proposition "Burnt child shuns fire." Its predicate might be regarded as all that is expressed, or as "has either not been burned or shuns fire," or "has not been burned," or "shuns fire," or "shuns," or "is true"; nor is this enumeration exhaustive. But where shall the line be most truly drawn? I reply that the purpose of this sentence being understood to be to communicate information, anything belongs to the interpretant that describes the quality or character of the fact, anything to the object that, without doing that, distinguishes this fact from others like it; while a third part of the proposition, *perhaps*, must be appropriated to information about the manner in which the assertion is made, what warrant is offered for its truth, etc. But I rather incline to think that all this goes to the subject. On this view, the predicate is, "is either not a child or has not been burned, or has no opportunity of shunning fire or does shun fire"; while the subject is "any individual object the interpreter may select from the universe of ordinary everyday experience."

I omit all I possibly can; but there is one fact extremely familiar in itself, that needs to be mentioned as being an indispensable point in the argument. It is that every man inhabits two worlds. These are directly distinguishable by their different appearances. But the greatest difference between them, by far, is that one of these two worlds, the Inner World, exerts a comparatively slight compulsion upon us, though we can, by direct efforts so slight as to be hardly noticeable, change it greatly, creating and destroying existent objects in it; while the other world, the Outer World, is full of irresistible compulsions for us, and we cannot modify it in the least, except by one peculiar kind of effort, muscular effort, and but very slightly even in that way.

Now the problem of what the "meaning" of an intellectual concept is can only be solved by the study of the interpretants, or proper significate effects, of signs. These we find to be of three general classes with some important subdivisions. The first proper significate effect of a sign is a feeling produced by it. There is almost always a feeling which we come to interpret as evidence that we comprehend the proper effect of the sign, although the foundation of truth in this is frequently very slight. This "emotional interpretant," as I call it, may amount to much more than that feeling of recognition; and in some cases, it is the only proper significate effect that the sign produces. Thus, the performance of a piece of concerted music is a sign. It conveys, and is intended to convey, the composer's musical ideas; but these usually consist merely in a series of feelings. If a sign produces any further proper significate effect, it will do so through the mediation of the emotional interpretant, and such further effect will always involve an effort. I call it the energetic interpretant. The effort may be a muscular one, as it is in the case of the command to ground arms; but it is much more usually an exertion upon the Inner World, a mental effort. It never can be the meaning of an intellectual concept, since it is a single act, [while] such a concept is of a general nature. But what further kind of effect can there be?

In advance of ascertaining the nature of this effect, it will be convenient to adopt a designation for it, and I will call it the *logical interpretant*, without as yet determining whether this term shall extend to anything beside the meaning of a general concept, though certainly closely related to that, or not. Shall we say that this effect may be a thought, that is to say, a mental sign? No doubt, it may be so; only, if this sign be of an intellectual kind—as it would have to be—it must itself have a logical interpretant; so that it cannot be the *ultimate* logical interpretant of the concept. It can be proved that the only mental effect that can be so produced and that is not a sign but is of a general application is a *habit-change*; meaning by a habit-change a modification of a person's tendencies toward action, resulting from previous experiences or from previous exertions of his will or acts, or from a complexus of both kinds of cause. It excludes natural dispositions, as the term "habit" does, when it is accurately used; but it includes beside associations, what may be called "transsociations," or alterations of association, and even includes *dissociation*, which has usually been looked upon by psychologists (I believe mistakenly), as of deeply contrary nature to association.

Habits have grades of strength varying from complete dissociation to inseparable association. These grades are mixtures of promptitude of action, say excitability and other ingredients not calling for separate examination here. The habit-change often consists in raising or lowering the strength of a habit. Habits also differ in their endurance (which is likewise a composite quality). But generally speaking, it may be said that the effects of habit-change last until time or some more definite cause produces new habit-changes. It naturally follows that repetitions of the actions that produce the changes increase the changes. [It] is noticeable that the iteration of the action is often said to be indispensable to the formation of a habit; but a very moderate exercise of observation suffices to refute this error. A single reading yesterday of a casual statement that the "shtar chindis" means in Romany "four shillings," though it is unlikely to receive any reinforcement beyond the recalling of it, at this moment, is likely to produce the habit of thinking that "four" in the Gypsy tongue is "shtar," that will last for months, if not for years, though I should never call it to mind in the interval. To be sure, there has been some iteration just now, while I dwelt on the matter long enough to write these sentences; but I do not believe any reminiscence like this was needed to create the habit; for such instances have been extremely numerous in acquiring different languages. There are, of course, other means than repetition of intensifying habit-changes. In particular, there is a peculiar kind of effort, which may be likened to an imperative command addressed to the future self. I suppose the psychologists would call it an act of auto-suggestion.

We may distinguish three classes of events causative of habit-change. Such events may, in the first place, not be acts of the mind in which the habit-change is brought about, but experiences forced upon [it]. Thus, surprise is very efficient in breaking up associations of ideas. On the other hand, each new instance that is brought to the experience that supports an induction goes to strengthen that association of ideas—that inward habit—in which the tendency to believe in the inductive conclusion consists. But careful examination has pretty thoroughly satisfied me that no new association, no entirely new habit, can be created by involuntary experiences.

In the second place, the event that causes a habit-change may be a muscular effort, apparently. If I wish to acquire the habit of speaking of "speaking, writing, thinking," etc., instead of "speakin', writin', thinkin'," as I suspect I now do (though I am not sure)—all I have to do is to make the desired enunciations a good many times; and to do this as thoughtlessly as possible, since it is an inattentive habit that I am trying to create. Everybody knows the facility with which habits may thus be acquired, even quite unintentionally. But I am persuaded that nothing like a concept can be acquired by muscular practice alone. When we seem to do that, it is not the muscular action but the accompanying inward efforts, the acts of imagination, that produce the habit. If a person who has never tried such a thing before undertakes to stand on one foot and to move the other round a horizontal circle, say, as being the easier way, clockwise if he is standing on the left foot, or counter-clockwise if he is standing on the right foot, and at the same time to move the fist of the same side as the moving foot round a horizontal circle in the opposite direction, that is, clockwise if the foot is moved counter-clockwise, and *vice versa*, he will, at first, find he cannot do it. The difficulty is that he lacks a unitary concept of the series of efforts that success requires. By practising the different parts of the movement, while attentively observing the kind of effort requisite in each part, he will, in a few minutes, catch the idea, and will then be able to perform the movements with perfect facility. But the proof that it is in no degree the muscular efforts, but only the efforts of the imagination that have been his teachers, is that if he does not perform the actual motions, but only imagines them vividly, he will acquire the same trick with only so much additional practice as is accounted for by the difficulty of imagining all the efforts that will have to be made in a movement one has not actually executed. There is an obvious difficulty of determining just how much allowance should be made for this, in the fact [that] when the feat is learned in either way, it cannot be unlearned, so as to compare that way with the other. The only resort is to learn a considerable number of feats which depend upon acquiring a unitary conception of a series of efforts, learning some with actual muscular exercise and others by unaided imagination, and then forming one's judgment of whether the greater facility afforded by the actual muscular contractions is, or is not, greater than the support this gives the imagination. Saying the verse about "Peter Piper"; spelling without an instant's hesitation, in the old way, the name Aldibirontifoscoforniocrononhotontothologes (that is, thus: *A-l*, al, and here's my *al*; *d-i*, di, and here's my *di*, and here's my *aldi*; *b-i*, bi, and here's my *bi*, and here's my *dibi*, and here's my *aldibi*, etc.); making the pass with one hand upon a pack of cards, playing the thimbles and ball, and other turns of legerdemain all largely depend for their success upon a unitary conception of all that has to be done and just when it must be done. It is from such experiments that I have been led to estimate as nil the power of mere muscular effort in contributing to the acquisition of ideas.

Every concept, doubtless, first arises when upon a strong, but more or less vague, sense of need is superinduced some involuntary experience of a suggestive nature; that being suggestive which has a certain occult relation to the build of the mind. We may assume that it is the same with the instinctive ideas of animals; and man's ideas are quite as miraculous as those of the bird, the beaver, and the ant. For a not insignificant percentage of them have turned out to be the keys of great secrets. With beasts, however, conditions are comparatively unchanging, and there is no further progress. With man these first concepts (first in the order of development, but emerging at all stages of mental life) take the form of conjectures, though they are by no means always recognized as such. Every concept, every general proposition of the great edifice of science, first came to us as a conjecture. These ideas are the *first logical interpretants* of the phenomena that suggest them, and which, as suggesting them, are signs, of which they are the (really conjectural) interpretants. But that they are no more than that is evidently an after-thought, the dash of cold doubt that awakens the sane judgment of the muser. Meantime, do not forget that every conjecture is equivalent to, or is expressive of, such a habit that having a certain desire one might accomplish it if one could perform a certain act. Thus, the primitive man must have been sometimes asked by his son whether the sun that rose in the morning was the same as the one that set the previous evening; and he may have replied, "I do not know, my boy; but I think that if I could put my brand on the evening sun, I should be able to see it on the morning sun again; and I once knew an old man who could look at the sun though he could hardly see anything else; and he told me that he had once seen a peculiarly shaped spot on the sun; and that it was to be recognized quite unmistakably for several days." [Readiness] to act in a certain way under given circumstances and when actuated by a given motive is a habit; and a deliberate, or self-controlled, habit is precisely a belief.

In the next step of thought, those first logical interpretants stimulate us to various voluntary performances in the inner world. We imagine ourselves in various situations and animated by various motives; and we proceed to trace out the alternative lines of conduct which the conjectures would leave open to us. We are, moreover, led, by the same inward activity, to remark different ways in which our conjectures could be slightly modified. The logical interpretant must, therefore, be in a relatively future tense.

To this may be added the consideration that it is not all signs that have logical interpretants, but only intellectual concepts and the like; and these are all either general or intimately connected with generals, as it seems to me. This shows that the species of future tense of the logical interpretant is that of the conditional mood, the "*would-be.*"

At the time I was originally puzzling over the enigma of the nature of the logical interpretant, and had reached about the stage where the discussion now is, being in a quandary, it occurred to me that if I only could find a moderate number of concepts which should be at once highly abstract and abstruse, and yet the whole nature of whose meanings should be quite unquestionable, a study of them would go far toward showing me how and why the logical interpretant should in all cases be a conditional future. I had no sooner framed a definite wish for such concepts, than I perceived that in mathematics they are as plenty as blackberries. I at once began running through the explications of them, which I found all took the following form: Proceed according to such and such a general rule. Then, if such and such a concept is applicable to such and such an object, the operation will have such and such a general result; and conversely. Thus, to take an extremely simple case, if two geometrical figures of dimensionality N should be equal in all their parts, an easy rule of construction would determine, in a space of dimensionality N containing both figures, an axis of rotation, such that a rigid body that should fill not only that space but also a space of dimensionality $N+1$, containing the former space, turning about that axis, and carrying one of the figures along with it while the other figure remained at rest, the rotation would bring the movable figure back into its original space of dimensionality, N, and when that event occurred, the movable figure would be in exact coincidence with the unmoved one, in all its parts; while if the two figures were not so equal, this would never happen.

Here was certainly a stride toward the solution of the enigma.

For the treatment of a score of intellectual concepts on that model, only a few of them being mathematical, seemed to me to be so refulgently successful as fully to convince me that to predicate any such concept of a real or imaginary object is equivalent to declaring that a certain operation, corresponding to the concept, if performed upon that object, would (certainly, or probably, or possibly, according to the mode of predication) be followed by a result of a definite general description.

Yet this does not quite tell us just what the nature is of the essential effect upon the interpreter, brought about by the sēmīo'sis of the sign, which constitutes the logical interpretant. (It is important to understand what I mean by *semiosis*. All dynamical action, or action of brute force, physical or psychical, either takes place between two subjects [whether they react equally upon each other, or one is agent and the other patient, entirely or partially] or at any rate is a resultant of such actions between pairs. But by "semiosis" I mean, on the contrary, an action, or influence, which is, or involves, a coöperation of *three* subjects, such as a sign, its object, and its interpretant, this tri-relative influence not being in any way resolvable into actions between pairs. Σημείωσις in Greek of the Roman period, as early as Cicero's time, if I remember rightly, meant the action of almost any kind of sign; and my definition confers on anything that so acts the title of a "sign.")

Although the definition does not require the logical interpretant (or, for that matter, either of the other two interpretants) to be a modification of consciousness, yet our lack of experience of any semiosis in which this is not the case, leaves us no alternative to beginning our inquiry into its general nature with a provisional assumption that the interpretant is, at least, in all cases, a sufficiently close analogue of a modification of consciousness to keep our conclusion pretty near to the general truth. We can only hope that, once that conclusion is reached, it may be susceptible of such a generalization as will eliminate any possible error due to the falsity of that assumption. The reader may well wonder why I do not simply confine my inquiry to psychical semiosis, since no other seems to be of much importance. My reason is that the too frequent practice, by those logicians who do not go to work [with] any method at all [or who follow] the method of basing propositions in the science of logic upon results of the science of psychology—as contradistinguished from common-sense observations concerning the workings of the mind, observations well-known even if little noticed, to all grown men and women, that are of sound minds—that practice is to my apprehension as unsound and insecure as was that bridge in the novel of "Kenilworth" that, being utterly without any sort of support, sent the poor Countess Amy to her destruction; seeing that, for the firm establishment of the truths of the science of psychology, almost incessant appeals to the results of the science of logic—as contradistinguished from natural perceptions that one relation evidently involves another—are peculiarly indispensable. Those logicians continually confound *psychical* truths with *psychological* truths, although the distinction between them is of that kind that takes precedence over all others as calling for the respect of anyone who would tread the strait and narrow road that leadeth unto exact truth.

Making that provisional assumption, then, I ask myself, since we have already seen that the logical interpretant is general in its possibilities of reference (*i.e.*, refers or is related to whatever there may be of a certain description), what categories of mental facts there be that are of general reference. I can find only these four: conceptions, desires (including hopes, fears, etc.), expectations, and habits. I trust I have made no important omission. Now it is no explanation of the nature of the logical interpretant (which, we already know, is a concept) to say that it is a concept. This objection applies also to desire and expectation, as explanations of the same interpretant; since neither of these is general otherwise than through connection with a concept. Besides, as to desire, it would be easy to show (were it worth the space), that the logical interpretant is an effect of the energetic interpretant, in the sense in which the latter is an effect of the emotional interpretant. Desire, however, is cause, not effect, of effort. As to expectation, it is excluded by the fact that it is not conditional. For that which might be mistaken for a conditional expectation is nothing but a judgment that, under certain conditions, there would be an expectation: there is no conditionality in the expectation itself, such as there is in the logical interpretant after it is actually produced. Therefore, there remains only habit, as the essence of the logical interpretant.

Let us see, then, just how, according to the rule derived from mathematical concepts (and confirmed by others), this habit is produced; and what sort of a habit it is. In order that this deduction may be rightly made, the following remark will be needed. It is not a result of scientific psychology, but is simply a bit of the catholic and undeniable common-sense of mankind, with no other modification than a slight accentuation of certain features.

Every sane person lives in a double world, the outer and the inner world, the world of percepts and the world of fancies. What chiefly keeps these from being mixed up together is (besides certain marks they bear) everybody's well knowing that fancies can be greatly modified by a certain non-muscular effort, while it is muscular effort alone (whether this be "voluntary," that is, preintended, or whether all the intended endeavour is to inhibit muscular action, as when one blushes, or when peristaltic action is set up on experience of danger to one's person) that can to any noticeable degree modify percepts. A man can be durably affected by his percepts and by his fancies. The way in which they affect him will be apt to depend upon his personal inborn disposition and upon his habits. Habits differ from dispositions in having been acquired as consequences of the principle, virtually well-known even to those whose powers of reflection are insufficient to its formulation, that multiple reiterated behaviour of the same kind, under similar combinations of percepts and fancies, produces a tendency—the *habit*—actually to behave in a similar way under similar circumstances in the future. Moreover—*here is the point*—every man exercises more or less control over himself by means of modifying his own habits; and the way in which he goes to work to bring this effect about in those cases in which circumstances will not permit him to practise reiterations of the desired kind of conduct in the outer world shows that he is virtually well-acquainted with the important principle that *reiterations in the inner world—fancied reiterations—if well-intensified by direct effort, produce habits*, just as do reiterations in the outer world; *and these habits will have power to influence actual behaviour in the outer world*; especially, if each reiteration be accompanied by a peculiar strong effort that is usually likened to issuing a command to one's future self.

I here owe my patient reader a confession. It is that when I said that those signs that have a logical interpretant are either general or closely connected with generals, this was not a scientific result, but only a strong impression due to a life-long study of the nature of signs. My excuse for not answering the question scientifically is that I am, as far as I know, a pioneer, or rather a back-woodsman, in the work of clearing and opening up what I call *semiotic*, that is, the doctrine of the essential nature and fundamental varieties of possible semiosis; and I find the field too vast, the labour too great, for a first-comer. I am, accordingly, obliged to confine myself to the most important questions. The questions of the same particular type as the one I answer on the basis of an impression, which are of about the same importance, exceed four hundred in number; and they are all delicate and difficult, each requiring much search and much caution. At the same time, they are very far from being among the most important of the questions of semiotic. Even if my answer is not exactly correct, it can lead to no great misconception as to the nature of the logical interpretant. There is my apology, such as it may be deemed.

It is not to be supposed that upon every presentation of a sign capable of producing a logical interpretant, such interpretant is actually produced. The occasion may either be too early or too late. If it is too early, the semiosis will not be carried so far, the other interpretants sufficing for the rude functions for which the sign is used.   On the other hand, the occasion will come too late if the interpreter be already familiar with the logical interpretant, since then it will be recalled to his mind by a process which affords no hint of how it was originally produced.   Moreover, the great majority of instances in which formations of logical interpretants do take place are very unsuitable to serve as illustrations of the process, because in them the essentials of this semiosis are buried in masses of accidental and hardly relevant semioses that are mixed with the former.   The best way that I have been able to hit upon for simplifying the illustrative example which is to serve as our matter upon which to experiment and observe is to suppose a man already skillful in handling a given sign (that has a logical interpretant) to begin now before our inner gaze for the first time, seriously to inquire what that interpretant is.   It will be necessary to amplify this hypothesis by a specification of what his *interest* in the question is supposed to be.   In doing this, I, by no means, follow Mr. Schiller's brilliant and seductive humanistic logic, according to which it is proper to take account of the whole personal situation in logical inquiries.   For I hold it to be very evil and harmful procedure to introduce into scientific investigation an unfounded hypothesis, without any definite prospect of its hastening our discovery of the truth.   Now such a hypothesis Mr. Schiller's rule seems to me, with my present lights, to be.   He has given a number of reasons for it; but, to my estimate, they seem to be of that quality that is well calculated to give rise to interesting discussions, and is consequently to be recommended to those who intend to pursue the study of philosophy as an entertaining exercise of the intellect, but is negligible [to] one whose earnest purpose is to do what in him lies toward bringing about a metamorphosis of philosophy into a genuine science.   I cannot turn aside into Mr. Schiller's charming lane.   When I ask what the interest is in seeking to discover a logical interpretant, it is not my fondness for strolling in paths where I can study the varieties of humanity that moves me, but the definite reflection that unless our hypothesis be rendered specific as to that interest, it will be impossible to trace out its logical consequences, since the way the interpreter will conduct the inquiry will greatly depend upon the nature of his interest in it.

I shall suppose, then, that the interpreter is not particularly interested in the theory of logic, which he may judge by examples to be profitless; but I shall suppose that he has embarked a great part of the treasures of his life in the enterprise of perfecting a certain invention; and that, for this end, it seems to him extremely desirable that he should acquire a demonstrative knowledge of the solution of a certain problem of reasoning. As to this problem itself, I shall suppose that it does not fall within any class for which any general method of handling is known, and that indeed it is indefinite in every respect which might afford any familiar kind of handle by which any image fairly representing it could be held firmly before the mind and examined; so that, in short, it seems to elude reason's application or to slip from its grasp.

In every case, after some preliminaries, the activity takes the form of experimentation in the inner world; and the conclusion (if it comes to a definite conclusion) is that under given conditions, the interpreter will have formed the habit of acting in a given way whenever he may desire a given kind of result. The real and living logical conclusion *is* that habit; the verbal formulation merely expresses it. I do not deny that a concept, proposition, or argument may be a logical interpretant. I only insist that it cannot be the final logical interpretant, for the reason that it is itself a sign of that very kind that has itself a logical interpretant. The habit alone, which though it may be a sign in some other way, is not a sign in that way in which that sign of which it is the logical inter- pretant is the sign. The habit conjoined with the motive and the conditions has the action for its energetic interpretant; but action cannot be a logical interpretant, because it lacks generality. The concept which is a logical interpretant is only imperfectly so. It somewhat partakes of the nature of a verbal definition, and is as inferior to the habit, and much in the same way, as a verbal defini- tion is inferior to the real definition. The deliberately formed, self- analyzing habit—self-analyzing because formed by the aid of analysis of the exercises that nourished it—is the living definition, the veritable and final logical interpretant. Consequently, the most perfect account of a concept that words can convey will consist in a description of the habit which that concept is calculated to produce. But how otherwise can a habit be described than by a description of the kind of action to which it gives rise, with the specification of the conditions and of the motive?

If we now revert to the psychological assumption originally made, we shall see that it is already largely eliminated by the consideration that habit is by no means exclusively a mental fact. Empirically, we find that some plants take habits. The stream of water that wears a bed for itself is forming a habit. Every ditcher so thinks of it. Turning to the rational side of the question, the excellent current definition of habit, due, I suppose, to some physiologist (if I can remember my bye-reading for nearly half a century unglanced at, Brown-Séquard much insisted on it in his book on the spinal cord), says not one word about the mind. Why should it, when habits in themselves are entirely unconscious, though feelings may be symptoms of them, and when consciousness alone—i.e., feeling —is the only distinctive attribute of mind?

What further is needed to clear the sign of its mental associations is furnished by generalizations too facile to arrest attention here, since nothing but feeling is exclusively mental.

But while I say this, it must not be inferred that I regard consciousness as a mere "epiphenomenon"; though I heartily grant that the hypothesis that it is so has done good service to science. To my apprehension, consciousness may be defined as that congeries of non-relative predicates, varying greatly in quality and in intensity, which are symptomatic of the interaction of the outer world—the world of those causes that are exceedingly compulsive upon the modes of consciousness, with general disturbance sometimes amounting to shock, and are acted upon only slightly, and only by a special kind of effort, muscular effort—and of the inner world, apparently derived from the outer, and amenable to direct effort of various kinds with feeble reactions; the interaction of these two worlds chiefly consisting of a direct action of the outer world upon the inner and an indirect action of the inner world upon the outer through the operation of habits. If this be a correct account of consciousness, i.e., of the congeries of feelings, it seems to me that it exercises a real function in self-control, since without it, or at least without that of which it is symptomatic, the resolves and exercises of the inner world could not affect the real determinations and habits of the outer world. I say that these belong to the outer world because they are not mere fantasies but are real agencies.

I have now outlined my own form of pragmatism; but there are other slightly different ways of regarding what is practically the same method of attaining vitally distinct conceptions, from which I should protest from the depths of my soul against being separated. In the first place, there is the pragmatism of James, whose definition differs from mine only in that he does not restrict the "meaning," that is, the ultimate logical interpretant, as I do, to a habit, but allows percepts, that is, complex feelings endowed with compulsiveness, to be such. If he is willing to do this, I do not quite see how

he need give any room at all to habit.   But practically, his view
and mine must, I think, coincide, except where he allows considerations not at all pragmatic to have weight.   Then there is Schiller,
who offers no less than seven alternative definitions of pragmatism.
The first is that pragmatism is the Doctrine that "truths are logical
values."   At first blush, this seems far too broad; for who, be he
pragmatist or absolutist, can fail to prefer truth to fiction?   But
no doubt what is meant is that the objectivity of truth really consists
in the fact that, in the end, every sincere inquirer will be led to
embrace it—and if he be not sincere, the irresistible effect of inquiry
in the light of experience will be to make him so.   This doctrine
appears to me, after one subtraction, to be a corollary of pragmatism.
I set it in a strong light in my original presentation of the method.[9]
I call my form of it "conditional idealism."   That is to say, I hold
that truth's independence of individual opinions is due (so far as
there is any "truth") to its being the predestined result to which
sufficient inquiry *would* ultimately lead.   I only object that, as
Mr. Schiller himself seems sometimes to say, there is not the smallest
scintilla of logical justification for any assertion that a given sort
of result will, as a matter of fact, either *always* or *never* come to
pass; and consequently we cannot know that there *is* any truth
concerning any given question; and this, I believe, agrees with the
opinion of M. Henri Poincaré, except that he seems to insist upon
the non-existence of any absolute truth for *all* questions, which is
simply to fall into the very same error on the opposite side.   But
practically, we know that questions do generally get settled in
time, when they come to be scientifically investigated; and that
is practically and pragmatically enough.   Mr. Schiller's second
definition is Captain Bunsby's that "the 'truth' of an assertion
depends on its application," which seems to me the result of a weak
analysis.   His third definition is that pragmatism is the doctrine
that "the meaning of a rule lies in its application," which would
make the "meaning" consist in the energetic interpretant and would
ignore the logical interpretant; another feeble analysis.   His fourth
definition is that pragmatism is the doctrine that "all meaning
depends on purpose."   I think there is much to be said in favour of
this, which would, however, make pragmatists of many thinkers
who do not consider themselves as belonging to our school of thought.
Their affiliations with us are, however, undeniable.   His fifth
definition is that pragmatism is the doctrine that "all mental life
is purposive."   His sixth definition is that pragmatism is "a
systematic protest against all ignoring of the purposiveness of actual

knowing." Mr. Schiller seems habitually to use the word "actual" in some peculiar sense. His seventh definition is that pragmatism is "a conscious application to epistemology (or logic) of a teleological psychology, which implies, ultimately, a voluntaristic metaphysics." Supposing by "psychology" he means *not* the science so called, but a critical acceptance of a sifted common-sense of mankind regarding mental phenomena, I might subscribe to this. I have myself called pragmatism "critical common-sensism"; but, of course, I do not mean this for a strict definition.

Signor Giovanni Papini goes a step beyond Mr. Schiller in maintaining [that] pragmatism is indefinable. But that seems to me to be a literary phrase. In the main, I much admire Papini's presentation of the subject.

There are certain questions commonly reckoned as metaphysical, and which certainly are so, if by metaphysics we mean ontology, which as soon as pragmatism is once sincerely accepted, cannot logically resist settlement. These are for example, What is reality? Are necessity and contingency real modes of being? Are the laws of nature real? Can they be assumed to be immutable or are they presumably results of evolution? Is there any real chance, or departure from real law? But on examination, if by metaphysics we mean the broadest positive truths of the psycho-physical universe—positive in the sense of not being reducible to logical formulae—then the very fact that these problems can be solved by a logical maxim is proof enough that they do not belong to metaphysics but to "epistemology," an atrocious translation of *Erkenntnislehre*. When we pass to consider the nature of Time, it seems that pragmatism is of aid, but does not of itself yield a solution. When we go on to the nature of Space, I boldly declare that Newton's view that it is a real entity is alone logically tenable; and that leaves such further questions as, Why should Space have three dimensions? quite unanswerable for the present. This, however, is a purely speculative question without much human interest. (It would, of course, be absurd to say that tridimensionality is without practical consequences.) For those metaphysical questions that have such interest, the question of a future life and especially that of One Incomprehensible but Personal God, not immanent in but creating the universe, I, for one, heartily admit that a Humanism, that does not pretend to be a science but only an instinct, like a bird's power of flight, but purified by meditation, is the most precious contribution that has been made to philosophy for ages.

19

CRITICAL COMMON-SENSISM *

I

PRAGMATICISM was originally enounced in the form of a maxim, as follows: Consider what effects that might *conceivably* have practical bearings you *conceive* the objects of your *conception* to have. Then, your *conception* of those effects is the whole of your *conception* of the object.

I will restate this in other words, since ofttimes one can thus eliminate some unsuspected source of perplexity to the reader. This time it shall be in the indicative mood, as follows: The entire intellectual purport of any symbol consists in the total of all general modes of rational conduct which, conditionally upon all the possible different circumstances and desires, would ensue upon the acceptance of the symbol.

Two doctrines that were defended by the writer about nine years before the formulation of pragmaticism may be treated as consequences of the latter belief. One of these may be called Critical Common-sensism. It is a variety of the Philosophy of Common Sense, but is marked by six distinctive characters, which had better be enumerated at once.

Character I. Critical Common-sensism admits that there not only are indubitable propositions but also that there are indubitable inferences. In one sense, anything evident is indubitable; but the propositions and inferences which Critical Common-sensism holds to be original, in the sense one cannot "go behind" them (as the lawyers say), are indubitable in the sense of being acritical. The term "reasoning" ought to be confined to such fixation of one belief by another as is reasonable, deliberate, self-controlled. A reasoning must be conscious; and this consciousness is not mere "immediate consciousness," which (as I argued in 1868) [18] is simple Feeling viewed from another side, but is in its ultimate nature (meaning in that characteristic element of it that is not reducible to anything

---

* [The first selection in I and both selections in II are from "Issues of Pragmaticism," *The Monist* 1905 (*CP* 5.438-46, 453, 457). The other selections in I are from ms. c. 1905 (*CP* 5.505-8, 511-16, 523-5).]

simpler), a sense of taking a habit, or disposition to respond to a given kind of stimulus in a given kind of way. . . . But the secret of rational consciousness is not so much to be sought in the study of this one peculiar nucleolus, as in the review of the process of self-control in its entirety. The machinery of logical self-control works on the same plan as does moral self-control, in multiform detail. The greatest difference, perhaps, is that the latter serves to inhibit mad puttings forth of energy, while the former most character-istically insures us against the quandary of Buridan's ass. The formation of habits under imaginary action (see the paper of January 1878) [9] is one of the most essential ingredients of both; but in the logical process the imagination takes far wider flights, proportioned to the generality of the field of inquiry, being bounded in pure mathematics solely by the limits of its own powers, while in the moral process we consider only situations that may be appre-hended or anticipated. For in moral life we are chiefly solicitous about our conduct and its inner springs, and the approval of con-science, while in intellectual life there is a tendency to value ex-istence as the vehicle of forms. Certain obvious features of the phenomena of self-control (and especially of habit) can be expressed compactly and without any hypothetical addition, except what we distinctly rate as imagery, by saying that we have an occult nature of which and of its contents we can only judge by the conduct that it determines, and by phenomena of that conduct. All will assent to that (or all but the extreme nominalist), but anti-synechistic [14] thinkers wind themselves up in a factitious snarl by falsifying the phenomena in representing consciousness to be, as it were, a skin, a separate tissue, overlying an unconscious region of the occult nature, mind, soul, or physiological basis. It appears to me that in the present state of our knowledge a sound methodeutic pre-scribes that, in adhesion to the appearances, the difference is only relative and the demarcation not precise.

According to the maxim of Pragmaticism, to say that determina-tion affects our occult nature is to say that it is capable of affecting deliberate conduct; and since we are conscious of what we do deliberately, we are conscious *habitualiter* of whatever hides in the depths of our nature; and it is presumable (and *only* presumable, although curious instances are on record) that a sufficiently ener-getic effort of attention would bring it out. Consequently, to say that an operation of the mind is controlled is to say that it is, in a special sense, a conscious operation; and this no doubt is the con-sciousness of reasoning. For this theory requires that in reasoning we should be conscious, not only of the conclusion, and of our deliberate approval of it, but also of its being the result of the premiss from which it does result, and furthermore that the inference is one of a possible class of inferences which conform to one guiding principle. Now in fact we find a well-marked class of mental operations, clearly of a different nature from any others which do possess just these properties. They alone deserve to be called *reasonings*; and if the reasoner is conscious, even vaguely, of what his guiding principle is, his reasoning should be called a *logical argumentation*. There are, however, cases in which we are conscious that a belief has been determined by another given belief, but are not conscious that it proceeds on any general principle. Such is St. Augustine's *"cogito, ergo sum."* Such a process should be called, not a reasoning, but an *acritical inference*. Again, there are cases in which one belief is determined by another, without our being at all aware of it. These should be called *associational suggestions of belief*.

Now the theory of Pragmaticism was originally based, as anybody will see who examines the papers of November 1877 and January 1878,[15] upon a study of that experience of the phenomena of self-control which is common to all grown men and women; and it seems evident that to some extent, at least, it must always be so based. For it is to conceptions of deliberate conduct that Pragmaticism would trace the intellectual purport of symbols; and deliberate conduct is self-controlled conduct. Now control may itself be controlled, criticism itself subjected to criticism; and ideally there is no obvious definite limit to the sequence. But if one seriously inquires whether it is possible that a completed series of actual efforts should have been endless or beginningless (I will spare the reader the discussion), I think he can only conclude that (with some vagueness as to what constitutes an effort) this must be regarded as impossible. It will be found to follow that there are, besides perceptual judgments, original (*i.e.*, indubitable because uncriticized) beliefs of a general and recurrent kind, as well as indubitable acritical inferences.

It is important for the reader to satisfy himself that genuine doubt always has an external origin, usually from surprise; and that it is as impossible for a man to create in himself a genuine doubt by such an act of the will as would suffice to imagine the condition of a mathematical theorem, as it would be for him to give himself a genuine surprise by a simple act of the will.

I beg my reader also to believe that it would be impossible for me to put into these articles over two per cent of the pertinent thought which would be necessary in order to present the subject as I have worked it out. I can only make a small selection of what it seems most desirable to submit to his judgment. Not only must all steps be omitted which he can be expected to supply for himself, but unfortunately much more that may cause him difficulty.

Character II. I do not remember that any of the old Scotch philosophers ever undertook to draw up a complete list of the original beliefs, but they certainly thought it a feasible thing, and that the list would hold good for the minds of all men from Adam down. For in those days Adam was an undoubted historical personage. Before any waft of the air of evolution had reached those coasts how could they think otherwise? When I first wrote, we were hardly orientated in the new ideas, and my impression was that the indubitable propositions changed with a thinking man from year to year. I made some studies preparatory to an investigation of the rapidity of these changes, but the matter was neglected, and it has been only during the last two years that I have completed a provisional inquiry which shows me that the changes are so slight from generation to generation, though not imperceptible even in that short period, that I thought to own my adhesion, under inevitable modification, to the opinion of that subtle but well-balanced intellect, Thomas Reid, in the matter of Common Sense (as well as in regard to immediate perception, along with Kant).

Character III. The Scotch philosophers recognized that the original beliefs, and the same thing is at least equally true of the acritical inferences, were of the general nature of instincts. But little as we know about instincts, even now, we are much better acquainted with them than were the men of the eighteenth century. We know, for example, that they can be somewhat modified in a very short time. The great facts have always been known; such as that instinct seldom errs, while reason goes wrong nearly half the time, if not more frequently. But one thing the Scotch failed to recognize is that the original beliefs only remain indubitable in their application to affairs that resemble those of a primitive mode of life. It is, for example, quite open to reasonable doubt whether the motions of electrons are confined to three dimensions, although it is good methodeutic to presume that they are until some evidence to the contrary is forthcoming. On the other hand, as soon as we find that a belief shows symptoms of being instinctive, although it may seem to be dubitable, we must suspect that experiment would show that it is not really so; for in our artificial life, especially in that of a student, no mistake is more likely than that of taking a paper-doubt for the genuine metal. Take, for example, the belief in the criminality of incest. Biology will doubtless testify that the practice is inadvisable; but surely nothing that it has to say could warrant the intensity of our sentiment about it. When, however, we consider the thrill of horror which the idea excites in us, we find reason in that to consider it to be an instinct; and from that we may infer that if some rationalistic brother and sister were to marry, they would find that the conviction of horrible guilt could not be shaken off.

In contrast to this may be placed the belief that suicide is to be classed as murder. There are two pretty sure signs that this is not an instinctive belief. One is that it is substantially confined to the Christian world. The other is that when it comes to the point of actual self-debate, this belief seems to be completely expunged and ex-sponged from the mind. In reply to these powerful arguments, the main points urged are the authority of the fathers of the church and the undoubtedly intense instinctive clinging to life. The latter phenomenon is, however, entirely irrelevant. For though it is a wrench to part with life, which has its charms at the very worst, just as it is to part with a tooth, yet there is no *moral* element in it whatever. As to the Christian tradition, it may be explained by the circumstances of the early Church. For Christianity, the most terribly earnest and most intolerant of religions (see *The Book of Revelations of St. John the Divine*)—and it remained so until diluted with civilization—recognized no morality as worthy of an instant's consideration except Christian morality. Now the early Church had need of martyrs, *i.e.*, witnesses, and if any man had done with life, it was abominable infidelity to leave it otherwise than as a witness to its power. This belief, then, should be set down as dubitable; and it will no sooner have been pronounced dubitable, than Reason will stamp it as false.

The Scotch School appears to have no such distinction concerning the limitations of indubitability and the consequent limitations of the jurisdiction of original belief.

Character IV. By all odds, the most distinctive character of the Critical Common-sensist, in contrast to the old Scotch philosopher, lies in his insistence that the acritically indubitable is invariably vague.

Logicians have too much neglected the study of *vagueness*, not suspecting the important part it plays in mathematical thought.

It is the antithetical analogue of generality. A sign is objectively *general*, in so far as, leaving its effective interpretation indeterminate, it surrenders to the interpreter the right of completing the determination for himself. "Man is mortal." "What man?" "Any man you like." A sign is objectively *vague*, in so far as, leaving its interpretation more or less indeterminate, it reserves for some other possible sign or experience the function of completing the determination. "This month," says the almanac-oracle, "a great event is to happen." "What event?" "Oh, we shall see. The almanac doesn't tell that." The *general* might be defined as that to which the principle of excluded middle does not apply. A triangle in general is not isosceles nor equilateral; nor is a triangle in general scalene. The *vague* might be defined as that to which the principle of contradiction does not apply. For it is false neither that an animal (in a vague sense) is male, nor that an animal is female. . . . No communication of one person to another can be entirely definite, *i.e.*, non-vague. We may reasonably hope that physiologists will some day find some means of comparing the qualities of one person's feelings with those of another, so that it would not be fair to insist upon their present incomparability as an inevitable source of misunderstanding. Besides, it does not affect the intellectual purport of communications. But wherever degree or any other possibility of continuous variation subsists, absolute precision is impossible. Much else must be vague, because no man's interpretation of words is based on exactly the same experience as any other man's. Even in our most intellectual conceptions, the more we strive to be precise, the more unattainable precision seems. It should never be forgotten that our own thinking is carried on as a dialogue, and though mostly in a lesser degree, is subject to almost every imperfection of language. I have worked out the logic of vagueness with something like completeness, but need not inflict more of it upon you, at present.

That veritably indubitable beliefs are especially vague could be proved *a priori*. But proof not being aimed at today, it will be simpler to say that the Critical Common-sensist's personal experience is that a suitable line of reflection, accompanied by imaginary experimentation, always excites doubt of any very broad proposition if it be defined with precision. Yet there are beliefs of which such a critical sifting invariably leaves a certain vague residuum unaffected.

One ought then to ask oneself, whether, since much of the original belief has disappeared under an attentive dissection, perseverance might not affect the destruction of what remains of it. This question always appears reasonable as long as one stands far enough away from the facts of the case, and views them as one would a painting of Monet.

But the answer that a closer scrutiny dictates in some cases is that it is not because insufficient pains have been taken to precide the residuum, that it is vague: it is that it is vague intrinsically. Take, for example, our belief in the Order of Nature. The criticisms of it [above], as well as by various other writers, of whom may be mentioned as long antecedent to the writer, Renouvier, Delboeuf, Fouillée, Blood, and James, and no doubt there were others, and since that time Dewey and I know not who else, appear to me to have stripped it of all rational precision. As precisely defined it can hardly be said to be absolutely indubitable considering how many thinkers there are who do not believe it. But who can think that there is *no* order in nature?

. . . While they never become dubitable in so far as our mode of life remains that of somewhat primitive man, yet as we develop *degrees of self-control* unknown to that man, occasions of action arise in relation to which the original beliefs, if stretched to cover them, have no sufficient authority. In other words, we outgrow the applicability of instinct—not altogether, by any manner of means, but in our highest activities. The famous Scotch philosophers lived and died out before this could be duly appreciated.

Doctor Y. What do you mean by "somewhat primitive"? And by what sort of reasoning can a dubitable proposition about experience become indubitable?

Pragmaticist. A searching question, because some of our beliefs, which seem as indubitable as any, are of such a character that they can hardly have entered the minds, say, of Neanderthal men, and in any case, cannot possibly have been transmitted to us from the first conscious animals. Consequently, Common-sensism has to grapple with the difficulty that if there are any indubitable beliefs, these beliefs must have grown up; and during the process, cannot have been indubitable beliefs. Still, I see no reason for thinking that beliefs that were dubitable became indubitable. Every decent house dog has been taught beliefs that appear to have no application to the wild state of the dog; and yet your trained dog has not, I guess, been observed to have passed through a period of scepticism on the subject. There is every reason to suppose that belief came first, and the power of doubting long after. Doubt, usually, perhaps always, takes its rise from surprise, which supposes previous belief;

and surprises come with novel environment. I will only add that though precise reasoning about precise experiential doubt could not entirely destroy doubt, any more than the action of finite conservative forces could leave a body in a continuous state of rest, yet vagueness, which is no more to be done away with in the world of logic than friction in mechanics, can have that effect.

As I was saying, a modern recognition of evolution must distinguish the Critical Common-sensist from the old school. Modern science, with its microscopes and telescopes, with its chemistry and electricity, and with its entirely new appliances of life, has put us into quite another world; almost as much so as if it had transported our race to another planet. Some of the old beliefs have no application except in extended senses, and in such extended senses they are sometimes dubitable and subject to just criticism. It is above all the normative sciences, esthetics, ethics, and logic, that men are in dire need of having severely criticized, in their relation to the new world created by science. Unfortunately, this need is as unconscious as it is great. The evils are in some superficial way recognized; but it never occurs to anybody that the study of esthetics, ethics, and logic can be seriously important, because these sciences are conceived by all, but their deepest students, in the old way. It only concerns my present purpose to glance at this state of things. The needed new criticism must know whereon it stands; namely, on the beliefs that remain indubitable; and young Critical Common-sensists of intellectual force who burn for a task in which they can worthily sacrifice their lives without encouragement, reward, recognition, or a hearing (and I trust such young men still live) can find in this field their heart's desire.

[*Character* V.] Yet a [fifth] mark of the Critical Common-sensist is that he has a high esteem for doubt. He may almost be said to have a *sacra fames* for it. Only, his hunger is not to be appeased with paper doubts: he must have the heavy and noble metal, or else belief.

He quite acknowledges that what has been indubitable one day has often been proved on the morrow to be false. He grants the presciss proposition that it may be so with any of the beliefs he holds. He really cannot admit that it may be so with all of them; but here he loses himself in vague unmeaning contradictions.

Doctor Y. Can indubitable propositions be demonstrable?

Pragmaticist. Indubitable propositions must be ultimate premisses, or at least, must be held without reference to precise proofs. For what one cannot doubt one cannot argue about; and no precise empirical argument can free its conclusion altogether from rational doubt.

Yet it is true that whenever one turns a critical glance upon one of our original beliefs—say, the belief in the order of nature—the mind at once seems vaguely to pretend to have reasons for believing it. One dreams of an inductive proof. One surmises that the belief results from something like an inductive proof that has been forgotten. Very likely it did, in a sense of the term "inductive process" that is so generalized as to include uncontrolled thought. But this admission must be accompanied by the emphatic denial that the indubitable belief is inferential, or is "accepted." It simply remains unshaken as it always was. That does not at all interfere with the theory that in the psychological process of its development, the occurrence of single experiences, such as might have been predictively deduced from it, were an indispensable factor, while an original potentiality of the belief-habit must have been a correlative factor. All this is perfectly consistent, too, with the necessity of criticizing the ordinary axioms of reasoning and of morals, as well as ordinarily developed ideals, as soon as they are extended so as to become applicable to the new world created by science.

Doctor Y. Is there any further peculiarity which distinguishes Critical Common-sensism from that of Reid and Dugald Stewart?

Pragmaticist. Yes [*Character* VI] ; for it criticizes the critical method, follows its footsteps, tracks it to its lair. To the accusation that Common-Sense accepts a proposition as indubitable because it has not been criticized, the answer is that this confounds two uses of the word "because." Neither the philosophy of Common-Sense nor the man who holds it accepts any belief *on the ground* that it has not been criticized. For, as already said, such beliefs are not "accepted." What happens is that one comes to recognize that one has had the belief-habit as long as one can remember; and to say that no doubt of it has ever arisen is only another way of saying the same thing. But it is quite true that the Common-sensist like everybody else, the Criticist included, believes propositions *because* they have not been criticized in the sense that he does not doubt certain propositions that he would have doubted if he had criticized them. For in the first place, to criticize is *ipso facto* to doubt, and in the second place criticism can only attack a proposition after it has given it some precise sense in which it is impossible entirely to remove the doubt. It is probably true, too, that the Common-sensist believes unquestioningly some propositions that might have been criticized and that are not true. We are all liable to do that; but perhaps he is more in danger of it than other men. Still, as a fact, it is difficult to find a Criticist who does not hold to more fundamental beliefs than any Critical Common-sensist does.

The Critical Philosopher seems to opine that the fact that he has not hitherto doubted a proposition is no reason why he should not henceforth doubt it. (At which Common-Sense whispers that, whether it be "reason" or no, it will be a well-nigh insuperable *obstacle* to doubt.) Accordingly, he will not stop to ask whether he actually does doubt it or not, but at once proceeds to examine it. Now if it happens that he *does* actually doubt the proposition, he does quite right in starting a critical inquiry. But in case he *does not* doubt, he virtually falls into the Cartesian error of supposing that one can doubt at will. A proposition that could be doubted at will is certainly not *believed*. For belief, while it lasts, is a strong habit, and as such, forces the man to believe until some surprise breaks up the habit. The breaking of a belief can only be due to some novel experience, whether external or internal. Now experience which could be summoned up at pleasure would not be experience.

Kant (whom I *more* than admire) is nothing but a somewhat confused pragmatist. A real is anything that is not affected by men's cognitions *about it*; which is a verbal definition, not a doctrine. An external object is anything that is not affected by any cognitions, whether about it or not, of the man to whom it is external. Exaggerate this, in the usual philosopher fashion, and you have the conception of what is not affected by any cognitions at all. Take the converse of this definition and you have the notion of what does not affect cognition, and in this indirect manner you get a hypostatically abstract notion of what the *Ding an sich* would be. In this sense, we also have a notion of a sky-blue demonstration; but in half a dozen ways the *Ding an sich* has been proved to be nonsensical; and here is another way. It has been shown that in the formal analysis of a proposition, after all that words can convey has been thrown into the predicate, there remains a subject that is indescribable and that can only be pointed at or otherwise indicated, unless a way, of finding what is referred to, be prescribed. The *Ding an sich*, however, can neither be indicated nor found. Consequently, no proposition can refer to it, and nothing true or false can be predicated of it. Therefore, all references to it must be thrown out as meaningless surplusage. But when that is done, we see clearly that Kant regards Space, Time, and his Categories just as everybody else does, and never doubts or has doubted their

objectivity. His limitation of them to possible experience is pragmatism in the general sense; and the pragmaticist, as fully as
Kant, recognizes the mental ingredient in these concepts. Only
(trained by Kant to define), he defines more definitely, and somewhat otherwise, than Kant did, just how much of this ingredient
comes from the mind of the individual in whose experience the
cognition occurs. The kind of Common-sensism which thus criticizes
the Critical Philosophy and recognizes its own affiliation to Kant
has surely a certain claim to call itself Critical Common-sensism.

II

Another doctrine which is involved in Pragmaticism as an
essential consequence of it, but which the writer defended . . . before
he had formulated, even in his own mind, the principle of pragmaticism, is the scholastic doctrine of realism. This is usually
defined as the opinion that there are real objects that are general,
among the number being the modes of determination of existent
singulars, if, indeed, these be not the only such objects. But the
belief in this can hardly escape being accompanied by the acknowledgment that there are, besides, real *vagues*, and especially real
possibilities. For possibility being the denial of a necessity, which
is a kind of generality, is vague like any other contradiction of a
general. Indeed, it is the reality of some possibilities that pragmaticism is most concerned to insist upon. The article of January
1878 [9] endeavoured to gloze over this point as unsuited to the
exoteric public addressed; or perhaps the writer wavered in his
own mind. He said that if a diamond were to be formed in a bed of
cotton-wool, and were to be consumed there without ever having
been pressed upon by any hard edge or point, it would be merely
a question of nomenclature whether that diamond should be said
to have been hard or not. No doubt this is true, except for the
abominable falsehood in the word MERELY, implying that symbols
are unreal. Nomenclature involves classification; and classification
is true or false, and the generals to which it refers are either reals
in the one case, or figments in the other. For if the reader will
turn to the original maxim of pragmaticism at the beginning of this
article, he will see that the question is, not what *did* happen, but
whether it would have been well to engage in any line of conduct
whose successful issue depended upon whether that diamond *would*
resist an attempt to scratch it, or whether all other logical means
of determining how it ought to be classed *would* lead to the conclusion

which, to quote the very words of that article, would be "the belief which alone could be the result of investigation carried *sufficiently far.*" Pragmaticism makes the ultimate intellectual purport of what you please to consist in conceived conditional resolutions, or their substance; and therefore, the conditional propositions, with their hypothetical antecedents, in which such resolutions consist, being of the ultimate nature of meaning, must be capable of being true, that is, of expressing whatever there be which is such as the proposition expresses, independently of being thought to be so in any judgment, or being represented to be so in any other symbol of any man or men. But that amounts to saying that possibility is sometimes of a real kind.

The question is, was that diamond *really* hard? It is certain that no discernible *actual* fact determined it to be so. But is its hardness not, nevertheless, a *real* fact? To say, as the article of January 1878 [9] seems to intend, that it is just as an arbitrary "usage of speech" chooses to arrange its thoughts, is as much as to decide against the reality of the property, since the real is that which is such as it is regardless of how it is, at any time, thought to be. Remember that this diamond's condition is not an isolated fact. There is no such thing; and an isolated fact could hardly be real. It is an unsevered, though presciss part of the unitary fact of nature. . . . But however this may be, how can the hardness of all other diamonds fail to bespeak *some* real relation among the diamonds without which a piece of carbon would not be a diamond? Is it not a monstrous perversion of the word and concept *real* to say that the accident of the non-arrival of the corundum prevented the hardness of the diamond from having the *reality* which it otherwise, with little doubt, would have had?

At the same time, we must dismiss the idea that the occult state of things (be it a relation among atoms or something else), which constitutes the reality of a diamond's hardness, can possibly consist in anything but in the truth of a general conditional proposition. For to what else does the entire teaching of chemistry relate except to the "behaviour" of different possible kinds of material substance? And in what does that behaviour consist except that if a substance of a certain kind should be exposed to an agency of a certain kind, a certain kind of sensible result *would* ensue, according to our experiences hitherto. As for the pragmaticist, it is precisely his position that nothing else than this can be so much as *meant* by saying that an object possesses a character.

20

PERCEPTUAL JUDGMENTS *

It now begins to look strongly as if perhaps all belief might involve expectation as its essence. That is as much as can justly be said. We have as yet no assurance that this is true of every kind of belief. One class of accepted truths which we have neglected is that of direct perceptual facts. I lay down a wafer, before me. I look at it, and say to myself, "That wafer looks red." What element of expectation is there in the belief that the wafer *looks* red at this moment?

It takes some time to write this sentence, to utter it, or even to think it. It must refer to the state of the percept at the time that it, the judgment, began to be made. But the judgment does not exist until it is completely made. It thus only refers to a memory of the past; and all memory is possibly fallible and subject to criticism and control. The judgment, then, can only mean that so far as the character of the percept can ever be ascertained, it will be ascertained that the wafer looked red.

Perhaps the matter may be stated less paradoxically. Everybody will agree that it would be perfectly meaningless to say that sulphur had the singular property of turning pink when nobody was looking at it, instantly returning to yellowness before the most rapid glance could catch its pink colour, or to say that copper was subject to the law that as long as there was no pressure upon it, it was perfectly yielding, becoming hard in proportion as it was pressed; and generally, a law which never should operate would be an empty formula. Indeed, something not very far from the assertion about copper is contained in all treatises on dynamics, although not limited to any particular substance. Namely, it is set down that no tangential force can be exerted upon a perfect fluid. But no writer puts it forth as a statement of fact; it is given as a definition merely. A law, then, which never will operate has no positive

* [The first two selections are from ms. c. 1902 (*CP* 5.542, 544-5), the next three from the Lectures on Pragmatism, at Harvard 1903 (*CP* 5.157, 181, 184-5), and the last from a review of William James's *Principles of Psychology* in the *Nation* Vol. 53 (1891) p. 32.]

existence. Consequently, a law which has operated for the last time has ceased to exist as a law, except as a mere empty formula which it may be convenient to allow to remain. Hence to assert that a law positively exists is to assert that it will operate, and therefore to refer to the future, even though only conditionally. But to say that a body is hard, or red, or heavy, or of a given weight, or has any other property, is to say that it is subject to law and therefore is a statement referring to the future.

In saying that perceptual judgments involve general elements I certainly never intended to be understood as enunciating any proposition in psychology. For my principles absolutely debar me from making the least use of psychology in logic. I am confined entirely to the unquestionable facts of everyday experience, together with what can be deduced from them. All that I can mean by a perceptual judgment is a judgment absolutely forced upon my acceptance, and that by a process which I am utterly unable to control and consequently am unable to criticize. Nor can I pretend to absolute certainty about any matter of fact. If with the closest scrutiny I am able to give, a judgment appears to have the characters I have described, I must reckon it among perceptual judgments until I am better advised. Now consider the judgment that one event C *appears to be* subsequent to another event A. Certainly, I may have inferred this; because I may have remarked that C was subsequent to a third event B which was itself subsequent to A. But then these premisses are judgments of the same description. It does not seem possible that I can have performed an infinite series of acts of criticism each of which must require a distinct effort. The case is quite different from that of Achilles and the tortoise because Achilles does not require to make an infinite series of distinct efforts. It therefore appears that I must have made some judgment that one event *appeared to be* subsequent to another without that judgment having been inferred from any premiss [*i.e.*] without any *controlled* and *criticized* action of reasoning. If this be so, it is a perceptual judgment in the only sense that the logician can recognize. But from that proposition that one event, Z, is subsequent to another event, J, I can at once deduce by necessary reasoning a universal proposition. Namely, the definition of the relation of apparent subsequence is well known, or sufficiently so for our purpose. Z will appear to be subsequent to Y if and only if Z appears to stand in a peculiar relation, R, to Y such that nothing can stand in the relation R to itself, and if, furthermore, whatever event, X, there may be to which Y stands in the relation R, to that same X, Z also stands in the relation R. This being implied in the meaning of subsequence, concerning which there is no room for doubt, it easily follows that whatever is subsequent to C is subsequent to anything, A, to which C is subsequent—which is a universal proposition.

Thus . . . Thirdness pours in upon us through every avenue of sense.

. . . Abductive inference shades into perceptual judgment without any sharp line of demarcation between them; or, in other words, our first premisses, the perceptual judgments, are to be regarded as an extreme case of abductive inferences, from which they differ in being absolutely beyond criticism. The abductive suggestion comes to us like a flash. It is an act of *insight*, although of extremely fallible insight. It is true that the different elements of the hypothesis were in our minds before; but it is the idea of putting together what we had never before dreamed of putting together which flashes the new suggestion before our contemplation.

On its side, the perceptive judgment is the result of a process, although of a process not sufficiently conscious to be controlled, or, to state it more truly, not controllable and therefore not fully conscious. If we were to subject this subconscious process to logical analysis, we should find that it terminated in what that analysis would represent as an abductive inference, resting on the result of a similar process which a similar logical analysis would represent to be terminated by a similar abductive inference, and so on *ad infinitum*. This analysis would be precisely analogous to that which the sophism of Achilles and the Tortoise applies to the chase of the Tortoise by Achilles, and it would fail to represent the real process for the same reason. Namely, just as Achilles does not have to make the series of distinct endeavours which he is represented as making, so this process of forming the perceptual judgment, because it is subconscious and so not amenable to logical criticism, does not have to make separate acts of inference, but performs its act in one continuous process.

If the percept or perceptual judgment were of a nature entirely unrelated to abduction, one would expect that the percept would be entirely free from any characters that are proper to *interpretations*, while it can hardly fail to have such characters if it be merely a continuous series of what, discretely and consciously performed, ' would be abductions. . . . The fact is that it is not necessary to go beyond ordinary observations of common life to find a variety of widely different ways in which perception is interpretative.

The whole series of hypnotic phenomena, of which so many fall within the realm of ordinary everyday observation—such as our waking up at the hour we wish to wake much nearer than our waking selves could guess it—involve the fact that we perceive what we are adjusted for interpreting, though it be far less perceptible than any express effort could enable us to perceive; while that, to the interpretation of which our adjustments are not fitted, we fail to perceive although it exceed in intensity what we should perceive with the utmost ease, if we cared at all for its interpretation. It is a marvel to me that the clock in my study strikes every half hour in the most audible manner, and yet I never hear it. I should not know at all whether the striking part were going, unless it is out of order and strikes the wrong hour. If it does that, I am pretty sure to hear it. . . .

I should tire you if I dwelt further on anything so familiar, especially to every psychological student, as the interpretativeness of the perceptive judgment. It is plainly nothing but the extremest case of Abductive Judgments.

[The form of the perceptual abduction is:]

A well-recognized kind of object, M, has for its ordinary predicates P_1, P_2, P_3, etc., indistinctly recognized.
The suggesting object, S, has these same predicates, P_1, P_2, P_3, etc.
Hence, S is of the kind M.

This is hypothetic inference in form. The first premiss is not actually thought, though it is in the mind habitually. This, of itself, would not make the inference unconscious. But it is so because it is not recognized as an inference; the conclusion is accepted without our knowing how.

21

TWO NOTES: ON MOTIVES, ON PERCEPTS *

I

A MAN may act with reference only to the momentary occasion, either from unrestrained desire, or from preference for one desideratum over another, or from provision against future desires, or from persuasion, or from imitative instinct, or from dread of blame, or in awed obedience to an instant command; or he may act according to some general rule restricted to his own wishes, such as the pursuit of pleasure, or self-preservation, or good-will toward an acquaintance, or attachment to home and surroundings, or conformity to the customs of his tribe, or reverence for a law; or, becoming a moralist, he may aim at bringing about an ideal state of things definitely conceived, such as one in which everybody attends exclusively to his own business and interest (individualism), or in which the maximum total pleasure of all beings capable of pleasure is attained (utilitarianism), or in which altruistic sentiments universally prevail (altruism), or in which his community is placed out of all danger (patriotism), or in which the ways of nature are as little modified as possible (naturalism); or he may aim at hastening some result not otherwise known in advance than as that, whatever it may turn out to be, to which some process seeming to him good must inevitably lead, such as whatever the dictates of the human heart may approve (sentimentalism), or whatever would result from every man's duly weighing, before action, the advantages of his every purpose (to which I will attach the nonce-name *entelism*, distinguishing it and others below by italics), or whatever the historical evolution of public sentiment may decree (*historicism*), or whatever the operation of cosmical causes may be destined to bring about (evolutionism); or he may be devoted to truth, and may be determined to do nothing not pronounced reasonable, either by his own cogitations (rationalism), or by public discussion (dialecticism), or by crucial experiment; or he may feel that the only thing really worth striving for is the generalizing or assimilating

* [Both I and II are from " Pearson's Grammar of Science," *Popular Science Monthly* Vol. 58 (1900-1901) pp. 298-9, 301-2.]

elements in truth, and that either as the sole object in which the mind can ultimately recognize its veritable aim (educationalism), or that which alone is destined to gain universal sway (pancratism); or, finally, he may be filled with the idea that the only reason that can reasonably be admitted as ultimate is that living reason for the sake of which the psychical and physical universe is in process of creation (*religionism*).

This list of ethical classes of motives may, it is hoped, serve as a tolerable sample upon which to base reflections upon the acceptability as ultimate of different kinds of human motives; and it makes no pretension to any higher value. The enumeration has been so ordered as to bring into view the various degrees of generality of motives. It would conduce to our purpose, however, to compare them in other respects. Thus, we might arrange them in reference to the degree to which an impulse of dependence enters into them, from express obedience, generalized obedience, conformity to an external exemplar, action for the sake of an object regarded as external, the adoption of a motive centring on something which is partially opposed to what is present, the balancing of one consideration against another, until we reach such motives as unrestrained desire, the pursuit of pleasure, individualism, sentimentalism, rationalism, educationalism, religionism, in which the element of otherness is reduced to a minimum. Again, we might arrange the classes of motives according to the degree in which immediate qualities of feeling appear in them, from unrestrained desire, through desire present but restrained, action for self, action for pleasure generalized beyond self, motives involving a retro-consciousness of self in outward things, the personification of the community, to such motives as direct obedience, reverence, naturalism, evolutionism, experimentalism, pancratism, religionism, in which the element of self-feeling is reduced to a minimum. But the important thing is to make ourselves thoroughly acquainted, as far as possible from the inside, with a variety of human motives ranging over the whole field of ethics.

I will not go further into ethics than simply to remark that all motives that are directed toward pleasure or self-satisfaction, of however high a type, will be pronounced by every experienced person to be inevitably destined to miss the satisfaction at which they aim. This is true even of the highest of such motives, that which Josiah Royce develops in his *World and Individual*. On the other hand, every motive involving dependence on some other leads us to ask for some ulterior reason. The only desirable object which is quite satisfactory in itself without any ulterior reason for desiring it, is the reasonable itself. I do not mean to put this forward as a demonstration; because, like all demonstrations about such matters, it would be a mere quibble, a sheaf of fallacies. I maintain simply that it is an experiential truth.

The only ethically sound motive is the most general one; and the motive that actually inspires the man of science, if not quite that, is very near to it—nearer, I venture to believe, than that of any other equally common type of humanity.

II

[Professor Pearson] will have it that knowledge is built up out of sense-impressions—a correct enough statement of a conclusion of psychology. Understood, however, as Professor Pearson understands and applies it, as a statement of the nature of our logical data, of "the facts of science," it is altogether incorrect. He tells us that each of us is like the operator at a central telephone office, shut out from the external world, of which he is informed only by sense-impressions. Not at all! Few things are more completely hidden from my observation than those hypothetical elements of thought which the psychologist finds reason to pronounce "immediate," in his sense. But the starting point of all our reasoning is not in those sense-impressions, but in our percepts. When we first wake up to the fact that we are thinking beings and can exercise some control over our reasonings, we have to set out upon our intellectual travels from the home where we already find ourselves. Now, this home is the parish of percepts. It is not inside our skulls, either, but out in the open. It is the external world that we directly observe. What passes within we only know as it is mirrored in external objects. In a certain sense, there is such a thing as introspection; but it consists in an interpretation of phenomena presenting themselves as external percepts. We first see blue and red things. It is quite a discovery when we find the eye has anything to do with them, and a discovery still more recondite when we learn that there is an *ego* behind the eye, to which these qualities properly belong. Our logically initial data are percepts. Those percepts are undoubtedly purely psychical, altogether of the nature of thought. They involve three kinds of psychical elements, their qualities of feelings, their reaction against my will, and their generalizing or associating element. But all that we find out afterward. I see an inkstand on the table: that is a percept. Moving my head, I get a different percept of the ink-stand. It coalesces with the other. What I call the inkstand is a generalized percept, a quasi-inference from percepts, perhaps I might say a composite-photograph of percepts. In this psychical product is involved an element of resistance to me, which I am obscurely conscious of from the first. Subsequently, when I accept the hypothesis of an inward subject for my thoughts, I yield to that consciousness of resistance and admit the inkstand to the standing of an external object. Still later, I may call this in question. But as soon as I do that, I find that the inkstand appears there in spite of me. If I turn away my eyes, other witnesses will tell me that it still remains. If we all leave the room and dismiss the matter from our thoughts, still a photographic camera would show the inkstand still there, with the same roundness, polish and trans-parency, and with the same opaque liquid within. Thus, or other-wise, I confirm myself in the opinion that its characters are what they are, and persist at every opportunity in revealing themselves, regardless of what you, or I, or any man, or generation of men, may think that they are. That conclusion to which I find myself driven, struggle against it as I may, I briefly express by saying that the inkstand is a *real* thing. Of course, in being real and external, it does not in the least cease to be a purely psychical product, a generalized percept, like everything of which I can take any sort of cognizance.

22

THE APPROACH TO METAPHYSICS *

LOGIC requires that the more abstract sciences should be developed earlier than the more concrete ones. For the more concrete sciences require as fundamental principles the results of the more abstract sciences, while the latter only make use of the results of the former as data; and if one fact is wanting, some other will generally serve to support the same generalization.

But notwithstanding this, there is one highly abstract science which is in a deplorably backward condition. I mean Metaphysics. There is and can be no doubt that this immature condition of Metaphysics has very greatly hampered the progress of one of the two great branches of special science, I mean the Moral or Psychical Sciences. Most immediately has it checked the development of psychology; while the backward state of psychology has been a great disadvantage to all the other psychical sciences, such as linguistics, anthropology, social science, etc. To my mind it is equally clear that defective and bad metaphysics has been almost as injurious to the physical sciences, and is the real reason why all that depends upon the science of the constitution of matter, even physiology, is more or less rolling in the trough of the sea in rudder-less fashion. The common opinion has been that Metaphysics is backward because it is intrinsically beyond the reach of human cognition. But that, I think I can clearly discern, is a complete mistake. Why should metaphysics be so difficult? Because it is abstract? But the abstracter a science is, the easier it is, both as a general rule of experience and as a corollary from logical principles. Mathematics, which is far more abstract than metaphysics, is certainly far more developed than any special science; and the same is true, though less tremendously so, of logic. But it will be said that metaphysics is inscrutable because its objects are not open to observation. This is doubtless true of some systems of metaphysics, though not to the extent that it is supposed to be true. The things that any science discovers are beyond the reach of direct observation. We cannot see energy, nor the attraction of gravitation, nor

* [The two selections are from mss. 1898 and c. 1903 respectively (CP 6.1-6).]

the flying molecules of gases, nor the luminiferous ether, nor the forests of the carbonaceous era, nor the explosions in nerve-cells. It is only the premisses of science, not its conclusions, which are directly observed. But metaphysics, even bad metaphysics, really rests on observations, whether consciously or not; and the only reason that this is not universally recognized is that it rests upon kinds of phenomena with which every man's experience is so saturated that he usually pays no particular attention to them. The data of metaphysics are not less open to observation, but immeasurably more so, than the data, say, of the very highly developed science of astronomy, to make any important addition to whose observations requires an expenditure of many tens of thousands of dollars. No, I think we must abandon the idea that metaphysics is backward owing to any intrinsic difficulty of it.

In my opinion the chief cause of its backward condition is that its leading professors have been theologians. Were they simply Christian ministers the effect of intrusting very important scientific business to their hands would be quite as bad as if the same number of Wall Street promoters and Broad Street brokers were appointed to perform the task. The unfitness in the one case, as in the other, would consist in those persons having no idea of any broader interests than the personal interests of some person or collection of persons. Both classes are practical men. Now it is quite impossible for a practical man to comprehend what science is about unless he becomes as a little child and is born again. Scientific men are made out of youths who during the plastic period of life are set to study science for a number of years. Most of these develop into mere teachers; only a minority imbibe the spirit of science. The practical man has a definite job which he sets himself to accomplish. For that purpose he has to adopt some consistent plan which must be based upon a theory, and to that theory he must be wedded before the work begins. Even if his practical problem is no more serious than playing a game of whist, when there are only three rounds of a hand to be played, he must go upon the supposition that the cards lie so that he can win the odd trick. If he is a judge presiding over the hearing of a cause, that cause must be decided somehow, no matter how defective the evidence may be; and consequently he is constrained to lay down a rule for the burden of proof. But the idea of science is to pile the ground before the foot of the outworks of truth with the carcasses of this generation, and perhaps of others to come after it, until some future generation, by treading on them, can storm the citadel. The difference comes to this, that the practical man stakes everything he cares for upon the hazard of a die, and must believe with all the force of his manhood that the object for which he strives is good and that the theory of his plan is correct; while the scientific man is above all things desirous of learning the truth and, in order to do so, ardently desires to have his present provisional beliefs (and all his beliefs are merely provisional) swept away, and will work hard to accomplish that object. This is the reason that a good practical man cannot do the best scientific work. The temperaments requisite for the two kinds of business are altogether contrary to one another. This is above all true of the practical teacher [who] has no calling for his work unless he thoroughly believes that he is already in possession of all-important truth, with which he seeks by every physiological means to imbue other minds, so that they shall be unable to give it up. But a scientific man, who has any such immovable beliefs to which he regards himself as religiously bound to be loyal, cannot at the same time desire to have his beliefs altered. In other words he cannot wish to learn the truth. Hence, I say that had the business of metaphysics been intrusted to ordinary parish priests it would have been performed unscientifically enough. But what has in fact been its fate has been far more tragic, in that it has been given over not to parish priests but to the caste of theologians. How much theologians may have contributed to the cause of Christianity, how far their writings and performances may have [been] the instruments of bringing home to men's hearts the truth of the Gospel of Love, or how far, on the other hand, they may have subserved the agencies that work to make Christians forget that truth, it is not in my province to inquire. I once bought and read through Dr. Schaff's three volumes upon the *Creeds of Christendom* for the purpose of ascertaining whether the theologians, who composed them, had ever once, from the first to the last, inserted a single clause in one of them by way of recognition of the principle of love; and I found that such a thing had never been done. But then we must remember that, that principle being fully admitted by all Christians, its insertion would not have served to damn anybody. Now the principal business of theologians is to make men feel the enormity of the slightest departure from the metaphysics they assume to be connected with the standard faith. Upon their religious side, however, I will not pretend to any opinion about the influence of theologians. But since theology pretends to be a science, they must also be judged as scientific men. And in that regard I must say that another so deplorably corrupt an influence as theirs upon the morals of science I do not believe has ever been operative. Theology, I am persuaded, derives its initial impulse from a religious wavering; for there is quite as much, or more, that is mysterious and calculated to awaken scientific curiosity in the intercourse of men with one another as in their intercourse with God, and it [is] a problem quite analogous to that of theology. Yet we do not find that theologians have cared much for those problems. They have taken human conversation as a matter of course, with rather a remarkable absence of all curiosity about it. But, as far as I can penetrate into the motive of theology, it begins in an effort of men who have joined the Christian army and sworn fidelity to it to silence the suggestions of their hearts that they renounce their allegiance. How far it is successful in that purpose I will not inquire. But nothing can be more unscientific than the attitude of minds who are trying to confirm themselves in early beliefs. The struggle of the scientific man is to try to see the errors of his beliefs—if he can be said to have any beliefs. The logic which observational science uses is not, like the logic that the books teach, quite independent of the motive and spirit of the reasoner. There is an ethics indissolubly bound up with it—an ethics of fairness and impartiality—and a writer, who teaches, by his example, to find arguments for a conclusion which he wishes to believe, saps the very foundations of science by trifling with its morals. To sum up, the case is this:

We should expect to find metaphysics, judging from its position in the scheme of the sciences, to be somewhat more difficult than logic, but still on the whole one of the simplest of sciences, as it is one whose main principles must be settled before very much progress can be gained either in psychics or in physics.

Historically we are astonished to find that it has been a mere arena of ceaseless and trivial disputation. But we also find that it has been pursued in a spirit the very contrary of that of wishing to learn the truth, which is the most essential requirement of the logic of science; and it is worth trying whether by proceeding modestly, recognizing in metaphysics an observational science, and applying to it the universal methods of such science, without caring one straw what kind of conclusions we reach or what their tendencies may be, but just honestly applying induction and hypothesis, we cannot gain some ground for hoping that the disputes and obscurities of the subject may at last disappear.

Metaphysics is the proper designation for the third, and completing department of cœnoscopy, which in places welds itself into idioscopy, or special science. Its business is to study the most general features of reality and real objects. But in its present condition it is, even more than the other branches of cœnoscopy, a puny, rickety, and scrofulous science. It is only too plain that those who pretend to cultivate it carry not the hearts of true men of science within their breast. Instead of striving with might and main to find out what errors they have fallen into, and exulting joyously at every such discovery, they are scared to look Truth in the face. They turn tail and flee her. Only a small number out of the great catalogue of problems which it is their business to solve have they ever taken up at all, and those few most feebly. Here let us set down almost at random a small specimen of the questions of metaphysics which press, not for hasty answers, but for industrious and solid investigation: Whether or no there be any real indefiniteness, or real possibility and impossibility? Whether or not there is any definite indeterminacy? Whether there be any strictly individual existence? Whether there is any distinction, other than one of more and less, between fact and fancy? Or between the external and the internal worlds? What general explanation or account can be given of the different qualities of feeling and their apparent connection with determinations of mass, space, and time ? Do all possible qualities of sensation, including, of course, a much vaster variety of which we have no experience than of those which we know, form one continuous system, as colours seem to do? What external reality do the qualities of sense represent, in general? Is Time a real thing, and if not, what is the nature of the reality that it represents? How about Space, in these regards? How far, and in what respects, is Time external or has immediate contents that are external? Are Time and Space continuous? What numerically are the Chorisy, Cyclosy, Periphraxy, and Apeiry of Space? Has Time, or has Space, any limit or node? Is hylozoism an opinion, actual or conceivable, rather than a senseless vocable; and if so, what is, or would be, that opinion? What is consciousness or mind like; meaning, is it a single continuum like Time and Space, which is for different purposes variously broken up by that which it contains; or is it composed of solid atoms, or is it more like a fluid? Has truth, in Kantian phrase, any "material" characteristics in general, by which it can, with any degree of probability, be recognized? Is there, for example, any general tendency in the course of events, any progress in one direction on the whole?

23

THE ARCHITECTURE OF THEORIES *

OF the fifty or hundred systems of philosophy that have been
advanced at different times of the world's history, perhaps the
larger number have been, not so much results of historical evolution,
as happy thoughts which have accidentally occurred to their authors.
An idea which has been found interesting and fruitful has been
adopted, developed, and forced to yield explanations of all sorts
of phenomena. The English have been particularly given to this
way of philosophizing; witness, Hobbes, Hartley, Berkeley, James
Mill. Nor has it been by any means useless labour; it shows us
what the true nature and value of the ideas developed are, and in
that way affords serviceable materials for philosophy. Just as if
a man, being seized with the conviction that paper was a good
material to make things of, were to go to work to build a *papier
mâché* house, with roof of roofing paper, foundations of pasteboard,
windows of paraffined paper, chimneys, bath tubs, locks, etc., all
of different forms of paper, his experiment would probably afford
valuable lessons to builders, while it would certainly make a de-
testable house, so those one-idea'd philosophies are exceedingly
interesting and instructive, and yet are quite unsound.

The remaining systems of philosophy have been of the nature of
reforms, sometimes amounting to radical revolutions, suggested by
certain difficulties which have been found to beset systems previously in vogue; and such ought certainly to be in large part the
motive of any new theory. This is like partially rebuilding a house.
The faults that have been committed are, first, that the repairs of
the dilapidations have generally not been sufficiently thorough-
going, and, second, that not sufficient pains have been taken to
bring the additions into deep harmony with the really sound parts
of the old structure.

When a man is about to build a house, what a power of thinking
he has to do before he can safely break ground! With what pains
he has to excogitate the precise wants that are to be supplied!

* [This chapter, with Peirce's title, and omitting matter principally where
the spatial division occurs, is the greater part of the first paper in a series of
five, *The Monist* 1891 (*CP* 6.7-25, 31-4).]

What a study to ascertain the most available and suitable materials, to determine the mode of construction to which those materials are best adapted, and to answer a hundred such questions! Now without riding the metaphor too far, I think we may safely say that the studies preliminary to the construction of a great theory should be at least as deliberate and thorough as those that are preliminary to the building of a dwelling house.

That systems ought to be constructed architectonically has been preached since Kant, but I do not think the full import of the maxim has by any means been apprehended. What I would recommend is that every person who wishes to form an opinion concerning fundamental problems should first of all make a complete survey of human knowledge, should take note of all the valuable ideas in each branch of science, should observe in just what respect each has been successful and where it has failed, in order that, in the light of the thorough acquaintance so attained of the available materials for a philosophical theory and of the nature and strength of each, he may proceed to the study of what the problem of philosophy consists in, and of the proper way of solving it. I must not be understood as endeavouring to state fully all that these preparatory studies should embrace; on the contrary, I purposely slur over many points, in order to give emphasis to one special recommendation, namely, to make a systematic study of the conceptions out of which a philosophical theory may be built, in order to ascertain what place each conception may fitly occupy in such a theory, and to what uses it is adapted.

The adequate treatment of this single point would fill a volume, but I shall endeavour to illustrate my meaning by glancing at several sciences and indicating conceptions in them serviceable for philosophy. As to the results to which long studies thus commenced have led me, I shall just give a hint at their nature.

We may begin with dynamics—field in our day of perhaps the grandest conquest human science has ever made—I mean the law of the conservation of energy. But let us revert to the first step taken by modern scientific thought—and a great stride it was—the inauguration of dynamics by Galileo. A modern physicist on examining Galileo's works is surprised to find how little experiment had to do with the establishment of the foundations of mechanics. His principal appeal is to common sense and *il lume naturale*. He always assumes that the true theory will be found to be a simple and natural one. And we can see why it should indeed be so in dynamics. For instance, a body left to its own inertia moves in a straight line, and a straight line appears to us the simplest of curves. In *itself*, no curve is simpler than another. A system of straight lines has intersections precisely corresponding to those of a system of like parabolas similarly placed, or to those of any one of an infinity of systems of curves. But the straight line appears to us simple, because, as Euclid says, it lies evenly between its extremities; that is, because viewed endwise it appears as a point. That is, again, because light moves in straight lines. Now, light moves in straight lines because of the part which the straight line plays in the laws of dynamics. Thus it is that, our minds having been formed under the influence of phenomena governed by the laws of mechanics, certain conceptions entering into those laws become implanted in our minds, so that we readily guess at what the laws are. Without such a natural prompting, having to search blindfold for a law which would suit the phenomena, our chance of finding it would be as one to infinity. The further physical studies depart from phenomena which have directly influenced the growth of the mind, the less we can expect to find the laws which govern them "simple," that is, composed of a few conceptions natural to our minds.

The researches of Galileo, followed up by Huygens and others, led to those modern conceptions of *Force* and *Law*, which have revolutionized the intellectual world. The great attention given to mechanics in the seventeenth century soon so emphasized these conceptions as to give rise to the Mechanical Philosophy, or doctrine that all the phenomena of the physical universe are to be explained upon mechanical principles. Newton's great discovery imparted a new impetus to this tendency. The old notion that heat consists in an agitation of corpuscles was now applied to the explanation of the chief properties of gases. The first suggestion in this direction was that the pressure of gases is explained by the battering of the particles against the walls of the containing vessel, which explained Boyle's Law of the compressibility of air. Later, the expansion of gases, Avogadro's chemical law, the diffusion and viscosity of gases, and the action of Crookes's radiometer were shown to be consequences of the same kinetical theory; but other phenomena, such as the ratio of the specific heat at constant volume to that at constant pressure, require additional hypotheses, which we have little reason to suppose are simple, so that we find ourselves quite afloat. In like manner with regard to light. That it consists of vibrations was almost proved by the phenomena of diffraction, while those of polarization showed the excursions of the particles to be perpendicular to the line of propagation; but the phenomena of dispersion, etc., require additional hypotheses which may be very complicated. Thus, the further progress of molecular speculation appears quite uncertain. If hypotheses are to be tried haphazard, or simply because they will suit certain phenomena, it will occupy the mathematical physicists of the world say half a century on the average to bring each theory to the test, and since the number of possible theories may go up into the trillions, only one of which can be true, we have little prospect of making further solid additions to the subject in our time. When we come to atoms, the presumption in favour of a simple law seems very slender. There is room for serious doubt whether the fundamental laws of mechanics hold good for single atoms, and it seems quite likely that they are capable of motion in more than three dimensions.

To find out much more about molecules and atoms we must search out a natural history of laws of nature which may fulfill that function which the presumption in favour of simple laws fulfilled in the early days of dynamics, by showing us what kind of laws we have to expect and by answering such questions as this: Can we, with reasonable prospect of not wasting time, try the supposition that atoms attract one another inversely as the seventh power of their distances, or can we not? To suppose universal laws of nature capable of being apprehended by the mind and yet having no reason for their special forms, but standing inexplicable and irrational, is hardly a justifiable position. Uniformities are precisely the sort of facts that need to be accounted for. That a pitched coin should sometimes turn up heads and sometimes tails calls for no particular explanation; but if it shows heads every time, we wish to know how this result has been brought about. Law is *par excellence* the thing that wants a reason.

Now the only possible way of accounting for the laws of nature and for uniformity in general is to suppose them results of evolution. This supposes them not to be absolute, not to be obeyed precisely. It makes an element of indeterminacy, spontaneity, or absolute chance in nature. Just as, when we attempt to verify any physical law, we find our observations cannot be precisely satisfied by it, and rightly attribute the discrepancy to errors of observation, so we must suppose far more minute discrepancies to exist owing to the imperfect cogency of the law itself, to a certain swerving of the facts from any definite formula.

Mr. Herbert Spencer wishes to explain evolution upon mechanical principles. This is illogical, for four reasons. First, because the principle of evolution requires no extraneous cause, since the tendency to growth can be supposed itself to have grown from an infinitesimal germ accidentally started. Second, because law ought more than anything else to be supposed a result of evolution. Third, because exact law obviously never can produce heterogeneity out of homogeneity; and arbitrary heterogeneity is the feature of the universe the most manifest and characteristic. Fourth, because the law of the conservation of energy is equivalent to the proposition that all operations governed by mechanical laws are reversible; so that an immediate corollary from it is that growth is not explicable by those laws, even if they be not violated in the process of growth. In short, Spencer is not a philosophical evolutionist, but only a half-evolutionist—or, if you will, only a semi-Spencerian. Now philosophy requires thoroughgoing evolutionism or none.

The theory of Darwin was that evolution had been brought about by the action of two factors: first, heredity, as a principle making offspring nearly resemble their parents, while yet giving room for "sporting" or accidental variations—for very slight variations often, for wider ones rarely; and, second, the destruction of breeds or races that are unable to keep the birth rate up to the death rate. This Darwinian principle is plainly capable of great generalization. Wherever there are large numbers of objects having a tendency to retain certain characters unaltered, this tendency, however, not being absolute but giving room for chance variations, then, if the amount of variation is absolutely limited in certain directions by the destruction of everything which reaches those limits, there will be a gradual tendency to change in directions of departure from them. Thus, if a million players sit down to bet at an even game, since one after another will get ruined, the average wealth of those who remain will perpetually increase. Here is indubitably a genuine formula of possible evolution, whether its operation accounts for much or little in the development of animal and vegetable species.

The Lamarckian theory also supposes that the development of species has taken place by a long series of insensible changes, but it supposes that those changes have taken place during the lives of the individuals, in consequence of effort and exercise, and that reproduction plays no part in the process except in preserving these modifications. Thus, the Lamarckian theory only explains the development of characters for which individuals strive, while the Darwinian theory only explains the production of characters really beneficial to the race, though these may be fatal to individuals. But more broadly and philosophically conceived, Darwinian evolution is evolution by the operation of chance, and the destruction of bad results, while Lamarckian evolution is evolution by the effect of habit and effort.

A third theory of evolution is that of Mr. Clarence King. The testimony of monuments and of rocks is that species are unmodified or scarcely modified, under ordinary circumstances, but are rapidly altered after cataclysms or rapid geological changes. Under novel circumstances, we often see animals and plants sporting excessively in reproduction, and sometimes even undergoing transformations during individual life, phenomena no doubt due partly to the enfeeblement of vitality from the breaking up of habitual modes of life, partly to changed food, partly to direct specific influence of the element in which the organism is immersed. If evolution has been brought about in this way, not only have its single steps not been insensible, as both Darwinians and Lamarckians suppose, but they are furthermore neither haphazard on the one hand, nor yet determined by an inward striving on the other, but on the contrary are effects of the changed environment, and have a positive general tendency to adapt the organism to that environment, since variation will particularly affect organs at once enfeebled and stimulated. This mode of evolution, by external forces and the breaking up of habits, seems to be called for by some of the broadest and most important facts of biology and paleontology; while it certainly has been the chief factor in the historical evolution of institutions as in that of ideas; and cannot possibly be refused a very prominent place in the process of evolution of the universe in general.

Passing to psychology, we find the elementary phenomena of mind fall into three categories. First, we have Feelings, comprising all that is immediately present. . . . Besides Feelings, we have Sensations of reaction. . . . Very different both from feelings and from reaction-sensations or disturbances of feeling are general conceptions. When we think, we are conscious that a connection between feelings is determined by a general rule, we are aware of being governed by a habit. Intellectual power is nothing but facility in taking habits and in following them in cases essentially analogous to, but in non-essentials widely remote from, the normal cases of connections of feelings under which those habits were formed.

The one primary and fundamental law of mental action consists in a tendency to generalization. Feeling tends to spread; connections between feelings awaken feelings; neighbouring feelings become assimilated; ideas are apt to reproduce themselves. These are so many formulations of the one law of the growth of mind. When a disturbance of feeling takes place, we have a consciousness of gain, the gain of experience; and a new disturbance will be apt to assimilate itself to the one that preceded it. Feelings, by being excited, become more easily excited, especially in the ways in which they have previously been excited. The consciousness of such a habit constitutes a general conception.

The cloudiness of psychological notions may be corrected by connecting them with physiological conceptions. Feeling may be supposed to exist wherever a nerve-cell is in an excited condition. The disturbance of feeling, or sense of reaction, accompanies the transmission of disturbance between nerve-cells, or from a nerve-cell to a muscle-cell, or the external stimulation of a nerve-cell. General conceptions arise upon the formation of habits in the nerve-matter, which are molecular changes consequent upon its activity and probably connected with its nutrition.

The law of habit exhibits a striking contrast to all physical laws in the character of its commands. A physical law is absolute. What it requires is an exact relation. Thus, a physical force introduces into a motion a component motion to be combined with the rest by the parallelogram of forces; but the component motion must actually take place exactly as required by the law of force. On the other hand, no exact conformity is required by the mental law. Nay, exact conformity would be in downright conflict with the law; since it would instantly crystallize thought and prevent all further formation of habit. The law of mind only makes a given feeling *more likely* to arise. It thus resembles the "non-conservative" forces of physics, such as viscosity and the like, which are due to statistical uniformities in the chance encounters of trillions of molecules.

The old dualistic notion of mind and matter, so prominent in Cartesianism, as two radically different kinds of substance, will hardly find defenders today. Rejecting this, we are driven to some form of hylopathy, otherwise called monism. Then the question arises whether physical laws on the one hand and the psychical law on the other are to be taken—

(*a*) as independent, a doctrine often called *monism*, but which I would name *neutralism*; or,

(*b*) the psychical law as derived and special, the physical law alone as primordial, which is *materialism*; or,

(c) the physical law as derived and special, the psychical law alone as primordial, which is *idealism*.

The materialistic doctrine seems to me quite as repugnant to scientific logic as to common sense; since it requires us to suppose that a certain kind of mechanism will feel, which would be a hypothesis absolutely irreducible to reason—an ultimate, inexplicable regularity; while the only possible justification of any theory is that it should make things clear and reasonable.

Neutralism is sufficiently condemned by the logical maxim known as Ockham's razor, *i.e.*, that not more independent elements are to be supposed than necessary. By placing the inward and outward aspects of substance on a par, it seems to render both primordial.

The one intelligible theory of the universe is that of objective idealism, that matter is effete mind, inveterate habits becoming physical laws. But before this can be accepted it must show itself capable of explaining the tridimensionality of space, the laws of motion, and the general characteristics of the universe, with mathematical clearness and precision; for no less should be demanded of every philosophy.

Had I more space, I now ought to show how important for philosophy is the mathematical conception of continuity. Most of what is true in Hegel is a darkling glimmer of a conception which the mathematicians had long before made pretty clear, and which recent researches have still further illustrated.

Among the many principles of Logic which find their application in Philosophy, I can here only mention one. Three conceptions are perpetually turning up at every point in every theory of logic, and in the most rounded systems they occur in connection with one another. They are conceptions so very broad and consequently indefinite that they are hard to seize and may be easily overlooked. I call them the conceptions of First, Second, Third. First is the conception of being or existing independent of anything else. Second is the conception of being relative to, the conception of reaction with, something else. Third is the conception of mediation, whereby a first and second are brought into relation. To illustrate these ideas, I will show how they enter into those we have been considering. The origin of things, considered not as leading to anything, but in itself, contains the idea of First, the end of things that of Second, the process mediating between them that of Third. A philosophy which emphasizes the idea of the One is generally a dualistic philosophy in which the conception of Second receives exaggerated attention; for this One (though of course involving the idea of First) is always the other of a manifold which is not one. The idea of the Many, because variety is arbitrariness and arbitrariness is repudiation of any Secondness, has for its principal component the conception of First. In psychology Feeling is First, Sense of reaction Second, General conception Third, or mediation. In biology, the idea of arbitrary sporting is First, heredity is Second, the process whereby the accidental characters become fixed is Third. Chance is First, Law is Second, the tendency to take habits is Third. Mind is First, Matter is Second, Evolution is Third.

Such are the materials out of which chiefly a philosophical theory ought to be built, in order to represent the state of knowledge to which the nineteenth century has brought us. Without going into other important questions of philosophical architectonic, we can readily foresee what sort of a metaphysics would appropriately be constructed from those conceptions. Like some of the most ancient and some of the most recent speculations it would be a Cosmogonic Philosophy. It would suppose that in the beginning —infinitely remote—there was a chaos of unpersonalized feeling, which being without connection or regularity would properly be without existence. This feeling, sporting here and there in pure arbitrariness, would have started the germ of a generalizing tendency. Its other sportings would be evanescent, but this would have a growing virtue. Thus, the tendency to habit would be started; and from this, with the other principles of evolution, all the regularities of the universe would be evolved. At any time, however, an element of pure chance survives and will remain until the world becomes an absolutely perfect, rational, and symmetrical system, in which mind is at last crystallized in the infinitely distant future.

That idea has been worked out by me with elaboration. It accounts for the main features of the universe as we know it—the characters of time, space, matter, force, gravitation, electricity, etc. It predicts many more things which new observations can alone bring to the test. May some future student go over this ground again, and have the leisure to give his results to the world.

24

THE DOCTRINE OF NECESSITY EXAMINED

I PROPOSE here to examine the common belief that every single fact in the universe is precisely determined by law. It must not be supposed that this is a doctrine accepted everywhere and at all times by all rational men. Its first advocate appears to have been Democritus, the atomist, who was led to it, as we are informed, by reflecting upon the "impenetrability, translation, and impact of matter (ἀντιτυπία καὶ φορὰ καὶ πληγὴ τῆς ὕλης)." That is to say, having restricted his attention to a field where no influence other than mechanical constraint could possibly come before his notice, he straightway jumped to the conclusion that throughout the universe that was the sole principle of action—a style of reasoning so usual in our day with men not unreflecting as to be more than excusable in the infancy of thought. But Epicurus, in revising the atomic doctrine and repairing its defences, found himself obliged to suppose that atoms swerve from their courses by spontaneous chance; and thereby he conferred upon the theory life and entelechy. For we now see clearly that the peculiar function of the molecular hypothesis in physics is to open an entry for the calculus of probabilities. Already, the prince of philosophers had repeatedly and emphatically condemned the dictum of Democritus (especially in the *Physics*, Book II, chapters 4, 5, 6), holding that events come to pass in three ways, namely, (1) by external compulsion, or the action of efficient causes, (2) by virtue of an inward nature, or the influence of final causes, and (3) irregularly without definite cause, but just by absolute chance; and this doctrine is of the inmost essence of Aristotelianism. It affords, at any rate, a valuable enumeration of the possible ways in which anything can be supposed to have come about. The freedom of the will, too, was admitted both by Aristotle and by Epicurus. But the Stoa, which in every department seized upon the most tangible, hard, and lifeless element, and blindly denied the existence of every other, which, for example, impugned the validity of the inductive

* [This chapter, with Peirce's title, is the entire second paper (minus a brief opening paragraph) in a series of five, *The Monist* 1892 (*CP* 6.36-65).]

method and wished to fill its place with the *reductio ad absurdum*, very naturally became the one school of ancient philosophy to stand by a strict necessitarianism, thus returning to a single principle of Democritus that Epicurus had been unable to swallow. Necessitarianism and materialism with the Stoics went hand in hand, as by affinity they should.   At the revival of learning, Stoicism met with considerable favour, partly because it departed just enough from Aristotle to give it the spice of novelty, and partly because its superficialities well adapted it for acceptance by students of literature and art who wanted their philosophy drawn mild.   Afterwards, the great discoveries in mechanics inspired the hope that mechanical principles might suffice to explain the universe; and, though without logical justification, this hope has since been continually stimulated by subsequent advances in physics.   Nevertheless, the doctrine was in too evident conflict with the freedom of the will and with miracles to be generally acceptable, at first.   But meantime there arose that most widely spread of philosophical blunders, the notion that associationalism belongs intrinsically to the materialistic family of doctrines; and thus was evolved the theory of motives; and libertarianism became weakened.   At present, historical criticism has almost exploded the miracles, great and small; so that the doctrine of necessity has never been in so great vogue as now.

The proposition in question is that the state of things existing at any time, together with certain immutable laws, completely determine the state of things at every other time (for a limitation to *future* time is indefensible).   Thus, given the state of the universe in the original nebula, and given the laws of mechanics, a sufficiently powerful mind could deduce from these data the precise form of every curlicue of every letter I am now writing.

Whoever holds that every act of the will as well as every idea of the mind is under the rigid governance of a necessity coördinated with that of the physical world will logically be carried to the proposition that minds are part of the physical world in such a sense that the laws of mechanics determine anything that happens according to immutable attractions and repulsions.   In that case, that instantaneous state of things, from which every other state of things is calculable, consists in the positions and velocities of all the particles at any instant.   This, the usual and most logical form of necessitarianism, is called the mechanical philosophy.

When I have asked thinking men what reason they had to believe that every fact in the universe is precisely determined by law, the first answer has usually been that the proposition is a "presupposition" or postulate of scientific reasoning. Well, if that is the best that can be said for it, the belief is doomed. Suppose it be "postulated": that does not make it true, nor so much as afford the slightest rational motive for yielding it any credence. It is as if a man should come to borrow money and, when asked for his security, should reply he "postulated" the loan. To "postulate" a proposition is no more than to hope it is true. There are, indeed, practical emergencies in which we act upon assumptions of certain propositions as true, because if they are not so, it can make no difference how we act. But all such propositions I take to be hypotheses of individual facts. For it is manifest that no universal principle can in its universality be comprised in a special case or can be requisite for the validity of any ordinary inference. To say, for instance, that the demonstration by Archimedes of the property of the lever would fall to the ground if men were endowed with free will is extravagant; yet this is implied by those who make a proposition incompatible with the freedom of the will the postulate of all inference. Considering, too, that the conclusions of science make no pretense to being more than probable, and considering that a probable inference can at most only suppose something to be most frequently, or otherwise approximately, true, but never that anything is precisely true without exception throughout the universe, we see how far this proposition in truth is from being so postulated.

But the whole notion of a postulate being involved in reasoning appertains to a bygone and false conception of logic. Non-deductive or ampliative inference is of three kinds: induction, hypothesis, and analogy.[19] If there be any other modes, they must be extremely unusual and highly complicated, and may be assumed with little doubt to be of the same nature as those enumerated. For induction, hypothesis, and analogy, as far as their ampliative character goes, that is, so far as they conclude something not implied in the premises, depend upon one principle and involve the same procedure. All are essentially inferences from sampling. Suppose a ship arrives at Liverpool laden with wheat in bulk. Suppose that by some machinery the whole cargo be stirred up with great thoroughness. Suppose that twenty-seven thimblefuls be taken equally from the forward, midships, and aft parts, from the starboard, centre, and larboard parts, and from the top, half depth, and lower parts of her hold, and that these being mixed and the grains counted, four-fifths of the latter are found to be of quality A. Then we infer, experientially and provisionally, that approximately four-fifths of all the grain in the cargo is of the same quality. I say we infer this *experientially* and *provisionally*. By saying that we infer it *experientially*, I mean that our conclusion makes no pretension to knowledge of wheat-in-itself, our ἀλήθεια, as the derivation of that word implies, has nothing to do with *latent* wheat. We are dealing only with the matter of possible experience—experience in the full acceptation of the term as something not merely affecting the senses but also as the subject of thought. If there be any wheat hidden on the ship, so that it can neither turn up in the sample nor be heard of subsequently from purchasers—or if it be half-hidden, so that it may, indeed, turn up, but is less likely to do so than the rest—or if it can affect our senses and our pockets, but from some strange cause or causelessness cannot be reasoned about—all such wheat is to be excluded (or have only its proportional weight) in calculating that true proportion of quality A, to which our inference seeks to approximate. By saying that we draw the inference *provisionally*, I mean that we do not hold that we have reached any assigned degree of approximation as yet, but only hold that if our experience be indefinitely extended, and if every fact of whatever nature, as fast as it presents itself, be duly applied, according to the inductive method, in correcting the inferred ratio, then our approximation will become indefinitely close in the long run; that is to say, close to the experience *to come* (not merely close by the exhaustion of a finite collection) so that if experience in general is to fluctuate irregularly to and fro, in a manner to deprive the ratio sought of all definite value, we shall be able to find out approximately within what limits it fluctuates, and if, after having one definite value, it changes and assumes another, we shall be able to find that out, and in short, whatever may be the variations of this ratio in experience, experience indefinitely extended will enable us to detect them, so as to predict rightly, at last, what its ultimate value may be, if it have any ultimate value, or what the ultimate law of succession of values may be, if there be any such ultimate law, or that it ultimately fluctuates irregularly within certain limits, if it do so ultimately fluctuate. Now our inference, claiming to be no more than thus experiential and provisional, manifestly involves no postulate whatever.

For what is a postulate? It is the formulation of a material fact which we are not entitled to assume as a premiss, but the truth of which is requisite to the validity of an inference. Any fact, then, which might be supposed postulated, must either be such that it would ultimately present itself in experience, or not. If it will present itself, we need not postulate it now in our provisional inference, since we shall ultimately be entitled to use it as a premiss. But if it never would present itself in experience, our conclusion is valid but for the possibility of this fact being otherwise than assumed, that is, it is valid as far as possible experience goes, and that is all that we claim. Thus, every postulate is cut off, either by the provisionality or by the experientiality of our inference. For instance, it has been said that induction postulates that, if an indefinite succession of samples be drawn, examined, and thrown back each before the next is drawn, then in the long run every grain will be drawn as often as any other, that is to say, postulates that the ratio of the numbers of times in which any two are drawn will indefinitely approximate to unity. But no such postulate is made; for if, on the one hand, we are to have no other experience of the wheat than from such drawings, it is the ratio that presents itself in those drawings and not the ratio which belongs to the wheat in its latent existence that we are endeavouring to determine; while if, on the other hand, there is some other mode by which the wheat is to come under our knowledge, equivalent to another kind of sampling, so that after all our care in stirring up the wheat some experiential grains will present themselves in the first sampling operation more often than others in the long run, this very singular fact will be sure to get discovered by the inductive method, which must avail itself of every sort of experience; and our inference, which was only provisional, corrects itself at last. Again, it has been said, that induction postulates that under like circumstances like events will happen, and that this postulate is at bottom the same as the principle of universal causation. But this is a blunder, or *bévue*, due to thinking exclusively of inductions where the concluded ratio is either 1 or 0. If any such proposition were postulated, it would be that under like circumstances (the circumstances of drawing the different samples) different events occur in the same proportions in all the different sets—a proposition which is false and even absurd. But in truth no such thing is postulated, the experiential character of the inference reducing the condition of validity to this, that if a certain result does not occur, the opposite result will be manifested, a condition assured by the provisionality of the inference. But it may be asked whether it is not conceivable that every instance of a certain class destined to be ever employed as a datum of induction should have one character, while every instance destined not to be so employed should have the opposite character. The answer is that, in that case, the instances excluded from being subjects of reasoning would not be experienced in the full sense of the word, but would be among these *latent* individuals of which our conclusion does not pretend to speak.

To this account of the rationale of induction I know of but one objection worth mention: it is that I thus fail to deduce the full degree of force which this mode of inference in fact possesses; that according to my view, no matter how thorough and elaborate the stirring and mixing process had been, the examination of a single handful of grain would not give me any assurance, sufficient to risk money upon, that the next handful would not greatly modify the concluded value of the ratio under inquiry, while, in fact, the assurance would be very high that this ratio was not greatly in error. If the true ratio of grains of quality A were 0·80 and the handful contained a thousand grains, nine such handfuls out of every ten would contain from 780 to 820 grains of quality A. The answer to this is that the calculation given is correct when we know that the units of this handful and the quality inquired into have the normal independence of one another, if for instance the stirring has been complete and the character sampled for has been settled upon in advance of the examination of the sample. But in so far as these conditions are not known to be complied with, the above figures cease to be applicable. Random sampling and predesignation of the character sampled for should always be striven after in inductive reasoning, but when they cannot be attained, so long as it is conducted honestly, the inference retains some value. When we cannot ascertain how the sampling has been done or the sample-character selected, induction still has the essential validity which my present account of it shows it to have.

I do not think a man who combines a willingness to be convinced with a power of appreciating an argument upon a difficult subject can resist the reasons which have been given to show that the principle of universal necessity cannot be defended as being a postulate of reasoning. But then the question immediately arises whether it is not proved to be true, or at least rendered highly probable, by observation of nature.

Still, this question ought not long to arrest a person accustomed to reflect upon the force of scientific reasoning. For the essence of the necessitarian position is that certain continuous quantities have certain exact values. Now, how can observation determine the value of such a quantity with a probable error absolutely *nil*? To one who is behind the scenes, and knows that the most refined comparisons of masses, lengths, and angles, far surpassing in precision all other measurements, yet fall behind the accuracy of bank accounts, and that the ordinary determinations of physical constants, such as appear from month to month in the journals, are about on a par with an upholsterer's measurements of carpets and curtains, the idea of mathematical exactitude being demonstrated in the laboratory will appear simply ridiculous. There is a recognized method of estimating the probable magnitudes of errors in physics —the method of least squares. It is universally admitted that this method makes the errors smaller than they really are; yet even according to that theory an error indefinitely small is indefinitely improbable; so that any statement to the effect that a certain continuous quantity has a certain exact value, if well founded at all, must be founded on something other than observation.

Still, I am obliged to admit that this rule is subject to a certain qualification. Namely, it only applies to continuous quantity. Now, certain kinds of continuous quantity are discontinuous at one or at two limits, and for such limits the rule must be modified. Thus, the length of a line cannot be less than zero. Suppose, then, the question arises how long a line a certain person had drawn from a marked point on a piece of paper. If no line at all can be seen, the observed length is zero; and the only conclusion this observation warrants is that the length of the line is less than the smallest length visible with the optical power employed. But indirect observations —for example, that the person supposed to have drawn the line was never within fifty feet of the paper—may make it probable that no line at all was made, so that the concluded length will be strictly zero. In like manner, experience no doubt would warrant the conclusion that there is absolutely *no* indigo in a given ear of wheat, and absolutely *no* attar in a given lichen. But such inferences can only be rendered valid by positive experiential evidence, direct or remote, and cannot rest upon a mere inability to detect the quantity in question. We have reason to think there is no indigo in the wheat, because we have remarked that wherever indigo is produced it is produced in considerable quantities, to mention only one argument. We have reason to think there is no attar in the lichen, because essential oils seem to be in general peculiar to single species. If the question had been whether there was iron in the wheat or the lichen, though chemical analysis should fail to detect its presence, we should think some of it probably was there, since iron is almost everywhere. Without any such information, one way or the other, we could only abstain from any opinion as to the presence of the substance in question. It cannot, I conceive, be maintained that we are in any *better* position than this in regard to the presence of the element of chance or spontaneous departures from law in nature.

Those observations which are generally adduced in favour of mechanical causation simply prove that there is an element of regularity in nature, and have no bearing whatever upon the question of whether such regularity is exact and universal or not. Nay, in regard to this *exactitude*, all observation is directly *opposed* to it; and the most that can be said is that a good deal of this observation can be explained away. Try to verify any law of nature, and you will find that the more precise your observations, the more certain they will be to show irregular departures from the law. We are accustomed to ascribe these, and I do not say wrongly, to errors of observation; yet we cannot usually account for such errors in any antecedently probable way. Trace their causes back far enough and you will be forced to admit they are always due to arbitrary determination, or chance.

But it may be asked whether if there were an element of real chance in the universe it must not occasionally be productive of signal effects such as could not pass unobserved. In answer to this question, without stopping to point out that there is an abundance of great events which one might be tempted to suppose were of that nature, it will be simplest to remark that physicists hold that the particles of gases are moving about irregularly, substantially as if by real chance, and that by the principles of probabilities there must occasionally happen to be concentrations of heat in the gases contrary to the second law of thermodynamics, and these concentrations, occurring in explosive mixtures, must sometimes have tremendous effects. Here, then, is in substance the very situation supposed; yet no phenomena ever have resulted which we are forced to attribute to such chance concentration of heat, or which anybody, wise or foolish, has ever dreamed of accounting for in that manner.

In view of all these considerations, I do not believe that anybody, not in a state of case-hardened ignorance respecting the logic of science, can maintain that the precise and universal conformity of facts to law is clearly proved, or even rendered particularly probable, by any observations hitherto made. In this way, the determined advocate of exact regularity will soon find himself driven to *a priori* reasons to support his thesis. These received such a socdolager from Stuart Mill in his examination of Hamilton, that holding to them now seems to me to denote a high degree of imperviousness to reason, so that I shall pass them by with little notice.

To say that we cannot help believing a given proposition is no argument, but it is a conclusive fact if it be true; and with the substitution of "I" for "we," it is true in the mouths of several classes of minds: the blindly passionate, the unreflecting and ignorant, and the person who has overwhelming evidence before his eyes. But that which has been inconceivable today has often turned out indisputable on the morrow. Inability to conceive is only a stage through which every man must pass in regard to a number of beliefs—unless endowed with extraordinary obstinacy and obtuseness. His understanding is enslaved to some blind compulsion which a vigorous mind is pretty sure soon to cast off.

Some seek to back up the *a priori* position with empirical arguments. They say that the exact regularity of the world is a natural belief, and that natural beliefs have generally been confirmed by experience. There is some reason in this. Natural beliefs, however, if they generally have a foundation of truth, also require correction and purification from natural illusions. The principles of mechanics are undoubtedly natural beliefs; but, for all that, the early formulations of them were exceedingly erroneous. The general approximation to truth in natural beliefs is, in fact, a case of the general adaptation of genetic products to recognizable utilities or ends. Now, the adaptations of nature, beautiful and often marvellous as they verily are, are never found to be quite perfect; so that the argument is quite *against* the absolute exactitude of any natural belief, including that of the principle of causation.

Another argument, or convenient commonplace, is that absolute chance is *inconceivable*. This word has eight current significations. The *Century Dictionary* enumerates six. Those who talk like this will hardly be persuaded to say in what sense they mean that chance is inconceivable. Should they do so, it would easily be shown either that they have no sufficient reason for the statement or that the inconceivability is of a kind which does not prove that chance is non-existent.

Another *a priori* argument is that chance is unintelligible; that is to say, while it may perhaps be conceivable, it does not disclose to the eye of reason the how or why of things; and since a hypothesis can only be justified so far as it renders some phenomenon intelligible, we never can have any right to suppose absolute chance to enter into the production of anything in nature. This argument may be considered in connection with two others. Namely, instead of going so far as to say that the supposition of chance can *never* properly be used to explain any observed fact, it may be alleged merely that no facts are known which such a supposition could in any way help in explaining. Or again, the allegation being still further weakened, it may be said that since departures from law are not unmistakably observed, chance is not a *vera causa*, and ought not unnecessarily to be introduced into a hypothesis.

These are no mean arguments, and require us to examine the matter a little more closely. Come, my superior opponent, let me learn from your wisdom. It seems to me that every throw of sixes with a pair of dice is a manifest instance of chance.

"While you would hold a throw of deuce-ace to be brought about by necessity?" (The opponent's supposed remarks are placed in quotation marks.)

Clearly one throw is as much chance as another.

"Do you think throws of dice are of a different nature from other events?"

I see that I must say that *all* the diversity and specificalness of events is attributable to chance.

"Would you, then, deny that there is any regularity in the world?"

That is clearly undeniable. I must acknowledge there is an approximate regularity, and that every event is influenced by it. But the diversification, specificalness, and irregularity of things I suppose is chance. A throw of sixes appears to me a case in which this element is particularly obtrusive.

"If you reflect more deeply, you will come to see that *chance* is only a name for a cause that is unknown to us."

Do you mean that we have no idea whatever what kind of causes could bring about a throw of sixes?

"On the contrary, each die moves under the influence of precise mechanical laws."

But it appears to me that it is not these *laws* which made the die turn up sixes; for these laws act just the same when other throws come up. The chance lies in the diversity of throws; and this diversity cannot be due to laws which are immutable.

"The diversity is due to the diverse circumstances under which the laws act. The dice lie differently in the box, and the motion given to the box is different. These are the unknown causes which produce the throws, and to which we give the name of chance; not the mechanical law which regulates the operation of these causes. You see you are already beginning to think more clearly about this subject."

Does the operation of mechanical law not increase the diversity?
"Properly not. You must know that the instantaneous state of a system of particles is defined by six times as many numbers as there are particles, three for the coördinates of each particle's position, and three more for the components of its velocity. This number of numbers, which expresses the amount of diversity in the system, remains the same at all times. There may be, to be sure, some kind of relation between the coördinates and component velocities of the different particles, by means of which the state of the system might be expressed by a smaller number of numbers. But, if this is the case, a precisely corresponding relationship must exist between the coördinates and component velocities at any other time, though it may doubtless be a relation less obvious to us. Thus, the intrinsic complexity of the system is the same at all times."

Very well, my obliging opponent, we have now reached an issue. You think all the arbitrary specifications of the universe were introduced in one dose, in the beginning, if there was a beginning, and that the variety and complication of nature has always been just as much as it is now. But I, for my part, think that the diversification, the specification, has been continually taking place. Should you condescend to ask me why I so think, I should give my reasons as follows:

(1) Question any science which deals with the course of time. Consider the life of an individual animal or plant, or of a mind. Glance at the history of states, of institutions, of language, of ideas. Examine the successions of forms shown by paleontology, the history of the globe as set forth in geology, of what the astronomer is able to make out concerning the changes of stellar systems. Everywhere the main fact is growth and increasing complexity. Death and corruption are mere accidents or secondary phenomena. Among some of the lower organisms, it is a moot point with biologists whether there be anything which ought to be called death. Races, at any rate, do not die out except under unfavourable circumstances. From these broad and ubiquitous facts we may fairly infer, by the most unexceptionable logic, that there is probably in nature some agency by which the complexity and diversity of things can be increased; and that consequently the rule of mechanical necessity meets in some way with interference.

(2) By thus admitting pure spontaneity or life as a character of the universe, acting always and everywhere though restrained within narrow bounds by law, producing infinitesimal departures

from law continually, and great ones with infinite infrequency, I account for all the variety and diversity of the universe, in the only sense in which the really *sui generis* and new can be said to be accounted for. The ordinary view has to admit the inexhaustible multitudinous variety of the world, has to admit that its mechanical law cannot account for this in the least, that variety can spring only from spontaneity, and yet denies without any evidence or reason the existence of this spontaneity, or else shoves it back to the beginning of time and supposes it dead ever since. The superior logic of my view appears to me not easily controverted.

(3) When I ask the necessitarian how he would explain the diversity and irregularity of the universe, he replies to me out of the treasury of his wisdom that irregularity is something which from the nature of things we must not seek to explain. Abashed at this, I seek to cover my confusion by asking how he would explain the uniformity and regularity of the universe, whereupon he tells me that the laws of nature are immutable and ultimate facts, and no account is to be given of them. But my hypothesis of spontaneity does explain irregularity, in a certain sense; that is, it explains the general fact of irregularity, though not, of course, what each lawless event is to be. At the same time, by thus loosening the bond of necessity, it gives room for the influence of another kind of causation, such as seems to be operative in the mind in the formation of associations, and enables us to understand how the uniformity of nature could have been brought about. That single events should be hard and unintelligible, logic will permit without difficulty: we do not expect to make the shock of a personally experienced earthquake appear natural and reasonable by any amount of cogitation. But logic does expect things *general* to be understandable. To say that there is a universal law, and that it is a hard, ultimate, unintelligible fact, the why and wherefore of which can never be inquired into, at this a sound logic will revolt, and will pass over at once to a method of philosophizing which does not thus barricade the road of discovery.

(4) Necessitarianism cannot logically stop short of making the whole action of the mind a part of the physical universe. Our notion that we decide what we are going to do, if, as the necessitarian says, it has been calculable since the earliest times, is reduced to illusion. Indeed, consciousness in general thus becomes a mere illusory aspect of a material system. What we call red, green, and violet are in reality only different rates of vibration. The sole reality is the distribution of qualities of matter in space

and time. Brain-matter is protoplasm in a certain degree and kind of complication—a certain arrangement of mechanical particles. Its feeling is but an inward aspect, a phantom. For, from the positions and velocities of the particles at any one instant, and the knowledge of the immutable forces, the positions at all other times are calculable; so that the universe of space, time, and matter is a rounded system uninterfered with from elsewhere. But, from the state of feeling at any instant, there is no reason to suppose the states of feeling at all other instants are thus exactly calculable; so that feeling is, as I said, a mere fragmentary and illusive aspect of the universe. This is the way, then, that necessitarianism has to make up its accounts. It enters consciousness under the head of sundries, as a forgotten trifle; its scheme of the universe would be more satisfactory if this little fact could be dropped out of sight. On the other hand, by supposing the rigid exactitude of causation to yield, I care not how little—be it but by a strictly infinitesimal amount—we gain room to insert mind into our scheme, and to put it into the place where it is needed, into the position which, as the sole self-intelligible thing, it is entitled to occupy, that of the fountain of existence; and in so doing we resolve the problem of the connection of soul and body.

(5) But I must leave undeveloped the chief of my reasons, and can only adumbrate it. The hypothesis of chance-spontaneity is one whose inevitable consequences are capable of being traced out with mathematical precision into considerable detail. Much of this I have done and find the consequences to agree with observed facts to an extent which seems to me remarkable. But the matter and methods of reasoning are novel, and I have no right to promise that other mathematicians shall find my deductions as satisfactory as I myself do, so that the strongest reason for my belief must for the present remain a private reason of my own, and cannot influence others. I mention it to explain my own position; and partly to indicate to future mathematical speculators a veritable gold mine, should time and circumstances and the abridger of all joys prevent my opening it to the world.

If now I, in my turn, inquire of the necessitarian why he prefers to suppose that all specification goes back to the beginning of things, he will answer me with one of those last three arguments which I left unanswered.

First, he may say that chance is a thing absolutely unintelligible, and therefore that we never can be entitled to make such a supposition. But does not this objection smack of naïve impudence? It is not mine, it is his own conception of the universe which leads abruptly up to hard, ultimate, inexplicable, immutable law, on the one hand, and to inexplicable specification and diversification of circumstances on the other. My view, on the contrary, hypothetizes nothing at all, unless it be hypothesis to say that all specification came about in some sense, and is not to be accepted as unaccountable. To undertake to account for anything by saying baldly that it is due to chance would, indeed, be futile. But this I do not do. I make use of chance chiefly to make room for a principle of generalization, or tendency to form habits, which I hold has produced all regularities. The mechanical philosopher leaves the whole specification of the world utterly unaccounted for, which is pretty nearly as bad as to baldly attribute it to chance. I attribute it altogether to chance, it is true, but to chance in the form of a spontaneity which is to some degree regular. It seems to me clear at any rate that one of these two positions must be taken, or else specification must be supposed due to a spontaneity which develops itself in a certain and not in a chance way, by an objective logic like that of Hegel. This last way I leave as an open possibility, for the present; for it is as much opposed to the necessitarian scheme of existence as my own theory is.

Secondly, the necessitarian may say there are, at any rate, no observed phenomena which the hypothesis of chance could aid in explaining. In reply, I point first to the phenomenon of growth and developing complexity, which appears to be universal, and which, though it may possibly be an affair of mechanism perhaps, certainly presents all the appearance of increasing diversification. Then, there is variety itself, beyond comparison the most obtrusive character of the universe: no mechanism can account for this. Then, there is the very fact the necessitarian most insists upon, the regularity of the universe which for him serves only to block the road of inquiry. Then, there are the regular relationships between the laws of nature—similarities and comparative characters, which appeal to our intelligence as its cousins, and call upon us for a reason. Finally, there is consciousness, feeling, a patent fact enough, but a very inconvenient one to the mechanical philosopher.

Thirdly, the necessitarian may say that chance is not a *vera causa*, that we cannot know positively there is any such element in the universe. But the doctrine of the *vera causa* has nothing to do with elementary conceptions. Pushed to that extreme, it at once cuts off belief in the existence of a material universe; and without that necessitarianism could hardly maintain its ground. Besides, variety is a fact which must be admitted; and the theory of chance merely consists in supposing this diversification does not antedate all time. Moreover, the avoidance of hypotheses involving causes nowhere positively known to act is only a recommendation of logic, not a positive command. It cannot be formulated in any precise terms without at once betraying its untenable character—I mean as rigid rule, for as a recommendation it is wholesome enough.

I believe I have thus subjected to fair examination all the important reasons for adhering to the theory of universal necessity, and have shown their nullity. I earnestly beg that whoever may detect any flaw in my reasoning will point it out to me, either privately or publicly; for, if I am wrong, it much concerns me to be set right speedily. If my argument remains unrefuted, it will be time, I think, to doubt the absolute truth of the principle of universal law; and when once such a doubt has obtained a living root in any man's mind, my cause with him, I am persuaded, is gained.

25

THE LAW OF MIND *

I

In an article published in *The Monist* for January 1891,[20] I endeavoured to show what ideas ought to form the warp of a system of philosophy, and particularly emphasized that of absolute chance. In the number of April 1892,[21] I argued further in favour of that way of thinking, which it will be convenient to christen *tychism* (from τύχη, chance). A serious student of philosophy will be in no haste to accept or reject this doctrine; but he will see in it one of the chief attitudes which speculative thought may take, feeling that it is not for an individual, nor for an age, to pronounce upon a fundamental question of philosophy. That is a task for a whole era to work out. I have begun by showing that *tychism* must give birth to an evolutionary cosmology, in which all the regularities of nature and of mind are regarded as products of growth, and to a Schelling-fashioned idealism which holds matter to be mere specialized and partially deadened mind. I may mention, for the benefit of those who are curious in studying mental biographies, that I was born and reared in the neighbourhood of Concord—I mean in Cambridge—at the time when Emerson, Hedge, and their friends were disseminating the ideas that they had caught from Schelling, and Schelling from Plotinus, from Boehm, or from God knows what minds stricken with the monstrous mysticism of the East. But the atmosphere of Cambridge held many an antiseptic against Concord transcendentalism; and I am not conscious of having contracted any of that virus. Nevertheless, it is probable that some cultured bacilli, some benignant form of the disease was implanted in my soul, unawares, and that now, after long incubation, it comes to the surface, modified by mathematical conceptions and by training in physical investigations.

The next step in the study of cosmology must be to examine the

---

* [I, with several pages omitted where the spatial division occurs, is "The Law of Mind," the third paper in a series of five, *The Monist* 1892 (*CP* 6.102-11, 126-44, 146-63). In II, the first two selections are from "Man's Glassy Essence," the fourth paper in this series (*CP* 6.264, 268) ; the third, from ms. c. 1893 (*CP* 6.277).]

general law of mental action. In doing this, I shall for the time drop my tychism out of view, in order to allow a free and independent expansion to another conception signalized in my first *Monist* paper as one of the most indispensable to philosophy, though it was not there dwelt upon; I mean the idea of continuity. The tendency to regard continuity, in the sense in which I shall define it, as an idea of prime importance in philosophy may conveniently be termed *synechism*. The present paper is intended chiefly to show what synechism is, and what it leads to. . . .

Logical analysis applied to mental phenomena shows that there is but one law of mind, namely, that ideas tend to spread continuously and to affect certain others which stand to them in a peculiar relation of affectibility. In this spreading they lose intensity, and especially the power of affecting others, but gain generality and become welded with other ideas.

I set down this formula at the beginning, for convenience, and now proceed to comment upon it.

We are accustomed to speak of ideas as reproduced, as passed from mind to mind, as similar or dissimilar to one another, and, in short, as if they were substantial things; nor can any reasonable objection be raised to such expressions. But taking the word "idea" in the sense of an event in an individual consciousness, it is clear that an idea once past is gone forever, and any supposed recurrence of it is another idea. These two ideas are not present in the same state of consciousness, and therefore cannot possibly be compared. To say, therefore, that they are similar can only mean that an occult power from the depths of the soul forces us to connect them in our thoughts after they are both no more. We may note, here, in passing, that of the two generally recognized principles of association, contiguity and similarity, the former is a connection due to a power without, the latter a connection due to a power within.

But what can it mean to say that ideas wholly past are thought of at all, any longer? They are utterly unknowable. What distinct meaning can attach to saying that an idea in the past in any way affects an idea in the future, from which it is completely detached? A phrase between the assertion and the denial of which there can in no case be any sensible difference is mere gibberish.

I will not dwell further upon this point, because it is a commonplace of philosophy.

We have here before us a question of difficulty, analogous to the question of nominalism and realism. But when once it has been clearly formulated, logic leaves room for one answer only. How can a past idea be present? Can it be present vicariously? To a certain extent, perhaps, but not merely so; for then the question would arise how the past idea can be related to its vicarious representation. The relation, being between ideas, can only exist in some consciousness: now that past idea was in no consciousness but that past consciousness that alone contained it; and that did not embrace the vicarious idea.

Some minds will here jump to the conclusion that a past idea cannot in any sense be present. But that is hasty and illogical. How extravagant, too, to pronounce our whole knowledge of the past to be mere delusion! Yet it would seem that the past is as completely beyond the bounds of possible experience as a Kantian thing-in-itself.

How can a past idea be present? Not vicariously. Then, only by direct perception. In other words, to be present, it must be *ipso facto* present. That is, it cannot be wholly past; it can only be going, infinitesimally past, less past than any assignable past date. We are thus brought to the conclusion that the present is connected with the past by a series of real infinitesimal steps.

It has already been suggested by psychologists that consciousness necessarily embraces an interval of time. But if a finite time be meant, the opinion is not tenable. If the sensation that precedes the present by half a second were still immediately before me, then, on the same principle, the sensation preceding that would be immediately present, and so on *ad infinitum*. Now, since there is a time, say a year, at the end of which an idea is no longer *ipso facto* present, it follows that this is true of any finite interval, however short.

But yet consciousness must essentially cover an interval of time; for if it did not, we could gain no knowledge of time, and not merely no veracious cognition of it, but no conception whatever. We are, therefore, forced to say that we are immediately conscious through an infinitesimal interval of time.

This is all that is requisite. For, in this infinitesimal interval, not only is consciousness continuous in a subjective sense, that is, considered as a subject or substance having the attribute of duration, but also, because it is immediate consciousness, its object is *ipso facto* continuous. In fact, this infinitesimally spread-out consciousness is a direct feeling of its contents as spread out. This will be further elucidated below. In an infinitesimal interval we directly perceive the temporal sequence of its beginning, middle, and end

—not, of course, in the way of recognition, for recognition is only of the past, but in the way of immediate feeling. Now upon this interval follows another, whose beginning is the middle of the former, and whose middle is the end of the former. Here, we have an immediate perception of the temporal sequence of its beginning, middle, and end, or say of the second, third, and fourth instants. From these two immediate perceptions, we gain a mediate, or inferential, perception of the relation of all four instants. This mediate perception is objectively, or as to the object represented, spread over the four instants; but subjectively, or as itself the subject of duration, it is completely embraced in the second moment. (The reader will observe that I use the word *instant* to mean a point of time, and *moment* to mean an infinitesimal duration.) If it is objected that, upon the theory proposed, we must have more than a mediate perception of the succession of the four instants, I grant it; for the sum of the two infinitesimal intervals is itself infinitesimal, so that it is immediately perceived. It is immediately perceived in the whole interval, but only mediately perceived in the last two-thirds of the interval. Now, let there be an indefinite succession of these inferential acts of comparative perception, and it is plain that the last moment will contain objectively the whole series. Let there be, not merely an indefinite succession, but a continuous flow of inference through a finite time, and the result will be a mediate objective consciousness of the whole time in the last moment. In this last moment, the whole series will be recognized, or known as known before, except only the last moment, which of course will be absolutely unrecognizable to itself. Indeed, even this last moment will be recognized like the rest, or, at least, be just beginning to be so. There is a little *elenchus*, or appearance of contradiction, here, which the ordinary logic of reflection quite suffices to resolve.

Suppose a surface to be part red and part blue; so that every point on it is either red or blue, and, of course, no part can be both red and blue. What, then, is the colour of the boundary line between the red and the blue? The answer is that red or blue, to exist at all, must be spread over a surface; and the colour of the surface is the colour of the surface in the immediate neighbourhood of the point. I purposely use a vague form of expression. Now, as the parts of the surface in the immediate neighbourhood of any ordinary point upon a curved boundary are half of them red and half blue, it follows that the boundary is half red and half blue.

In like manner, we find it necessary to hold that consciousness essentially occupies time; and what is present to the mind at any ordinary instant is what is present during a moment in which that instant occurs. Thus, the present is half past and half to come. Again, the colour of the parts of a surface at any finite distance from a point has nothing to do with its colour just at that point; and, in the parallel, the feeling at any finite interval from the present has nothing to do with the present feeling, except vicariously. Take another case: the velocity of a particle at any instant of time is its mean velocity during an infinitesimal instant in which that time is contained. Just so my immediate feeling is my feeling through an infinitesimal duration containing the present instant.

One of the most marked features about the law of mind is that it makes time to have a definite direction of flow from past to future. The relation of past to future is, in reference to the law of mind, different from the relation of future to past. This makes one of the great contrasts between the law of mind and the law of physical force, where there is no more distinction between the two opposite directions in time than between moving northward and moving southward.

In order, therefore, to analyze the law of mind, we must begin by asking what the flow of time consists in. Now, we find that in reference to any individual state of feeling, all others are of two classes, those which affect this one (or have a tendency to affect it, and what this means we shall inquire shortly), and those which do not. The present is affectible by the past but not by the future.

Moreover, if state A is affected by state B, and state B by state C, then A is affected by state C, though not so much so. It follows, that if A is affectible by B, B is not affectible by A.

If, of two states, each is absolutely unaffectible by the other, they are to be regarded as parts of the same state. They are contemporaneous.

To say that a state is *between* two states means that it affects one and is affected by the other. Between any two states in this sense lies an innumerable series of states affecting one another; and if a state lies between a given state and any other state which can be reached by inserting states between this state and any third state, these inserted states not immediately affecting or being affected by either, then the second state mentioned immediately affects or is affected by the first, in the sense that in the one the other is *ipso facto* present in a reduced degree.

These propositions involve a definition of time and of its flow.

Over and above this definition they involve a doctrine, namely, that every state of feeling is affectible by every earlier state.

Time with its continuity logically involves some other kind of continuity than its own. Time, as the universal form of change, cannot exist unless there is something to undergo change and to undergo a change continuous in time there must be a continuity of changeable qualities. Of the continuity of intrinsic qualities of feeling we can now form but a feeble conception. The development of the human mind has practically extinguished all feelings, except a few sporadic kinds, sound, colours, smells, warmth, etc., which now appear to be disconnected and disparate. In the case of colours, there is a tridimensional spread of feelings. Originally, all feelings may have been connected in the same way, and the presumption is that the number of dimensions was endless. For development essentially involves a limitation of possibilities. But given a number of dimensions of feeling, all possible varieties are obtainable by varying the intensities of the different elements. Accordingly, time logically supposes a continuous range of intensity in feeling. It follows, then, from the definition of continuity, that when any particular kind of feeling is present, an infinitesimal continuum of all feelings differing infinitesimally from that is present.

Consider a gob of protoplasm, say an amoeba or a slime-mould. It does not differ in any radical way from the contents of a nerve-cell, though its functions may be less specialized. There is no doubt that this slime-mould, or this amoeba, or at any rate some similar mass of protoplasm, feels. That is to say, it feels when it is in its excited condition. But note how it behaves. When the whole is quiescent and rigid, a place upon it is irritated. Just at this point, an active motion is set up, and this gradually spreads to other parts. In this action, no unity nor relation to a nucleus, or other unitary organ can be discerned. It is a mere amorphous continuum of protoplasm, with feeling passing from one part to another. Nor is there anything like a wave-motion. The activity does not advance to new parts just as fast as it leaves old parts. Rather, in the beginning, it dies out at a slower rate than that at which it spreads. And while the process is going on, by exciting the mass at another point, a second quite independent state of excitation will be set up. In some places, neither excitation will exist, in others each separately, in still other places, both effects will be added together. Whatever there is in the whole phenomenon to make us think there is feeling in such a mass of protoplasm—

feeling, but plainly no *personality*—goes logically to show that that feeling has a subjective, or substantial, spatial extension, as the excited state has. This is, no doubt, a difficult idea to seize, for the reason that it is a subjective, not an objective, extension. It is not that we have a feeling of bigness; though Professor James, perhaps rightly, teaches that we have. It is that the feeling, as a subject of inhesion, is big. Moreover, our own feelings are focused in attention to such a degree that we are not aware that ideas are not brought to an absolute unity; just as nobody not instructed by special experiment has any idea how very, very little of the field of vision is distinct. Still, we all know how the attention wanders about among our feelings; and this fact shows that those feelings that are not coördinated in attention have a reciprocal externality, although they are present at the same time. But we must not tax introspection to make a phenomenon manifest which essentially involves externality.

Since space is continuous, it follows that there must be an immediate community of feeling between parts of mind infinitesimally near together. Without this, I believe it would have been impossible for minds external to one another ever to become coördinated, and equally impossible for any coördination to be established in the action of the nerve-matter of one brain.

But we are met by the question, what is meant by saying that one idea affects another. The unravelment of this problem requires us to trace out phenomena a little further.

Three elements go to make up an idea. The first is its intrinsic quality as a feeling. The second is the energy with which it affects other ideas, an energy which is infinite in the here-and-nowness of immediate sensation, finite and relative in the recency of the past. The third element is the tendency of an idea to bring along other ideas with it.

As an idea spreads, its power of affecting other ideas gets rapidly reduced; but its intrinsic quality remains nearly unchanged. It is long years now since I last saw a cardinal in his robes; and my memory of their colour has become much dimmed. The colour itself, however, is not remembered as dim. I have no inclination to call it a dull red. Thus, the intrinsic quality remains little changed; yet more accurate observation will show a slight reduction of it. The third element, on the other hand, has increased. As well as I can recollect, it seems to me the cardinals I used to see wore robes more scarlet than vermillion is, and highly luminous. Still, I know the colour commonly called cardinal is on the crimson side of vermillion and of quite moderate luminosity, and the original idea calls up so many other hues with it, and asserts itself so feebly, that I am unable any longer to isolate it.

A finite interval of time generally contains an innumerable series of feelings; and when these become welded together in association, the result is a general idea. For we have just seen how by continuous spreading an idea becomes generalized.

The first character of a general idea so resulting is that it is living feeling. A continuum of this feeling, infinitesimal in duration, but still embracing innumerable parts, and also, though infinitesimal, entirely unlimited, is immediately present. And in its absence of boundedness a vague possibility of more than is present is directly felt.

Second, in the presence of this continuity of feeling, nominalistic maxims appear futile. There is no doubt about one idea affecting another, when we can directly perceive the one gradually modified and shaping itself into the other. Nor can there any longer be any difficulty about one idea resembling another, when we can pass along the continuous field of quality from one to the other and back again to the point which we had marked.

Third, consider the insistency of an idea. The insistency of a past idea with reference to the present is a quantity which is less the further back that past idea is, and rises to infinity as the past idea is brought up into coinci-dence with the present. Here we must make one of those inductive applications of the law of continuity which have produced such great results in all the positive sciences. We must extend the law of insist-ency into the future. Plainly, the insistency of a future idea with reference to the present is a quantity affected by the minus sign; for it is the pres-ent that affects the future, if there be any effect, not the future that affects the present.

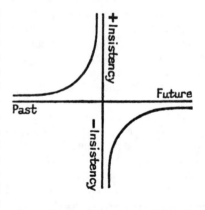

Accordingly, the curve of insist-ency is a sort of equilateral hyperbola. Such a conception is none the less mathematical, that its quantification cannot now be exactly specified.

Now consider the induction which we have here been led into. This curve says that feeling which has not yet emerged into immediate consciousness is already affectible and already affected. In fact, this is habit, by virtue of which an idea is brought up into present consciousness by a bond that had already been established between it and another idea while it was still *in futuro*.

We can now see what the affection of one idea by another consists in. It is that the affected idea is attached as a logical predicate to the affecting idea as subject. So when a feeling emerges into immediate consciousness, it always appears as a modification of a more or less general object already in the mind. The word suggestion is well adapted to expressing this relation. The future is suggested by, or rather is influenced by the suggestions of, the past.

That ideas can nowise be connected without continuity is sufficiently evident to one who reflects upon the matter. But still the opinion may be entertained that after continuity has once made the connection of ideas possible, then they may get to be connected in other modes than through continuity. Certainly, I cannot see how anyone can deny that the infinite diversity of the universe, which we call chance, may bring ideas into proximity which are not associated in one general idea. It may do this many times. But then the law of continuous spreading will produce a mental association; and this I suppose is an abridged statement of the way the universe has been evolved. But if I am asked whether a blind ἀνάγκη cannot bring ideas together, first I point out that it would not remain blind. There being a continuous connection between the ideas, they would infallibly become associated in a living, feeling, and perceiving general idea. Next, I cannot see what the mustness or necessity of this ἀνάγκη would consist in. In the absolute uniformity of the phenomenon, says the nominalist. Absolute is well put in; for if it merely happened so three times in succession, or three million times in succession, in the absence of any reason, the coincidence could only be attributed to chance. But absolute uniformity must extend over the whole infinite future; and it is idle to talk of that except as an idea. No, I think we can only hold that wherever ideas come together they tend to weld into general ideas; and wherever they are generally connected, general ideas govern the connection; and these general ideas are living feelings spread out.

The three main classes of logical inference are Deduction, Induction, and Hypothesis. These correspond to three chief modes of action of the human soul.

. . . By induction, a number of sensations followed by one reaction become united under one general idea followed by the same reaction; while, by the hypothetic process, a number of reactions called for by one occasion get united in a general idea which is called out by the same occasion. By deduction, the habit fulfills its function of calling out certain reactions on certain occasions.

The inductive and hypothetic forms of inference are essentially probable inferences, not necessary; while deduction may be either necessary or probable.

But no mental action seems to be necessary or invariable in its character. In whatever manner the mind has reacted under a given sensation, in that manner it is the more likely to react again; were this, however, an absolute necessity, habits would become wooden and ineradicable and, no room being left for the formation of new habits, intellectual life would come to a speedy close. Thus, the uncertainty of the mental law is no mere defect of it, but is on the contrary of its essence. The truth is, the mind is not subject to "law" in the same rigid sense that matter is. It only experiences gentle forces which merely render it more likely to act in a given way than it otherwise would be. There always remains a certain amount of arbitrary spontaneity in its action, without which it would be dead.

Some psychologists think to reconcile the uncertainty of reactions with the principle of necessary causation by means of the law of fatigue. Truly for a *law*, this law of fatigue is a little lawless. I think it is merely a case of the general principle that an idea in spreading loses its insistency. Put me tarragon into my salad, when I have not tasted it for years, and I exclaim, "What nectar is this!" But add it to every dish I taste for week after week, and a habit of expectation has been created; and in thus spreading into habit, the sensation makes hardly any more impression upon me; or, if it be noticed, it is on a new side, from which it appears as rather a bore. The doctrine that fatigue is one of the primordial phenomena of mind I am much disposed to doubt. It seems a somewhat little thing to be allowed as an exception to the great principle of mental uniformization. For this reason, I prefer to explain it in the manner here indicated, as a special case of that great principle. To consider it as something distinct in its nature, certainly somewhat strengthens the necessitarian position; but even if it be distinct, the hypothesis that all the variety and apparent arbitrariness of mental action ought to be explained away in favour of absolute determinism does not seem to me to recommend itself to a sober and sound judgment, which seeks the guidance of observed facts and not that of prepossessions.

Let me now try to gather up all these odds and ends of commentary and restate the law of mind, in a unitary way.

First, then, we find that when we regard ideas from a nominalistic, individualistic, sensualistic way, the simplest facts of mind become utterly meaningless. That one idea should resemble another or influence another, or that one state of mind should so much as be thought of in another, is, from that standpoint, sheer nonsense.

Second, by this and other means we are driven to perceive, what is quite evident of itself, that instantaneous feelings flow together into a continuum of feeling, which has in a modified degree the peculiar vivacity of feeling and has gained generality. And in reference to such general ideas, or continua of feeling, the difficulties about resemblance and suggestion and reference to the external cease to have any force.

Third, these general ideas are not mere words, nor do they consist in this, that certain concrete facts will every time happen under certain descriptions of conditions; but they are just as much, or rather far more, living realities than the feelings themselves out of which they are concreted. And to say that mental phenomena are governed by law does not mean merely that they are describable by a general formula; but that there is a living idea, a conscious continuum of feeling, which pervades them, and to which they are docile.

Fourth, this supreme law, which is the celestial and living harmony, does not so much as demand that the special ideas shall surrender their peculiar arbitrariness and caprice entirely; for that would be self-destructive. It only requires that they shall influence and be influenced by one another.

Fifth, in what measure this unification acts, seems to be regulated only by special rules; or, at least, we cannot in our present knowledge say how far it goes. But it may be said that, judging by appearances, the amount of arbitrariness in the phenomena of human minds is neither altogether trifling nor very prominent.

Having thus endeavoured to state the law of mind, in general, I descend to the consideration of a particular phenomenon which is remarkably prominent in our own consciousnesses, that of personality. A strong light is thrown upon this subject by recent observations of double and multiple personality. The theory, which at one time seemed plausible, that two persons in one body corresponded to the two halves of the brain will, I take it, now be universally acknowledged to be insufficient. But that which these cases make quite manifest is that personality is some kind of coördination or connection of ideas. Not much to say, this, perhaps. Yet when we consider that, according to the principle which we are tracing out, a connection between ideas is itself a general idea, and that a general idea is a living feeling, it is plain that we have at least taken an appreciable step toward the understanding of personality. This personality, like any general idea, is not a thing to be apprehended in an instant. It has to be lived in time; nor can any finite time embrace it in all its fullness. Yet in each infinitesimal interval it is present and living, though specially coloured by the immediate feelings of that moment. Personality, so far as it is apprehended in a moment, is immediate self-consciousness.

But the word coördination implies somewhat more than this; it implies a teleological harmony in ideas, and in the case of personality this teleology is more than a mere purposive pursuit of a predeterminate end; it is a developmental teleology. This is personal character. A general idea, living and conscious now, it is already determinative of acts in the future to an extent to which it is not now conscious.

This reference to the future is an essential element of personality. Were the ends of a person already explicit, there would be no room for development, for growth, for life; and consequently there would be no personality. The mere carrying out of predetermined purposes is mechanical. This remark has an application to the philosophy of religion. It is that a genuine evolutionary philosophy, that is, one that makes the principle of growth a primordial element of the universe, is so far from being antagonistic to the idea of a personal creator that it is really inseparable from that idea; while a necessitarian religion is in an altogether false position and is destined to become disintegrated. But a pseudo-evolutionism which enthrones mechanical law above the principle of growth is at once scientifically unsatisfactory, as giving no possible hint of how the universe has come about, and hostile to all hopes of personal relations to God.

Consistently with the doctrine laid down in the beginning of this paper, I am bound to maintain that an idea can only be affected by an idea in continuous connection with it. By anything but an idea, it cannot be affected at all. This obliges me to say, as I do say, on other grounds, that what we call matter is not completely dead, but is merely mind hidebound with habits. It still retains the element of diversification; and in that diversification there is life. When an idea is conveyed from one mind to another, it is by forms of combination of the diverse elements of nature, say by some curious symmetry, or by some union of a tender colour with a refined odour. To such forms the law of mechanical energy has no application. If they are eternal, it is in the spirit they embody; and their origin cannot be accounted for by any mechanical necessity. They are embodied ideas; and so only can they convey ideas. Precisely how primary sensations, as colours and tones, are excited, we cannot tell, in the present state of psychology. But in our ignorance, I think that we are at liberty to suppose that they arise in essentially the same manner as the other feelings, called secondary. As far as sight and hearing are in question, we know that they are only excited by vibrations of inconceivable complexity; and the chemical senses are probably not more simple. Even the least psychical of peripheral sensations, that of pressure, has in its excitation conditions which, though apparently simple, are seen to be complicated enough when we consider the molecules and their attractions. The principle with which I set out requires me to maintain that these feelings are communicated to the nerves by continuity, so that there must be something like them in the excitants themselves. If this seems extravagant, it is to be remembered that it is the sole possible way of reaching any explanation of sensation, which otherwise must be pronounced a general fact, absolutely inexplicable and ultimate. Now absolute inexplicability is a hypothesis which sound logic refuses under any circumstances to justify.

I may be asked whether my theory would be favourable or otherwise to telepathy. I have no decided answer to give to this. At first sight, it seems unfavourable. Yet there may be other modes of continuous connection between minds other than those of time and space.

The recognition by one person of another's personality takes place by means to some extent identical with the means by which he is conscious of his own personality. The idea of the second personality, which is as much as to say that second personality itself, enters within the field of direct consciousness of the first person, and is as immediately perceived as his ego, though less strongly. At the same time, the opposition between the two persons is perceived, so that the externality of the second is recognized.

The psychological phenomena of intercommunication between

two minds have been unfortunately little studied. So that it is impossible to say, for certain, whether they are favourable to this theory or not. But the very extraordinary insight which some persons are able to gain of others from indications so slight that it is difficult to ascertain what they are is certainly rendered more comprehensible by the view here taken.

A difficulty which confronts the synechistic philosophy is this. In considering personality, that philosophy is forced to accept the doctrine of a personal God; but in considering communication, it cannot but admit that if there is a personal God, we must have a direct perception of that person and indeed be in personal communication with him. Now, if that be the case, the question arises how it is possible that the existence of this being should ever have been doubted by anybody. The only answer that I can at present make is that facts that stand before our face and eyes and stare us in the face are far from being, in all cases, the ones most easily discerned. That has been remarked from time immemorial.

I have thus developed as well as I could in a little space the *synechistic* philosophy, as applied to mind. I think that I have succeeded in making it clear that this doctrine gives room for explanations of many facts which without it are absolutely and hopelessly inexplicable; and further that it carries along with it the following doctrines: first, a logical realism of the most pronounced type; second, objective idealism; third, tychism, with its consequent thoroughgoing evolutionism. We also notice that the doctrine presents no hindrances to spiritual influences, such as some philosophies are felt to do.

II

If consciousness belongs to all protoplasm, by what mechanical constitution is this to be accounted for? The slime is nothing but a chemical compound. There is no inherent impossibility in its being formed synthetically in the laboratory, out of its chemical elements; and if it were so made, it would present all the characters of natural protoplasm. No doubt, then, it would feel. To hesitate to admit this would be puerile and ultra-puerile. By what element of the molecular arrangement, then, would that feeling be caused? This question cannot be evaded or pooh-poohed. Protoplasm certainly does feel; and unless we are to accept a weak dualism, the property must be shown to arise from some peculiarity of the mechanical system. Yet the attempt to deduce it from the three laws of mechanics, applied to never so ingenious a mechanical contrivance, would obviously be futile. It can never be explained, unless we admit that physical events are but degraded or undeveloped forms of psychical events. But once grant that the phenomena of matter are but the result of the sensibly complete sway of habits upon mind, and it only remains to explain why in the protoplasm these habits are to some slight extent broken up, so that, according to the law of mind, in that special clause of it sometimes called the principle of accommodation, feeling becomes intensified.

It may be well here to reflect that if matter has no existence except as a specialization of mind, it follows that whatever affects matter according to regular laws is itself matter. But all mind is directly or indirectly connected with all matter, and acts in a more or less regular way; so that all mind more or less partakes of the nature of matter. Hence, it would be a mistake to conceive of the psychical and the physical aspects of matter as two aspects absolutely distinct. Viewing a thing from the outside, considering its relations of action and reaction with other things, it appears as matter. Viewing it from the inside, looking at its immediate character as feeling, it appears as consciousness. These two views are combined when we remember that mechanical laws are nothing but acquired habits, like all the regularities of mind, including the tendency to take habits, itself; and that this action of habit is nothing but generalization, and generalization is nothing but the spreading of feelings.

Now, in obedience to the principle, or maxim, of continuity, that we ought to assume things to be continuous as far as we can . . . the reaction between mind and matter would be of no essentially different kind from the action between parts of mind that are in continuous union, and would thus come directly under the great law of mental association. . . . This hypothesis might be called materialistic, since it attributes to mind one of the recognized properties of matter, extension, and attributes to all matter a certain excessively low degree of feeling, together with a certain power of taking habits. But it differs essentially from materialism, in that, instead of supposing mind to be governed by blind mechanical law, it supposes the one original law to be the recognized law of mind, the law of association, of which the laws of matter are regarded as mere special results.

26

SYNECHISM, FALLIBILISM, AND EVOLUTION *

I

[SYNECHISM is] that tendency of philosophical thought which insists upon the idea of continuity as of prime importance in philosophy and, in particular, upon the necessity of hypotheses involving true continuity.

A true continuum is something whose possibilities of determination no multitude of individuals can exhaust. Thus, no collection of points placed upon a truly continuous line can fill the line so as to leave no room for others, although that collection had a point for every value towards which numbers, endlessly continued into the decimal places, could approximate; nor if it contained a point for every possible permutation of all such values. It would be in the general spirit of synechism to hold that time ought to be supposed truly continuous in that sense. The term was suggested and used by C. S. Peirce in 1892.

The general motive is to avoid the hypothesis that this or that is inexplicable. For the synechist maintains that the only possible justification for so much as entertaining a hypothesis is that it affords an explanation of the phenomena. Now, to suppose a thing inexplicable is not only to fail to explain it, and so to make an un-justifiable hypothesis, but, much worse, it is to set up a barrier across the road of science, and to forbid all attempt to understand the phenomenon.

To be sure, the synechist cannot deny that there is an element of the inexplicable and ultimate, because it is directly forced upon him; nor does he abstain from generalizing from this experience. True generality is, in fact, nothing but a rudimentary form of true continuity. Continuity is nothing but perfect generality of a law of relationship.

It would, therefore, be most contrary to his own principle for

* [I is the article " Synechism " in Baldwin's *Dict. of Philos. and Psychol.* 1902 (*CP* 6.169-73). II is from ms. c. 1897 (*CP* 1.170, 171-5), III from ms. c. 1890 (*CP* 1.409), IV from the article " Uniformity " in Baldwin's (*CP* 6.101).]

the synechist not to generalize from that which experience forces upon him, especially since it is only so far as facts can be generalized that they can be understood; and the very reality, in his way of looking at the matter, is nothing else than the way in which facts must ultimately come to be understood. There would be a contradiction here, if this ultimacy were looked upon as something to be absolutely realized; but the synechist cannot consistently so regard it. Synechism is not an ultimate and absolute metaphysical doctrine; it is a regulative principle of logic, prescribing what sort of hypothesis is fit to be entertained and examined. The synechist, for example, would never be satisfied with the hypothesis that matter is composed of atoms, all spherical and exactly alike. If this is the only hypothesis that the mathematicians are as yet in condition to handle, it may be supposed that it may have features of resemblance with the truth. But neither the eternity of the atoms nor their precise resemblance is, in the synechist's view, an element of the hypothesis that is even admissible hypothetically. For that would be to attempt to explain the phenomena by means of an absolute inexplicability. In like manner, it is not a hypothesis fit to be entertained that any given law is absolutely accurate. It is not, upon synechist principles, a question to be asked, whether the three angles of a triangle amount precisely to two right angles, but only whether the sum is greater or less. So the synechist will not believe that some things are conscious and some unconscious, unless by consciousness be meant a certain grade of feeling. He will rather ask what are the circumstances which raise this grade; nor will he consider that a chemical formula for protoplasm would be a sufficient answer. In short, synechism amounts to the principle that inexplicabilities are not to be considered as possible explanations; that whatever is supposed to be ultimate is supposed to be inexplicable; that continuity is the absence of ultimate parts in that which is divisible; and that the form under which alone anything can be understood is the form of generality, which is the same thing as continuity.

II

How can one mind act upon another mind? How can one particle of matter act upon another at a distance from it? The nominalists tell us this is an ultimate fact—it cannot be explained. Now, if this were meant in [a] merely practical sense, if it were only meant that we know that one thing does act on another but that how it takes place we cannot very well tell, up to date, I should have nothing to say, except to applaud the moderation and good logic of the statement. But this is not what is meant; what is meant is that we come up, bump against actions absolutely unintelligible and inexplicable, where human inquiries have to stop. Now that is a mere *theory*, and nothing can justify a theory except its explaining observed facts. It is a poor kind of theory which in place of performing this, the sole legitimate function of a theory, merely supposes the facts to be inexplicable. It is one of the peculiarities of nominalism that it is continually supposing things to be absolutely inexplicable. That blocks the road of inquiry. But if we adopt the theory of continuity we escape this illogical situation. We may then say that one portion of mind acts upon another, because it is in a measure immediately present to that other; just as we suppose that the infinitesimally past is in a measure present. And in like manner we may suppose that one portion of matter acts upon another because it is in a measure in the same place. . . .

The principle of continuity is the idea of fallibilism objectified. For fallibilism is the doctrine that our knowledge is never absolute but always swims, as it were, in a continuum of uncertainty and of indeterminacy. Now the doctrine of continuity is that *all things* so swim in continua.

The doctrine of continuity rests upon observed fact as we have seen. But what opens our eyes to the significance of that fact is fallibilism. The ordinary scientific infallibilist—of which sect Büchner in his *Kraft und Stoff* affords a fine example—cannot accept *synechism*, or the doctrine that all that exists is continuous—because he is committed to discontinuity in regard to all those things which he fancies he has exactly ascertained, and especially in regard to that part of his knowledge which he fancies he has exactly ascertained to be *certain*. For where there is continuity, the exact ascertainment of real quantities is too obviously impossible. No sane man can dream that the ratio of the circumference to the diameter could be exactly ascertained by measurement. As to the quantities he has not yet exactly ascertained, the Büchnerite is naturally led to separate them into two distinct classes, those which may be ascertained hereafter (and there, as before, continuity must be excluded), and those absolutely unascertainable—and these in their utter and everlasting severance from the other class present a new breach of continuity. Thus scientific infallibilism draws down a veil before the eyes which prevents the evidences of continuity from being discerned.

But as soon as a man is fully impressed with the fact that absolute exactitude never can be known, he naturally asks whether there are any facts to show that hard discrete exactitude really exists. That suggestion lifts the edge of that curtain and he begins to see the clear daylight shining in from behind it.

But fallibilism cannot be appreciated in anything like its true significancy until evolution has been considered. This is what the world has been most thinking of for the last forty years—though old enough is the general idea itself. Aristotle's philosophy, that dominated the world for so many ages and still in great measure tyrannizes over the thoughts of butchers and bakers that never heard of him—is but a metaphysical evolutionism.

Evolution means nothing but *growth* in the widest sense of that word. Reproduction, of course, is merely one of the incidents of growth. And what is growth? Not mere increase. Spencer says it is the passage from the homogeneous to the heterogeneous—or, if we prefer English to Spencerese—*diversification*. That is certainly an important factor of it. Spencer further says that it is a passage from the unorganized to the organized; but that part of the definition is so obscure that I will leave it aside for the present. But think what an astonishing idea this of *diversification* is! Is there such thing in nature as increase of variety? Were things simpler, was variety less in the original nebula from which the solar system is supposed to have grown than it is now when the land and sea swarms with animal and vegetable forms with their intricate anatomies and still more wonderful economies? It would seem as if there were an increase in variety, would it not? And yet mechanical law, which the scientific infallibilist tells us is the only agency of nature, mechanical law can never produce diversification. That is a mathematical truth—a proposition of analytical mechanics; and anybody can see without any algebraical apparatus that mechanical law out of like antecedents can only produce like consequents. It is the very idea of law. So if observed facts point to real growth, they point to another agency, to spontaneity for which infallibilism provides no pigeon-hole. And what is meant by this passage from the less organized to the more organized? Does it mean a passage from the less bound together to the more bound together, the less connected to the more connected, the less regular to the more regular? How can the regularity of the world increase, if it has been absolutely perfect all the time?

. . . Once you have embraced the principle of continuity no kind of explanation of things will satisfy you except that they *grew*. The infallibilist naturally thinks that everything always was substantially as it is now. Laws at any rate being absolute could not grow. They either always were, or they sprang instantaneously into being by a sudden fiat like the drill of a company of soldiers. This makes the laws of nature absolutely blind and inexplicable. Their why and wherefore can't be asked. This absolutely blocks the road of inquiry. The fallibilist won't do this. He asks may these *forces* of nature not be somehow amenable to reason? May they not have naturally grown up? After all, there is no reason to think they are absolute. If all things are continuous, the universe must be undergoing a continuous growth from non-existence to existence. There is no difficulty in conceiving existence as a matter of degree. The reality of things consists in their persistent forcing themselves upon our recognition. If a thing has no such persistence, it is a mere dream. Reality, then, is persistence, is regularity. In the original chaos, where there was no regularity, there was no existence. It was all a confused dream. This we may suppose was in the infinitely distant past. But as things are getting more regular, more persistent, they are getting less dreamy and more real.

Fallibilism will at least provide a big pigeon-hole for facts bearing on that theory.

III

Uniformities in the modes of action of things have come about by their taking habits. At present, the course of events is approximately determined by law. In the past that approximation was less perfect; in the future it will be more perfect. The tendency to obey laws has always been and always will be growing. We look back toward a point in the infinitely distant past when there was no law but mere indeterminacy; we look forward to a point in the infinitely distant future when there will be no indeterminacy or chance but a complete reign of law. But at any assignable date in the past, however early, there was already some tendency toward uniformity; and at any assignable date in the future there will be some slight aberrancy from law. Moreover, all things have a tendency to take habits. For atoms and their parts, molecules and groups of molecules, and in short every conceivable real object, there is a greater probability of acting as on a former like occasion than otherwise. This tendency itself constitutes a regularity, and is continually on the increase. In looking back into the past we are looking toward periods when it was a less and less decided tendency. But its own essential nature is to grow. It is a generalizing tendency; it causes actions in the future to follow some generalization of past actions; and this tendency is itself something capable of similar generalizations; and thus, it is self-generative. We have therefore only to suppose the smallest spoor of it in the past, and that germ would have been bound to develop into a mighty and over-ruling principle, until it supersedes itself by strengthening habits into absolute laws regulating the action of all things in every respect in the indefinite future.

According to this, three elements are active in the world: first, chance; second, law; and third, habit-taking.

IV

The hypothesis suggested by the present writer is that all laws are results of evolution; that underlying all other laws is the only tendency which can grow by its own virtue, the tendency of all things to take habits. Now since this same tendency is the one sole fundamental law of mind, it follows that the physical evolution works towards ends in the same way that mental action works towards ends, and thus in one aspect of the matter it would be perfectly true to say that final causation is alone primary. Yet, on the other hand, the law of habit is a simple formal law, a law of efficient causation; so that either way of regarding the matter is equally true, although the former is more fully intelligent. Meantime, if law is a result of evolution, which is a process lasting through all time, it follows that no law is absolute. That is, we must suppose that the phenomena themselves involve departures from law analogous to errors of observation. But the writer has not supposed that this phenomenon had any connection with free will. In so far as evolution follows a law, the law of habit, instead of being a movement from homogeneity to heterogeneity, is growth from difformity to uniformity. But the chance divergences from law are perpetually acting to increase the variety of the world, and are checked by a sort of natural selection and otherwise (for the writer does not think the selective principle sufficient), so that the general result may be described as "organized heterogeneity," or, better, rationalized variety. In view of the principle of continuity, the supreme guide in framing philosophical hypotheses, we must, under this theory, regard matter as mind whose habits have become fixed so as to lose the powers of forming them and losing them, while mind is to be regarded as a chemical genus of extreme complexity and instability. It has acquired in a remarkable degree a habit of taking and laying aside habits. The fundamental divergences from law must here be most extraordinarily high, although probably very far indeed from attaining any directly observable magnitude. But their effect is to cause the laws of mind to be themselves of so fluid a character as to simulate divergences from law. All this, according to the writer, constitutes a hypothesis capable of being tested by experiment.

27

EVOLUTIONARY LOVE *

PHILOSOPHY, when just escaping from its golden pupa-skin, mythology, proclaimed the great evolutionary agency of the universe to be Love.   Or, since this pirate-lingo, English, is poor in such-like words, let us say Eros, the exuberance-love.   Afterwards, Empedocles set up passionate-love and hate as the two coördinate powers of the universe.   In some passages, kindness is the word. But certainly, in any sense in which it has an opposite, to be senior partner of that opposite, is the highest position that love can attain. Nevertheless, the ontological gospeller, in whose days those views were familiar topics, made the One Supreme Being, by whom all things have been made out of nothing, to be cherishing-love.   What, then, can he say to hate?   Never mind, at this time, what the scribe of the apocalypse, if he were John, stung at length by persecution into a rage unable to distinguish suggestions of evil from visions of heaven, and so become the Slanderer of God to men, may have dreamed.   The question is rather what the sane John thought, or ought to have thought, in order to carry out his idea consistently. His statement that God is love seems aimed at that saying of Ecclesiastes that we cannot tell whether God bears us love or hatred.   "Nay," says John, "we can tell, and very simply!   We know and have trusted the love which God hath in us.   God is love." There is no logic in this, unless it means that God loves all men. In the preceding paragraph, he had said, "God is light and in him is no darkness at all."   We are to understand, then, that as darkness is merely the defect of light, so hatred and evil are mere imperfect stages of ἀγάπη and ἀγαθόν, love and loveliness.   This concords with that utterance reported in John's Gospel: "God sent not the Son into the world to judge the world; but that the world should through him be saved.   He that believeth on him is not judged: he that believeth not hath been judged already. . . . And this is the judgment, that the light is come into the world, and that men

* [This chapter, with Peirce's title (the two spatial divisions each indicating an omission of some paragraphs), is the greater part of the last paper in a series of five, *The Monist* 1893 (*CP* 6.287-90, 293-5, 302-17).]

loved darkness rather than the light." That is to say, God visits
no punishment on them; they punish themselves, by their natural
affinity for the defective. Thus, the love that God is, is not a love
of which hatred is the contrary; otherwise Satan would be a coördinate power; but it is a love which embraces hatred as an
imperfect stage of it, an Anteros—yea, even needs hatred and
hatefulness as its object. For self-love is no love; so if God's self
is love, that which he loves must be defect of love; just as a
luminary can light up only that which otherwise would be dark.
Henry James, the Swedenborgian, says: "It is no doubt very
tolerable finite or creaturely love to love one's own in another, to
love another for his conformity to one's self: but nothing can be in
more flagrant contrast with the creative Love, all whose tenderness
ex vi termini must be reserved only for what intrinsically is most
bitterly hostile and negative to itself." This is from *Substance and
Shadow: an Essay on the Physics of Creation.* It is a pity he had
not filled his pages with things like this, as he was able easily to
do, instead of scolding at his reader and at people generally, until
the physics of creation was wellnigh forgot. I must deduct, however,
from what I just wrote: obviously no genius could make his every
sentence as sublime as one which discloses for the problem of evil
its everlasting solution.

The movement of love is circular, at one and the same impulse
projecting creations into independency and drawing them into
harmony. This seems complicated when stated so; but it is fully
summed up in the simple formula we call the Golden Rule. This
does not, of course, say, Do everything possible to gratify the
egoistic impulses of others, but it says, Sacrifice your own perfection to the perfectionment of your neighbour. Nor must it
for a moment be confounded with the Benthamite, or Helvetian,
or Beccarian motto, Act for the greatest good of the greatest
number. Love is not directed to abstractions but to persons; not
to persons we do not know, nor to numbers of people, but to our
own dear ones, our family and neighbours. "Our neighbour," we
remember, is one whom we live near, not locally perhaps, but in
life and feeling.

Everybody can see that the statement of St. John is the formula
of an evolutionary philosophy, which teaches that growth comes
only from love, from—I will not say self-*sacrifice*, but from the
ardent impulse to fulfill another's highest impulse. Suppose, for
example, that I have an idea that interests me. It is my creation.
It is my creature . . . it is a little person. I love it; and I will

sink myself in perfecting it. It is not by dealing out cold justice to the circle of my ideas that I can make them grow, but by cherishing and tending them as I would the flowers in my garden. The philosophy we draw from John's gospel is that this is the way mind develops; and as for the cosmos, only so far as it yet is mind, and so has life, is it capable of further evolution. Love, recognizing germs of loveliness in the hateful, gradually warms it into life, and makes it lovely. That is the sort of evolution which every careful student of my essay " The Law of Mind " must see that *synechism* calls for.

The nineteenth century is now fast sinking into the grave, and we all begin to review its doings and to think what character it is destined to bear as compared with other centuries in the minds of future historians. It will be called, I guess, the Economical Century; for political economy has more direct relations with all the branches of its activity than has any other science. Well, political economy has its formula of redemption, too. It is this: Intelligence in the service of greed ensures the justest prices, the fairest contracts, the most enlightened conduct of all the dealings between men, and leads to the *summum bonum*, food in plenty and perfect comfort. Food for whom? Why, for the greedy master of intelligence. I do not mean to say that this is one of the legitimate conclusions of political economy, the scientific character of which I fully acknowledge. But the study of doctrines, themselves true, will often temporarily encourage generalizations extremely false, as the study of physics has encouraged necessitarianism. What I say, then, is that the great attention paid to economical questions during our century has induced an exaggeration of the beneficial effects of greed and of the unfortunate results of sentiment, until there has resulted a philosophy which comes unwittingly to this, that greed is the great agent in the elevation of the human race and in the evolution of the universe.

The *Origin of Species* of Darwin merely extends politico-economical views of progress to the entire realm of animal and vegetable life. The vast majority of our contemporary naturalists hold the opinion that the true cause of those exquisite and marvellous adaptations of nature for which, when I was a boy, men used to extol the divine wisdom is that creatures are so crowded together that those of them that happen to have the slightest advantage force those less pushing into situations unfavourable to multiplication or even kill them before they reach the age of reproduction.

Among animals, the mere mechanical individualism is vastly re-enforced as a power making for good by the animal's ruthless greed. As Darwin puts it on his title-page, it is the struggle for existence; and he should have added for his motto: Every individual for himself, and the Devil take the hindmost! Jesus, in his sermon on the Mount, expressed a different opinion.

Here, then, is the issue. The gospel of Christ says that progress comes from every individual merging his individuality in sympathy with his neighbours. On the other side, the conviction of the nineteenth century is that progress takes place by virtue of every individual's striving for himself with all his might and trampling his neighbour under foot whenever he gets a chance to do so. This may accurately be called the Gospel of Greed.

Much is to be said on both sides. I have not concealed, I could not conceal, my own passionate predilection. Such a confession will probably shock my scientific brethren. Yet the strong feeling is in itself, I think, an argument of some weight in favour of the agapastic theory of evolution,—so far as it may be presumed to bespeak the normal judgment of the Sensible Heart. Certainly, if it were possible to believe in agapasm without believing it warmly, that fact would be an argument against the truth of the doctrine. At any rate, since the warmth of feeling exists, it should on every account be candidly confessed; especially since it creates a liability to one-sidedness on my part against which it behooves my readers and me to be severally on our guard.

Three modes of evolution have . . . been brought before us: evolution by fortuitous variation, evolution by mechanical necessity, and evolution by creative love.[22] We may term them *tychastic* evolution, or *tychasm*, *anancastic* evolution, or *anancasm*, and *agapastic* evolution, or *agapasm*. The doctrines which represent these as severally of principal importance, we may term *tychasticism*, *anancasticism*, and *agapasticism*. On the other hand the mere propositions that absolute chance, mechanical necessity, and the law of love, are severally operative in the cosmos, may receive the names of *tychism*, *anancism*, and *agapism*.

All three modes of evolution are composed of the same general elements. Agapasm exhibits them the most clearly. The good result is here brought to pass, first, by the bestowal of spontaneous energy by the parent upon the offspring, and, second, by the disposition of the latter to catch the general idea of those about it and thus to subserve the general purpose. In order to express the relation that tychasm and anancasm bear to agapasm, let me borrow a word from geometry. An ellipse crossed by a straight line is a sort of cubic curve; for a cubic is a curve which is cut thrice by a straight line; now a straight line might cut the ellipse twice and its associated straight line a third time. Still the ellipse with the straight line across it would not have the characteristics of a cubic. It would have, for instance, no contrary flexure, which no true cubic wants; and it would have two nodes, which no true cubic has. The geometers say that it is a *degenerate* cubic. Just so, tychasm and anancasm are degenerate forms of agapasm.

Men who seek to reconcile the Darwinian idea with Christianity will remark that tychastic evolution, like the agapastic, depends upon a reproductive creation, the forms preserved being those that use the spontaneity conferred upon them in such wise as to be drawn into harmony with their original, quite after the Christian scheme. Very good! This only shows that just as love cannot have a contrary, but must embrace what is most opposed to it, as a degenerate case of it, so tychasm is a kind of agapasm. Only, in the tychastic evolution progress is solely owing to the distribution of the napkin-hidden talent of the rejected servant among those not rejected, just as ruined gamesters leave their money on the table to make those not yet ruined so much the richer. It makes the felicity of the lambs just the damnation of the goats, transposed to the other side of the equation. In genuine agapasm, on the other hand, advance takes place by virtue of a positive sympathy among the created springing from continuity of mind. This is the idea which tychasticism knows not how to manage.

The anancasticist might here interpose, claiming that the mode of evolution for which he contends agrees with agapasm at the point at which tychasm departs from it. For it makes development go through certain phases, having its inevitable ebbs and flows, yet tending on the whole to a foreordained perfection. Bare existence by this its destiny betrays an intrinsic affinity for the good. Herein, it must be admitted, anancasm shows itself to be in a broad acception a species of agapasm. Some forms of it might easily be mistaken for the genuine agapasm. The Hegelian philosophy is such an anancasticism. With its revelatory religion, with its synechism (however imperfectly set forth), with its "reflection," the whole idea of the theory is superb, almost sublime. Yet, after all, living freedom is practically omitted from its method. The whole movement is that of a vast engine, impelled by a *vis a tergo*, with a blind and mysterious fate of arriving at a lofty goal. I mean that such an engine it *would* be, if it really worked; but in point of fact, it is a Keely motor. Grant that it really acts as it professes to act, and there is nothing to do but accept the philosophy. But never was there seen such an example of a long chain of reasoning,—shall I say with a flaw in every link?—no, with every link a handful of sand, squeezed into shape in a dream. Or say, it is a pasteboard model of a philosophy that in reality does not exist. If we use the one precious thing it contains, the idea of it, introducing the tychism which the arbitrariness of its every step suggests, and make that the support of a vital freedom which is the breadth of the spirit of love, we may be able to produce that genuine agapasticism, at which Hegel was aiming.

In the very nature of things, the line of demarcation between the three modes of evolution is not perfectly sharp. That does not prevent its being quite real; perhaps it is rather a mark of its reality. There is in the nature of things no sharp line of demarcation between the three fundamental colours, red, green, and violet. But for all that they are really different. The main question is whether three radically different evolutionary elements have been operative; and the second question is what are the most striking characteristics of whatever elements have been operative.

I propose to devote a few pages to a very slight examination of these questions in their relation to the historical development of human thought. I first formulate for the reader's convenience the briefest possible definitions of the three conceivable modes of development of thought, distinguishing also two varieties of anancasm and three of agapasm. The tychastic development of thought, then, will consist in slight departures from habitual ideas in different directions indifferently, quite purposeless and quite unconstrained whether by outward circumstances or by force of logic, these new departures being followed by unforeseen results which tend to fix some of them as habits more than others. The anancastic development of thought will consist of new ideas adopted without foreseeing whither they tend, but having a character determined by causes either external to the mind, such as changed circumstances of life, or internal to the mind as logical developments of ideas already accepted, such as generalizations. The agapastic development of thought is the adoption of certain mental tendencies, not altogether heedlessly, as in tychasm, nor quite blindly by the mere force of circumstances or of logic, as in anancasm, but by an immediate attraction for the idea itself, whose nature is divined before the mind possesses it, by the power of sympathy, that is, by virtue of the continuity of mind; and this mental tendency may be of three varieties, as follows. First, it may affect a whole people or community in its collective personality, and be thence communicated to such individuals as are in powerfully sympathetic connection with the collective people, although they may be intellectually incapable of attaining the idea by their private understandings or even perhaps of consciously apprehending it. Second, it may affect a private person directly, yet so that he is only enabled to apprehend the idea, or to appreciate its attractiveness, by virtue of his sympathy with his neighbours, under the influence of a striking experience or development of thought. The conversion of St. Paul may be taken as an example of what is meant. Third, it may affect an individual, independently of his human affections, by virtue of an attraction it exercises upon his mind, even before he has comprehended it. This is the phenomenon which has been well called the *divination* of genius; for it is due to the continuity between the man's mind and the Most High.

Let us next consider by means of what tests we can discriminate between these different categories of evolution. No absolute criterion is possible in the nature of things, since in the nature of things there is no sharp line of demarcation between the different classes. Nevertheless, quantitative symptoms may be found by which a sagacious and sympathetic judge of human nature may be able to estimate the approximate proportions in which the different kinds of influence are commingled.

So far as the historical evolution of human thought has been tychastic, it should have proceeded by insensible or minute steps; for such is the nature of chances when so multiplied as to show phenomena of regularity. For example, assume that of the native-born white adult males of the United States in 1880, one-fourth part were below 5 feet 4 inches in stature and one-fourth part above 5 feet 8 inches. Then by the principles of probability, among the whole population, we should expect

216 under 4 feet 6 inches				216 above 6 feet 6 inches			
48	,,	4 ,, 5	,,	48	,,	6 ,, 7	,,
9	,,	4 ,, 4	,,	9	,,	6 ,, 8	,,
less than 2	,,	4 ,, 3	,,	less than 2	,,	6 ,, 9	,,

I set down these figures to show how insignificantly few are the cases in which anything very far out of the common run presents itself by chance. Though the stature of only every second man is included within the four inches between 5 feet 4 inches and 5 feet

8 inches, yet if this interval be extended by thrice four inches above and below, it will embrace all our 8 millions odd of native-born adult white males (of 1880), except only 9 taller and 9 shorter.

The test of minute variation, if *not* satisfied, absolutely negatives tychasm. If it *is* satisfied, we shall find that it negatives anancasm but not agapasm. We want a positive test, satisfied by tychasm, only. Now wherever we find men's thought taking by imperceptible degrees a turn contrary to the purposes which animate them, in spite of their highest impulses, there, we may safely conclude, there has been a tychastic action.

Students of the history of mind there be of an erudition to fill an imperfect scholar like me with envy edulcorated by joyous admiration, who maintain that ideas when just started are and can be little more than freaks, since they cannot yet have been critically examined, and further that everywhere and at all times progress has been so gradual that it is difficult to make out distinctly what original step any given man has taken. It would follow that tychasm has been the sole method of intellectual development. I have to confess I cannot read history so; I cannot help thinking that while tychasm has sometimes been operative, at others great steps covering nearly the same ground and made by different men independently, have been mistaken for a succession of small steps, and further that students have been reluctant to admit a real entitative "spirit" of an age or of a people, under the mistaken and unscrutinized impression that they should thus be opening the door to wild and unnatural hypotheses. I find, on the contrary, that, however it may be with the education of individual minds, the historical development of thought has seldom been of a tychastic nature, and exclusively in backward and barbarizing movements. I desire to speak with the extreme modesty which befits a student of logic who is required to survey so very wide a field of human thought that he can cover it only by a reconnaissance, to which only the greatest skill and most adroit methods can impart any value at all; but, after all, I can only express my own opinions and not those of anybody else; and in my humble judgment, the largest example of tychasm is afforded by the history of Christianity, from about its establishment by Constantine, to, say, the time of the Irish monasteries, an era or eon of about 500 years. Undoubtedly the external circumstance which more than all others at first inclined men to accept Christianity in its loveliness and tenderness, was the fearful extent to which society was broken up into units by the unmitigated greed and hard-heartedness into which the Romans had seduced the world. And yet it was that very same fact, more than any other external circumstance, that fostered that bitterness against the wicked world of which the primitive Gospel of Mark contains not a single trace. At least, I do not detect it in the remark about the blasphemy against the Holy Ghost, where nothing is said about vengeance, nor even in that speech where the closing lines of Isaiah are quoted, about the worm and the fire that feed upon the "carcasses of the men that have transgressed against me." But little by little the bitterness increases until in the last book of the New Testament, its poor distracted author represents that all the time Christ was talking about having come to save the world, the secret design was to catch the entire human race, with the exception of a paltry 144,000, and souse them all in a brimstone lake, and as the smoke of their torment went up for ever and ever, to turn and remark, "There is no curse any more." Would it be an insensible smirk or a fiendish grin that should accompany such an utterance? I wish I could believe St. John did not write it; but it is his gospel which tells about the "resurrection unto condemnation,"—that is of men's being resuscitated just for the sake of torturing them;—and, at any rate, the Revelation is a very ancient composition. One can understand that the early Christians were like men trying with all their might to climb a steep declivity of smooth wet clay; the deepest and truest element of their life, animating both heart and head, was universal love; but they were continually, and against their wills, slipping into a party spirit, every slip serving as a precedent, in a fashion but too familiar to every man. This party feeling insensibly grew until by about A.D. 330 the lustre of the pristine integrity that in St. Mark reflects the white spirit of light was so far tarnished that Eusebius (the Jared Sparks of that day), in the preface to his History, could announce his intention of exaggerating everything that tended to the glory of the church and of suppressing whatever might disgrace it. His Latin contemporary Lactantius is worse, still; and so the darkling went on increasing until before the end of the century the great library of Alexandria was destroyed by Theophilus, until Gregory the Great, two centuries later, burnt the great library of Rome, proclaiming that "Ignorance is the mother of devotion" (which is true, just as oppression and injustice is the mother of spirituality), until a sober description of the state of the church would be a thing our not too nice newspapers would treat as "unfit for publication." All this movement is shown by the application of the test given above to have been

tychastic.   Another very much like it on a small scale, only a
hundred times swifter, for the study of which there are documents
by the library-full, is to be found in the history of the French
Revolution.

Anancastic evolution advances by successive strides with pauses
between. The reason is that in this process a habit of thought having
been overthrown is supplanted by the next strongest. Now this
next strongest is sure to be widely disparate from the first, and as
often as not is its direct contrary. It reminds one of our old rule
of making the second candidate vice-president. This character,
therefore, clearly distinguishes anancasm from tychasm. The character which distinguishes it from agapasm is its purposelessness.
But external and internal anancasm have to be examined separately.
Development under the pressure of external circumstances, or cata-
clasmine evolution, is in most cases unmistakable enough. It has
numberless degrees of intensity, from the brute force, the plain war,
which has more than once turned the current of the world's thought,
down to the hard fact of evidence, or what has been taken for it,
which has been known to convince men by hordes. The only hesitation that can subsist in the presence of such a history is a quantitative one. Never are external influences the only ones which affect
the mind, and therefore it must be a matter of judgment for which
it would scarcely be worth while to attempt to set rules, whether a
given movement is to be regarded as principally governed from
without or not. In the rise of medieval thought, I mean scholasticism and the synchronistic art developments, undoubtedly the
crusades and the discovery of the writings of Aristotle were powerful
influences. The development of scholasticism from Roscellin to
Albertus Magnus closely follows the successive steps in the knowledge
of Aristotle. Prantl thinks that that is the whole story, and few
men have thumbed more books than Carl Prantl. He has done good
solid work, notwithstanding his slap-dash judgments. But we shall
never make so much as a good beginning of comprehending scholasticism until the whole has been systematically explored and digested
by a company of students regularly organized and held under rule
for that purpose. But as for the period we are now specially considering, that which synchronized the Romanesque architecture,
the literature is easily mastered. It does not quite justify Prantl's
dicta as to the slavish dependence of these authors upon their
authorities. Moreover, they kept a definite purpose steadily before
their minds, throughout all their studies. I am, therefore, unable
to offer this period of scholasticism as an example of pure external

anancasm, which seems to be the fluorine of the intellectual elements. Perhaps the recent Japanese reception of western ideas is the purest instance of it in history. Yet in combination with other elements, nothing is commoner. If the development of ideas under the influence of the study of external facts be considered as external anancasm—it is on the border between the external and the internal forms—it is, of course, the principal thing in modern learning. But Whewell, whose masterly comprehension of the history of science critics have been too ignorant properly to appreciate, clearly shows that it is far from being the overwhelmingly preponderant influence, even there.

Internal anancasm, or logical groping, which advances upon a predestined line without being able to foresee whither it is to be carried nor to steer its course, this is the rule of development of philosophy. Hegel first made the world understand this; and he seeks to make logic not merely the subjective guide and monitor of thought, which was all it had been ambitioning before, but to be the very mainspring of thinking, and not merely of individual thinking but of discussion, of the history of the development of thought, of all history, of all development. This involves a positive, clearly demonstrable error. Let the logic in question be of whatever kind it may, a logic of necessary inference or a logic of probable inference (the theory might perhaps be shaped to fit either), in any case it supposes that logic is sufficient of itself to determine what conclusion follows from given premises; for unless it will do so much, it will not suffice to explain why an individual train of reasoning should take just the course it does take, to say nothing of other kinds of development. It thus supposes that from given premises, only one conclusion can logically be drawn, and that there is no scope at all for free choice. That from given premises only one conclusion can logically be drawn, is one of the false notions which have come from logicians' confining their attention to that Nantucket of thought, the logic of non-relative terms. In the logic of relatives, it does not hold good.

One remark occurs to me. If the evolution of history is in considerable part of the nature of internal anancasm, it resembles the development of individual men; and just as 33 years is a rough but natural unit of time for individuals, being the average age at which man has issue, so there should be an approximate period at the end of which one great historical movement ought to be likely to be supplanted by another. Let us see if we can make out anything of the kind. Take the governmental development of Rome as being sufficiently long and set down the principal dates.

B.C.   753, Foundation of Rome.
B.C.   510, Expulsion of the Tarquins.
B.C.   27, Octavius assumes title Augustus.
A.D.   476, End of Western Empire.
A.D.   962, Holy Roman Empire.
A.D. 1453, Fall of Constantinople.

The last event was one of the most significant in history, especially for Italy. The intervals are 243, 483, 502, 486, 491 years. All are rather curiously near equal, except the first which is half the others. Successive reigns of kings would not commonly be so near equal. Let us set down a few dates in the history of thought.

B.C.   585, Eclipse of Thales. Beginning of Greek philosophy.
A.D.   30, The crucifixion.
A.D.   529, Closing of Athenian schools. End of Greek philosophy.
A.D. 1125, (Approximate) Rise of the Universities of Bologna and Paris.
A.D. 1543, Publication of the *De Revolutionibus* of Copernicus. Beginning of Modern Science.

The intervals are 615, 499, 596, 418 years. In the history of metaphysics, we may take the following:

B.C.   322, Death of Aristotle.
A.D. 1274, Death of Aquinas.
A.D. 1804, Death of Kant.

The intervals are 1595 and 530 years. The former is about thrice the latter.

From these figures, no conclusion can fairly be drawn. At the same time, they suggest that perhaps there may be a rough natural era of about 500 years. Should there be any independent evidence of this, the intervals noticed may gain some significance.

The agapastic development of thought should, if it exists, be distinguished by its purposive character, this purpose being the development of an idea. We should have a direct agapic or sympathetic comprehension and recognition of it, by virtue of the continuity of thought. I here take it for granted that such continuity of thought has been sufficiently proved by the arguments used in my paper on the "Law of Mind." . . . Even if those arguments are not quite convincing in themselves, yet if they are reënforced by an apparent agapasm in the history of thought, the two propositions will lend one another mutual aid. The reader will, I trust, be too well grounded in logic to mistake such mutual support for a vicious circle in reasoning. If it could be shown directly that there is such an entity as the "spirit of an age" or of a people, and that mere individual intelligence will not account for all the phenomena, this would be proof enough at once of agapasticism and of synechism. I must acknowledge that I am unable to produce a cogent demonstration of this; but I am, I believe, able to adduce such arguments as will serve to confirm those which have been drawn from other facts. I believe that all the greatest achievements of mind have been beyond the powers of unaided individuals; and I find, apart from the support this opinion receives from synechistic considerations, and from the purposive character of many great movements, direct reason for so thinking in the sublimity of the ideas and in their occurring simultaneously and independently to a number of individuals of no extraordinary general powers. The pointed Gothic architecture in several of its developments appears to me to be of such a character. All attempts to imitate it by modern architects of the greatest learning and genius appear flat and tame, and are felt by their authors to be so. Yet at the time the style was living, there was quite an abundance of men capable of producing works of this kind of gigantic sublimity and power. In more than one case, extant documents show that the cathedral chapters, in the selection of architects, treated high artistic genius as a secondary consideration, as if there were no lack of persons able to supply that; and the results justify their confidence. Were individuals in general, then, in those ages possessed of such lofty natures and high intellect? Such an opinion would break down under the first examination.

How many times have men now in middle life seen great discoveries made independently and almost simultaneously! The first instance I remember was the prediction of a planet exterior to Uranus by Leverrier and Adams. One hardly knows to whom the principle of the conservation of energy ought to be attributed, although it may reasonably be considered as the greatest discovery science has ever made. The mechanical theory of heat was set forth by Rankine and by Clausius during the same month of February 1850; and there are eminent men who attribute this great step to Thomson. The kinetical theory of gases, after being started by John Bernoulli and long buried in oblivion, was reinvented and applied to the explanation not merely of the laws of Boyle, Charles, and Avogadro, but also of diffusion and viscosity, by at least three modern physicists separately. It is well known that the doctrine of natural selection was presented by Wallace and by Darwin at the same meeting of the British Association; and Darwin in his "Historical Sketch" prefixed to the later editions of his book shows that both were anticipated by obscure forerunners. The method of spectrum analysis was claimed for Swan as well as for Kirchhoff, and there were others who perhaps had still better claims. The authorship of the Periodical Law of the Chemical Elements is disputed between a Russian, a German, and an Englishman; although there is no room for doubt that the principal merit belongs to the first. These are nearly all the greatest discoveries of our times. It is the same with the inventions. It may not be surprising that the telegraph should have been independently made by several inventors, because it was an easy corollary from scientific facts well made out before. But it was not so with the telephone and other inventions. Ether, the first anæsthetic, was introduced independently by three different New England physicians. Now ether had been a common article for a century. It had been in one of the pharmacopœias three centuries before. It is quite incredible that its anæsthetic property should not have been known; it was known. It had probably passed from mouth to ear as a secret from the days of Basil Valentine; but for long it had been a secret of the Punchinello kind. In New England, for many years, boys had used it for amusement. Why then had it not been put to its serious use? No reason can be given, except that the motive to do so was not strong enough. The motives to doing so could only have been desire for gain and philanthropy. About 1846, the date of the introduction, philanthropy was undoubtedly in an unusually active condition. That sensibility, or sentimentalism, which had been introduced in the previous century, had undergone a ripening process, in consequence of which, though now less intense than it had previously been, it was more likely to influence unreflecting people than it had ever been. All three of the ether-claimants had probably been influenced by the desire for gain; but nevertheless they were certainly not insensible to the agapic influences.

I doubt if any of the great discoveries ought, properly, to be considered as altogether individual achievements; and I think many will share this doubt. Yet, if not, what an argument for the continuity of mind, and for agapasticism is here! I do not wish to be very strenuous. If thinkers will only be persuaded to lay aside their prejudices and apply themselves to studying the evidences of this doctrine, I shall be fully content to await the final decision.

28

THE CONCEPT OF GOD *

"Do you believe in the existence of a Supreme Being?" Hume, in his *Dialogues Concerning Natural Religion*, justly points out that the phrase "Supreme Being" is not an equivalent of "God," since it neither implies infinity nor any of the other attributes of God, excepting only Being and Supremacy. This is important; and another distinction between the two designations is still more so. Namely, "God" is a vernacular word and, like all such words, but more than almost any, is *vague*. No words are so well understood as vernacular words, in one way; yet they are invariably vague; and of many of them it is true that, let the logician do his best to substitute precise equivalents in their places, still the vernacular words alone, for all their vagueness, answer the principal purposes. This is emphatically the case with the very vague word "God," which is not made less vague by saying that it imports "infinity," etc., since those attributes are at least as vague. I shall, therefore, if you please, substitute "God," for "Supreme Being" in the question.

I will also take the liberty of substituting "reality" for "existence." This is perhaps overscrupulosity; but I myself always use *exist* in its strict philosophical sense of "react with the other like things in the environment." Of course, in that sense, it would be fetichism to say that God "exists." The word "reality," on the contrary, is used in ordinary parlance in its correct philosophical sense. . . . So, then, the question being whether I believe in the reality of God, I answer, Yes. I further opine that pretty nearly everybody more or less believes this, including many of the scientific men of my generation who are accustomed to think the belief is entirely unfounded. The reason they fall into this extraordinary error about their own belief is that they precide (or render precise) the conception, and, in doing so, inevitably change it; and such precise conception is easily shown not to be warranted, even if it cannot be quite refuted. Every concept that is vague is liable to

---

* [The first two selections are from ms. c. 1906 (*CP* 6.494-6, 502-3), the third from ms. c. 1896 (*CP* 6.492-3).]

be self-contradictory in those respects in which it is vague. *No* concept, not even those of mathematics, is absolutely precise; and some of the most important for everyday use are extremely vague. Nevertheless, our instinctive beliefs involving such concepts are far more trustworthy than the best established results of science, if these be precisely understood. For instance, we all think that there is an element of order in the universe. Could any laboratory experiments render that proposition more certain than instinct or common sense leaves it? It is ridiculous to broach such a question. But when anybody undertakes to say *precisely* what that order consists in, he will quickly find he outruns all logical warrant. Men who are given to defining too much inevitably run themselves into confusion in dealing with the vague concepts of common sense.

If a pragmaticist is asked what he means by the word "God," he can only say that just as long acquaintance with a man of great character may deeply influence one's whole manner of conduct, so that a glance at his portrait may make a difference, just as almost living with Dr. Johnson enabled poor Boswell to write an immortal book and a really sublime book, just as long study of the works of Aristotle may make him an acquaintance, so if contemplation and study of the physico-psychical universe can imbue a man with principles of conduct analogous to the influence of a great man's works or conversation, then that analogue of a mind—for it is impossible to say that *any* human attribute is *literally* applicable— is what he means by "God." Of course, various great theologians explain that one cannot attribute *reason* to God, nor perception (which always involves an element of surprise and of learning what one did not know), and, in short, that his "mind" is necessarily so unlike ours, that some—though wrongly—high in the church say that it is only negatively, as being entirely different from everything else, that we can attach any meaning to the Name. This is not so; because the discoveries of science, their enabling us to *predict* what will be the course of nature, is proof conclusive that, though we cannot think any thought of God's, we can catch a fragment of His Thought, as it were.

Now such being the pragmaticist's answer to the question what he means by the word "God," the question whether there really *is* such a being is the question whether all physical science is merely the figment—the arbitrary figment—of the students of nature, and further whether the *one* lesson of Gautama Boodha, Confucius,

Socrates, and all who from any point of view have had their ways of conduct determined by meditation upon the physico-psychical universe, be only their arbitrary notion or be the Truth behind the appearances which the frivolous man does not think of; and whether the superhuman courage which such contemplation has conferred upon priests who go to pass their lives with lepers and refuse all offers of rescue is mere silly fanaticism, the passion of a baby, or whether it is strength derived from the power of the truth. Now the only guide to the answer to this question lies in the power of the passion of love which more or less overmasters every agnostic scientist and everybody who seriously and deeply considers the universe. But whatever there may be of *argument* in all this is as nothing, the merest nothing, in comparison to its force as an appeal to one's own instinct, which is to argument what substance is to shadow, what bed-rock is to the built foundations of a cathedral.

By experience must be understood the entire mental product. Some psychologists whom I hold in respect will stop me here to say that, while they admit that experience is more than mere sensation, they cannot extend it to the whole mental product, since that would include hallucinations, delusions, superstitious imaginations and fallacies of all kinds; and that they would limit experience to sense-perceptions. But I reply that my statement is the logical one. Hallucinations, delusions, superstitious imaginations, and fallacies of all kinds are experiences, but experiences misunderstood; while to say that all our knowledge relates merely to sense-perception is to say that we can know nothing—not even mistakenly—about higher matters, as honour, aspirations, and love.

Where would such an idea, say as that of God, come from, if not from direct experience? Would you make it a result of some kind of reasoning, good or bad? Why, reasoning can supply the mind with nothing in the world except an estimate of the value of a statistical ratio, that is, how often certain kinds of things are found in certain combinations in the ordinary course of experience. And scepticism, in the sense of doubt of the validity of elementary ideas —which is really a proposal to turn an idea out of court and permit no inquiry into its applicability—is doubly condemned by the fundamental principle of scientific method—condemned first as obstructing inquiry, and condemned second because it is treating some other than a statistical ratio as a thing to be argued about. No: as to God, open your eyes—and your heart, which is also a perceptive organ—and you see him. But you may ask, Don't you admit there are any delusions? Yes: I may think a thing is black, and on close examination it may turn out to be bottle-green. But I cannot think a thing is black if there is no such thing to be seen as black. Neither can I think that a certain action is self-sacrificing, if no such thing as self-sacrifice exists, although it may be very rare. It is the nominalists, and the nominalists alone, who indulge in such scepticism, which the scientific method utterly condemns.

NOTES

¹ Ch. 2.

² Cf. ch. 19, part II.

³ Ch. 12, part I.

⁴ See ch. 11.

⁵ E.g., "pedagogics, gold-beating, etiquette, pigeon-fancying, vulgar arithmetic, horology, surveying, navigation, telegraphy, printing, bookbinding . . . librarian's work, engraving, etc." (*CP* 1.243).

⁶ Cf. p. 99 and note 7 below.

⁷ Cf. p. 62 above. Cf. also: "Logic . . . has three departments. . . . *Critical Logic* is the theory of the general conditions of the reference of Symbols and other Signs to their professed Objects, that is, it is the theory of the conditions of truth. . . . *Speculative Grammar* is the doctrine of the general conditions of symbols and other signs having the significant character. It is this department of general logic with which we are, at this moment [e.g., ch. 7], occupying ourselves. . . . *Speculative Rhetoric* is substantially what goes by the name of methodology, or better, of *methodeutic*. It is the doctrine of the general conditions of the reference of Symbols and other Signs to the Interpretants which they aim to determine. . . ." (*CP* 2.93). The earliest statement is : "The first would treat of the formal conditions of symbols having meaning, that is, of the reference of symbols in general to their grounds or imputed characters, and this might be called formal grammar ; the second, logic, would treat of the formal conditions of the truth of symbols ; and the third would treat of the formal conditions of the force of symbols, or their power of appealing to a mind, that is, of their reference in general to interpretants, and this might be called formal rhetoric " (*CP* 1.559).

⁸ The constituent letters are symbols, the subscript numbers indices.

⁹ Ch. 3.

¹⁰ Ch. 12.

¹¹ "Hypothesis," "Hypothetic Inference," "Abduction," and "Retroduction" are synonymous; but the accounts of this form of inference and its relation to induction vary (e.g., cf. ch. 11).

¹² See pp. 181-2 above.

¹³ See ch. 15.

¹⁴ See ch. 25 and 26.

¹⁵ Ch. 2 and 3.

¹⁶ See ch. 23, 24, 25, 27.

¹⁷ See p. 92 above.

¹⁸ P. 236 above.

¹⁹ Analogy is ordinarily regarded by Peirce as a composite of induction, hypothesis, and deduction (cf. *CP* 2.513, 733).

²⁰ Ch. 23.

²¹ Ch. 24.

²² These modes of evolution are, respectively, generalized expressions of Darwinian, cataclysmic, and Lamarckian evolution. See pp. 49, 319-20 above.

INDEX

A CATALOG OF SELECTED
DOVER BOOKS
IN ALL FIELDS OF INTEREST

A CATALOG OF SELECTED DOVER
BOOKS IN ALL FIELDS OF INTEREST

CONCERNING THE SPIRITUAL IN ART, Wassily Kandinsky. Pioneering work by father of abstract art. Thoughts on color theory, nature of art. Analysis of earlier masters. 12 illustrations. 80pp. of text. 5⅝ x 8½.   23411-8 Pa. $3.95

ANIMALS: 1,419 Copyright-Free Illustrations of Mammals, Birds, Fish, Insects, etc., Jim Harter (ed.). Clear wood engravings present, in extremely lifelike poses, over 1,000 species of animals. One of the most extensive pictorial sourcebooks of its kind. Captions. Index. 284pp. 9 x 12.   23766-4 Pa. $12.95

CELTIC ART: The Methods of Construction, George Bain. Simple geometric techniques for making Celtic interlacements, spirals, Kells-type initials, animals, humans, etc. Over 500 illustrations. 160pp. 9 x 12. (USO)   22923-8 Pa. $9.95

AN ATLAS OF ANATOMY FOR ARTISTS, Fritz Schider. Most thorough reference work on art anatomy in the world. Hundreds of illustrations, including selections from works by Vesalius, Leonardo, Goya, Ingres, Michelangelo, others. 593 illustrations. 192pp. 7⅛ x 10¼.   20241-0 Pa. $9.95

CELTIC HAND STROKE-BY-STROKE (Irish Half-Uncial from "The Book of Kells"): An Arthur Baker Calligraphy Manual, Arthur Baker. Complete guide to creating each letter of the alphabet in distinctive Celtic manner. Covers hand position, strokes, pens, inks, paper, more. Illustrated. 48pp. 8¼ x 11.   24336-2 Pa. $3.95

EASY ORIGAMI, John Montroll. Charming collection of 32 projects (hat, cup, pelican, piano, swan, many more) specially designed for the novice origami hobbyist. Clearly illustrated easy-to-follow instructions insure that even beginning papercrafters will achieve successful results. 48pp. 8¼ x 11.   27298-2 Pa. $3.50

THE COMPLETE BOOK OF BIRDHOUSE CONSTRUCTION FOR WOODWORKERS, Scott D. Campbell. Detailed instructions, illustrations, tables. Also data on bird habitat and instinct patterns. Bibliography. 3 tables. 63 illustrations in 15 figures. 48pp. 5¼ x 8½.   24407-5 Pa. $2.50

BLOOMINGDALE'S ILLUSTRATED 1886 CATALOG: Fashions, Dry Goods and Housewares, Bloomingdale Brothers. Famed merchants' extremely rare catalog depicting about 1,700 products: clothing, housewares, firearms, dry goods, jewelry, more. Invaluable for dating, identifying vintage items. Also, copyright-free graphics for artists, designers. Co-published with Henry Ford Museum & Greenfield Village. 160pp. 8¼ x 11.   25780-0 Pa. $10.95

HISTORIC COSTUME IN PICTURES, Braun & Schneider. Over 1,450 costumed figures in clearly detailed engravings—from dawn of civilization to end of 19th century. Captions. Many folk costumes. 256pp. 8⅜ x 11¾.   23150-X Pa. $12.95

STICKLEY CRAFTSMAN FURNITURE CATALOGS, Gustav Stickley and L. & J. G. Stickley. Beautiful, functional furniture in two authentic catalogs from 1910. 594 illustrations, including 277 photos, show settles, rockers, armchairs, reclining chairs, bookcases, desks, tables. 183pp. 6½ x 9¼. 23838-5 Pa. $11.95

AMERICAN LOCOMOTIVES IN HISTORIC PHOTOGRAPHS: 1858 to 1949, Ron Ziel (ed.). A rare collection of 126 meticulously detailed official photographs, called "builder portraits," of American locomotives that majestically chronicle the rise of steam locomotive power in America. Introduction. Detailed captions. xi + 129pp. 9 x 12. 27393-8 Pa. $12.95

AMERICA'S LIGHTHOUSES: An Illustrated History, Francis Ross Holland, Jr. Delightfully written, profusely illustrated fact-filled survey of over 200 American lighthouses since 1716. History, anecdotes, technological advances, more. 240pp. 8 x 10¾. 25576-X Pa. $12.95

TOWARDS A NEW ARCHITECTURE, Le Corbusier. Pioneering manifesto by founder of "International School." Technical and aesthetic theories, views of industry, economics, relation of form to function, "mass-production split" and much more. Profusely illustrated. 320pp. 6⅛ x 9¼. (USO) 25023-7 Pa. $9.95

HOW THE OTHER HALF LIVES, Jacob Riis. Famous journalistic record, exposing poverty and degradation of New York slums around 1900, by major social reformer. 100 striking and influential photographs. 233pp. 10 x 7⅞. 22012-5 Pa. $11.95

FRUIT KEY AND TWIG KEY TO TREES AND SHRUBS, William M. Harlow. One of the handiest and most widely used identification aids. Fruit key covers 120 deciduous and evergreen species; twig key 160 deciduous species. Easily used. Over 300 photographs. 126pp. 5⅜ x 8½. 20511-8 Pa. $3.95

COMMON BIRD SONGS, Dr. Donald J. Borror. Songs of 60 most common U.S. birds: robins, sparrows, cardinals, bluejays, finches, more—arranged in order of increasing complexity. Up to 9 variations of songs of each species.
Cassette and manual 99911-4 $8.95

ORCHIDS AS HOUSE PLANTS, Rebecca Tyson Northen. Grow cattleyas and many other kinds of orchids—in a window, in a case, or under artificial light. 63 illustrations. 148pp. 5⅜ x 8½. 23261-1 Pa. $4.95

MONSTER MAZES, Dave Phillips. Masterful mazes at four levels of difficulty. Avoid deadly perils and evil creatures to find magical treasures. Solutions for all 32 exciting illustrated puzzles. 48pp. 8¼ x 11. 26005-4 Pa. $2.95

MOZART'S DON GIOVANNI (DOVER OPERA LIBRETTO SERIES), Wolfgang Amadeus Mozart. Introduced and translated by Ellen H. Bleiler. Standard Italian libretto, with complete English translation. Convenient and thoroughly portable—an ideal companion for reading along with a recording or the performance itself. Introduction. List of characters. Plot summary. 121pp. 5¼ x 8½. 24944-1 Pa. $3.95

TECHNICAL MANUAL AND DICTIONARY OF CLASSICAL BALLET, Gail Grant. Defines, explains, comments on steps, movements, poses and concepts. 15-page pictorial section. Basic book for student, viewer. 127pp. 5⅜ x 8½. 21843-0 Pa. $4.95

BRASS INSTRUMENTS: Their History and Development, Anthony Baines. Authoritative, updated survey of the evolution of trumpets, trombones, bugles, cornets, French horns, tubas and other brass wind instruments. Over 140 illustrations and 48 music examples. Corrected and updated by author. New preface. Bibliography. 320pp. 5⅜ x 8½. 27574-4 Pa. $9.95

HOLLYWOOD GLAMOR PORTRAITS, John Kobal (ed.). 145 photos from 1926-49. Harlow, Gable, Bogart, Bacall; 94 stars in all. Full background on photographers, technical aspects. 160pp. 8⅜ x 11¼. 23352-9 Pa. $12.95

MAX AND MORITZ, Wilhelm Busch. Great humor classic in both German and English. Also 10 other works: "Cat and Mouse," "Plisch and Plumm," etc. 216pp. 5⅜ x 8½. 20181-3 Pa. $6.95

THE RAVEN AND OTHER FAVORITE POEMS, Edgar Allan Poe. Over 40 of the author's most memorable poems: "The Bells," "Ulalume," "Israfel," "To Helen," "The Conqueror Worm," "Eldorado," "Annabel Lee," many more. Alphabetic lists of titles and first lines. 64pp. 5$\frac{3}{16}$ x 8¼. 26685-0 Pa. $1.00

PERSONAL MEMOIRS OF U. S. GRANT, Ulysses Simpson Grant. Intelligent, deeply moving firsthand account of Civil War campaigns, considered by many the finest military memoirs ever written. Includes letters, historic photographs, maps and more. 528pp. 6⅛ x 9¼. 28587-1 Pa. $12.95

AMULETS AND SUPERSTITIONS, E. A. Wallis Budge. Comprehensive discourse on origin, powers of amulets in many ancient cultures: Arab, Persian Babylonian, Assyrian, Egyptian, Gnostic, Hebrew, Phoenician, Syriac, etc. Covers cross, swastika, crucifix, seals, rings, stones, etc. 584pp. 5⅜ x 8½. 23573-4 Pa. $12.95

RUSSIAN STORIES/PYCCKNE PACCKA3bl: A Dual-Language Book, edited by Gleb Struve. Twelve tales by such masters as Chekhov, Tolstoy, Dostoevsky, Pushkin, others. Excellent word-for-word English translations on facing pages, plus teaching and study aids, Russian/English vocabulary, biographical/critical introductions, more. 416pp. 5⅜ x 8½. 26244-8 Pa. $9.95

PHILADELPHIA THEN AND NOW: 60 Sites Photographed in the Past and Present, Kenneth Finkel and Susan Oyama. Rare photographs of City Hall, Logan Square, Independence Hall, Betsy Ross House, other landmarks juxtaposed with contemporary views. Captures changing face of historic city. Introduction. Captions. 128pp. 8¼ x 11. 25790-8 Pa. $9.95

AIA ARCHITECTURAL GUIDE TO NASSAU AND SUFFOLK COUNTIES, LONG ISLAND, The American Institute of Architects, Long Island Chapter, and the Society for the Preservation of Long Island Antiquities. Comprehensive, well-researched and generously illustrated volume brings to life over three centuries of Long Island's great architectural heritage. More than 240 photographs with authoritative, extensively detailed captions. 176pp. 8¼ x 11. 26946-9 Pa. $14.95

NORTH AMERICAN INDIAN LIFE: Customs and Traditions of 23 Tribes, Elsie Clews Parsons (ed.). 27 fictionalized essays by noted anthropologists examine religion, customs, government, additional facets of life among the Winnebago, Crow, Zuni, Eskimo, other tribes. 480pp. 6⅛ x 9¼. 27377-6 Pa. $10.95

FRANK LLOYD WRIGHT'S HOLLYHOCK HOUSE, Donald Hoffmann. Lavishly illustrated, carefully documented study of one of Wright's most controversial residential designs. Over 120 photographs, floor plans, elevations, etc. Detailed perceptive text by noted Wright scholar. Index. 128pp. 9¼ x 10¾. 27133-1 Pa. $11.95

THE MALE AND FEMALE FIGURE IN MOTION: 60 Classic Photographic Sequences, Eadweard Muybridge. 60 true-action photographs of men and women walking, running, climbing, bending, turning, etc., reproduced from rare 19th-century masterpiece. vi + 121pp. 9 x 12. 24745-7 Pa. $10.95

1001 QUESTIONS ANSWERED ABOUT THE SEASHORE, N. J. Berrill and Jacquelyn Berrill. Queries answered about dolphins, sea snails, sponges, starfish, fishes, shore birds, many others. Covers appearance, breeding, growth, feeding, much more. 305pp. 5¼ x 8¼. 23366-9 Pa. $8.95

GUIDE TO OWL WATCHING IN NORTH AMERICA, Donald S. Heintzelman. Superb guide offers complete data and descriptions of 19 species: barn owl, screech owl, snowy owl, many more. Expert coverage of owl-watching equipment, conservation, migrations and invasions, etc. Guide to observing sites. 84 illustrations. xiii + 193pp. 5⅜ x 8½. 27344-X Pa. $8.95

MEDICINAL AND OTHER USES OF NORTH AMERICAN PLANTS: A Historical Survey with Special Reference to the Eastern Indian Tribes, Charlotte Erichsen-Brown. Chronological historical citations document 500 years of usage of plants, trees, shrubs native to eastern Canada, northeastern U.S. Also complete identifying information. 343 illustrations. 544pp. 6½ x 9¼. 25951-X Pa. $12.95

STORYBOOK MAZES, Dave Phillips. 23 stories and mazes on two-page spreads: Wizard of Oz, Treasure Island, Robin Hood, etc. Solutions. 64pp. 8¼ x 11. 23628-5 Pa. $2.95

NEGRO FOLK MUSIC, U.S.A., Harold Courlander. Noted folklorist's scholarly yet readable analysis of rich and varied musical tradition. Includes authentic versions of over 40 folk songs. Valuable bibliography and discography. xi + 324pp. 5⅜ x 8½. 27350-4 Pa. $9.95

MOVIE-STAR PORTRAITS OF THE FORTIES, John Kobal (ed.). 163 glamor, studio photos of 106 stars of the 1940s: Rita Hayworth, Ava Gardner, Marlon Brando, Clark Gable, many more. 176pp. 8⅜ x 11¼. 23546-7 Pa. $12.95

BENCHLEY LOST AND FOUND, Robert Benchley. Finest humor from early 30s, about pet peeves, child psychologists, post office and others. Mostly unavailable elsewhere. 73 illustrations by Peter Arno and others. 183pp. 5⅜ x 8½. 22410-4 Pa. $6.95

YEKL and THE IMPORTED BRIDEGROOM AND OTHER STORIES OF YIDDISH NEW YORK, Abraham Cahan. Film Hester Street based on Yekl (1896). Novel, other stories among first about Jewish immigrants on N.Y.'s East Side. 240pp. 5⅜ x 8½. 22427-9 Pa. $6.95

SELECTED POEMS, Walt Whitman. Generous sampling from *Leaves of Grass.* Twenty-four poems include "I Hear America Singing," "Song of the Open Road," "I Sing the Body Electric," "When Lilacs Last in the Dooryard Bloom'd," "O Captain! My Captain!"–all reprinted from an authoritative edition. Lists of titles and first lines. 128pp. 5³⁄₁₆ x 8¼. 26878-0 Pa. $1.00

THE BEST TALES OF HOFFMANN, E. T. A. Hoffmann. 10 of Hoffmann's most important stories: "Nutcracker and the King of Mice," "The Golden Flowerpot," etc. 458pp. 5⅜ x 8½. 21793-0 Pa. $9.95

FROM FETISH TO GOD IN ANCIENT EGYPT, E. A. Wallis Budge. Rich detailed survey of Egyptian conception of "God" and gods, magic, cult of animals, Osiris, more. Also, superb English translations of hymns and legends. 240 illustrations. 545pp. 5⅜ x 8½. 25803-3 Pa. $13.95

FRENCH STORIES/CONTES FRANÇAIS: A Dual-Language Book, Wallace Fowlie. Ten stories by French masters, Voltaire to Camus: "Micromegas" by Voltaire; "The Atheist's Mass" by Balzac; "Minuet" by de Maupassant; "The Guest" by Camus, six more. Excellent English translations on facing pages. Also French-English vocabulary list, exercises, more. 352pp. 5⅜ x 8½. 26443-2 Pa. $9.95

CHICAGO AT THE TURN OF THE CENTURY IN PHOTOGRAPHS: 122 Historic Views from the Collections of the Chicago Historical Society, Larry A. Viskochil. Rare large-format prints offer detailed views of City Hall, State Street, the Loop, Hull House, Union Station, many other landmarks, circa 1904-1913. Introduction. Captions. Maps. 144pp. 9⅜ x 12¼. 24656-6 Pa. $12.95

OLD BROOKLYN IN EARLY PHOTOGRAPHS, 1865-1929, William Lee Younger. Luna Park, Gravesend race track, construction of Grand Army Plaza, moving of Hotel Brighton, etc. 157 previously unpublished photographs. 165pp. 8⅞ x 11¾. 23587-4 Pa. $13.95

THE MYTHS OF THE NORTH AMERICAN INDIANS, Lewis Spence. Rich anthology of the myths and legends of the Algonquins, Iroquois, Pawnees and Sioux, prefaced by an extensive historical and ethnological commentary. 36 illustrations. 480pp. 5⅜ x 8½. 25967-6 Pa. $10.95

AN ENCYCLOPEDIA OF BATTLES: Accounts of Over 1,560 Battles from 1479 B.C. to the Present, David Eggenberger. Essential details of every major battle in recorded history from the first battle of Megiddo in 1479 B.C. to Grenada in 1984. List of Battle Maps. New Appendix covering the years 1967-1984. Index. 99 illustrations. 544pp. 6½ x 9¼. 24913-1 Pa. $16.95

SAILING ALONE AROUND THE WORLD, Captain Joshua Slocum. First man to sail around the world, alone, in small boat. One of great feats of seamanship told in delightful manner. 67 illustrations. 294pp. 5⅜ x 8½. 20326-3 Pa. $6.95

ANARCHISM AND OTHER ESSAYS, Emma Goldman. Powerful, penetrating, prophetic essays on direct action, role of minorities, prison reform, puritan hypocrisy, violence, etc. 271pp. 5⅜ x 8½. 22484-8 Pa. $7.95

MYTHS OF THE HINDUS AND BUDDHISTS, Ananda K. Coomaraswamy and Sister Nivedita. Great stories of the epics; deeds of Krishna, Shiva, taken from puranas, Vedas, folk tales; etc. 32 illustrations. 400pp. 5⅜ x 8½. 21759-0 Pa. $12.95

BEYOND PSYCHOLOGY, Otto Rank. Fear of death, desire of immortality, nature of sexuality, social organization, creativity, according to Rankian system. 291pp. 5⅜ x 8½. 20485-5 Pa. $8.95

A THEOLOGICO-POLITICAL TREATISE, Benedict Spinoza. Also contains unfinished Political Treatise. Great classic on religious liberty, theory of government on common consent. R. Elwes translation. Total of 421pp. 5⅜ x 8½. 20249-6 Pa. $9.95

MY BONDAGE AND MY FREEDOM, Frederick Douglass. Born a slave, Douglass became outspoken force in antislavery movement. The best of Douglass' autobiographies. Graphic description of slave life. 464pp. 5⅜ x 8½. 22457-0 Pa. $8.95

FOLLOWING THE EQUATOR: A Journey Around the World, Mark Twain. Fascinating humorous account of 1897 voyage to Hawaii, Australia, India, New Zealand, etc. Ironic, bemused reports on peoples, customs, climate, flora and fauna, politics, much more. 197 illustrations. 720pp. 5⅜ x 8½. 26113-1 Pa. $15.95

THE PEOPLE CALLED SHAKERS, Edward D. Andrews. Definitive study of Shakers: origins, beliefs, practices, dances, social organization, furniture and crafts, etc. 33 illustrations. 351pp. 5⅜ x 8½. 21081-2 Pa. $8.95

THE MYTHS OF GREECE AND ROME, H. A. Guerber. A classic of mythology, generously illustrated, long prized for its simple, graphic, accurate retelling of the principal myths of Greece and Rome, and for its commentary on their origins and significance. With 64 illustrations by Michelangelo, Raphael, Titian, Rubens, Canova, Bernini and others. 480pp. 5⅜ x 8½. 27584-1 Pa. $9.95

PSYCHOLOGY OF MUSIC, Carl E. Seashore. Classic work discusses music as a medium from psychological viewpoint. Clear treatment of physical acoustics, auditory apparatus, sound perception, development of musical skills, nature of musical feeling, host of other topics. 88 figures. 408pp. 5⅜ x 8½. 21851-1 Pa. $10.95

THE PHILOSOPHY OF HISTORY, Georg W. Hegel. Great classic of Western thought develops concept that history is not chance but rational process, the evolution of freedom. 457pp. 5⅜ x 8½. 20112-0 Pa. $9.95

THE BOOK OF TEA, Kakuzo Okakura. Minor classic of the Orient: entertaining, charming explanation, interpretation of traditional Japanese culture in terms of tea ceremony. 94pp. 5⅜ x 8½. 20070-1 Pa. $3.95

LIFE IN ANCIENT EGYPT, Adolf Erman. Fullest, most thorough, detailed older account with much not in more recent books, domestic life, religion, magic, medicine, commerce, much more. Many illustrations reproduce tomb paintings, carvings, hieroglyphs, etc. 597pp. 5⅜ x 8½. 22632-8 Pa. $12.95

SUNDIALS, Their Theory and Construction, Albert Waugh. Far and away the best, most thorough coverage of ideas, mathematics concerned, types, construction, adjusting anywhere. Simple, nontechnical treatment allows even children to build several of these dials. Over 100 illustrations. 230pp. 5⅜ x 8½. 22947-5 Pa. $8.95

DYNAMICS OF FLUIDS IN POROUS MEDIA, Jacob Bear. For advanced students of ground water hydrology, soil mechanics and physics, drainage and irrigation engineering, and more. 335 illustrations. Exercises, with answers. 784pp. 6⅛ x 9¼. 65675-6 Pa. $19.95

SONGS OF EXPERIENCE: Facsimile Reproduction with 26 Plates in Full Color, William Blake. 26 full-color plates from a rare 1826 edition. Includes "TheTyger," "London," "Holy Thursday," and other poems. Printed text of poems. 48pp. 5¼ x 7. 24636-1 Pa. $4.95

OLD-TIME VIGNETTES IN FULL COLOR, Carol Belanger Grafton (ed.). Over 390 charming, often sentimental illustrations, selected from archives of Victorian graphics—pretty women posing, children playing, food, flowers, kittens and puppies, smiling cherubs, birds and butterflies, much more. All copyright-free. 48pp. 9¼ x 12¼. 27269-9 Pa. $7.95

PERSPECTIVE FOR ARTISTS, Rex Vicat Cole. Depth, perspective of sky and sea, shadows, much more, not usually covered. 391 diagrams, 81 reproductions of drawings and paintings. 279pp. 5⅜ x 8½. 22487-2 Pa. $7.95

DRAWING THE LIVING FIGURE, Joseph Sheppard. Innovative approach to artistic anatomy focuses on specifics of surface anatomy, rather than muscles and bones. Over 170 drawings of live models in front, back and side views, and in widely varying poses. Accompanying diagrams. 177 illustrations. Introduction. Index. 144pp. 8⅜ x11¼. 26723-7 Pa. $8.95

GOTHIC AND OLD ENGLISH ALPHABETS: 100 Complete Fonts, Dan X. Solo. Add power, elegance to posters, signs, other graphics with 100 stunning copyright-free alphabets: Blackstone, Dolbey, Germania, 97 more–including many lower-case, numerals, punctuation marks. 104pp. 8⅛ x 11. 24695-7 Pa. $8.95

HOW TO DO BEADWORK, Mary White. Fundamental book on craft from simple projects to five-bead chains and woven works. 106 illustrations. 142pp. 5⅜ x 8. 20697-1 Pa. $4.95

THE BOOK OF WOOD CARVING, Charles Marshall Sayers. Finest book for beginners discusses fundamentals and offers 34 designs. "Absolutely first rate . . . well thought out and well executed."–E. J. Tangerman. 118pp. 7¾ x 10⅝. 23654-4 Pa. $6.95

ILLUSTRATED CATALOG OF CIVIL WAR MILITARY GOODS: Union Army Weapons, Insignia, Uniform Accessories, and Other Equipment, Schuyler, Hartley, and Graham. Rare, profusely illustrated 1846 catalog includes Union Army uniform and dress regulations, arms and ammunition, coats, insignia, flags, swords, rifles, etc. 226 illustrations. 160pp. 9 x 12. 24939-5 Pa. $10.95

WOMEN'S FASHIONS OF THE EARLY 1900s: An Unabridged Republication of "New York Fashions, 1909," National Cloak & Suit Co. Rare catalog of mail-order fashions documents women's and children's clothing styles shortly after the turn of the century. Captions offer full descriptions, prices. Invaluable resource for fashion, costume historians. Approximately 725 illustrations. 128pp. 8⅜ x 11¼. 27276-1 Pa. $11.95

THE 1912 AND 1915 GUSTAV STICKLEY FURNITURE CATALOGS, Gustav Stickley. With over 200 detailed illustrations and descriptions, these two catalogs are essential reading and reference materials and identification guides for Stickley furniture. Captions cite materials, dimensions and prices. 112pp. 6½ x 9¼. 26676-1 Pa. $9.95

EARLY AMERICAN LOCOMOTIVES, John H. White, Jr. Finest locomotive engravings from early 19th century: historical (1804–74), main-line (after 1870), special, foreign, etc. 147 plates. 142pp. 11⅜ x 8¼. 22772-3 Pa. $10.95

THE TALL SHIPS OF TODAY IN PHOTOGRAPHS, Frank O. Braynard. Lavishly illustrated tribute to nearly 100 majestic contemporary sailing vessels: Amerigo Vespucci, Clearwater, Constitution, Eagle, Mayflower, Sea Cloud, Victory, many more. Authoritative captions provide statistics, background on each ship. 190 black-and-white photographs and illustrations. Introduction. 128pp. 8⅞ x 11¾. 27163-3 Pa. $14.95

EARLY NINETEENTH-CENTURY CRAFTS AND TRADES, Peter Stockham (ed.). Extremely rare 1807 volume describes to youngsters the crafts and trades of the day: brickmaker, weaver, dressmaker, bookbinder, ropemaker, saddler, many more. Quaint prose, charming illustrations for each craft. 20 black-and-white line illustrations. 192pp. 4⅝ x 6.   27293-1 Pa. $4.95

VICTORIAN FASHIONS AND COSTUMES FROM HARPER'S BAZAR, 1867–1898, Stella Blum (ed.). Day costumes, evening wear, sports clothes, shoes, hats, other accessories in over 1,000 detailed engravings. 320pp. 9⅜ x 12¼.
22990-4 Pa. $15.95

GUSTAV STICKLEY, THE CRAFTSMAN, Mary Ann Smith. Superb study surveys broad scope of Stickley's achievement, especially in architecture. Design philosophy, rise and fall of the Craftsman empire, descriptions and floor plans for many Craftsman houses, more. 86 black-and-white halftones. 31 line illustrations. Introduction 208pp. 6½ x 9¼.   27210-9 Pa. $9.95

THE LONG ISLAND RAIL ROAD IN EARLY PHOTOGRAPHS, Ron Ziel. Over 220 rare photos, informative text document origin (1844) and development of rail service on Long Island. Vintage views of early trains, locomotives, stations, passengers, crews, much more. Captions. 8⅞ x 11¾.   26301-0 Pa. $13.95

THE BOOK OF OLD SHIPS: From Egyptian Galleys to Clipper Ships, Henry B. Culver. Superb, authoritative history of sailing vessels, with 80 magnificent line illustrations. Galley, bark, caravel, longship, whaler, many more. Detailed, informative text on each vessel by noted naval historian. Introduction. 256pp. 5⅜ x 8½.
27332-6 Pa. $7.95

TEN BOOKS ON ARCHITECTURE, Vitruvius. The most important book ever written on architecture. Early Roman aesthetics, technology, classical orders, site selection, all other aspects. Morgan translation. 331pp. 5⅜ x 8½.   20645-9 Pa. $8.95

THE HUMAN FIGURE IN MOTION, Eadweard Muybridge. More than 4,500 stopped-action photos, in action series, showing undraped men, women, children jumping, lying down, throwing, sitting, wrestling, carrying, etc. 390pp. 7⅞ x 10⅝.
20204-6 Clothbd. $27.95

TREES OF THE EASTERN AND CENTRAL UNITED STATES AND CANADA, William M. Harlow. Best one-volume guide to 140 trees. Full descriptions, woodlore, range, etc. Over 600 illustrations. Handy size. 288pp. 4½ x 6⅜.
20395-6 Pa. $6.95

SONGS OF WESTERN BIRDS, Dr. Donald J. Borror. Complete song and call repertoire of 60 western species, including flycatchers, juncoes, cactus wrens, many more–includes fully illustrated booklet.   Cassette and manual 99913-0 $8.95

GROWING AND USING HERBS AND SPICES, Milo Miloradovich. Versatile handbook provides all the information needed for cultivation and use of all the herbs and spices available in North America. 4 illustrations. Index. Glossary. 236pp. 5⅜ x 8½.
25058-X Pa. $6.95

BIG BOOK OF MAZES AND LABYRINTHS, Walter Shepherd. 50 mazes and labyrinths in all–classical, solid, ripple, and more–in one great volume. Perfect inexpensive puzzler for clever youngsters. Full solutions. 112pp. 8⅛ x 11.
22951-3 Pa. $4.95

PIANO TUNING, J. Cree Fischer. Clearest, best book for beginner, amateur. Simple repairs, raising dropped notes, tuning by easy method of flattened fifths. No previous skills needed. 4 illustrations. 201pp. 5⅜ x 8½. 23267-0 Pa. $6.95

A SOURCE BOOK IN THEATRICAL HISTORY, A. M. Nagler. Contemporary observers on acting, directing, make-up, costuming, stage props, machinery, scene design, from Ancient Greece to Chekhov. 611pp. 5⅜ x 8½. 20515-0 Pa. $12.95

THE COMPLETE NONSENSE OF EDWARD LEAR, Edward Lear. All nonsense limericks, zany alphabets, Owl and Pussycat, songs, nonsense botany, etc., illustrated by Lear. Total of 320pp. 5⅜ x 8½. (USO) 20167-8 Pa. $7.95

VICTORIAN PARLOUR POETRY: An Annotated Anthology, Michael R. Turner. 117 gems by Longfellow, Tennyson, Browning, many lesser-known poets. "The Village Blacksmith," "Curfew Must Not Ring Tonight," "Only a Baby Small," dozens more, often difficult to find elsewhere. Index of poets, titles, first lines. xxiii + 325pp. 5⅜ x 8¼. 27044-0 Pa. $8.95

DUBLINERS, James Joyce. Fifteen stories offer vivid, tightly focused observations of the lives of Dublin's poorer classes. At least one, "The Dead," is considered a masterpiece. Reprinted complete and unabridged from standard edition. 160pp. 5 3/16 x 8¼. 26870-5 Pa. $1.00

THE HAUNTED MONASTERY and THE CHINESE MAZE MURDERS, Robert van Gulik. Two full novels by van Gulik, set in 7th-century China, continue adventures of Judge Dee and his companions. An evil Taoist monastery, seemingly supernatural events; overgrown topiary maze hides strange crimes. 27 illustrations. 328pp. 5⅜ x 8½. 23502-5 Pa. $8.95

THE BOOK OF THE SACRED MAGIC OF ABRAMELIN THE MAGE, translated by S. MacGregor Mathers. Medieval manuscript of ceremonial magic. Basic document in Aleister Crowley, Golden Dawn groups. 268pp. 5⅜ x 8½. 23211-5 Pa. $9.95

NEW RUSSIAN-ENGLISH AND ENGLISH-RUSSIAN DICTIONARY, M. A. O'Brien. This is a remarkably handy Russian dictionary, containing a surprising amount of information, including over 70,000 entries. 366pp. 4½ x 6⅛. 20208-9 Pa. $9.95

HISTORIC HOMES OF THE AMERICAN PRESIDENTS, Second, Revised Edition, Irvin Haas. A traveler's guide to American Presidential homes, most open to the public, depicting and describing homes occupied by every American President from George Washington to George Bush. With visiting hours, admission charges, travel routes. 175 photographs. Index. 160pp. 8¼ x 11. 26751-2 Pa. $11.95

NEW YORK IN THE FORTIES, Andreas Feininger. 162 brilliant photographs by the well-known photographer, formerly with *Life* magazine. Commuters, shoppers, Times Square at night, much else from city at its peak. Captions by John von Hartz. 181pp. 9¼ x 10¾. 23585-8 Pa. $12.95

INDIAN SIGN LANGUAGE, William Tomkins. Over 525 signs developed by Sioux and other tribes. Written instructions and diagrams. Also 290 pictographs. 111pp. 6⅛ x 9¼. 22029-X Pa. $3.95

CATALOG OF DOVER BOOKS

ANATOMY: A Complete Guide for Artists, Joseph Sheppard. A master of figure drawing shows artists how to render human anatomy convincingly. Over 460 illustrations. 224pp. 8⅜ x 11¼. 27279-6 Pa. $11.95

MEDIEVAL CALLIGRAPHY: Its History and Technique, Marc Drogin. Spirited history, comprehensive instruction manual covers 13 styles (ca. 4th century thru 15th). Excellent photographs; directions for duplicating medieval techniques with modern tools. 224pp. 8⅜ x 11¼. 26142-5 Pa. $12.95

DRIED FLOWERS: How to Prepare Them, Sarah Whitlock and Martha Rankin. Complete instructions on how to use silica gel, meal and borax, perlite aggregate, sand and borax, glycerine and water to create attractive permanent flower arrangements. 12 illustrations. 32pp. 5⅜ x 8½. 21802-3 Pa. $1.00

EASY-TO-MAKE BIRD FEEDERS FOR WOODWORKERS, Scott D. Campbell. Detailed, simple-to-use guide for designing, constructing, caring for and using feeders. Text, illustrations for 12 classic and contemporary designs. 96pp. 5⅜ x 8½.
25847-5 Pa. $2.95

SCOTTISH WONDER TALES FROM MYTH AND LEGEND, Donald A. Mackenzie. 16 lively tales tell of giants rumbling down mountainsides, of a magic wand that turns stone pillars into warriors, of gods and goddesses, evil hags, powerful forces and more. 240pp. 5⅜ x 8½. 29677-6 Pa. $6.95

THE HISTORY OF UNDERCLOTHES, C. Willett Cunnington and Phyllis Cunnington. Fascinating, well-documented survey covering six centuries of English undergarments, enhanced with over 100 illustrations: 12th-century laced-up bodice, footed long drawers (1795), 19th-century bustles, 19th-century corsets for men, Victorian "bust improvers," much more. 272pp. 5⅜ x 8¼. 27124-2 Pa. $9.95

ARTS AND CRAFTS FURNITURE: The Complete Brooks Catalog of 1912, Brooks Manufacturing Co. Photos and detailed descriptions of more than 150 now very collectible furniture designs from the Arts and Crafts movement depict davenports, settees, buffets, desks, tables, chairs, bedsteads, dressers and more, all built of solid, quarter-sawed oak. Invaluable for students and enthusiasts of antiques, Americana and the decorative arts. 80pp. 6½ x 9¼. 27471-3 Pa. $8.95

HOW WE INVENTED THE AIRPLANE: An Illustrated History, Orville Wright. Fascinating firsthand account covers early experiments, construction of planes and motors, first flights, much more. Introduction and commentary by Fred C. Kelly. 76 photographs. 96pp. 8¼ x 11. 25662-6 Pa. $8.95

THE ARTS OF THE SAILOR: Knotting, Splicing and Ropework, Hervey Garrett Smith. Indispensable shipboard reference covers tools, basic knots and useful hitches; handsewing and canvas work, more. Over 100 illustrations. Delightful reading for sea lovers. 256pp. 5⅜ x 8½. 26440-8 Pa. $7.95

FRANK LLOYD WRIGHT'S FALLINGWATER: The House and Its History, Second, Revised Edition, Donald Hoffmann. A total revision—both in text and illustrations—of the standard document on Fallingwater, the boldest, most personal architectural statement of Wright's mature years, updated with valuable new material from the recently opened Frank Lloyd Wright Archives. "Fascinating"—*The New York Times*. 116 illustrations. 128pp. 9¼ x 10¾. 27430-6 Pa. $11.95

CATALOG OF DOVER BOOKS

PHOTOGRAPHIC SKETCHBOOK OF THE CIVIL WAR, Alexander Gardner. 100 photos taken on field during the Civil War. Famous shots of Manassas Harper's Ferry, Lincoln, Richmond, slave pens, etc. 244pp. 10⅝ x 8¼. 22731-6 Pa. $9.95

FIVE ACRES AND INDEPENDENCE, Maurice G. Kains. Great back-to-the-land classic explains basics of self-sufficient farming. The one book to get. 95 illustrations. 397pp. 5⅜ x 8½. 20974-1 Pa. $7.95

SONGS OF EASTERN BIRDS, Dr. Donald J. Borror. Songs and calls of 60 species most common to eastern U.S.: warblers, woodpeckers, flycatchers, thrushes, larks, many more in high-quality recording. Cassette and manual 99912-2 $9.95

A MODERN HERBAL, Margaret Grieve. Much the fullest, most exact, most useful compilation of herbal material. Gigantic alphabetical encyclopedia, from aconite to zedoary, gives botanical information, medical properties, folklore, economic uses, much else. Indispensable to serious reader. 161 illustrations. 888pp. 6½ x 9¼. 2-vol. set. (USO) Vol. I: 22798-7 Pa. $9.95
Vol. II: 22799-5 Pa. $9.95

HIDDEN TREASURE MAZE BOOK, Dave Phillips. Solve 34 challenging mazes accompanied by heroic tales of adventure. Evil dragons, people-eating plants, blood-thirsty giants, many more dangerous adversaries lurk at every twist and turn. 34 mazes, stories, solutions. 48pp. 8¼ x 11. 24566-7 Pa. $2.95

LETTERS OF W. A. MOZART, Wolfgang A. Mozart. Remarkable letters show bawdy wit, humor, imagination, musical insights, contemporary musical world; includes some letters from Leopold Mozart. 276pp. 5⅜ x 8½. 22859-2 Pa. $7.95

BASIC PRINCIPLES OF CLASSICAL BALLET, Agrippina Vaganova. Great Russian theoretician, teacher explains methods for teaching classical ballet. 118 illustrations. 175pp. 5⅜ x 8½. 22036-2 Pa. $5.95

THE JUMPING FROG, Mark Twain. Revenge edition. The original story of The Celebrated Jumping Frog of Calaveras County, a hapless French translation, and Twain's hilarious "retranslation" from the French. 12 illustrations. 66pp. 5⅜ x 8½. 22686-7 Pa. $3.95

BEST REMEMBERED POEMS, Martin Gardner (ed.). The 126 poems in this superb collection of 19th- and 20th-century British and American verse range from Shelley's "To a Skylark" to the impassioned "Renascence" of Edna St. Vincent Millay and to Edward Lear's whimsical "The Owl and the Pussycat." 224pp. 5⅜ x 8½. 27165-X Pa. $5.95

COMPLETE SONNETS, William Shakespeare. Over 150 exquisite poems deal with love, friendship, the tyranny of time, beauty's evanescence, death and other themes in language of remarkable power, precision and beauty. Glossary of archaic terms. 80pp. 5³⁄₁₆ x 8¼. 26686-9 Pa. $1.00

BODIES IN A BOOKSHOP, R. T. Campbell. Challenging mystery of blackmail and murder with ingenious plot and superbly drawn characters. In the best tradition of British suspense fiction. 192pp. 5⅜ x 8½. 24720-1 Pa. $6.95

CATALOG OF DOVER BOOKS

THE INFLUENCE OF SEA POWER UPON HISTORY, 1660–1783, A. T. Mahan. Influential classic of naval history and tactics still used as text in war colleges. First paperback edition. 4 maps. 24 battle plans. 640pp. 5⅜ x 8½. 25509-3 Pa. $14.95

THE STORY OF THE TITANIC AS TOLD BY ITS SURVIVORS, Jack Winocour (ed.). What it was really like. Panic, despair, shocking inefficiency, and a little heroism. More thrilling than any fictional account. 26 illustrations. 320pp. 5⅜ x 8½. 20610-6 Pa. $8.95

FAIRY AND FOLK TALES OF THE IRISH PEASANTRY, William Butler Yeats (ed.). Treasury of 64 tales from the twilight world of Celtic myth and legend: "The Soul Cages," "The Kildare Pooka," "King O'Toole and his Goose," many more. Introduction and Notes by W. B. Yeats. 352pp. 5⅜ x 8½. 26941-8 Pa. $8.95

BUDDHIST MAHAYANA TEXTS, E. B. Cowell and Others (eds.). Superb, accurate translations of basic documents in Mahayana Buddhism, highly important in history of religions. The Buddha-karita of Asvaghosha, Larger Sukhavativyuha, more. 448pp. 5⅜ x 8½. 25552-2 Pa. $12.95

ONE TWO THREE . . . INFINITY: Facts and Speculations of Science, George Gamow. Great physicist's fascinating, readable overview of contemporary science: number theory, relativity, fourth dimension, entropy, genes, atomic structure, much more. 128 illustrations. Index. 352pp. 5⅜ x 8½. 25664-2 Pa. $8.95

ENGINEERING IN HISTORY, Richard Shelton Kirby, et al. Broad, nontechnical survey of history's major technological advances: birth of Greek science, industrial revolution, electricity and applied science, 20th-century automation, much more. 181 illustrations. ". . . excellent . . ."–*Isis*. Bibliography. vii + 530pp. 5⅜ x 8¼. 26412-2 Pa. $14.95

DALÍ ON MODERN ART: The Cuckolds of Antiquated Modern Art, Salvador Dalí. Influential painter skewers modern art and its practitioners. Outrageous evaluations of Picasso, Cézanne, Turner, more. 15 renderings of paintings discussed. 44 calligraphic decorations by Dalí. 96pp. 5⅜ x 8½. (USO) 29220-7 Pa. $4.95

ANTIQUE PLAYING CARDS: A Pictorial History, Henry René D'Allemagne. Over 900 elaborate, decorative images from rare playing cards (14th–20th centuries): Bacchus, death, dancing dogs, hunting scenes, royal coats of arms, players cheating, much more. 96pp. 9¼ x 12¼. 29265-7 Pa. $12.95

MAKING FURNITURE MASTERPIECES: 30 Projects with Measured Drawings, Franklin H. Gottshall. Step-by-step instructions, illustrations for constructing handsome, useful pieces, among them a Sheraton desk, Chippendale chair, Spanish desk, Queen Anne table and a William and Mary dressing mirror. 224pp. 8⅛ x 11¼. 29338-6 Pa. $13.95

THE FOSSIL BOOK: A Record of Prehistoric Life, Patricia V. Rich et al. Profusely illustrated definitive guide covers everything from single-celled organisms and dinosaurs to birds and mammals and the interplay between climate and man. Over 1,500 illustrations. 760pp. 7½ x 10⅛. 29371-8 Pa. $29.95

Prices subject to change without notice.

Available at your book dealer or write for free catalog to Dept. GI, Dover Publications, Inc., 31 East 2nd St., Mineola, N.Y. 11501. Dover publishes more than 500 books each year on science, elementary and advanced mathematics, biology, music, art, literary history, social sciences and other areas.